A HEART FOR ANY FATE

PUBLICATION OF THIS BOOK IS MADE POSSIBLE BY

A GENEROUS GRANT FROM

THE WATSON-BROWN FOUNDATION, INC.

A HEART FOR ANY FATE

THE BIOGRAPHY OF RICHARD BREVARD RUSSELL SR.

Sally Russell

Uncle Remus Regional Library System

Eatonton–Putnam County Library

309 North Madison Avenue

Eatonton, Georgia 31024

www.uncleremus.org

Mercer University Press
Macon, Georgia
25th Anniversary

ISBN 0-86554-957-5
MUP/H628

© 2004 Mercer University Press
1400 Coleman Avenue
Macon, Georgia 31207
All rights reserved

First Edition.

8The paper used in this publication meets the minimum
requirements of American National Standard for
Information Sciences—Permanence of Paper for Printed
Library Materials, ANSI Z39.48-1992.

Library of Congress Cataloging-in-Publication Data

Russell, Sally, 1942-
A heart for any fate : the biography of Richard Brevard Russell, Sr. /
Sally Russell.-- 1st ed.
    p. cm.
Includes bibliographical references and index.
ISBN 0-86554-957-5 (alk. paper)
1. Russell, Richard Brevard, 1861-1938. 2. Judges—Georgia—Biography.
3. Politicians—Georgia—Biography. 4. Georgia—Biography. I. Title.
CT275.R8855A5 2004
975.8'041'092--dc22

                                                      2004014603

To
Susan Way Russell Reynolds
and
Nancy Carolyn Russell Black
sisters
soul-mates
support systems extraordinaire

CONTENTS

PREFACE

At first glance, the life of Richard Brevard Russell Sr. appeals as the subject of a fascinating novel of the post-Civil War South. Born in 1861 into a prosperous family that lost everything material in the war, Richard Russell was handsome, brilliant, ambitious, romantic, eccentric, and consumed with the ambition to make a name for himself. A closer examination of how he went about attaining this goal reveals, unfortunately, that his story would not work as a novel because it does not fit the first requirement of good fiction, that is, credibility. Few would willingly suspend disbelief and accept a protagonist who was a hard-hitting but humane public prosecutor, a passionate, ambition-driven politician (he ran for public office seventeen times), a pioneering, long-serving appellate court judge of dedication and wisdom, yet a home-loving man with a breadth and depth of tender emotions that would inspire heart's core love and loyalty in two wives and thirteen children.

Although Richard Russell's parents lost literally everything material in the sanguinary conflict between the Blue and the Gray of 1861–1865, they retained an earnest determination not to bow in defeat. Rearing five sons and one daughter in the patriarchal tradition, his mother taught Richard fiercely that family came first, that his place as eldest was privileged, that others below him, especially women and children, were dependent, and that he must be dependable. The culture of his day insisted that the South's young men restore its vaunted honor, but how this could be accomplished was unclear. His ambitions and his ideals proved equal to the myriad challenges of this setting, and his achievements in the public and the domestic arenas stand a tribute to the virtues of the masculine.

An important factor in his success is that he knew how to pick out a good wife. His first wife, chosen when he was twenty-two years old, was intelligent, accomplished, and deeply family-oriented, and her love for and devotion to him was complete. His love for her was so all-embracing that when she died after three years and three children, who also died, he swore he would never risk that crucible again. Fortunately, five years later, at the age of thirty, he met another woman of like character and reconsidered his decision. With this extraordinary woman he formed a tender and true marriage relationship that produced fifteen children, thirteen of whom survived to become responsible adults, credits to effective parenting. This wife's love and respect for her husband waxed throughout their forty-seven-year marriage, as did his love and respect for her.

I first came to consider the life of Richard Russell while editing the letters of his second wife, Ina Dillard Russell, to their thirteen children. Ina saw Christian wife- and motherhood as a high calling, and she took this major career of women in her day to its zenith. Among her thirteen children she claimed three lawyers, one of whom became governor of Georgia and the state's most distinguished United States Senator. Another became, like his father, a respected judge. The third lawyer, a daughter, worked as a civil servant in Washington, DC, for nearly forty years. Four other daughters became teachers and another a self-taught legal secretary. One son became a Presbyterian minister, another a college English professor. One made business and the military his career and another went into business and farming. Their youngest son and fourteenth child became a medical doctor. All were decent human beings who contributed to their communities in positive ways. While these children were away at school, Ina wrote an estimated three thousand letters, of which over 1200 survive. Her book, *Roots and Ever Green* (Georgia, 1999), chronicles her superior work.

In the past three decades we have taken pains, and rightly so, to recognize the important labor of domesticity, its trials and rewards, for women. Yet it is easy to be so impressed with Ina's record that Richard Russell, the father she chose for these children, the man whose work provided for them, is overlooked. We ought not to overlook the masculine side of the home. This biography is an illustration of how white Southern men in the period following the Civil War responded to the challenges of patriarchy.

I am constrained to say that I do not see Richard and Ina Russell as my grandparents. I offer them as all our grandparents, representatives of the lives and work of countless men and women who lived in a time when role models were comfortingly solid but also in a time of great social upheaval when the physical aspects of daily living were much more difficult than they are today. Men and women in the upper classes were reared to high ideals of human conduct, and their efforts to measure up to challenging values of family love and loyalty and religious duty and faith, show in their history. We may postulate that such ideal behavior was not the norm, but that it is a norm devoutly to be wished for human happiness can hardly be in dispute.

We are accustomed to thinking of the white male as the privileged one in this social setting, the person with all the power. My study of this remarkable couple in no way leads to the conclusion that the role of the male was easier than that of the female. When he took his responsibilities seriously, as most did, his work required industry, determination, tenderness, imagination, nerve, and plain old grit. Valor, from the Latin root *valere*, to be strong, comes to mind. I offer three books by colleagues of Richard's who were in like circumstances, responsible family men trying to be effective public servants. They are Nat Harris' *The Autobiography of an Old Man*, Arthur Powell's *I Can Go Home Again*, and S. Price Gilbert's *A Georgia Lawyer*. Richard Russell's distinguishing mark is perhaps in the quantity of his production, both as a politician and as a patriarch. That he maintained admirable quality of work along with profuse quantity is undeniable.

Richard Russell's story is a true one, and I have tried to be thorough in its documentation. Fortunately for social historians, Sheryl Vogt of the Richard B. Russell Library for Political Research and Studies at the University of Georgia saved the papers of Richard B. Russell Sr. and of Ina Dillard Russell when those of their most famous son, Richard B. Russell Jr., were first gathered. She also saved those of Lewis Carolyn Russell, youngest brother and life-long right-hand man of Richard Sr., and those of their brother US naval captain Robert Lee Russell that were in Lewis' papers. Most of them personal in nature, these papers, carefully catalogued and clearly marked, are a pleasure to work with. The papers of Ina Dillard Russell Stacy, the lawyer daughter, were given to the Russell Library at a later time and also provide detailed family information.

A voluminous and sprawling collection that informed this work I can only call the Russell Family Papers. These consist of letters and other documents such as wills, obituaries, inscriptions in books, photographs, albums, school notebooks, receipts, bills and the like, left until recently at the Russell homeplace. On an optimistic day a good description of these is chaos forming a dim idea of order. Digging here invariably brought up gold, but when I first began to mine these papers I was working on Ina's book and had not yet conceived the idea of Richard's. Thus I have not always been able to relocate an item. For example, I have not found again a lovely photograph of Richard's first wife, Minnie Tyler, or a memorable letter in which he tells about choosing the gravesite for his grandparents when he was fourteen years old.

This native confusion was multiplied by the fact that the family gave the remaining papers to the Russell Library around 1998 and some of them are now at the Russell, but not yet inventoried, and a few are still at the Russell homeplace. The record exists, nonetheless, and will be inventoried so that future scholars can search there.

Another rich source for the life of Richard B. Russell Sr. is the collection of oral histories done with family and friends following the death of Richard B. Russell Jr. I knew, loved, and admired all thirteen children—they were the finest father and collection of aunts and uncles anyone could hope for—and I never tired of hearing their stories. It is fair to say, I think, that I have spent my entire life interviewing them. I and numerous cousins (there were thirty-nine grandchildren) have myriad stories in our hearts that I have chosen to document simply as family history. Tribal memory counts.

For ten years, 1991–2000, I edited the family newsletter, which grew into a magazine of one to two hundred pages each year, as I researched the family collection. We call this publication the *Russell Herald*, and it is available at the Russell Library.

As the editor of and amanuensis for Ina Dillard Russell's book *Roots and Ever Green*, I lived in deep intimacy with her for more than five years. I have read countless letters from her numerous times, and I still get a letter or a card from her occasionally, as they surface from various family memorabilia. I believe I know her better than anyone did in her life except perhaps Richard. This work supports a position of authority in writing his book.

Richard Russell's life and career paralleled those of many prominent political figures in Georgia history from 1861 to 1938. To keep this information simple, I have used two main sources: the *Dictionary of Georgia Biography*, edited by Kenneth Coleman and Steve Gurr, and *The Governors of Georgia* by James Cook.

For the political development and campaigns of Richard Brevard Russell Jr. I have used Gilbert Fite's biography, *Richard B. Russell Jr., Senator from Georgia*. I do not challenge anything in Professor Fite's thorough work, but it is my hope that the father's story will illustrate that the responsible white Southerner's attitude toward family and white-dominated social order was not universally one of careless racism and abuse of power. A sincere belief in hierarchy that required much of those in the top ranks permeated their lives. The Richard B. Russells abhorred demagoguery and blind racism, and both felt deeply the plight of all humankind. Like other Southern politicians of this ilk, they walked a razor's edge to stay in office and bring progressive ideas to fruition, for any politician branded as pro-black was soon out of a job. Working within the system with compassion and patience was the wisest choice if one wished to retain any influence. Certainly these two prominent Georgians struggled with the responsibilities and the temptations of power, but believing public service more important than individual aggrandizement, they avoided the abuse of power and remained modest about significant accomplishments. Richard B. Russell Jr.'s sustained success in the United States Senate worked to huge advantages for Georgia that today benefit blacks and whites. He would be pleased with that outcome.

I am confident that a thorough examination of the life of Richard B. Russell Sr. reveals an honest and accurate picture of the social and familial structures that both restricted and strengthened conscientious middle- and upper-class white men of the post-Civil War South. Their story, like those of other races and classes, deserves its day in court.

ACKNOWLEDGMENTS

No matter how difficult it is to take up the tools of words and create a story, re-create a life, chronicle an era, the honest writer pales more at the difficulty of thanking those who have helped her in this daunting task. I humbly admit that I am incapable of saying adequate thanks for the innumerable deeds of kindness, words of encouragement, and generous financial support that have made telling the remarkable story of Richard B. Russell Sr. possible. Nevertheless, I joyfully take this opportunity to name my benefactors.

The project would never have got off the ground without the interest and commitment of Marc Jolley at Mercer University Press. Throughout the writing, Marc has been a constant source of encouragement and humor. We writers are given to calling an editor, rather selfishly, "my editor." It is a privilege and an honor to think of Marc Jolley as my editor.

With Marc in favor of the project, I canvassed family members for financial support. Because I live in England, travel expenses for research in Georgia loomed costly. More than a dozen of Richard Russell's direct living descendants are occupied in the profession of law and among these Hugh Peterson Jr., Robert Bruce Russell Sr., and Harriette Russell Coleman offered ready financial aid that set me on my way. Other legally-engaged relatives have given time and attention in various ways, and I thank Betty Russell Vandiver, Richard B. Russell III, John Davidson Russell, and Ann Russell Parker for their valuable help.

Financial and moral support through Rosemary DePaolo and staff at Georgia College/State University is also deeply appreciated. Raymond H. Reynolds Jr. and library staff at the Georgia Institute of Technology sent useful material for which I am grateful.

To the staff at the Russell Library for Political Research and Studies at the University of Georgia I acknowledge an unpayable debt, especially to Sheryl Vogt and Jill Severn for their unflagging interest and exceptional professional expertise.

Friends and family whose belief in this project kept me going, literally and figuratively, are Raymond and Susan Russell Reynolds, Ted and Lynn Smith Roberts, Frank and Nancy Russell Black, Steve and Rebecca Gurr, and Carolyn Russell Nelson. These dear ones furnished food, shelter, clothing (no kidding), and transportation in abundance, with constant smiles and cheerful words.

It is impossible to name all family and friends who furnished information but I must thank especially our "Old Guard" Ala Joanna Brewton Russell, Virginia Wilson Russell, Carolyn Russell Nelson, and before her death in 2002, Patience Elizabeth Russell Peterson. In the next generation, Virginia Russell Black, Jane Bowden Moore, Richard Russell Bowden, and Kathryn Hairston Green have given useful stories. Kathy produced an interview with Mary Willie Russell Green, my beloved Aunt Billie, who has been dead twenty years. We Russells believe in "mystic sweet communion with those whose rest is won." Hugh Peterson III, a great-grandson, did research in Atlanta. Mary Bondurant Lanier arranged an unhoped-for interview with her remarkable father, Frank Bondurant, a contemporary of Walter Brown Russell Sr.

Nancy Jackson O'Neill and Jessica Jackson Keeley have been patient in giving up Grandmother to the work. I owe thanks to Jessica's husband Howard Keeley, a Princeton doctorate in English and Irish literature, who read and critiqued the manuscript with academic skill and, more importantly, with the diplomacy needed to tackle such a project for one's mother-in-law. He ought to be high up in the state department.

My husband, Les Warrington, remains the backbone of my writing projects. Money, taming of recalcitrant computers, proofreading, untiring patience, bedrock faith and abundant love, he provides them all. This is the third time I am left with the insurmountable task of thanking him for our children.

FREQUENTLY USED ABBREVIATIONS:

RLPRS — Russell Library for Political Research and Studies
from the Russell Library:

IDR Collection—Ina Dillard Russell Collection

IDRS Collection—Ina Dillard Russell Stacy Collection

LCR Collection—Lewis Carolyn Russell Collection

RBR Sr. Collection—Richard Brevard Russell Sr. Collection

RBR Jr. Collection—Richard Brevard Russell Jr. Collection

RLR Collection—Robert Lee Russell (son) Collection

RFH— Russell Family Herald

RFP—Russell Family Papers

Let us then be up and doing,
With a heart for any fate,
Still achieving, still pursuing,
Learn to labor and to wait.

Henry Wadsworth Longfellow
"A Psalm of Life"

A RUSSELL PHOTOGRAPH ALBUM

Ruins of Sweetwater/New Manchester Mill, the factory operated by William John Russell from 1859–1864, when it was burned by Union troops. Courtesy Les Warrington.

The Russell home at Princeton, near Athens, about 1875. Courtesy Richard B. Russell Library for Political Research and Studies at the University of Georgia.

The house in Athens, Georgia, that Richard Russell bought for his first wife, Minnie Tyler, about 1884. Courtesy Richard B. Russell Library for Political Research and Studies at the University of Georgia.

The William John Russell family, 1890. Standing, left to right: Richard Brevard, Robert Lee, William John, Edward Gaston. Seated, left to right: Mary Brevard, William John the elder, Harriette Brumbly, Lewis Carolyn. Courtesy Russell Family Collection.

Ina Dillard and Richard Russell on their honeymoon at Niagara
Falls, June 1891. Courtesy RBRLPRS at UGA.

The William John Russell family, June 1894. Standing left to right:
Richard, Ina, and Lewis. Seated in chairs, left to right: William
John, holding Mary Willie, and Harriette, holding Ina Jr. Seated on
steps, left to right: Edward, John, Robert, and Mary. Courtesy
RLPRS at UGA

Richard Brevard Russell Sr., about 1904.
Courtesy RLPRS at UGA.

Richard Brevard Russell Sr., about 1906. Courtesy RLPRS at UGA.

The Russell homeplace, soon after completion in the summer of 1912. Courtesy RLPRS at UGA.

Thirty-ninth annual session Grand Council Royal Arcanum, Savannah, Georgia, 18 April 1917. Courtesy RLPRS at UGA.

Campaign poster, 1922 Chief Justice race. Courtesy RLPRS at UGA.

The Russell brothers, 1923. Seated, left to right: Richard, Robert, and William John; standing left to right: Edward, Lewis. Courtesy RLPRS at UGA

Judge and Mrs. Russell with their children, 1926. front row, seated left to right: Patience, Mary Willie, Ina Jr., Carolyn; middle row, seated left to right: Alex, Harriette, Ina Sr., Richard Sr., Marguerite, Walter; back row left to right: Fielding, William, Richard Jr., Rob, and Edward. Courtesy RLPRS at UGA.

Richard and Ina Russell with their daughters, about 1927. Seated, Judge and Mrs. Russell. Standing left to right: Carolyn, Ina Jr., Harriette, Billie, Marguerite, and Patience. Courtesy Russell Family Collection.

Russell family reunion, 1929. First row, seated, left to right: Alex Russell, Betty Russell, Bobby Russell Jr., Jane Bowden, Nancy Green, Peggy Bowden, Richard Russell Green, Walter Russell; middle row, seated left to right: Harriette Russell Sharpton, Marguerite Russell Bowden, holding James Harris Bowden Jr., Carolyn Russell, Judge Russell, Ina Russell, Billie Russell Green, holding Samuel Gordon Green Jr., Ina Russell Jr., Patience Russell, Sybil Milsaps Russell; back row, standing left to right: Ralph Sharpton, James Harris Bowden Sr., Henry Edward Russell, Richard B. Russell Jr., William John Russell, Fielding Russell, Robert Lee Russell. Courtesy RLPRS at UGA.

Richard B. Russell Sr., Chief Justice of the Georgia Supreme Court, about 1930. Courtesy RLPRS at UGA.

The dirt-digging judge, Richard B. Russell Sr., 1930 or 1931. Courtesy Private Collection of Richard Russell Bowden and Jane Bowden Moore.

Gubernatorial Inaugural Parade, Atlanta, 27 June 1931. Left to right: Gov. Richard B. Russell Jr., Mrs. Ina Dillard Russell, and Chief Justice Richard B. Russell Sr. Georgia State Special Collections.

Richard B. Russell Sr., Chief Justice of the Georgia Supreme Court, swears in his son, Richard B. Russell Jr., as governor of Georgia, Atlanta, 27 June 1931. UPI/Corbis.

Russell family in-laws, Russell Reunion, June 1938. Seated left to right: Virginia Wilson Russell, Jean K. Stacy, Ala Jo Brewton Russell, Hugh Peterson. Standing left to right: Ralph Sharpton, S. Gordon Green Sr., Sybil Milsaps Russell, Dorothea (Dolly) Bealer Russell, James Harris Bowden Sr., Sarah Eaton Russell. Courtesy RLPRS at UGA

1

LIABLE TO HEAVY PAINS AND PENALTIES

1861–1866

By June 1864, the ominous thunder of Confederate and Union artillery reaching the city limits of Marietta, Georgia, grew louder daily. Like many other citizens in the little town just north of Atlanta, Harriette Brumby Russell had to consider leaving her home to refugee with her two young sons. She could flee to the mountains of North Carolina where her mother had relatives or to south Georgia where her husband's people lived. Yet she lingered. Her husband, William John Russell, was in Augusta, and she was loathe to leave him. A prospering thirty-nine-year-old Marietta businessman, engaged in war work of manufacturing shoes and cloth for the Confederate army, William John had enlisted in the state militia in February 1864 and was assigned to Augusta, supposedly to guard an arsenal there.[1]

Like others in Marietta and Atlanta, Harriette could hardly grasp the possibility that General Joe Johnston would fail to halt the Union forces under General William T. Sherman. Born a Brumby, Harriette showed the legendary stubborn nature of her family, especially where family was concerned. She and John had married in December 1859, when she was thirty and he thirty-four, and it was an affectionate union. Their first son, Richard Brumby, named for Harriette's father, was born on April 27, 1861, and the second, William Edward, named for John's father, arrived on March 7, 1863. Harriette had not sent William John off to the militia in February without a tender farewell. She was expecting another baby in late November.[2]

Harriette's parents and two younger sisters also lived in Marietta. Her father, Richard Trapier Brumby, an early acclaimed Southern academic, professor of science at the universities of Alabama and South Carolina, had retired from South Carolina in 1857 for health reasons, but after moving to Marietta, Professor Brumby recovered enough to teach at Marietta Military Institute, a school founded by his younger brother Arnoldus Vanderhorst Brumby. This school became the state-funded Georgia Military Institute in the late 1850s. The Brumbys soon became part of upper Marietta society. A few days after the war began in April 1861, Harriette's sister Sarah married John Heyward Glover III, a young man prominent in Marietta business and social life. The Italianate home built in 1851 by his father, John Heyward Glover Jr., the first mayor of Marietta, and the stately Greek-Revival style home of the Brumbys were the scenes of pleasant pre-war social gatherings for the courting couple. Uncle Arnoldus was known not only for his school but also for the many varieties of roses in the garden of his home, where cadets were often entertained.[3]

Professor Brumby, long an ardent states-rightist, was at first in no mood to encourage his daughters to leave Marietta; nor was he disposed to leave himself. Having invested almost everything in Confederate bonds, like many other Southerners he continued to hope Sherman would be held back long enough for Peace Democrats to unseat Lincoln and sue for peace before total defeat brought the South back into the Union against its will.[4]

Confronting this dream of peace was the reality that Russell and Brumby properties could not be expected to escape the wrath of a Union Army grinding into north Georgia from Tennessee. The Russells owned interests in a brickyard in Marietta and, with the Glovers, in a tannery, consisting of three buildings, one of which housed fifteen workers. The tannery, one mile from the square in Marietta, processed leather and manufactured shoes for the Confederate army. John and Harriette's home and servants' quarters, purchased only a few years earlier from Judge George N. Lester, stood nearby.[5]

With Arnoldus Brumby, his wife's uncle, William John also was leasing an important interest in New Manchester Mill on Sweetwater Creek west of Atlanta. First named Sweetwater Factory, the mill was an imposing five-story brick structure, the tallest textile manufacturing building north of Macon. Working for former Georgia Governor Charles McDonald, who built the factory, William John laid out the mill village, millrace and factory, supervising construction in 1854. Over a hundred people lived in the mill village, a prospering community where the mill building itself served as a social hall and sometimes a wedding chapel.[6]

William John had been working for Charles McDonald for more than ten years when he laid out Sweetwater village, having begun as a civil servant when McDonald was governor of Georgia (1839 –1843). As a superintendent at the mill, William John had helped earn enormous profits during the cotton boom of the 1850s. Anyone with his enterprising abilities and inclinations would have felt fortunate to acquire McDonald's considerable interest in the mill in 1859. William John's fortune seemed, if not made, at least well on its way to the bank. Indeed, the advent of war only made prodigious profits more likely for Brumby and Russell, for the coarse osnaburg cloth they produced soon was demanded for blankets, tents and uniforms for Confederate soldiers. During the war they continued to keep the machinery in good condition and to purchase new machines when necessary.[7] By the late spring of 1864, however, as the war shifted into north Georgia, they could only hope that this mill, miles from Atlanta down a rough road, in a remote, hilly, almost mountainous area, might escape detection.

When William Tecumseh Sherman turned his armies towards Georgia on May 6, 1864, he had but one goal: to take Atlanta, the Gate City of the South, its second most important manufacturing center. His advance, swift and deadly, swept along in three columns that inexorably flanked defending General Joseph T. Johnston, especially with the fast-moving Army of the Tennessee, headed by General James McPherson. Outgunned, outsupplied, outnumbered almost two to one, Johnston and his lieutenants could only try to slow the Union advance, watching for a chance to lure Sherman into making a doomed frontal attack.[8]

Sherman would not be lured. He would have Atlanta, and then devastate Georgia in the kind of scorched-earth warfare that shows no mercy. He determined to break Georgia's economic back and her heart and spirit as well. "War is the remedy our enemies have chosen," he said, "and I say let us give them all they want."

Refugees pouring into the Atlanta area reported that the Yanks were devouring everything in their path. A Confederate soldier, victim of another successful flanking motion, told his Yankee captors, "Sherman'll never go to hell; he will flank the devil and make heaven in spite of the guards."

As if possessed by an evil pride, Sherman wrote, "All people retire before us and desolation is behind. To realize what war is one should follow our tracks." Ahead of the main army came ragtag, lawless troops who smashed everything they did not steal. These were followed by more orderly regular soldiers and officers who sometimes commiserated with the local population, while claiming to be powerless to stop the marauding troops. This sequence of troop arrival, however, was a deliberate tactic and was perceived as such by the soldiers participating in it.[9]

On May 31 the King family, important textile manufacturers in Roswell, near Marietta, abandoned their home, taking wealth and furnishings in great haste, including, it was rumored, a wagonload of gold. They left their mill in the hands of a French supervisor.[10] Although the Brumbys must have known of this precipitous flight, it seems likely they held their ground until the Battle of Kennesaw Mountain on June 27, when Sherman was at last lured into a frontal assault. Thirteen thousand Union soldiers stormed the Confederates on Kennesaw Mountain but failed to break the Confederate line. The slaughter was so savage that an armistice had to be declared for burying the dead, not from respect for the fallen, but to get rid of the sickening stench. Sherman resumed flanking movements and on July 5, Union troops were reported advancing on Roswell.[11]

By this time, the Brumbys had decided to move. Professor and Mrs. Brumby put their unmarried daughter Ann Eliza on a train for Griffin, about sixty miles south of Marietta, and it seems likely that Harriette and her two children went along, accompanied by a young black servant named Paul Glover. The Professor and his wife loaded supplies of yarn and leather from William John's factories into a carriage and headed for Griffin themselves, spending the first night in Smyrna, in a brick church. They were reunited with their daughters in Griffin, where they proceeded with Ann Eliza to Lincolnton, North Carolina, site of Mary Brumby's ancestral home. Mary was the youngest daughter of Alexander Brevard, a celebrated North Carolina patriot of the American Revolution. The yarn and leather the Brumbys had been prudent enough to save would serve as valuable barter as the war wore on.[12]

Clinging to her determination to remain near her husband, Harriette continued with Paul and the children to an unidentified place near Augusta. She carried with her a few valuables, including some gold, and the family Bible. The gold was intended for the education of her eldest son, Richard, whom she dreamed would study at Princeton Theological Seminary in New Jersey and become a Presbyterian minister.[13]

It might seem strange, even irresponsible, of William John Russell to find himself in Augusta, when the enemy army for months had been headed for Atlanta via a path that led directly past his front door. William John, however, had two important reasons for enlisting, and February 1864 seemed the right time to do it, while Sherman was still holed up in Chattanooga, with hope strong, if unrealistic, among Georgians that he could be contained there.

One reason William John Russell felt compelled to enlist in the Confederate Army was almost surely because of his grandfather, for whom he was named. Although this elder William John Russell had been a prosperous shipbuilder in Charleston, SC, a man of considerable wealth, little was ever said of him because he had had the poor judgement to side with the king during the American Revolution. Forced to flee to the Bahamas near the end of that conflict, this illustrious ancestor lost almost everything except one ship and a few slaves and household possessions. In the Bahamas he married Mary Hogg, also from a refugeeing Tory family. Because shipbuilding was vital to the expanding British Empire and because he was industrious, he prospered in the Bahamas and later in north Florida, where he acquired a land grant from the Spanish king.

This early William John Russell died in mysterious circumstances during the War of 1812, perhaps in a skirmish with neighbors who knew of his Tory background.[14] His eldest son, Edward Russell, father of the younger William John Russell, had been sent to school in England, first at the famed Rugby School and then at Oxford University. He was called home at his father's death, and the family sold up in Florida and moved to south Georgia where they owned lands that had not been confiscated and where they may have hoped their Tory background was not known. Edward Russell, having spent so many formative years in England, was not lauded in family lore as a particularly stalwart American. With this family history, the younger William John Russell was determined never to stand accused of not doing all he could for his country.[15]

Idealism aside, the keen businessman likely had a more practical reason for joining the militia assigned to Augusta. With Savannah blockaded, Augusta had become the main "port city" of Georgia. Goods that merchants and manufacturers hoped could be shipped when the war ended were accumulating on the Savannah River at Augusta. William John Russell arrived in Augusta with cloth and yarn from New Manchester Mill and with leather from his tannery. There is no record that he transported bricks from his brickyard. He stored these goods in various places, hoping to be ready to start up trade again as soon as the war ended.[16]

His factory and mill continued production. His mill superintendent, Joshua Welch, knew of local stockpiles of yarn and was instructed how to dispose of them in the case of the enemy's arrival. William John also left instructions that if abandoning the mill became necessary, the mill workers should carry away goods.[17]

On July 5 Union troops under General Kenner Dudley Garrard advanced on Roswell. At the King factory, the supervisor ran up a French flag and declared the factory French territory, immune from acts of aggression by the US Army. Union soldiers marched directly into the "territory." Not amused, on July 7 Sherman wrote to General Garrard that he had permission to hang those who tried to turn Georgia acres to French soil.[18]

Sherman had spent his early days as a young army lieutenant surveying for the government in Georgia. He boasted that he knew Georgia better than most Georgians.[19] He was thus undoubtedly aware of the somewhat unique geological feature through which Sweetwater Creek ran, and there is no question that he wanted mills in the area destroyed for practical and psychological reasons. Other mills at Roswell and tanneries near Marietta were targets. Garrard had written orders to burn all such mills in the vicinity and to take the mill workers, mostly white women and children, prisoner. Sherman knew that such an action would cause consternation and criticism, but he did not want these skilled workers left to work for the Confederacy again.[20]

Union troops gained control of New Manchester Mill on July 9, and about one hundred women and children were taken prisoners, along with three hundred workers from the Roswell King factory. The men had felt safe in leaving. Their women most likely had encouraged them to go, because in such cases, it was the men who were in danger of being shot or imprisoned. It was a shock to see women and children herded like animals, while drunken Union soldiers "tried to make ardent love" to several of the women.[21]

On July 10 the prisoners were housed on the grounds of the Georgia Military Institute. Union cavalrymen quartered their horses in the Glover homes nearby, after they trampled the roses in Uncle Arnoldus' garden. A few days later these four hundred prisoners were loaded onto railroad cars and shipped north, first to Chattanooga, Tennessee, then to Louisville, Kentucky, and finally across the Ohio River into southern Indiana. Many of the deported mill workers were never able to find their way home to Georgia after the war. Their unknown fate, shrouded in mystery for more than sixty years, would remain a source of heartache, chagrin and shame for the Russell family.[22]

On July 20, Joshua Welch wrote to report to William John in Augusta what he had done to dispose of the yarn and two mule teams. He also gave him the bad news that the "yanks have taken all our operatives, men, women & children, to Big Shantus & Burnt the Factory before they left."[23]

Union troops also burned the tannery and the Russell home and slave cabins nearby, as well as Professor Brumby's home and that of Arnoldus Brumby. The Georgia Military Institute was burned to the ground.[24]

On July 22 what became known as the Battle of Atlanta began, and Sherman hammered at the gates of the Gate City until the end of August, when the Confederates finally evacuated the doomed town. On September 2 Union troops marched into Atlanta.[25]

On September 27, with Atlanta in Union hands, William John wrote to his wife, still somewhere near Augusta: "I now think it best for you to go to NoCar and if you prefer you can go by Rail Rd or I will try and [get] Ted [his brother] to go along with you by land. I think the Yankees will to overrun Geo. and I don't know of but one secure place and that is out in the wild woods about twenty five miles from any where and any body which I know would not suit you....I hope by this you have heard from your Pa about getting you a House, or a good boarding place...[we must]try and get you where you will be more comfortable and at the same time nearer your Father & Mother..."[26]

On September 28 William John wrote again, a fact that shows Harriette was close enough to receive frequent communications. He was fearful for her health as she entered the final trimester of her pregnancy: "I recd yours this morning will get the ham of a Mr. Conrad. Also the Hose for you and meal. I recd a letter from your Papa. He has done nothing about getting you a House... I recd a letter from Ted. He...[is] willing to go with you where ever you want to go if I cant leave. I now think it is best to go to Liberty County or South West Geo. You must choose between the two points. Or if you prefer to NoCarolina. But you ought to decide soon...The House at the Factory has been *burned*, and *no* out House, *No stable, Corn House* or *Negro Houses*."[27]

Although their home was burned two months earlier, John tells her of it now, perhaps hoping this catastrophe will be his trump to insure her flight. Harriette did not take her husband's advice. She remained close to Augusta.

In mid-November General Sherman ordered a large part of Atlanta burned, and several thousand Atlantans, black and white, fled the city, clogging the roads for miles. On November 16 the Union army left Atlanta in ruins, heading towards Savannah, under orders to leave desolation and destruction in a path sixty miles wide.

On November 24, 1864, Harriette's third son was born, according to a notation in the family Bible, on the sandflats of Edgefield County, South Carolina, west of Augusta. Although according to tradition in this strongly patriarchal family it was time for a son to be named for her husband, Harriette showed the fierce pride of the Brumbys in the Confederacy. She named the baby Robert Lee.

Following the birth of this child, Harriette traveled back into Georgia to spend the winter in Hancock County, at a settlement called Mount Zion, near Sparta. She was about fifty miles from Augusta, living in the home of William John and Martha Neal Northen. The Northens were South Carolina educators who, around 1857, had taken over Mount Zion Academy, one of the most respected boys' schools in Georgia. They were probably friends of Professor Brumby. The Northens had acquired a plantation, for John Northen was also interested in agriculture. Mount Zion community, with the Northen home at its center, was a prospering, self-sufficient one before the war, famed for its emphasis on religion and education.[28]

This area of Hancock County escaped the Union raids, and Harriette may well have spent her time without serious deprivation, caring for her three sons and helping Martha Northen in the school. Then tragedy struck. On April 10, 1865, the day after Lee surrendered to Grant at Appomatox Court House, Virginia, little Willie died of a childhood ailment. The child was buried in the churchyard of the Mount Zion Presbyterian Church in a coffin fashioned from the doors of a walnut cupboard, donated by the Northens.[29] In the family Bible, the heartbroken mother wrote the hour of death and the years, months and days of her child's life.

On April 21, Harriette received a letter from her husband, still in Augusta, announcing the news of Lee's surrender. Defeat was bitter, and he feared for his two brothers, Henry with General Lee and Ted with General Johnston. Nevertheless, the thought of peace and reunion with loved ones was sweet.

William John's instructions regarding money and food indicate that they possessed sufficient of both, as well as cloth, yarn, and a team of mules. Aware of their privileged status, he wrote: "Send Mrs. Dana what ever we have that will contribute to her comfort, also send Mrs. Palmer some Okra and Sugar, Bacon, Flour, &c. Don't let her want any thing while God is so munificent and Kind in supplying our every want."

They shared deeply their loss, as William John writes:

> My Dear, you request me to pray for you. I pray for you alway but not with that hope and faith that I know I should

possess. I will not make the same request of you for I feel too
confident that you have been fervent and constant in your
petitions for your sinful and unworthy husband and must believe
God has heard your prayers else I too would long ere this been
cut off from the earth. I thank God that since he was pleased to
take away our Darling I have been permitted to enjoy my Bible
now and to think less of the things of this life and more of those
things that make for our eternal peace. Write me often and pour
out your heart to me. It does me good.[30]

About ten days later Union troops arrived in Augusta, and not a
moment too soon. Confederate soldiers, boys and 'low women' had
begun to pillage the town. William John's prudence in storing his goods
at four different places paid off, and neither authorities nor marauding
crowds uncovered them. He was optimistic that the cloth and yarn would
be saleable as soon as Southern ports opened. He also had managed to
hold onto about $2000 in gold, a considerable amount given his
circumstances.[31]

On August 28, 1865, William John Russell, like most other
rebellious Southerners, submitted to the bitterness of seeking pardon. By
signing the amnesty oath prescribed in the President's Proclamation of
May 29, 1865, he agreed that his participation in the late rebellion
against the Government of the United States had made him "liable to
heavy pains and penalties." Surely his war troubles were over.[32]

The family moved back to Marietta later in the year, to stay with
Harriette's sisters, whose homes had not escaped the Yankee horses but
had escaped the fires. Hopeful and enterprising, William John
determined to take the cash they had saved and open a lumber business
in the Florida panhandle. Although the tannery and mill property had
passed back into the hands of the owners from whom they were being
purchased, John managed to sell other property he owned in Atlanta and
Marietta in order to have money to put into the new business. He
persuaded Harriette that there was no risk to the gold she was saving for
Richard's Princeton seminary education, and she surrendered it to his
investments. Early in 1866 he went to the Gulf of Mexico, at a point
called Escambra Bay, not far from Pensacola, with an unnamed partner.

Within a few months his partner absconded to a foreign country with another man's wife and, what was worse from the Russells' point of view, with all their money.[33]

Harriette gave birth to their fourth child, Mary Brevard, on October 4, 1866, in the Marietta home of one of her sisters, two of whom were now married to Glover brothers. Ann Eliza had married James Bolon Glover at the end of the war, brother to her sister Sarah's husband, John Heyword Glover III. Strong family loyalty was an undeniable part of the Brumby creed, and so Professor Brumby and his wife, now virtually penniless and in ailing health, were also residing in the Glover homes. James Bolan Glover, a worn, tired, returning soldier, found he was responsible for fifteen women and children.[34]

Harriette and William John determined to move on soon. They were from come-back stock, from people not given to giving up, nor to excessive complaint. William John knew of his Tory grandfather's struggles after he lost great wealth in the Revolution. Harriette's father had battled with debilitating asthma attacks all his life, having been forced to give up employment three times for health reasons, but each time he had returned to a productive life. Harriette and John realized that although they were bereft of property and cash, John's skill in managing factories and people was a valuable asset. When a position as manager and general agent for the directors of the Princeton Manufacturing Company of Athens, Georgia, became available, William John applied and was hired to take charge of this established textile factory. A plain but large house in the mill village was available for the manager's family.[35]

2

THE BIBLE IS TRUE, AWFULLY TRUE

1867-1874

The Princeton factory on McNutt Creek, three miles from Athens, was established as early as 1833. By 1866, when William John Russell moved his family there, the mill was an imposing structure, a solid, many-windowed brick building, and an example of John Quincy Adams's "palaces of the poor." No houses could claim palatial size or appearance. The manager's house was a three-story, plain structure of white clapboard. Workers' homes were unpainted clapboard shacks of one or two unsealed rooms, on rock foundations without underpinning. At Princeton there was no school, church, or post office. There was a village store. Athens, despite its distance, was the town center for Princeton residents.[1]

The natural beauty of the site, where the vigorous creek had cut ravines through wooded hills, could not have offset the bleak village for Harriette Brumby Russell. She had lived in pleasing faculty housing on picturesque college campuses in Alabama and South Carolina, where her father was a respected professor with a comfortable salary. The Greek Revival-style homes in Athens echoed the lost family homes in Marietta. In Alabama, South Carolina and Georgia, the Brumbys and the Russells had had black servants for difficult household and gardening tasks. Living at the heart of their thriving communities, they enjoyed attending social events and initiated entertainments themselves. Professor Brumby's excellent reputation and charismatic personality, not to mention Mary Brevard Brumby's kindly and sweet nature, made the family popular wherever they lived.[2] Athens, however, had not always had a kind attitude towards Princeton Factory, and an elevated social status for the manager's family was far from assured. [3]

The eldest child of twelve, of whom eight lived to adulthood, Harriette had spent her girlhood and young womanhood looking after younger siblings and also her parents, who were plagued with health problems. The caregiver role was the duty of daughters in Southern culture, especially eldest daughters, who might be expected not to marry but to remain at home to care for aging parents. Harriette appears to have accepted her work with a will. She was quick to learn anything, including home remedies and child-rearing. Left in charge, she took charge.[4]

Harriette was, in addition, an intensely intellectual woman. Although Professor Richard Brumby had three living sons, Harriette was the strongest heir to her father's intellectual depth. After receiving her early education from her father, she attended girls' seminaries in Alabama, but she was not satisfied with schools that taught more embroidery and tea-pouring than sciences and languages. When the family moved to South Carolina, she petitioned the faculty at the University of South Carolina to be allowed to take her father's chemistry class. At first they refused, but she persisted until at last they agreed, provided she sit behind a screen to insure she would not be a source of disturbance to the male class.[5] Being made to sit hidden did not improve Harriette's imperious disposition, but the importance of a woman's being attractive and charming did not escape her. At a prestigious social gathering in honor of the famous South Carolina statesman John C. Calhoun, the senator presented Harriette with the bloom of a century plant, honoring her as the most brilliant and gracious woman at the party.[6]

By the time Harriette met William John Russell in Marietta, she was almost thirty years old, had had one broken engagement and was almost surely assigned and was perhaps herself resigned to old maidenhood. When she fell deeply in love with John Russell, she approached marital life with joy, bringing to it superior education and home-making skills. As babies and troubles arrived in rapid succession, Harriette showed she was made of tough fiber, a woman determined, spirited and capable enough to make a good life for her family, wherever they were. At

Princeton, however barren the social landscape, she developed a routine for teaching and running her household, having as her philosophy that it was better to neglect dirt and dust than to neglect people. Sensitive to those among Brumby relatives who seemed to think themselves better than the William Russell Factory agent group, she drew a protective circle around her family, and the Russells of Princeton kept much to themselves.[7]

Devoted to all her children, from the first Harriette was aware that in her eldest son she had an unusual child. Intense, highly intelligent, he was eager to please. With skills learned under her father, Harriette taught young Richard, and his progress thrilled her mother's and her teacher's heart. He was beginning to read at about the age of two, and before he was seven years old he was reading in English and Latin. Harriette liked to have Richard read the Bible aloud to her, for she had retained her high hope that he become a Presbyterian minister. From an early age she instilled in him an ambition to achieve, to do something wonderful to the glory of God and the improvement of mankind, even if his Princeton school was a homebound one in a Georgia mill village and not the famed New Jersey seminary where she had hoped to send him with salvaged Confederate gold. This child was characterized as puny and delicate until his teens, and Harriette's concern for him, coupled with pride in his mental prowess, forged an intense bond she would find difficult to loosen.[8]

In late 1867, war troubles came back to haunt the Russells. Heirs and business associates of Charles McDonald sued Arnoldus Brumby and John Russell for defaulting on terms of their lease of McDonald's interests in the Sweetwater (New Manchester) factory. They charged that the factory was not returned in a condition commensurate with its condition at time of purchase, that Russell and Brumby had not kept the factory in good running order, and that they could have prevented the Union assault if they had remained at the factory. It was questioned why the machinery at least was not moved from the factory site and thus saved.

In court, former employees testified to improvements Russell and Brumby had made after purchasing McDonald's lease and to the good condition of the mill and machinery right up to the moment the Union soldiers poured kerosene over everything and threw in the torches. Testimony claimed that cams, spinning frames, rollers and belting had been well worn when Russell and Brumby took over in 1860, but added that these had been repaired or replaced with modern, high quality stock by 1864. Only sperm or peanut oil, considered the best type, was used to grease all but the heaviest machinery. Two machinists worked constantly to keep material repaired and running. The lawsuit dragged on but was finally thrown out of the courts on the grounds that individuals are not responsible for acts of war.[9]

In spite of being thus reminded of their wartime turmoil, William John took advantage of current events to bring record profits to the Princeton factory. A Congressional repeal of the cotton tax in February 1868, coupled with an East Indian cotton failure, raised the price of an abundant American crop from the fall of 1867. 1868 saw another bumper cotton crop in the South, and cotton bales barricaded both sides of Clayton and Broad Streets in Athens by the first week in December. With three textile mills in the vicinity, Athens was well supplied to turn such a crop into thread. By the summer of 1871, Princeton was running sixty-two looms and employed one hundred and sixty hands. It paid dividends of fifteen percent that year, one of its best years ever.[10]

Harriette was not idle on the home front. In 1868 she gave birth to William John, in 1869 to Edward Gaston, and in 1871 to Lewis Carolyn.

On April 17, 1872, ten days before his eleventh birthday, Richard Russell found time from his studies to write a letter to his cousin John Gaston in Marietta. It was not easy for Richard to take time off from his studies because by 1872 his teacher was a stern taskmaster with total authority, and he was loathe to see his charge with his nose at any appreciable distance from the grindstone. It is altogether likely the letter was, in fact, an assignment, and that in it the lad was showing his teacher that he could observe the world around him and make intelligent comments on what he saw. The maturity of his observations and his method of self-expression would have pleased any teacher. The tone shows he enjoyed writing it in his clear, script-like hand, in ink. He blotched the paper only slightly.

Family life went on, with births, deaths, and house purchases reported. A new baby in his mother's sister's household was declared pretty, but the budding patriarch noted with ironic humor: "Of course, babies are generally considered by their own parents sweeter and prettier than other peoples babies."

Education news was always important to Brumbys. "The Legislature has endowed the 'University' with Sand Scrip which is a sum of money, given by the legislature to some educational institution in the State the int[erest]. of which is to be used to establish an Agricultural, Mechanical and Military College, the money itself amounts to about $250,000 the only money to be used is the int[erest], which at legal rate of int. will amount to about 17,000 per anum none of which is to be used in buildings."

Of particular note to everyone in the Brumby family was that Athens had a new drugstore: R.T. Brumby Jr. & Co. Although Athens was a town of only 4800 people, this was her fourth drugstore. It was sponsored by Richard Trapier Brumby Sr., in order that his youngest child, Richard T. Brumby Jr., might have employment. Grandson and nephew Richard Brumby reported that "they have a very nice assortment of Drugs, medicines, paint, oils, glass, putty, Chemicals &c. and a fine stock of Fancy articles such as hair brushes, watch chains, Knives, combs, tooth picks, &c. they also have pocket lanterns, that are made of tin so constructed as to fold up in your pocket, & then you may take them out & use them like lanterns. Grandpa furnishes entire capital & uncle has entire management of the store."[11]

"Trippie," as R.T. Brumby Jr. was sometimes called in the family, was having difficulty realizing his potential. Grandpa had already sponsored an unsuccessful drugstore in Marietta with this son, and now, with the last of his scant capital, was trying again to establish him in work. Unfortunately, Brumby Jr. developed a serious drinking problem and the drugstore became known as a place to view the effects of a questionable "medicine."

At home, Harriette, embarrassed by the reputation of her brother in Athens society and pained at watching her father's money disappear in these last years of his life, railed against the evils of drink. She urged her sons never to touch a drop of the vile liquid. So voracious were her attacks that her eldest son asked her if he were snake-bitten, should he take whiskey, as was commonly done, to stave off the effects of the poison. She paused for thought, then shook her head. The poison of whiskey was worse than that of a mere rattlesnake.[12]

Richard Trapier Brumby Sr. was at this time living at Princeton with the Russells, and it was he who was teaching young Richard, keeping him heavily occupied with school work. From his earliest days as a teacher at the fledgling University of Alabama, Professor Brumby had reveled in academic endeavor.[13] A South Carolina native and graduate of its state college, he had migrated to Alabama about 1833 for his health, following two years of trying to practice law in North Carolina. After a brief period editing a nullification newspaper, Richard Brumby accepted a professorship in chemistry, mineralogy, and geology, subjects with which his acquaintance was slight, at the new University of Alabama.

Immediately he began delving into every branch of science, becoming deeply intimate with his main subjects. In addition, he became a good friend to physiology, conchology, and agricultural chemistry and introduced these into the curriculum. The hours he spent in the laboratory were legendary. In an academic career of more than two decades, he collected, analyzed, classified and displayed over seven thousand rocks, minerals, shells and fossils. He predicted his discovery of hugely profitable iron and coal deposits in the northern part of the state would make Birmingham the Pittsburgh of the South, and he was right. His portrait hung in the state capitol at Montgomery in honor of his achievement. After fifteen years in Alabama he accepted a call from his home state to teach science at the University of South Carolina and moved his family to Columbia in 1848.

His colleagues at the Universities of Alabama and South Carolina admired and respected Brumby for the way he consecrated his time and talents to the pursuits of science. They found, perhaps not without irritation, that he exalted science above every other department of collegiate instruction and this in a time when a classical education was a calcified norm. In fact, Brumby himself had a classical education. Yet he passionately believed that the highest interests of man were involved in scientific development. His colleagues felt that in the fervor of his devotion, he would sometimes push the claims of science beyond their legitimate limits, but his sincerity and innate charm kept him a favorite on the faculty.

Professor Brumby was also an intensely religious man of the Presbyterian persuasion, known for faithful church attendance and devout living. When Francis Lieber, a brilliant German scholar and liberal thinker, came to the University of South Carolina to teach, his ideas became popular with many students, causing alarm in the community. The character of faculty member Richard Brumby was held up as the suitable antidote to Lieber's influence.

Professor Brumby's students at Alabama and at South Carolina did not find him as charming as his colleagues did. Himself a worker who needed not to be ashamed, he expected no less from his students, and his reputation as a notorious slave-driver increased with time. He clashed often with the young men who came to the new universities of the South, often from frontier plantations where they had lived as wild princes. These New World aristocrats were less malleable than the iron and coal of northern Alabama. His students protested the work and exams heaped upon them, and open warfare between students and professor sometimes erupted. Alabama students attacked Professor Brumby with rotten tomatoes, eggs, and, more dangerously, stones, as he headed across campus to check on their shenanigans in the dormitories and dining room. In South Carolina his students burned him in effigy on campus before his own home, on a pyre fueled by their chemistry books.

Although Richard Brumby had a brilliant mind, his life experiences had taught him that there is only one genius and that is hard work.[14] He did not back down in confrontations with students regarding their need to work. Once the entire faculty of four at Alabama resigned because of student unrest—all, that is, except Richard Brumby. When South Carolina students thought a walk-out would thwart his tyranny, the faculty supported his requirements and expelled nearly a third of the protesting class.

Under this professorial grandfather, now concentrating all his talents on one student, the young namesake could not fail to notice the importance of work, nor was he likely to miss the significance of having convictions and the courage to sustain them. He never rebelled against his stern taskmaster, but worked diligently, apparently craving the sparse praise he received for precocious accomplishments.[15]

In his early studies, before her father's arrival, Harriette drilled her son in Latin declensions but not more than in principles of religious belief and moral behavior based on sound Presbyterian doctrine. Not only was he reading the Bible aloud to her, but he also could recite the Child's Catechism and the Shorter Catechism at an early age.

The Shorter Catechism, consisting of one hundred and seven questions, defined God and the Godhead, sin, God's works of providence, justification, sanctification, and many other doctrinal terms. It reaffirmed the Ten Commandments and explained what is forbidden and required in each one. It identified the chief end of man, man's fall from grace, his resulting state of misery and sin, and the way in which he may achieve again a state of grace. Through this catechism Richard learned that the word of God was made effectual to salvation through reading, but especially through preaching.

By the age of fourteen the boy could recite the Larger Catechism, wherein thorny theological concerns introduced in the Shorter version were further expounded. He had inherited his grandfather's prodigious memory and ability to focus.

Richard may have missed the lessons of intimacy and praise that he shared with his mother, but he could never have complained about his teacher to her with impunity. Harriette's father was her hero in both intellectual and spiritual matters, a revered and honored patriarch. Although when Harriette and John first moved to Princeton, the elder Brumbys continued to live with their daughters in Marietta, by 1870 Harriette had asked them to live with her and John because her star pupil was outstripping his teacher's knowledge. In addition, by 1871 she had five children younger than ten-year-old Richard, and these needed her attention.

At first Professor Brumby worked only with Richard, giving Harriette more time to teach the other children. The latter were not neglected, but according to patriarchal tradition, Richard, as the eldest son, received first attention. He was the only child allowed to go into the parlor, and the other children were shushed so that he could study.[16]

Young Richard's privileged rank put him in grave danger of becoming a spoiled brat, and he developed plutocratic tendencies from an early age. He escaped total depravity because the Brumby/Russell patriarchal creed did not offer indiscriminate respect and deference to patriarchs and patriarchs-in-waiting. It emphasized equally their solemn obligation to bring honor to the position through their work and character, and it took for granted their responsibility for the security of those beneath them in the hierarchy. *Noblesse oblige* was much more than French vocabulary. It was a way of life. Harriette drilled her eldest son on his duties towards his siblings, and she highlighted the importance of family love and tolerance. Mutual family support adhered to Southern wisdom that counted family as strength, a first and necessary line of defense against life's inevitable troubles and the world's other tribes.

Although Professor Brumby was without doubt the strongest influence in young Richard's formative years, praised and held up as supreme example, patriarchs of admirable character and achievement were not lacking on either side of Richard's genealogy. In addition to the achievements of his Brumby grandfather, he knew that his Russell grandfather, Edward, was educated at Rugby School in England, and also at Oxford, a fact which Richard would quote with great pride all his life. Edward married Susan Sarah Way, the daughter of an early and prominent Liberty County family whose patriarch was William Way. Edward Russell owned a large tract of land near Walthourville, at the western edge of Liberty County, and although there is little to suggest he was a particularly successful planter, his was a respected family in that community, active in founding the Presbyterian Church.[17]

It is not likely that Richard would have vaunted the accomplishments, however considerable, of his shipbuilding great-grandfather on the Russell side. The Tory epithet was nothing to highlight even a hundred years after the American Revolution. On the other hand, his Brumby grandmother gave him plenty of revolutionary glory to bask in. Mary Isabella Brevard Brumby was the youngest daughter of Sarah Davidson and Alexander Brevard. Alexander Brevard was a North Carolina revolutionary patriot who served with George Washington at Valley Forge and fought in several important battles, including Brandywine, Germantown, Princeton, and Camden. His brother Ephraim was one of the authors of the Mecklenburg Declaration of Independence. The Davidsons also figured in this historic document's creation and signing and in distinguished service during the American Revolution. The family enjoyed recounting the heroic deeds of these lines.[18]

That Harriette held up his father to her son as an admirable example of what a man should be is certain. Her husband's hard luck did not dim his accomplishments in her affectionate eyes. Although without significant formal education, he had become, before the age of seventeen, a clerk to Governor Charles McDonald at Milledgeville. The governor had been so impressed with the young man that he had hired him to go into North Georgia with him as early as 1847 to investigate the possibilities of setting up a textile mill there. No doubt Harriette pointed out to her children that their father's work in the noisy, dusty environment of a textile mill was no easy way to provide for his family. Workdays were long for workers and manager alike with twelve- to fourteen-hour shifts. She wanted her sons to follow his example of industrious, straight-forward, high-minded living.[19]

William John Russell was a quiet man, less fiery than his wife, though not meek. His nature was more tolerant and openly affectionate than hers. During the early years of their marriage an attack of pneumonia had settled in his throat, permanently affecting his voice. Unable to speak above a whisper, he was known in Athens as "the whispering Mr. Russell." In addition, millwork took an inexorable toll on his hearing. In spite of this accidental insulation, he remained a strong figure. Richard thought him as brave as a lion, yet capable of great tenderness. In a quarrel he was not afraid of fisticuffs and urged his sons to fight both figuratively and literally if honor was at stake.[20]

During his time as manager of the Princeton factory, William John Russell produced reasonably profitable returns, including a few especially good years. On the other hand, the Russells would never enjoy great wealth or the security and status that the properties they had owned before the war might have given. Although chief executive of the mill, William John was not an owner. Thus he could provide few of the paternalistic benefits common in the day for workers. He had vegetable plots plowed and planted each spring and gave the workers free access to these, but he could not sponsor yearly picnics on the lawn of his mansion in town as wealthy factory owners in Athens did.[21] It seems likely that the Russells remained aloof from the people of the mill village, and that they would not have seen these workers as oppressed or exploited. Rather they were fortunate to have steady, paying work in these harsh, post-war years when farming families faced ruin from season to season.

Family life at Princeton in the 1870s revolved around the studies of the children, and with age Professor Brumby softened, deciding that at seven or eight years a child could play and grow, be happy and study, too. By 1874 he had become the chief teacher of all the children, finding pleasure in the early reading efforts of little Mary and Edward. At the age of eleven, Richard was reading the Gospels in Latin and could recite the whole of the Gospel of Matthew in Latin. The lad started his studies in Greek in early 1873. By the time he was fourteen, he was riding on horseback into Athens daily for lessons in French and writing.[22]

Harriette was no longer the head teacher, but she remained the head of Christian education. Daily Bible reading was part of the children's work, and the Professor advised them to read habitually and reverently. Harriette also taught them to sing hymns from memory. They loved to go into their grandfather's room, especially on Sunday evenings, to sing for him, and he thrived on their efforts.

Besides their schoolwork, the children were busy with household chores and even the aged professor and dear grandma did not escape these tasks. Although accustomed to servants for menial work before the war, at Princeton the professor found his time taken in making fires and getting in wood and water. Grandma Mary did housecleaning, in spite of his efforts to stop her. [23] The two older boys, Richard and Robbie, had the arduous task of cutting, loading, and hauling firewood from the hilly woods around the factory.[24]

In 1872 Professor Brumby traveled to New York City to try to sell his mineral collections, and young Richard was allowed to accompany his grandfather. Brumby preferred to place his collection at the University of South Carolina, but this school was unable to afford it, and it was sold to the Cooper Union Museum in New York City.[25] While in New York City with his grandfather, Richard asked to visit the American

Bible Society and was allowed to go alone with a letter of introduction from his grandfather.[26] Although the elder Brumbys were desperate for cash and the Russells stretched to the limit of their means with their large family, they made the effort to enable Richard to see more of the world.

Activities at the First Presbyterian Church in Athens, where Richard sang in the choir, continued to be important to the family. Professor Brumby liked to have the boy summarize the sermons of Dr. Charles Lane, in oral and written form. Brumby urged his grandson to listen to Lane's expositions and to remember that "the Bible is true, awfully true…[Men] do not believe it…because they will not study properly the evidence of its Divine origin and authority."[27]

The boy was reminded that he must try to do all things well. When he apologized to his grandfather for a letter written hastily, he was admonished to "form the habit *now* of doing deliberately & well & at the right time, whatever you undertake to do. This is especially important to you in letter writing. A neat, well-written letter, always makes a favorable impression—and *vice versa*…"[28] As years passed, Richard learned to write neat and artful letters, but he pushed to the limit "the right time" to do whatever he undertook. Procrastination became a hateful habit.

3

THE SAME WORM THAT EATS THE PAUPER

1875-1880

The year 1875 brought dramatic change for Richard Brumby Russell. His religious studies under his mother were continuing apace, and at that time he had twice read the entire Bible aloud to her in English. Effective oratory was a primary objective, and the boy enjoyed speaking, but in their limited social surroundings there was little opportunity for public discourse.

Richard's road to the ministry was paved not only with Scripture verses, with prayers, with Catechism questions and answers, but also with less divine directives. Harriette urged her children to "seize every shining hour," "take time by the forelock," "consider the report your hours bear to heaven." "Remember no matter where you go," she pronounced, "you always take yourself with you." She frequently reminded them that "experience is the best teacher," and that by examining their mistakes they might "through faults arrive at perfection." Perfection in life as well as in schoolwork was not considered unattainable. Sometime during this period she had the children commit to memory Longfellow's "A Psalm of Life," written when the poet was only twenty-one. This ringing call to high purpose and heroic struggle was a favorite family recitation.[1]

Dr. Lane at the Presbyterian Church was pleased with this precocious apprentice. When Alexander Stephens, former vice-president of the Confederacy, was in town for a Board of Trustees meeting at the University, Dr. Lane told him about the boy.[2] Alexander Hamilton

Stephens had himself as a youth been bound for the Presbyterian ministry, and when he heard about a fourteen-year-old boy who could recite the Shorter and the Larger Catechisms of his faith, he wanted to hear it done. Richard Brumby Russell was invited to Stephens' home, Liberty Hall, at Crawfordville, famed for informal hospitality, to spend a few days with Georgia's foremost pre-war Congressman and one of the greatest heroes of the Lost Cause.

Stephens' unimpeachable code of personal honor and his imprisonment for four months at Fort Warren in Boston Harbor at the end of the war had endeared him to his people.[3] "Little Alex" was so frail when Union soldiers came for him at Liberty Hall on May 11, 1865, that his black servant had to carry him to the wagon, and the servant was allowed to remain with his master to care for him. Georgians were proud of how the long-suffering little giant, then fifty-three years of age and already tormented by the rheumatism that would eventually completely cripple his body, endured and survived prison to return home and continue a life of service. In 1866 the Georgia legislature elected him to the US Senate, but being from an ex-Confederate state, Stephens was not allowed to take his seat.

By 1868 he had completed the first volume of a two-volume history of the war, which people bought by the thousands and were disappointed to find it was what its title claimed: *A Constitutional View of the Late War between the States*. Young Richard, only seven years old, received a copy of this book at Christmas 1868, the gift of his father.[4]

Excitement must have been high in the Russell household as they prepared the boy for his train journey to Crawfordville, and he might have been nervous. He had had little social experience outside his nuclear and extended family, yet he had never been given the slightest hint that he was inferior to anyone else. On the contrary, although the Russells' Tory history made the subject of aristocracy one to be avoided, they were not without family pride, an element certainly not lacking on the Brumby side. In addition, Brumbys and Russells, although undeniably clannish, were good company. When they wished, they knew how to behave with charm and grace.

Harriette, who had fiercely protected her young in her nest, must have felt a twinge of maternal regret at the recognition of her first-born's flutters of independence. She could not have imagined, however, that her dreams for her son would be corrupted by a man whose well-publicized speeches declared he was "afraid of nothing on earth, or above the earth, or under the earth, except to do wrong," a man who, like her father, had been willing to suffer for his beliefs when they were contrary to popular opinion. Stephens had been unpopular in Athens in the few months preceding the war because of his Unionist stand, but his statesmanship was never in question. He was chosen vice president of the Confederacy in spite of his Unionist views.[5]

Known as the Great Commoner, Alexander Hamilton Stephens was born in 1812 to a farming family in Wilkes County Georgia. Orphaned at the age of fourteen, he became the recipient of local charity in Washington, Georgia. Impressed with the youth's mental acuity and devoutness, some of the town's citizens united to send him to Washington Academy and the University of Georgia, with the understanding that he would become a Presbyterian minister. After four exciting years at the university, Stephens decided to enter the profession of law instead of that of the ministry. He taught school for two years in order to repay his debts, then moved to Crawfordville and had established himself as a capable lawyer and up-and-coming young politician by 1836, when he won a seat in the Georgia legislature. Elected to Congress in 1843, Stephens supported the Compromise of 1850 and along with Robert Toombs and Howell Cobb was instrumental in persuading the voters of Georgia to accept it.

By the late 1850s, Stephens, a redoubtable orator of striking appearance, had become the foremost Southerner in the House. About five feet nine inches in height, he weighed a scant ninety-eight pounds and looked like a frail adolescent boy, but his shrill voice could easily be heard at the edges of crowds of five or six thousand people.

Having bought the farm that his parents owned and having acquired other land around his home at Crawfordville, in 1860 he owned almost a thousand acres and thirty-four slaves. His hospitality was legendary. After the war, Liberty Hall—so-named because he wanted guests to feel free there—continued to be a gathering place for his numerous friends and political colleagues. They came and went at all hours of the day and night, with almost every train bringing new guests and bearing away others. Five of the six bedrooms in the house were reserved for guests.

By the time young Richard's train was speeding down the tracks to Crawfordville, the great man was white-haired and crippled, permanently dependent on crutches and wheelchair, yet he had been elected to Congress in 1873. In Washington he attracted much attention, but not content to be a mere relic of the past, he spoke out sharply on the deepening plight of farmers and the injustices of tax laws. When Congress was not in session, he returned home to write and to entertain.

Arriving on a summer's day at Liberty Hall, Richard saw an unpretentious mansion, half-hidden by the magnificent grove of oaks in which it stood, on an elevated hill. Large oaks and hickories and many transplanted trees and choice exotics, scattered over an enclosure of about three acres, cast delightful shade over a grassy lawn. The house was spacious and furnished with elegant simplicity. Black servants ran the house, greeting guests and showing them to their rooms, seeing that meals were prepared and served in proper order.

Entering the front hall, the lad saw only an iron hat rack and a gigantic barometer. As he waited in the parlor, he must have noticed the engraving on the mantel of the United States Senate in 1830, during the great speech of Daniel Webster. Lithographs of Mr. Stephens himself in younger times and an excellent likeness of his life-long friend, the superb and unbending Robert Toombs, adorned one wall. Beside the fireplace, fine old family portraits reigned. On a small table that also held the family Bible, a pillar of green and white marble supported a bust of the great statesman of Liberty Hall.

In the back passage, the boy passed the cedar pail of pure cold drinking water on his way to his simply furnished upper room. In summer everything was open and the master of the house was often on the wide, columned veranda built at the rear, separating two rooms from the main house. There Stephens liked to have a game of whist or to engage his guests in lively conversation. A huge brown mastiff named Troup and a little black terrier called Frank ruled the lawns.

The two rooms off the veranda were the library and the study, which also served as master bedroom. The boy must have been almost overwhelmed by the sight of the library: a room fifteen by twenty feet, where trunks containing the letters of a lifetime also took up space, was crammed with fifteen hundred volumes of law-related books and five thousand volumes of other books, many of them rare ones, collected over a long and studious lifetime. A bronze bust of Daniel Webster presided on a shelf over the inner door.

Meals were taken in the dining room, which contained an extension table and an ancient sideboard. Mr. Stephens dined with his guests only at the mid-day meal, taking his place at the head of the table and directing conversation, which might continue for a long time after the meal was finished. Richard was seeing a side of life he had never dreamed of. He listened with awe to the lively discussions of politics and law by practitioners from the lowest to the highest levels of each discipline. Tales of days before the war when Stephens entertained the entire bar each court week surely brought laughter and amazement.

Because Stephens liked to have a guest read to him after he had retired, it is likely that Richard gave his catechism recitations in the great man's study, perhaps over several evenings. Witty, well-read and eager to please, Richard entertained the older man. The master of Liberty Hall had a genuine affection for children, and his pleasure in young Richard's company would not have gone unnoticed by the sensitive boy. There was sympathy between them. Stephens may have reminisced about his own pre-college days and his early aspirations to the ministry. His satisfaction with his choice of a law career was evident. Outspoken and frank, the statesman may have questioned the boy about his true feelings towards the life's work his mother had chosen for him.

Whatever their topics of conversation, it is no wonder that Richard Russell fell under a powerful spell cast by the unique personality and high reputation of Alexander Hamilton Stephens. Others of greater experience and worldliness stood in awe at this husk of a human being, small, sick and sorrowful, who could hold an audience of one or one hundred with his burning eyes and high thought. A kindness that triumphed over acute pain showed in his face. Patient suffering was written there as well. His friends felt that in his last years his countenance became angelic.

In the presence of this invincible soul, the boy was overcome with a desire to attain what Stephens had attained. He felt the indomitable spirit in the shrunken and aching frame and judged him to be the greatest man the South had ever produced.[6] Through Stephens' example, he saw that to be a leader among men in the political rather than the spiritual sphere could be a high calling indeed. A passion to study law and become a famous and respected public servant took light within him. A real desire to serve accompanied his dream of fame and power. At Liberty Hall he knew what he wanted to become, what his life's work must be.

His own youthful experience may have helped Stephens to suspect some of the awakening desires in the boy's heart and mind. Perhaps he saw the admiration and awe in Richard's looks, the reverence with which he followed the old hero's words and movements, and he felt he must offer some advice. Before the boy departed, Stephens invited him one last time into the study, and drawing him close to his side, as he lay on his couch, he said, "Never forget, Richard, that the same worm that eats the pauper eats the prince."[7]

Richard may not have understood that the old man was sharing an ancient truth about ambition, but he was never to forget those words or his time at Liberty Hall.

The visit to Stephens was not the last event to set Richard on a course free of his mother's well-meaning influence. In the autumn of 1875, his grandfather and grandmother fell desperately ill. Because both had suffered many illnesses, at first the latest installments were not thought serious.

Harriette gave herself completely to the care of her beloved parents, and by early October, her days and nights ran together as the crisis deepened. When at last the end was near, Harriette, overcome with grief and labor, turned to her eldest son for help. It was to be his responsibility to purchase a cemetery lot in the Oconee Hill Cemetery.

Although only fourteen years old, he accomplished his errand with confidence. He chose a lot on a hillside overlooking the Oconee River, with a restful view, one to encourage visitors to the grave to contemplate life and death with serenity. He carried out the necessary legal work with gravity and assurance. Being grown up was not an uncomfortable state.[8]

Mary Brevard Brumby died on October 5, 1875. On October 6, her husband followed her across the Great Divide, into that House not Made with Hands. Harriette recorded in the family Bible: "Mary M. Brevard Brumby died at Princeton Factory near Athens. Tuesday aft. 2 oclock, Oct. 5, 1875; Prof. Rich T. Brumby died at Princeton Factory Wednesday night 10:30 ock. Oct. 6, 1875 age 71 yrs. 2 mos. & 2 days." The Brumbys were buried the same day in the lot their grandson chose for them. Professors at the University of Georgia acted as pall bearers.

Someone, perhaps one of the grandchildren, scratched the death dates on the window pane of their bedroom and nearly seventy years later the story of how two faithful old lovers lay corpses at the same time was a well-known tale in the area known as Princeton.[9]

Without her father, Harriette no longer tried to carry on home schooling. Georgia had no publicly-funded schools at this time, and so the younger children would attend a local private academy. But what should they do with Richard?

By this time Richard had dared to tell his mother that he did not believe he was called to preach the Gospel and that he wanted to study law. His school of choice was the University of Georgia. Devastated, Harriette could hardly be persuaded that this change of heart had happened. Although her son grieved over her disappointment and ached to cause his mother pain, he could not be dissuaded.[10] William John agreed to send him to UGA but only as long as he remained in the top four of his class. If he did not, his father said, he would have to go to work in a textile mill in Columbus. Richard believed his father meant this threat, for these were days when most boys of his age would be working. The luxury of spending several years as a student was one afforded to only a privileged few. He promised to work hard.[11]

Richard was growing in another sense. He was becoming increasingly attracted to the opposite sex. Faced with bringing up five sons, Harriette was well aware of the need to civilize virility, and true to form, she was diligent in instructing her sons in proper amatory attitudes. Love and marriage could be the only setting for sexual thoughts, much less activity. Marriage was held up as a holy and desirable institution wherein all one's needs, spiritual and physical, would be met. Within the patriarchal family circle, Harriette's work of wife and mother was highly venerated, and her role was in no way considered 'lower' than that of her husband. Her children recognized that she was an exceptional mother and that her self-sacrifice made their lives better and happier. Sister Mary was a favorite with her brothers, and because she never enjoyed good health, they were protective of her. Richard was especially fond of Mary. He early developed a sincere respect and regard for women.[12]

In the social and political chaos in the South following the Civil War, all classes were struggling to understand the changes in their lives. For the white elite, including planters, professionals and business people, rigid domestic standards as well as personalized standards of manly and womanly conduct were the subject of many articles intended to guide this class adrift in dangerous waters. These articles, in local papers and in magazines, continually lobbied for the proper roles and respective duties of white males and females. The essential ingredient in creating proper homes and an orderly society, the domestic literature assured its readers, was neither wealth nor power but good character. This attitude underlined and re-enforced Harriette and John's stern biblical values and their worthwhile examples.[13]

Richard's early pre-occupation with the idea of love and marriage, not to mention his tender nature, are evident in his entry in the friendship book of his cousin Mamie Glover. Friendship books gave friends a page on which to answer questions that described their personalities and dreams. To the question "What is your idea of happiness?" the fourteen-year-old Richard answered, "A sweet and amiable wife." There is scant evidence that Harriette qualified for either of these epithets, but amiability and sweetness were the ideals for Southern women of the day and at fourteen, Richard's rose-colored view admitted only the ideal.[14] In his opinion, the sweetest words in the world were "I will be thine," while the saddest were "I cannot love you, no never." The sublimest passion of which human nature is capable? Richard wrote "Love & Fidelity." While he thought the most important character trait for a man was truthfulness, for a woman it was modesty. In both men and women what he most detested was deceit.

Richard's growing reputation for wit and adroit word play was also revealed in this document. Asked what book (not religious) would he part with last, he wrote: "My pocket book."[15]

In spite of her desire to keep her son near her, Harriette decided that to assure his passing the university's entrance exams, he ought to attend an academy in Lawrenceville, Georgia, run by her brother, Alexander Brevard Brumby, and accordingly he was sent there in 1876. Richard suffered a few pangs at this separation from his mother, but soon gloried in making new friends and tasting the delicious freedom to roam with them in a small but growing community. Within the narrow confines of life at Princeton he had learned the value of family. In Lawrenceville he first tasted the joys of friendship.[16]

In the autumn of 1876, Richard Russell entered the University of Georgia. His entrance exams placed him in the Sophomore class, and remembering what his father had said about working in the Columbus textile mill, he settled in to prove he could be an outstanding student. His father's injunction to remain in the top four of his class "or else" probably stemmed from the tales William John had heard of Professor Brumby's rambunctious and rebellious students. Without question education would be nothing but a high-minded pursuit in this Russell-Brumby household.

William John need not have worried. The war had radically altered peer pressure in Southern universities. Although Franklin College students in Athens had been no different from the rowdy antebellum students at Alabama and South Carolina, the days were past when students could indulge in idle and frivolous pursuits. Post-war young men who were lucky enough to afford and to get places in higher education worked hard. The first students to come back to Athens after the war were in the majority returning soldiers who, having survived a terrible crucible, were loathe to waste study time. Gratified professors at the University felt this changed attitude could be counted one positive outcome of the war.[17]

By the autumn of 1876, the war veterans had gone, but young men still felt privileged to have a chance to go on to school. The flickering torch of white Southern culture had been passed to them, and they were eager to honor their defeated fathers by making good in a new South. Boys did not forego being boys, of course, but when they disobeyed rules, disrupted assemblies, cut classes to attend unauthorized circuses, blew up chemistry labs, and the like, they accepted their discipline as deserved.[18]

For Richard, participating in campus social activities, approved or otherwise, was difficult because he lived at home, walking or riding a beloved horse, Charlie, the three miles to and from Athens each day. His course work included chemistry, physics, mathematics, Greek, Latin, French, German, history and Belles Lettres (English language and literature). It was not unusual for him to stay up studying until two or three o'clock in the morning or to have his mother wake him at four or five a.m. to study. He began several diaries during his school years, intending to record his successes for future pleasure of recall and his failures as learning experiences, but he wrote only sporadically. A former candidate for the cloth, he recorded with mixed pride and despair his use of bad words and yieldings to other carefully unnamed temptations.[19]

From his first days at college, he was an ardent member of the Phi Kappa literary society and soon became one of its most competitive orators. Oratory in the South both before and after the Civil War was a high-profile sport, and those who excelled at it were the modern-day equivalent of star athletes. A man able to influence others through the spoken word, to stir the emotions and stimulate the minds of large crowds, was a man likely to become important in his community, state and nation.[20] Many former graduates testified to the importance of the literary societies in their education, some feeling they learned more from their activities than from classes. Interested crowds filled the Chapel for various events, and until about 1880, the societies remained the most important social organization on campus.[21]

Richard Russell recognized immediately how important the skills of declaiming, orating and debating would be to him in his legal and political career, and he was not ignorant of how the ladies, especially young women from Lucy Cobb Institute, enjoyed the competitions between the Phi Kappas and the Demosthenians. His early schooling in Latin, Greek, and the Holy Scriptures stood him in good stead in this arena. At ease with Horace and Cicero, Aristotle and Socrates, the ringing, poetic phrases and powerful metaphors of the King James version of the Bible part of his blood and bone, he possessed the tools needed to become a champion orator. Deeply emotional and sensitive, he was a handsome young man, tall, straight, dark-haired, blue-eyed. His riding, walking and wood cutting gave him a sturdy physique in contrast to his earlier delicate frame. He was not likely to be upstaged regarding appearances. He longed for a new suit but was forced by his parents' economic situation to wear the same old short-tailed "sock coat" day in and day out.[22]

He was not the only one, student or professor, to wear worn clothing. The professors wore high hats and dark swallowtail coats, and in winter capes or shawls. The shawl of a favorite math professor, William Rutherford, became so decrepit that the boys took up a collection to buy their professor the finest overcoat to be had in Athens for Christmas. When it was presented, a large crowd of boys gathered from all classes, and Professor Rutherford accepted their gift with such appreciation and kindness that every student present felt touched and uplifted.[23]

The campus itself was in a shabby condition, so much so that when the Board of Trustees met in 1878, prior to Commencement, it called attention to the dilapidated and unseemly condition of the dormitories, the neglected appearance of the Phi Kappa and Demosthenian Halls, and to the shocking condition of the sanitary arrangements on campus. There was little money for improvements. Attendance for the year was one hundred and sixteen students and only about thirty of these paid fees. Forty were Agricultural students exempt from fees and under law fifty students were admitted free to Franklin College, which had forty-six students.[24]

Alexander H. Stephens, who was on the Board of Trustees, was in Athens to attend the 1878 meetings and was a guest of Dr. John A. Hunnicutt on Milledge Avenue. Many students, surely Richard among them, took this chance to speak to the great man, calling at the Hunnicutt home. Perhaps Richard was comforted to note during the Commencement exercises, that Stephens' beaver hat showed considerable age. Huge crowds came to the Commencement activities, countrymen in linen dusters with palmetto fans and straw hats, city fellows with dark suits and swallowtails.

Another Georgian growing in importance was at this Commencement week. It was the tenth reunion of Henry W. Grady's class, and the young scion was on campus. Everywhere he went or stopped, a crowd would gather around him, talking and laughing. Grady's reputation as an orator was established, and the students watched with admiration as he captivated crowds all over town.[25]

In the autumn of 1878, at the start of Richard's senior year, a Congressional election attracted attention on campus. One of the candidates, Emory Speer, an Athens lawyer, thirty years old, a young man of splendid appearance, made a memorable impression among the students. Budding orators observed he had a keen sense of irony, ready wit and quickness of reply, especially when he was interrupted. Although most students disapproved of Speer because he was running as an Independent instead of as a Democrat, they admired his brilliancy and resistless power of oratory. They were not surprised when he was elected by a narrow majority.[26]

Campus improvements were going on in 1879. Some of the buildings were repaired and painted and many trees were set out. An especially unsightly area in front of Moore College, the Agricultural building completed in 1875, was graded, terraced and partially sodded with Bermuda grass. A measles epidemic made class attendance slack in the winter term, but as Commencement approached in the summer of 1879, there was great excitement. Alexander Stephens would be back and this time he was the principal speaker, scheduled to give the Alumni Society address.

Richard was one of three Phi Kappas representing the society at the Champion Debate. The honorable O. A. Lochrane, who was to become the fourth Chief Justice of the state of Georgia, presided. The subject: *Resolved, That there should be a property or educational qualification on suffrage.* The Phi Kappas had the affirmative, deemed the unpopular side, and the Demosthenians won. The *Augusta Chronicle*, in a special from Athens, said it was a great debate but praised especially only the speeches by Mell, Felker, and Smith.[27]

Nevertheless, nothing could dim these glorious days for Richard, for he was to make another speech. One of four graduates to speak at the Commencement exercises, he had made good his promise to his father to remain at the top of his class: he was ranked second. In addition, his rigorous course of study had earned him two degrees, the A. B. and the Ph B. He was the only student awarded two degrees.[28]

Athens was again aglow at the presence of Alexander Stephens. Two military companies arrived on the morning he was to speak: the Oglethorpe Light Infantry from Savannah, and the mounted Richmond Hussars from Augusta. The companies arrived on the Georgia Railroad and were met at the depot beyond the Oconee River by the Athens Guards with the Burns Silver Cornet Band, to be escorted to a champagne lunch at the Hope Fire Hall on Market (now Washington) Street. Then both companies went through drill exercises on Campus, with the cavalry coming out crowd favorite.

In the afternoon, the largest crowd ever seen gathered at the chapel for Stephens' speech. There was no question of the chapel's holding the throng, and many stood outside, waiting to catch a glimpse of the statesman. He spoke for an hour and a half on "Objects and Aims in Life and the Chief End of Man."[29] Richard would have recognized the reference to a Catechism question in the title and would have been pleased to tell friends of his first meeting with the great man.

Wheeling his chair right and left on the podium, the orator spoke ex tempore, in a tone reminiscent of an old patriarch returning home from a long journey, talking to his kin and neighbors. He was sixty-eight years old, but there was no hollowness in his voice. When he became impassioned of a subject, his high-keyed, penetrating voice was as stirring as the sound of fifes. Although disruption during speakers' presentations was common at commencements, while Stephens spoke, no one else moved or spoke. When he concluded, the rapt audience rose cheering and clapping in a thrilling ovation.[30] Young Richard's blood must have coursed with pride in his hero and with hope for his own great destiny.

Thirty-three graduates received their diplomas the next day. Richard made his speech on the subject of "Young Men" and likely received many congratulations on it and on his future prospects at an evening reception when the Chancellor's home was thronged with graduates, parents, and other visitors. Refreshments graced the tables in the parlors and halls, and guests enjoyed promenading outside in the large grove of trees lit with hundreds of Chinese lanterns.   These Commencement exercises were judged among the greatest in many years for enthusiasm and stirring speeches.[31]

Law school required only one year, and Richard received his degree at the 1880 Commencement exercises, along with three other candidates. He was admitted to the Georgia bar in Watkinsville, Oconee County, before Superior Court Judge Alex S. Irwin, on July 21, 1880.[32]

It was about this time that the young man made the decision to change his name. Since his grandfather's death, two Brumby uncles had continued to gain reputations in Athens for heavy drinking. Looking to his political career, Richard feared potential electors would hear the Brumby name and assume he was a drunkard. He had long ceased to write Brumby as part of his name, giving only the "B" as a middle initial. Thinking of having his entire name in the public eye, he changed his middle name to Brevard, his grandmother Mary Brumby's maiden name. This change saddened Harriette, but given her attitude towards the evils of drink, she could hardly disapprove.[33]

4

I AM RESOLVED TO MARRY
AND MARRY I WILL

1881-1885

As a rising young solicitor, Richard Brevard Russell could have set up shop anywhere, and he was determined to make his mark, even if he had to go west, but he did not want to leave home.[1] Harriette's well-drilled code of conduct reminded him to honor his father and mother, and he was sensitive to the manifold demands upon his parents as they struggled to educate six children in a poverty-stricken region. Certainly he enjoyed his heir-apparent status, but he stayed near the family fortress where he might be useful as well as honored.

By 1880 his brother Rob, a tall, robust, good-looking lad, was a sophomore at the university. Harriette had transferred her hopes for a Presbyterian minister to her second son, who was her right-hand man at the home, helping her with milking and other chores. Rob, however, had his eye on an appointment to Annapolis and a naval career. When he won the drilling medal in the end-of-term military exercises in the spring of 1880, he pinned his prize to his uniform as he walked the three miles home, hoping the girls out Cobham way would notice it. He tucked it away when he reached home, and surprised the family with the news at the supper table, waiting until Mary finally asked who had won the contest.[2]

Mary, bright and witty, attended Lucy Cobb Institute in Athens, where she studied rules of etiquette and the latest fashion as avidly as lessons in math and English. The younger sons, John, Edward and Lewis, were in school at Grove School, located between Athens and Princeton. Richard referred to them affectionately as 'the small fry' and enjoyed scuffling with them until early hours of the morning when Harriette, tolerant of this affectionate male bonding, would finally call out, to Richard's delight, "Peace, be still."[3]

All young lawyers could expect a 'waiting period' when they started out. They had to wait for clients to appear.[4] Richard wanted to be on hand when they did show. As soon as he had passed the bar, he rented an office at the corner of Clayton Street and College Avenue and set up a cot in the back room. He cooked and ate in this small room when he could not afford boarding house meals. Athens had upwards of fifteen lawyers and competition was keen. Few clients appeared in the beginning, so with time to spare and an agile pen, he wrote articles for Athens papers, the *Banner-Watchman* and the *Chronicle*, to supplement his income. He used this experience to plump out his resume, declaring himself an associate editor.[5]

A few evenings each week and after church on Sunday, Richard was at Princeton, relishing Harriette's home-cooked meals. Sometimes he slept at home, and if he had court or other business in Jackson or Oconee Counties, he took the family horse and buggy after he delivered the brothers to their schools. Renting a horse and buggy cost $1.50, a prohibitive expense. When working in Athens, he walked to town, leaving the school run to Rob, who liked horses and was better at managing them than was Richard. Lewis enjoyed working with horses alongside Rob, and these two sons thought of themselves as Harriette's special forces.[6]

Richard did not find these binding family ties unpleasant. The Brumbys and the Russells adhered to the code of family loyalty prevalent in the South, and he was proud of his blood. In his world the importance of kinship could not be underestimated. Second and third cousins, both Brumbys and Russells, were known and valued, whether living or dead. Graves of those who had passed to a fairer shore were objects to revere. The Brumby lot, in Oconee Hill Cemetery, which he had chosen at his grandparents' deaths was swept and raked regularly. For years Harriette and John paid Paul Glover, the former slave who had accompanied

Harriette when she refugeed to Hancock County, to tend little Willie's grave at Mt. Zion. The little brother was gone but not forgotten. Although Richard had no money, in Southern church-directed and kin-dominated society, the young man was reassured that the determining element in social relationships was kin, not wealth. In this view, he was rich in respectability and numerous kin. By his own success, he intended to bring honor to the line and to waste no time in achieving this distinction.[7]

On a snowy January 1, 1881, confined to his room at Princeton with a sore throat after an extensive trip to Jackson County, Richard spent time going through his old examinations, speeches and letters. Recognizing the success and the skill of these papers acted as an elixir, urging him on in the pursuit of his ambition. In his diary he declared:

> Ambition? did I say shall I admit I am ambitious? Ay in this diary written for my eye alone I shall make any admission of any thought I feel so that in future days when I shall be known and honored by all I shall look back with pleasure to this recaller of my past pleasures and joys when unknown to fame, or if it be my sad fate to fail, I shall rejoice oh so greatly in my bitterness of spirit and misery that I once had at least a hope of doing great things...I have but one ambition but as I know I could not forget... I shall not record it.

Richard's ambitions were political, but politics was not what the virile young man dreamed of most often. Much more prevalent in his diary entries was the theme of love. Richard Russell was in search of a bride.

Frustrated and lonely, he longed for a mate. Following his mother's and his society's teachings, he looked to the institution of marriage to fulfill his desires and dreams. His attitude towards women was typical of the white South at this period. Women were the fairer and better sex, and their reason for being was to make life comfortable for men. While his mother was a woman of strong intellect, she willingly spent her talents and energies in the care of her husband and children, as she had spent them in the care of her parents and siblings. She saw nothing belittling in this choice. Not only was it God-ordained in her view, but there were few other spheres in which women could achieve or find even a quiet niche. Perhaps it was unconscious practicality, but Harriette Brumby Russell urged all her sons to aspire to greatness, knowing she would make her mark through them. They longed to please her, and Richard's desire to establish his own home seems to have sprung at least partly from Harriette's veneration of her husband and her hearth.[8]

In January 1881, Richard had been practicing law only six months, and he had not reached his twenty-first birthday. Yet he had already fixed upon his 'dulcina,' the memory of whose sweet smile, silvery voice, and plait of light hair hanging down her back, haunted him. He had not yet declared his intentions, but, he wrote, "I have made up my mind to marry before this time next year." If his beloved refuses him, he has two or three others he will try, and "though they can not ever supply a thousandth part of the void in my heart and my life which she could, still I am resolved to marry and marry I will."[9]

He believed marriage would ease his frustration and loneliness:

> I can never overcome my bad habits and evil propensities without a companion to cheer my loneliness and urge me on to greatness…[O]h! how great the pleasure to be derived from companionship with one whose every interest is identical with your own, to whom you can reveal, if you like, every thought and working of your inmost heart…If I could get Miss B. she would make a most congenial companion, friend, counsellor, guide and a guardian *angel* through life….

On January 6, he discovered new delights in the person of "Miss Lily"[Moss], the daughter of an influential local businessman whose family was prominent in Athens society.[10] Competition for her company was vigorous. He often found two or three other young men visiting at her home in the evenings or on Sunday afternoons, and Lily did not fear disappointing one suitor, so numerous were her admirers. He persevered, comparing himself with the others, confident in the impression he had made, feeling he had held his own. When her father had to remind him it was time to go home, he tried to derive comfort that she whispered to him 'not to mind.' He went to Methodist revival meetings in order to please Lily, and was miserable when he met her on his way to Presbyterian services on a Sunday, sure she was angry. They attended plays and minstrels, and he was anxious that she seemed offended once because they had to sit among a "nest of Jews."

Before leaving on a trip to St. Louis, he tried to build up his courage to "pop the question." She gave him a violet and played the piano charmingly for him on their last night together, but he lost his nerve. When he returned from St. Louis, he grieved that she was not as warm to him as she had been before he left.

Longing to see Lily's bright sunny face during his time in St. Louis, he came home via Atlanta and visited a second cousin on the Brumby side, who seemed charmed with him. When Cousin Rena invited him to come calling, he considered her secure economic position and the delight of 'striking a rich wife.' Thinking of Rena reminded him of Susie, and he asked himself whether she cared for him or not. It was rumored earlier among Brumby cousins that they might marry.[11]

Lily remained the favorite, however, in spite of his being only one of five suitors in her parlor. Hoping for marriage with her did not prevent his daydreaming over the girls in his church to the extent that he admitted in his diary that he did not hear one word of the sermon. His friend Sylvanus Morris, another young lawyer in town, agreed that the Presbyterian girls were a distraction sufficient to sink the words of even the finest biblical scholar.[12]

In addition to his romantic activities, Richard pursued less happily another kind of courting. Harriette urged her sons to get and keep in first class society, not to waste time with 'little' people, and Richard tried hard to follow her advice.[13] Accustomed to the comfort zones of clan life at Princeton and in Marietta and Atlanta with Brumby and Russell kin, he found it distasteful to court people in order to secure work or recognition. Although he early realized he could hold his own in any company for wit, repartee, stories, and intellectual discussion, he preferred not to compete. Harriette warned her sons that it was a Russell failing to associate with subordinates in order to be admired, yet Richard preferred to work in the smaller and, by Athens standards, less cultured towns in the region, such as Watkinsville, Jefferson, Mt. Airy, Homer, and Carnesville.[14] Athens had long held an elevated opinion of her central place in the cultural universe that was Georgia, and the Russells, exiled at Princeton, had not entered that heady atmosphere except as members of the Presbyterian Church and briefly as part of the university community while Professor Brumby was alive. In these early years Richard Russell chaffed under what he saw as his great disadvantage of living near Athens all his life, yet not entitled to be 'from' Athens. He was sure older lawyers and businessmen snubbed him for his less-than-native status as well as for his youth.[15]

On the other hand, his talent for friendship endeared him to the younger men in town, including rival swains for Miss Lily's hand. Friends were often in his office early in the mornings and late in the evenings, where they told jokes, talked politics and even read and discussed law cases. Richard relished these sessions, but after everyone had gone, felt that he was 'not himself' in these circumstances, again likely a reflection of his sheltered life. He also went into local saloons with friends to drink beer, but worried whether respectable people would frown on him or if he met Miss Lily, would she suspect he'd been to an improper place?

Two especially close and life-long friends emerged from this time. One was Joseph Jacobs, a young druggist who had apprenticed in Crawford W. Long's Athens drugstore in the 1870s and opened his own establishment in 1882. The other was Sylvanus Morris, six years Richard's senior and well-established as a young lawyer in whom the yeast of hard work was producing noticeable leavening. Joe Jacobs understood Richard's misgivings that the Brumby reputation for drinking might rub off on him and listened for hours as Richard went over quarrels with 'Uncle Eph.' Sylvanus was a companion on trips to and from Jefferson, in Jackson County, and the young men shared hopes and dreams as they covered the twenty-mile journey, whether travelling in a horse and buggy or, when neither had enough money for wheels, walking. It was during one of these walks that Richard first told his friend at least part of his political ambition.[16]

What was this ambition? Although he told Sylvanus that he wanted only to become chief justice of the Supreme Court of Georgia, Richard Russell declared to himself that he would also become governor of

Georgia and United States senator from Georgia. Because no Southerner of his day could hope to become president, these offices covered the highest he could achieve in all branches of government, judicial, executive and legislative. He wanted to win the whole shooting match.[17]

What inspired a near-penniless young man to such heights? Richard's upbringing had assured him he could do anything he set out to do. As his mother urged him to greatness, she no doubt cited examples of successful men who had risen from nothing. No other theme is more American. In addition, the social, economic, and political situation in the South spurred Richard's entire generation of white men, for they were the dispossessed, destined to fight to regain what their fathers had lost. As the poverty of the South deepened following the war, the loss of the Russell factories, home and prestige must have weighed heavily on the young man. The lawsuit brought upon his father by a governor's family may have made him yearn for power. Not to be discredited as motivation was his sincere desire to serve. He longed for fame, for recognition, but he must deserve it. He was prepared to work and to work hard. The tradition of labor producing achievement was also part of his inheritance. Brumbys and Russells believed that "Labor omnia vincit." He wanted, like the poet, to leave footprints on the sands of time, to make his life sublime. Thus he must be up and doing, with a heart for any fate. He must learn to labor (for work conquers all) and to wait.

At the age of twenty-one, he was not adept at waiting, and there were many days when he felt that he had chosen the wrong profession, that he was ill-suited to the law and that he would never have any true friends in Athens. He detested examining every act for political or social advancement. In his diary he confessed: "God only knows the yearning of my soul for friendly sympathy. How hard to wear day after day a smile and look as if you had been successful in getting friends so as to draw friends! Oh, I am ambitious too ambitious."

By mid-1881 his despair had deepened, not principally from his work, but from the bitter memory that when he declared his love to Miss Lily, she coolly made fun of his 'fancied love.' Resigning himself to her lack of interest in him, he recorded philosophically: "I have suffered all that a sensitive unloved and doting nature could, but I regret it not since I have luxuriated in anticipations fraught with heavenly joys when to be in her presence was sweeter to me than nectar to Gods." Nevertheless, her refusal sent him to his friend Woodward and the local saloon, where he drank too much and later made drunken speeches at a Sigma Alpha Epsilon fraternity meeting. He paced in his room all night and soon after he and Woodward went to Atlanta and "got on a most terrible spree."

In behavior typical of white Southern men of his class, he also attended the state Sunday School Association meeting in Atlanta at the same time and took a leadership position in the organization. He was already treasurer of the First Presbyterian Church, and he sang in the choir each Sunday. In his diary he catalogued his church activities as signs of not only duty fulfilled but also of honor and accomplishment.

In spite of relinquishing his dream of domestic bliss with Miss Lily, Richard was determined to build a pleasant home in which to spend his lonely hours and to house a good library. He bought two lots in Athens, probably on Milledge Avenue, and through a mighty effort of industry and economy paid $228, the first of three payments. He was proud of these financial achievements.[18]

Resigned to the loss of love, he decided his political ambition was all that was left to him. When he learned that the Honorable Pope Barrow would be vacating his General Assembly seat to take an appointment to the United States Senate, Richard Russell decided, in spite of his youth, to run for the General Assembly from Clarke County. If he could win the support of fellow Democrats, he could become the unofficial party choice before the election and discourage other candidates from entering the race. This anointing of a candidate for the legislature was not uncommon in the decade following Reconstruction because Democrats wanted as little opposition as possible. Clarke County had had Republican black representatives during Reconstruction, and white citizens were anxious to prevent a recurrence. Richard Russell nevertheless, made friends with Madison Davis, a black man from Athens, who had served as a representative in the state legislature during Reconstruction. Davis had retained the respect of white Athenians, including Congressman Emory Speer, and Davis and Richard Russell formed an alliance that both considered beneficial.[19]

Georgia politics was at this time firmly in the grip of three men who have been called the Bourbon Triumvirate. Alfred H. Colquitt, John B.

Gordon, and Joseph E. Brown played musical chairs with the offices of governor and senator for more than twenty years following the return to home rule in 1872. They were originally named Bourbons in recognition of their conservatism. As an antidote to Reconstruction, the battle cry was a return to the ways of the Old South, but in fact, their outlook was far from agrarian. They favored sectional reconciliation, industrialization, low taxes, and frugal government.

These ideas, especially those regarding an industrialized New South and cordial relations with Northern business interests, were popularized by Henry Grady and the *Atlanta Constitution*. Grady, while never entering the political ring as a candidate, influenced politics heavily through his oratory and his newspaper. With Grady as their manager, the Bourbon trio was unbeatable. Brown, governor during the Civil War and a highly successful businessman, provided the brains; Gordon, a genuine war hero, provided the looks and charm; and Colquitt, a licensed Methodist minister, provided the religion, a necessary element in the politics of the South.

Colquitt, a lawyer and planter as well as a minister, was elected governor for a four-year term in 1876 and re-elected for two years in 1880. The revised Georgia Constitution of 1877, which endured with amendments until 1945, was passed during his first term. His gubernatorial tenure was stormy, however, and he met with strong criticism at every turn. Many scandals were exposed among his officers, but none touched him. His character was certain to appeal to the Brumby ideal of moral rectitude. Gordon and Brown had clearly entered the political arena not only for loudly declared service to their downtrodden people but also for a less well-advertised desire for material gain. Brown added to his considerable wealth while in office, and the gallant Gordon gained and lost fortunes as if they were marbles. Colquitt's political career, on the other hand, did not glitter with acquired gold. A strong advocate of temperance, interested in all religious and moral issues, an unpretentious and mild-mannered Christian, Colquitt was appointed United States Senator at the death of Benjamin H. Hill, and served in the Senate for twelve years. He would ultimately be considered one of Georgia's greatest political leaders of the nineteenth century. Here, in tandem with Alexander Stephens, was a man Richard Russell could admire.

By this time opposition outside the Democratic party was almost defunct. Emory Speer, whose oratory had thrilled Richard in 1878 when the lawyer spoke on the university campus, was associated with Sylvanus Morris in legal offices in the 1880s. Speer had won election to Congress in 1878 as an independent Democrat, and was re-elected in 1880, but by 1881, local Democrats were becoming alarmed at his Republican associations and his tolerance of blacks.[20] A concerted Democratic effort to unseat Speer in 1882 succeeded, and Richard, watching this defeat at close quarters through his friend Sylvanus, must have decided that in Georgia politics the better part of valor and good sense was to stick close to the party line. He would become well-known for his independence but within the Democratic fold.

Late in the year 1881 he began canvassing for support in his campaign for the legislature among his friends and acquaintances in Clarke County. He met with opposition. He was "too young," "not the man for the place," the idea was "simply ridiculous." Determined to be tough, he steeled his sensitive nature to take unkind cuts, and although he recorded the criticism in his diary, he refused to be discouraged. When the election was held in the autumn of 1882, he was elected, receiving 776 of 791 votes cast. At the same time, his idol, Alexander Stephens, was elected governor of Georgia.

Richard Russell did not go to Atlanta unprepared. He studied the legislature and determined which committees he wished to serve on, both for his own advancement and for the good of his county, and he made a daring plan that would assure his appointments. It was an idea an older, more experienced political servant, aware of the territory, would have trembled to contemplate, but the young whippersnapper in blissful ignorance rushed boldly in. When candidates for Speaker of the House wrote him with their campaign claims, he wrote back, saying he would consider their candidacy but expect some favors in the way of committee assignments. Seasoned legislators may have considered this reply a sign of naivete or audacity, but Richard Russell knew what he was doing.[21]

On November 4 the honorable Mr. Russell of Clarke arrived in Atlanta for the inauguration of the governor and his first session of the General Assembly of Georgia. He was twenty-one years old, the youngest member of that august body. At ten in the morning, Governor Colquitt addressed the Assembly in joint session, speaking about matters of public concern dealt with in his tenure: public schools, railroad regulation, agriculture, the state penitentiary, the asylums for the deaf, dumb and blind, pardons, the State Board of Health, the state university, and myriad financial matters. Then they adjourned and reconvened at three in the afternoon to inaugurate the new governor.

The legislature met in the old Kimball Opera House at Marietta and Forsythe Streets, a building secured for the capitol when Atlanta replaced Milledgeville as the seat of government in 1868. Legislators usually stayed at the Kimball Hotel, where as much politicking went on as in the State House. In this era superior and supreme court judges, solicitors general and US senators were elected by the legislature in joint session, and election fever burned high in the opening days of the session. Only after these offices had been filled could the business of lawmaking be carried on. A young man would be assaulted by others seeking his vote. In addition, special interest groups would be after him, hoping to secure legislation favorable to them. Keeping a clear head and a clear conscience would not be easy. Keeping a low-profile might be considered prudent.[22]

Richard wanted to be a member of the powerful Rules Committee, and also the committees on judiciary, finance, and education. He knew that as a new representative, he would be ignored in this request unless he could make himself indispensable in some way. Because the campaign for Speaker of the House, one of the most powerful positions in all of state government, would be close between L. F. Garrard of Muscogee county and W. R. Rankin of Gordon county, Richard decided to run for Speaker of the House himself and to get a few colleagues from counties close to Clarke to support him. He persuaded four others to promise to vote for him, believing if they could hold out, they would have a powerful trading tool. Only the candidate for Speaker who was willing to give them their chosen committee assignments would get their votes.

The contest between Garrard and Rankin for Speaker proved as close as Richard predicted. As the temperature rose over the voting, it became obvious that the Russell votes did indeed control the election. Russell and his colleagues frankly asked for committee assignments in exchange for their votes, but at first neither Garrard nor Rankin was disposed to consider the matter serious. However, Russell could not be swayed to withdraw nor his colleagues to abandon him. He wittily suggested that if things went on this way for long, he himself would become Speaker because Rankin supporters would vote for him before they voted for Garrard and vice versa.

The contest waxed warmer and warmer, yet Russell remained unperturbed. Finally, Garrard gave in, promising Richard Russell an appointment on the Rules Committee, and was elected Speaker of the House of Representatives by a two-vote margin.[23] Russell was also assigned to the Special Judiciary Committee and the Committee on Wild Lands. This show of political sagacity and nerve would later earn him places on the education and finance committees.

Richard Russell showed early and far-reaching vision in the causes of education in his beloved home state. He was from a county that was the center of state higher education, and his family example of the importance of education could scarcely have been stronger. Consequently, in his first session, he participated in a fight for appropriation of $20,000 to replace the mint at Dahlonega and thus enable Dahlonega and North Georgia to get the North Georgia Agricultural College.[24]

In his first session he allied himself with Nathaniel E. Harris of Bibb County whose goal was the establishment of a technological school in Georgia. Harris, himself a newly elected representative, was grateful for Richard's interest because he knew that opposition from university forces, which was sure to come, could be fatal to his project. On November 24, 1882, Harris introduced a resolution to provide for a committee of seven to "investigate and consider the propriety and expediency of establishing in this State a School of Technology, under the supervision and direction of the State University."[25] Richard Russell was one of seven named to this committee, which was to return to the summer session of 1883 with recommendations.

Russell of Clarke missed no sessions during this first term and worked hard on bills covering a wide variety of subjects: roads and bridges, business incorporations, education, and prohibition. He served with able colleagues, who would later rise in state politics. William J. Northen, from Hancock County, in whose home Harriette had refugeed during the war, Joe Terrell, W. Y. Atkinson, and Nat Harris shared his commitment to education during these first years. All would become governors of Georgia. He roomed during one session with a man who was to become a bizarre kingmaker in Georgia politics for two decades, the legendary Tom Watson. When Watson grew impatient with what he considered his lack of achievement in the final days of the session, he left for home, instructing Richard to draw his pay and send it on to him.[26]

When the legislature adjourned on December 8, 1882, Richard had earned his four dollars per diem, and he was certain that his record would vindicate him before his critics. He wrote with obvious satisfaction in his diary that he had fulfilled his first political goal. He wrote nothing about his progress in obtaining a wife.

On March 4, 1883, Alexander Stephens' frail body could no longer take the demands of its proud spirit, and the venerable statesman died. The Legislature reconvened for his funeral in Atlanta, an occasion of great sorrow and ceremony. Robert Toombs, in one of his last public appearances, bade farewell to his life-long friend with tear-bedimmed eyes and husky voice. The curtain was coming down on the old warriors.

By law James S. Boynton, the president of the Senate, became governor. Boynton called an election for April 24 and summoned the General Assembly to meet, count the votes, and install the new governor. In an exciting contest between Boynton and A. O. Bacon, a former Speaker of the House, no candidate was chosen after seventeen ballots. A compromise candidate had to be found in Henry D. McDaniel, who was nominated by acclamation and elected. It was for young Richard to note the vagaries of politics and the possibilities of little-known men achieving the high office of governor. McDaniel did not even have the skill of oratory but instead had a terrible stutter.

Between McDaniel's election in late April and his inauguration on May 10, Richard Russell went to Newnan, Georgia, to the wedding of a friend. There he met Marie Louise Tyler, a dark-haired, dark-eyed beauty whom her friends and family called Minnie. Small in stature and slight of build, Minnie was pretty and personable. Her family enjoyed music and theater, and perhaps there was a little of the actress about her for she sometimes performed in amateur opera with her father and brother in her hometown of Barnesville. She was a member of the Mozart Club there, which had presented musical comedies and light operas, works like "Pinafore," "The Pirates of Penzance" and "The Mikado." When she met Richard Russell, she was twenty-three years old. He had celebrated his twenty-second birthday on April 27.

The lightning bolt struck. Richard and Minnie fell wildly in love, and as the wedding festivities drew to a close, Richard could hardly bear the thought of leaving her to return to Atlanta. Nevertheless, the new governor must be inaugurated and the honorable Mr. Russell of Clarke must be present. Before taking his train, he invited Minnie for a buggy ride that lasted into the warm May night. It grew late, but he drove on, refusing to bring her home until she promised to marry him. Minnie promised.[27]

On May 10, 1883, the inauguration of Henry Dickerson McDaniel took place, and Russell of Clarke was present. Afterwards, rather than go home to Athens, he went to Barnesville, and the couple decided they would not wait for parental approval and a delayed wedding date. They eloped to Griffin, where they were married on May 13. The next day Richard and Minnie arrived in Athens on a late train.

Richard could hardly ask Minnie to share his cot in the back room of his office, and he was eager to introduce his bride to his family. He had achieved another goal. A sweet and amiable wife, his guardian angel through life, was by his side. They may have walked the three miles to Princeton. What did miles matter? They were floating on air.

It was past bedtime when they arrived at the old white clapboard house and roused the residents. Sister Mary came downstairs, and when Richard announced he had brought home a bride, she ran back upstairs to tell Harriette and John.

Harriette would not take this announcement in. She refused to get out of bed and meet the new Mrs. Russell. It was left to Mary to go down and tell Richard that his mother did not wish to see them. The younger boys must have been looking on, all except Rob, by then a student at the US Naval Academy in Annapolis, and the tense scene sent a mixed message about the advisability of marriage. On the one hand, here was brother Richard about to take a beautiful young woman to bed. On the other, they trembled before the knowledge of an angry and hurt Harriette, shut away in her room. It would be a long, long time before another Russell son would take a bride.

Too fond of Richard to do anything but welcome Minnie warmly, Mary put fresh sheets on the bed in his room and readied the bridal chamber as best she could. Richard had always loved Mary, but her loyalty on that night endeared her more than ever to his sensitive heart.[28]

The wedding announcement in the Athens *Banner/Watchman* of May 15 declared that "Mr. Russell is a rising young lawyer, while his bride is one of Georgia's most loveable and amiable daughters."

It can scarcely be doubted that in the beginning the Tylers looked with noticeable disfavor upon Richard Russell. Had he not come into their midst and stolen their daughter away? For her part, Harriette Russell kept to her bed for several days before finally agreeing to meet Minnie. The young couple would have amends to make in both houses.

They were not long in making them. Minnie's sweet nature and sunny disposition soon won her mother-in-law and all Richard's family over. They watched with interest and pride as the pair set about establishing their home.[29] Richard's open adoration of Minnie, coupled with his success in law and politics, must have reassured the Tylers. Within the next year Richard was forgiven enough in Barnesville to be invited as orator to the joint meeting of the Eunomian and Lysium Societies of the city, and he did not neglect to extol the virtues of the classic city of Middle Georgia for several pages before getting into his main topic, "Advice to Young People." He was twenty-three.[30]

William Patterson Tyler, Minnie's father, called Captain Tyler, had died in 1880, but he had been a strong father figure. He had had two daughters by earlier marriages, losing his wife with the birth of each child. He then had three sons and five daughters by Martha A. R.

Redding, his third wife. Minnie was the fifth child of this union. The Tylers, having suffered the deaths of young mothers, were accustomed to taking in children who had lost either home or caretaker, and two of Minnie's cousins would begin, in Macon, Georgia, the Hephzibah Orphanage, which is extant. In love and veneration of family, Minnie and Richard were well-matched.

Richard's two lots on Milledge Avenue, bought in his discouragement over earlier courtships, proved providential. He was prosperous enough to provide a rather large house for his bride, and the young couple seemed set to prove that wedded bliss does exist.

Richard continued his law practice and his politicking with fervor. Although he was becoming more and more at home in these combative masculine arenas, where men must prove themselves in battles of words, wits and even fists, he found the returns to his home with its attachment of feminine graces as sweet as he had dreamed. He could appreciate and recognize Minnie as a gifted and beautiful woman in her own right, but her loyalty to him and his interests, her unswerving admiration, was what most endeared her to him.[31]

Richard's legislative duties kept him away from home during the summer of 1883. The legislative committee on the technological school traveled to the Northeast by sea, convening in New York City on June 9 to inspect several engineering schools. It is certain that Richard Russell influenced these choices, for one was Cooper Union in New York City, where Richard Trapier Brumby had taken his grandson when the professor sold his mineral collection. They also visited Stevens Institute of Technology in New Jersey, Boston Tech (later MIT) and the Worcester Free Institute in Massachusetts. At the General Assembly summer session on July 24, the committee report recommended a school modeled after the Worcester Free Institute, and House Bill No. 732 was introduced and referred to the committee on finance. Although the idea was a favorable one, the struggle for a technological school was to be long and its outcome uncertain. Russell of Clarke would have to show political courage in order to stick with Nat Harris in this fight.[32]

On August 13, 1883, in the early hours of the morning, the Kimball Hotel caught fire and burned to the ground in less than five hours, leaving a shell of the building that was home-away-from-home to the

General Assembly. Fortunately, the fire was spotted in time to evacuate all guests and servants. Although no one was killed, Western Union received four hundred anxious telegrams, and four hundred assurances were sent out.

Among the lucky, Richard Russell escaped wearing an entire suit of clothes, but all his other things burned. Others got away in night-shirts or odd assortments of garments. As they milled about in the street, Richard shared his collar buttons with a man who looked particularly addled. This kind of shirt-off-his-back gesture created long-lasting friendships. On the day after the fire, the Atlanta paper noted that Russell of Clarke moved that the Assembly suspend roll call and the motion passed. No one blamed anyone for going home after such an horrific night, and under the circumstances it seemed hardly fair that their per diem should be lost.[33]

Journalistic approval of legislators was not common, however. Legislators worked all week but came home on Saturdays. They received free railroad passes, a perk disputed in the local press because it was feared the railroads had too much power over state politics. The *Banner-Watchman* reported that returning legislators tended to spend the week-ends swaggering about the town 'or up and down the air line road.' The *Banner* also criticized the $1000-per-day cost of the legislature, calling it an 'extended frolic' at which legislators went to nearby resorts (on their donated railroad passes), drinking and airing their dignity instead of being at their posts of duty. They were 'hanging onto the public teat like grim death to a dead nigger.' It printed a joke about a captain not wanting to be mistaken for a member of the legislature, 'those free-pass gents and canine protectors.'[34] In fact Richard Russell had steered through the Assembly a bill requiring that all dogs in Clarke County be taxed. He had to learn early that in politics it is not possible to please all of the people all of the time, even on the most trivial matters.

Athens in the 1880s was one of the most civilized places in Georgia for a young couple to start out. Only Savannah, Atlanta and Augusta were her rivals. Athens' location as a center of education, farming, industry, and railroads gave the city a strong economy in spite of hard times. Social life bustled with teas, dances, operas and minstrel shows. In 1884 the town gave a gala party in honor of Grover Cleveland's Inauguration.

Church on Sundays and revival meetings at other times provided social as well as religious interest. The university, although not growing in numbers, continued to emphasize Athens as a place of culture and refinement. By 1881, Athens had a police force of three, and in 1882 modern utilities appeared when Bell Telephone installed lines to its first thirty-six subscribers.[35]

It is doubtful that Richard and Minnie were telephone subscribers since telephones were expensive and new. Richard Russell rarely embraced "modern conveniences", especially if they increased household expenses. Although in his early courting days he felt he had made his living and then had thrown away enough to support a wife, he found supporting two challenging.[36] There were building expenses and furniture to buy. Minnie picked out an ornate, carved walnut bedroom suite, with an elegant marble top to the wash stand and a vast headboard that would have been frightening to almost anyone but blissful honeymooners. They needed a set of chairs, a washstand, a wardrobe, and lamps. It would take them two years to pay for all this.[37]

Merchants, thanks to Athens' general prosperity, could afford to advance credit. Richard became experienced at owing money, borrowing for everything from houses to harness. Although he eventually paid every debt, he was often late in payments as he juggled income in order to meet his many obligations.[38]

This indifferent attitude toward debt in a son of Harriette Brumby and John Russell is understandable in view of the fact that the South was a place where everyone owed everyone else, for there was little money anywhere. Farmers owed merchants from season to season, and merchants owed their suppliers. In the case of share-cropping, the tenant farmer owed the landowner. The merchant or landowner had the advantage of the lien system, which meant the farmer had to buy from him as long as the farmer was indebted to him, and merchants consistently overcharged the farmers and kept them virtually enslaved. On the other hand, without the merchant's risking debt for supplies, the farmer would have had no seed or fertilizer, no flour and sugar to feed his family. A bad crop year could wipe out not only the farmer but also the merchant or land owner who was in debt to the bank or to wholesalers. The South's sharecropping system has been likened to the tar baby of her own Uncle Remus tales. All who touched it became stuck.[39]

Professional people in this scene grew accustomed to waiting months and years for payments from others saddled with debt. Although young lawyers could make a little money through collection of debt, Richard hated this work. Chasing down a farmer's cotton in order to impound it before he could sell it away from his creditor was not pleasant work.[40] It is small wonder in such a climate that men like Henry Grady championed attracting Northern capital to the South. Richard Russell understood the needs of the New South, but in his own life, he could not make accumulating money a goal. His political ledger called him more insistently than his bank book.

When not in the legislature, Richard worked hard at his law practice but his law income was not adequate for his ambition. Diversification was the name of survival for young men of the South, and he tried business ventures. The merchant image was not a tarnished one to the son of William John Russell. Richard sold guano and fertilizer to farmers, perhaps with his father's help. On his trips to the remote towns of the judicial circuit, places like Homer and Carnesville, he hauled goods such as canned fruit, cloth, buttons, miscellaneous household items (syrup pitchers, glasses, teapots and washbowls) and sold them to merchants at a ten percent commission. He could pay for his horse and buggy and make a little extra.[41]

He joined a group of businessmen to organize the Athens Street Railway Company's passenger service and introduced the bill to incorporate it in the General Assembly on August 28, 1883. In the 1870s the railway was established to transport goods only from the train station into town, but in the 1880s it was thought in the public interest to establish a passenger system. There were three cars on the line, pulled by small Texas mules. The mules arrived in boxcar loads, untamed, and until they learned the job, provided exciting entertainment on the streets of Athens. They might be seen as likely behind the car as in front of it, and on a few occasions mules had chosen to join passengers inside the cars. The *Athens Banner* reported that a bulldog took hold of an errant railway mule and refused to release his prize. Unfortunately, between bulldogs and belly-deep mud, the mules found the work more than they could stand, and the business floundered. When electric cars were introduced, profits improved, but by this time Richard had got out of the scheme. He was retained as attorney for the Classic City Street Railway Company when it was reorganized and remained proud of his association with this venture.[42]

Richard and Minnie enjoyed a pleasant life in Athens, for they were congenial, attractive, and sociable. Their home was likely a gathering place for those of their age and for Richard's family as well. All their dreams of a happy family seemed to be coming true when they learned they were expecting a baby.

The birth of their first child, probably in February or March 1884, was not the joyful event they anticipated. The child was stillborn, leaving them heartbroken but not discouraged. Losing a first baby was painful but not unusual, and Minnie's sunny disposition returned quickly. By the end of the summer, she was expecting another baby.

Richard was re-elected to the House of Representatives in the autumn of 1884, over two other contenders. His chief interest and accomplishment in the Assembly continued to be in education, where his projects would lead to long-lasting and beneficial effects at the local and the state level.

As he had feared, Nat Harris's technology school bill did indeed generate opposition among university advocates. Branches of the university had been established over the years, some had proven failures, and all were unpopular with the university alumni, including its board of trustees, who saw them as "stepchildren" whom the legislature forced upon the state. They claimed every dollar given to such schools was a dollar taken from the university itself, thus preventing its progress and development. The technology school would require an appropriation of nearly half a million dollars.

Richard Russell's determination to see this project through in this climate showed vision for his state and personal political courage. In the beginning the idea was most unpopular in Athens. The report of the committee of nine was published in large extracts state-wide during 1884, and soon after, the university chancellor and prominent members of the university faculty came around to supporting the school bill. According to Harris, these men were too great to let the old animosity towards branch colleges stand in the way of an institution that would bring about so great an advantage to the state. Self-interest might also have been at work as the *Banner-Watchman* suggested in July 1885 that the school should be built in Athens. There was fierce competition for towns to become the sites of new public schools, for schools brought jobs and money.

In fact, scant state money was allotted to education of any kind during the post-bellum period, when money was in short supply. Every debt weighed heavily on the citizenry, and the Bourbon triumvirate discouraged new projects. Harris believed that legislators were sleeplessly vigilant in trying to cut off anything like the expenditure of public money, in the interest either of education, pensions, or otherwise. In addition, Georgia was constructing a new capitol building, and this necessitated a dreaded extra tax for the expenditure of one million dollars.

Athens itself had been trying to establish a public school system since 1879 and Richard was a keen advocate. There had been much public debate, with opponents arguing that "what was good enough for our parents [that is, private education] is good enough for today" and that "the public school is a Massachusetts invention and we are becoming Yankeeized fast enough." Progressives argued that all growing cities, of which Athens was one, had public schools and that what the country needed was systematic education for the public good and thus the public must pay for it.[43] In 1885 a bond issue was passed, and in the 1885 session Russell of Clarke introduced and guided through the state legislature, a bill that authorized the public school system of Athens.

In early 1885, Minnie gave birth to another stillborn child. To signify their grief, the young wife wore mourning, black in winter and white in summer, and struggled to regain her equilibrium after this new loss. Between the pages of her *Peale's Popular Educator Cyclopedia*, along with a few pressed carnations, she saved a news story of a mother who killed herself when her child died.[44] Although the doctor recommended time to recover, they were determined to try again.

The summer of 1885 was an exciting time in the Legislature for Richard. Nat Harris was jousting full tilt to get his bill for the technology school passed, and because there was still heavy opposition to the bill, he would need to call on every lieutenant he had. Four of the nine young men who had gone with Harris to the North to study technical education had not returned to the House for the 1885 session. Richard became more than ever a highly valued ally. Harris counted on him to persuade the opposing university elements from his district that this kind of technical education was absolutely vital to the prosperous future of the state.

The bill, Number Eight, was first referred to the Finance Committee, of which Harris was chairman, but it did not go through unresisted. Numerous amendments were offered and numerous parliamentary schemes inaugurated to defeat it, but it finally emerged on July 22 for consideration. Russell made an impassioned speech in favor of the bill, referring to the university objections but declaring that although he loved the university and its purpose, it was his duty and the duty of all present to take the state forward into the new age with this different character of education.

The supporters of Bill Number Eight sat with anxious hearts as the roll call was made for the vote on July 29. They needed eighty-eight yea votes for passage. Tension mounted as the yeas and the nays rang out. When the eighty-eighth yea vote sounded, the enthusiasm of the House could not be controlled. Supporters of Bill Number Eight shouted and pounded their desks and threw papers into the air, yelling like Georgia Tech sports fans in training. The adrenaline of political battle is a powerful potion for the winning team. Such moments confirmed Richard's feeling that politics was a glorious profession and his ambitions worthy of the struggle.

In spite of this enthusiastic celebration, the bill had the gauntlet of the senate to run. William J. Northen, a powerful ally of education, was on the senate education committee, and the bill made it through the upper chamber with only two amendments. Nevertheless, its House opponents had a surprise in store for Harris. They managed to persuade a few of his supporters to vote against taking the bill up with its amendments, and it looked as if Number Eight would die quietly as the session ended. Harris refused to let this happen and through skillful parliamentary procedure, managed to get the amended bill passed. Governor McDaniel approved the bill on October 17, 1885, but it would be almost two years before the fight for its appropriations would be finished. This fight would not be won without a memorable sacrifice from Russell of Clarke.

5

THE WING OF WOE HANGS LOW
ITS SABLE SHADOW

1886-1890

By the end of the summer of 1885 Richard and Minnie were again hopeful for the arrival of a little Russell in early spring. Richard, busy with his law practice, was active in business enterprises such as the Athens Savings Bank, and he was serving on the newly-formed school board. The board set up schools for whites and blacks, and plans were underway for construction of a large new school building on Washington Street. Although his financial situation improved, he continued to write for the *Banner-Watchman* and the *Chronicle*.[1]

Early on Richard took up membership in a number of fraternal organizations, including the Masons, Oddfellows, Knights of Phythias, and Royal Arcanum. These associations flourished in the post-bellum South among males of both races. Their emphasis on brotherhood and on honoring members with flowery phrases and hierarchy provided a means of gratifying needs for friendship and recognition.[2] Exulting in elections to offices of any kind, Richard did not resist those with such titles as Grand Master, Grand Representative and Supreme Regent. He was perennially an officer of some degree. At the district meetings of fraternal organizations he was in demand as an orator and thus had the opportunity to speak to large crowds. Such speeches increased his name recognition with the voting population and nourished his ego as well.[3]

As Christmas of 1885 approached, Minnie began to have trouble with her pregnancy. Dr. Gerdine, a beloved and respected doctor of Athens, sent her to bed, and she seemed to improve. She felt well enough to greet Harriette and young John from her bed on Christmas morning. Minnie insisted Richard accept their invitation to have Christmas dinner at Princeton, and he went home with John and Harriette.[4]

By the time he returned Christmas night, Minnie was much worse. Dr. Gerdine declared the situation grave, and Richard was obliged to send to Barnesville for Minnie's sister Ida to help with the constant nursing. The baby came prematurely and stillborn, and Minnie was stricken with what must have been childbed fever. The weather turned cruelly cold. Water froze in buckets not ten feet from the fire, while Minnie's life burned out in a raging fever.

At five o'clock on the morning of January 6, Minnie Tyler Russell died, leaving her young husband crushed under the desolate weight of the shadow of death. He carried out his duties with dignity, that he might honor his wife, but his grief-stricken face rent the hearts of his family and friends.

Minnie was laid out in her coffin in a black silk dress with white lace collar, her abundant black hair loose upon the pillows. If ever a corpse could be called beautiful, hers would have deserved the adjective. Harriette and son John once again came to see Minnie, this time to bid final farewell. Harriette found her daughter-in-law sublimely beautiful. Young John, seventeen, volunteered to go with Richard to Barnesville with the body. Father John could not go because the cold weather meant he had to be at the mill around the clock. He thought it best for Ephraim Brumby, Harriette's brother, to go. Old quarrels were laid aside as the older man supported his nephew with his sorrowful burden.

The funeral was to be in the Methodist church, and Minnie would be buried in the Greenwood Street Cemetery, in the little town where she had spent her life except for the thirty-one months of her marriage.

The small party of Richard, Ida, and Uncle Eph went by train to Barnesville, and because of the cold they had to spend the night in Atlanta, where Mary was visiting Brumby relatives. Letters from Harriette had gone astray, and Mary had not heard of Minnie's illness. When she received a telegram informing her that Minnie's body would pass through Atlanta, she was profoundly shocked. She met her beloved Richard and his sister-in-law at the station, intent upon doing what she could to console them. Her offer to stay with Ida that night was gratefully accepted, and the young women mourned Minnie together. Friends and relatives gathered. In spite of the cold, they found fresh flowers to brighten the dark night. Mary was proud of her brother's composure, but in his face, she saw that he was suffering a grief the young do not suspect or expect. She tried to remind herself that death can come at any time, and she resolved to be ready.

Richard arrived with his beloved wife in Barnesville at ten o'clock on the morning of January 7.[5] By eleven o'clock the church was crowded with sorrowing friends and family. While the choir sang "Refuge" as a voluntary, the casket was brought up the aisle, covered with fresh flowers. Most of the congregation could not hold back tears.

Three ministers directed the service, the Reverend Mr. Timmons, and Drs. Kendall and Cook. After Mr. Timmons read the burial service and spoke of the beautiful life of Mrs. Russell, the eulogy was delivered by Dr. Kendall, who had known Minnie from her earliest childhood. He spoke of her as a sunbeam, bright, sparkling, never dimmed by cares and sorrow. His illustrations of her irrepressible good nature, perhaps taken from the desolate days when she mourned her lost babies, seemed striking and appropriate to her friends. While the choir sang "In the Sweet Bye and Bye," the congregation filed past the open casket to look for the last time on the mortal remains of Minnie Tyler Russell.

The *Barnesville Mail* published a lengthy obituary and a poignant poem written by one of Minnie's Athens friends. Richard clipped these articles and slipped them into the family Bible. In the first grief-stricken weeks after Minnie's death they must have pained and consoled him, as he wept "for the days that would come no more, for his sunbeam flown from hearth and door." When it had been washed and ironed, he pinned a note to a white night-gown: "These are the clothes in which my precious Minnie died." He would keep the box holding this treasure for the rest of his life.[6]

The wing of woe hung low its sable shadow over the heart and home of Richard Russell. Minnie's friend's poem, "She Will Sleep Tonight," sought to console with the thought that although he suffered because his love would not wake "for tears, nor prayers, nor love's sweet sake," he must remember she had ceased to suffer. She was at perfect rest. The intellect does not comfort at such times. He was struck dumb with hopeless anguish, the knowledge of his loss unavoidable, yet too terrible to bear.[7]

The Brumbys were given to melancholia, and Richard had shown this penchant to depression even when times were good. In one of life's most stressful situations, the loss of a spouse, he endured black depressions, but he struggled against the enemy despair. Relying on precept and example from his father and his grandfather, he turned to his work. Without Minnie, life would be bleak, but fulfilled ambitions of glory and service offered a reason for being.

During the winter of 1886, Richard's friends, mindful of his grief, gave a dinner in appreciation of his work for Athens in the legislature. During his remarks, he discussed with pleasure the successful passing of the bill to establish a technical school in Georgia, and he reiterated the need for Georgia's young men to have the opportunity for industrial education, in addition to educational opportunities already provided at the university.

Afterwards a woman visiting from Mississippi sought him out to tell him his remarks had struck a sour note with her. She introduced herself as Mrs. Strong, an appropriate appellation, for she took him to task for his failure to see that Georgia's young women needed education as badly as her young men. No, the women needed it worse. Could not he see that woman has no way to support herself unless she has education? Many women are forced to support themselves and their families for various reasons, and it was a shame and a disgrace that the state of Georgia gave no thought to her daughters' welfare. Even those women who are fulfilling the all-important role of wife and mother, supported financially by their husbands, could not be said to lack a need for higher education.

Richard Russell saw as a truth revealed in a flash that this ardent woman was right. He felt keenly the sense of shame she sought to arouse. It was so obvious, why had no one thought of it? He determined to do something for the education of Georgia's daughters at the next session of the legislature, and asked her what she thought he might do.

She gave him the example of a recently formed normal and industrial college for women in Mississippi.[8]

While the boys' technical school bill had passed in 1885, its appropriations, an initial $65,000, were not to be available until after January 1887, and the wording of the approval meant that technically they should come out of any surplus in state funds. Since state funds were never in surplus, in the summer session of 1887 the opponents of the bill saw another chance to shoot down the school. Nat Harris had not returned to the legislature, and thus his former lieutenants would have to return fire in this unexpected fight.

Richard Russell was indeed determined to do something for girls' education in Georgia, and he drafted, in his own hand, House Bill Number 680 of the 1887-1888 session, to establish a state-supported college for women that would give them the same amount from the treasury of the state that was afforded and had long been furnished to boys at the University of Georgia. The school he proposed would offer normal training for teachers and other industrial and technical skills such as typing, stenography, telegraphy, as well as domestic science. He determined that the best way to get the bill through was to attach it to the appropriations vote of the Industrial School for boys, and when this bill came up in the summer session of 1887, "Russell's Girl College bill" was duly attached.

The Russell bill had received favorable publicity state-wide during the session. Henry Grady of the *Atlanta Constitution*, Patrick Walsh, of the *Augusta Chronicle*, Albert R. Lamar, of the *Macon Telegraph*, and John H. Estill, of the *Savannah Morning News* endorsed it and encouraged its adoption. The *Athens Banner-Watchman* reported it on September 6 as another 'branch college' and, not surprisingly, was not particularly in favor of the idea, but recommended to voters to read the bill itself for particulars. Once again Richard Russell found himself with a project that the university community, his principal constituents, frowned upon.

The principal opposition to the industrial school for boys had been led by a Judge Harrell of Webster County, a rural county in southwest Georgia. When his renewed opposition came in September 1887, there was a bitter struggle to repeal the bill. One of the main arguments against it was that the state simply could not afford it. Also there was entrenched in many from the deeply rural counties that education was for the elite, a perception not entirely false where the university was concerned. Although it was an attempt to make education more available to the masses that motivated Harris and others in their vision, Harrell played on the idea of inequality, and some were willing to listen. Now that a large number of those in favor of the bill had left the House, the scheme was in serious jeopardy. The Speaker of the House, Judge W. A. Little, a long-time friend of Nat Harris, left the chair and with energy, eloquence and power, marshaled the forces in favor of the measure. In order to be sure of defeating its repeal, however, he had to make a compromise: He had to agree to drop the girls' school bill, which was, in fact, not part of the original bill. This would reassure those who were worried about the state's ability to finance even one school.

When the matter was thus presented to Russell of Clarke, he knew he would have to abdicate. It would be foolish to sacrifice the hard work that had brought them so far with the boys' school. If the girls' school had to accept a delay, it could and would be brought back at the next session. Like Harris, he would have patience and perseverance. He agreed to withdraw Bill No. 680, and the appropriations for Georgia's first school of technology for boys went through.[9]

Although Richard reveled in his work in the legislature, the time had come to leave it.[10] For one so young, legislative duty was only one step in legal training and political service. A frequent reason for running against opponents in Georgia politics at this time was that the office holder had been in too long, was 'homesteading' the office. To remain was a sign that one's career was not going well or worse, that one's ambitions were modest. In spite of his desire to re-introduce the girls' school bill, Richard Russell decided in 1888 not to seek re-election to the General Assembly but to run for solicitor general of the Western Circuit.

The solicitor general's office was, like service in the legislature, a stepping stone.[11] Ambitious young lawyers filling this role could hope to become Superior Court judges. Because Richard Russell knew so many legislators, the fact that the office was elected by the General Assembly gave him a strong advantage. Solicitor general hopefuls with attendant family and friends as extra campaigners converged on Atlanta at the opening of the General Assembly, took up residence at the re-built Kimball, and endured or enjoyed, depending on their temperaments, two weeks of vigorous campaigning.

Another advantage to being solicitor general was money. The office paid two hundred and fifty dollars per annum, not an entirely negligible sum, considering that many respectable jobs paid only twenty-five dollars per month. More importantly, the solicitor general was entitled to various court fines, which might grow to two hundred dollars or more per session.[12] In his diversified efforts to make a living and in his efforts to become known as an ambitious politician, Richard had not built up a thriving law practice. Bored with financial matters and the solicitation of clients, he needed a job that would provide not only political advancement, but also ready cases and pay.

The first two weeks of the legislative session were given over to the task of choosing judges and solicitors general, so that the elections could be disposed of along with the throngs they attracted. A dozen judges and a dozen solicitors general were elected to four-year terms, with perhaps two or three candidates for election to each office. In 1888 four men were running for Solicitor General of the Western Circuit.

Richard knew his chances were good. Lawmakers considered it an advantage of the system that they had two weeks in which to get to know the candidates, observe their conduct, and discuss their characters with people who knew them. Richard's acquaintance with so many members of the Assembly would put him far ahead within this custom.

Before the legislature convened, Richard did his homework, writing by hand to men all over the state to ask for their support. Two of his opponents, Albert Mitchell, a former Solicitor General and E.T. Brown, the incumbent, were also from Athens. T. W. Hill of Jefferson was running on the platform that Athens ought not to have the monopoly on the office. Richard ran on his service in the legislature and his desire to serve further.

He kept a little book with the names of all legislators, senators and representatives, and canvassed every man during the opening two weeks of the session.[13] The entire business of the Assembly during this time concerned these elections, and campaigners could walk freely on the House and Senate floors to talk with the lawmakers. Richard was indefatigable in this work, and proved a hard man to resist. An accomplished storyteller, he loved to swap jokes, a favorite activity in these circumstances. Although prohibition was already a rising issue and tee-totallers were plentiful, Richard negotiated this razor's edge with finesse. He would take a drink with the boys but was not known for drunkenness. He had also picked up a convivial habit common to law work in those days: he chewed tobacco. He cultivated an image as a common man, self-made, working hard for every achievement and every dollar. He wanted no taint of "privilege" attached to his name.[14]

Richard Russell reveled in these contests, and by this time it seems certain he was addicted to politics. Especially after his home life was destroyed, he needed the buzz that campaigning gave him, and he became increasingly unable to give up any activity that promised it to him.

When the votes were counted for Solicitor General of the Western Circuit, Richard Russell's book showed he received one hundred and forty, E.T. Brown forty-seven, Albert Mitchell fifteen, and T.W. Hill six.

Although the election ended Richard's official involvement with the legislature of 1889-1890, he saw with satisfaction a girls' school bill re-introduced in 1889 by his friend William Y. Atkinson, whose wife, Susie Cobb Milton, encouraged him in this move. The Atkinsons conducted a campaign to awaken the minds of the people to favor the ideal of widening the sphere of female education. Enlisting women's organizations in the effort proved successful, and in spite of Bourbon conservatism and fear over paying for the new capitol, the girls' school bill as Richard Russell envisioned it passed the General Assembly and was signed into law by Governor Gordon on November 8, 1889. To be located in Milledgeville, the school was called the Georgia Normal and Industrial College.[15]

Becoming solicitor general meant Richard Russell began riding the judicial circuit in earnest in 1888. As a free-lance lawyer he knew both the excitement and the weariness of this venue. Now he had to be at every court, and this necessity meant long weeks away from Athens. The

Western Circuit, composed of the counties of Banks, Clarke, Franklin, Gwinnett, Jackson, Oconee and Walton, was one of the largest in land area in Georgia. Before railroads became common, young lawyers wore out their shoes in getting to and from court, and they had no need for fitness rooms. In his earliest days of practice Richard had often walked the twenty-six miles between Athens and Jefferson. In his diary he recorded walking from Carnesville to Harmony Grove (re-named Commerce), a distance of more than twenty miles, in five hours. By 1888, there were railroads connecting some of the courthouse towns of the circuit, and he was more able to afford a horse and buggy than he had been in the early 1880s. Nevertheless, this nomadic lawyer's life was demanding physically, mentally, and emotionally. In his loneliness after Minnie's death, it suited him to stay in hotels or boarding houses in the towns where court was held, to submerge himself in the masculine world of work, and thus to suppress painful memories of the sacred but lost joys of home.

From the earliest days of courts in Georgia, entertaining the court and its entourage was a principal delight of the local population in all court house towns. Trade and social activities would increase during the week before court, and the pace and excitement of life sped up during court week as lawyers and clients descended on the town. In Carnesville, near the mountain resort of Franklin Springs, in summer the social whirl could be dazzling. Richard Russell received invitations to parties, picnics, and other outings, some from young women, others from their parents, but he did not cultivate the idea that he was an eligible bachelor. He could not avoid social gatherings—they offered too much scope for politicking—but he preferred going alone or with male friends. He told family and close friends that he would never marry again.[16]

In spite of sorrow and loneliness, he practiced law in earnest. The decade of the 1880s saw the rise of many new courthouses in Georgia, symbolic of the return to law and order after a chaotic time in which rules of social and legal restraint had often been suspended or disregarded. Pre- and early post-war courts had been held in mills, homes, stores, even in the open air under shade trees on hot summer days. The imposing new courthouses were comparable in importance to the European cathedral of the Middle Ages. The courthouse was at the center of town and visible at great distances, proclaiming the majesty of the law and the pride of the people who had built this edifice to it. The cross plan was often used, with doors opening onto each side of the courthouse square, showing accessibility, and encouraging businesses on all sides.[17] New courthouses were built in Clarke (1876), Jackson (1879) and Walton (1883) while Richard was studying law and beginning his practice. The Banks County courthouse, started in 1859 and finished in 1865, with distinctive architecture of double stairway, porches and overhanging eaves, does not illustrate the cross plan, but it was undeniably the finest building in the little community of Homer in the first decades after the war. The excitement of court week was a recurring feast for the solicitor general, and the gratifying prestige that came with being part of this important element of his society must have given Richard deep satisfaction in his professional life.

Meanwhile he continued with his fertilizer and guano business, and speculated in town real estate, a booming business nationwide from 1887-1890. In Athens he bought rental houses and vacant lots on which to build houses. Caught up in the boom, Athens citizens could not find the skilled labor to build needed houses fast enough.[18] He was making money during this period and investing it in solid projects.

When the *Athens Chronicle* went out of business, he decided to start his own newspaper, the *Evening Ledger*. He was the titular editor, but had to hire someone to do the real work because he did not have time to do such a daily grind and keep his law practice thriving. This move was likely more political than commercial. Successful political candidates needed a powerful newspaper behind them.

Richard's account book for the *Evening Ledger* showed a slight profit at the end of 1890.[19] The newspaper had advertising accounts with local insurance companies, banks, the Athens Chemical Works, the Athens Steam Laundry, the University of Georgia and the First Baptist Church. Barnum and Bailey Circus paid the enormous sum of fifty dollars for advertising when it came to town. Yet Richard Russell does not seem to have been much better at collecting debts regularly than he was at paying them. Many accounts remained unpaid or partially paid. Nevertheless, 1890 was a respectable year for the *Ledger*, with family members, brother John and father John, coming in to help with it. Both received respectable payment for their work. Richard drew only occasionally from paper funds.

In the autumn of 1889, William John Russell retired from his work at Princeton factory. He was sixty-five years old, and he hoped to have a few years to dabble in other things. This decision meant that the elder Russells were without a home, for their manager's house went with the job. There was an anxious time as they searched for a house. John found only one he considered suitable, but Harriette, after all these exiled years, held out to live near the university campus, and the house John wanted was sold to someone else. When they moved to Athens in October, they took up residence at 319 Milledge Avenue, quite possibly one of Richard's houses.[20] Richard kept his office with sleeping quarters, but he spent much time in his parents' home. John, Edward, Lewis, and Mary were still at home. Edward, following Rob, had tried Annapolis, but unable to endure the intense discipline of military life, dropped out and came back to Athens.[21] He was a junior at the university in 1890. Only Rob, who graduated from Annapolis in 1885, had left home.

On May 20, 1890, while Ensign Robert Russell was home on leave, Harriette arranged for a family photograph to be made. Standing before screens of quiet oriental decor, Richard and Robert, her oldest, are straight, tall young men, handsome and at ease in dark suits, shining black top hats and bow ties. Richard, undeniably thin, has grown a bushy black moustache, and Robert, more robust, sports a neat beard. Beside their older brothers, William John and Edward Gaston, clean-shaven and shorter, have chosen light bowler hats and cravat type ties with light suits. Edward has draped his right hand rakishly on John's shoulder and pushed his hat back. While the other men have their jackets tightly buttoned, Edward's is open.

On the front row, seated beside her beloved father, Mary, in a fashionable velvet and satin dress, is pretty, dark and slim, but she looks hollow-eyed, as if she has suffered one of her migraines. Richard has laid his hand on her shoulder.

The venerable patriarch, in a dark bowler hat and dark suit, wears a white beard that reaches to his top jacket button. His expression is worried, perhaps reflecting anxiety over being able to support Mary and

Harriette, but perhaps he is only struggling to hear the photographer's instructions. At sixty-one, Harriette is wearing a dark, heavy cotton dress and a velvet bonnet tied with a remarkable bow. Her hair has not been allowed to gray, and her face does not show as much care as her husband's. Beside her, Lewis, the youngest, not yet nineteen, wears a straw panama and a jacket with slacks. His dark curls brim beneath his hat. He is slightly chubby, as if he has not lost his baby fat yet.

Unsure whether hats put the men in their best light, someone must have asked that hats be removed for a second photo. In this version, Harriette and William John are holding hands. Harriette kept copies of both photos.[22]

No one is smiling in the photographs, but they do not look unhappy. They look serious and determined. Harriette's sons look, as their mother intended, ready, willing and able.

6

SHE LEFT HONEY IN HER FOOTPRINTS

1891-1892

Five years after Minnie's death, John and Lewis conceived a project to help Richard find another bride. All the family worried about the eldest son's melancholia and his obsession with politics, and they remembered how happy he had been as a married man. There was some self-interest in the idea. William John Jr. enjoyed the company of the ladies and was sure he would want to marry someday, but in the patriarchal tradition it would be inappropriate for him to do so unless his older brother had re-married. When he and Lewis began to frequent the home of a group of seven women who lived near the university campus, the two brothers agreed they might have found a bride for Richard. It is possible both men were a little in love with the girl themselves, but they were in no position to court. John lacked regular employment, while Lewis was still a student.[1]

The seven women called their home on Jackson Street "Cottage Content." Several were of a venerable and unmentionable chaperone age, perhaps widowed, and the others were young, sheltering under the wings of their elders.[2] By repute, all enjoyed independence and earned their livelihoods teaching and making their home a pleasant gathering place. One of the young women was called Birdie and another Ruby. The woman the Russell brothers admired most John called Miss Dilly, or, when he dared, Dilly. Lewis called her by her real name, Ina Dillard, and it was he who first urged Richard to go with him to Cottage Content and make her acquaintance.

At first Richard declined, but his brothers continued to extol the virtues of Miss Dillard: the sweet look in her blue eyes, a diminutive but curvaceous figure, ready wit, quick laughter, sincere piety (she was a Methodist, but it had not hurt him to be a Methodist for Minnie), her love of children, a good education.[3] Finally Richard went with Lewis to Cottage Content. Miss Dillard, upon the introduction, noted that he was her boss, as he was on the city Board of Education, her official employers. She taught fourth grade at the Meigs/Washington Street School, which Richard had worked to create when he began serving on the new school board in 1887.[4] Lewis thought the evening passed successfully.

Whatever Richard Russell felt when he left Cottage Content that first time was apparently too painful to contemplate. Perhaps the fear of losing again a precious happiness made him decline to return when next Lewis suggested they go. Exasperated, Lewis declared he had better not let a girl like that slip through his fingers. She surely would, Lewis added, because Cottage Content was not lacking in desirable suitors. Richard shrugged.

A few days later—it was early spring—Richard met Miss Dillard on the streets of Athens. He must have seen her coming from a distance, walking in her sprightly, graceful way, head up, her face serious beneath the brim of her bonnet.

"Good day, Mist'Russell," she said, running the words Mister and Russell together in a charming contraction.

He tipped his hat and returned her greeting, and as she passed, lightning struck Richard Russell again. He stopped in the street and turned to watch Ina Dillard going away from him. Overwhelmed with a sensation of her sweetness, he remarked a phenomenon: she left honey in her footprints. His desire to share in this sweetness triumphed over his fear of the heartache that might come with it. He determined to return to Cottage Content.[5]

Christened Blandina in honor of a Christian martyr of the second century, Ina Dillard was born into a favored position as the youngest of thirteen children in a close, loving family.[6] She ran considerable risk of being spoiled, for she was a child of energy, wit, intelligence, and beauty, and her parents, Fielding and America Dillard, were prosperous by the standards of the post-war South. The Dillards farmed several hundred acres in Oglethorpe County, next to Clarke, with sons working alongside black laborers, some of whom had been slaves of the family. The Dillards were unpretentious, made no claims to being planters. They called their home Farm Hill.

The family was deeply religious. Devout, grateful for their blessings, the Dillards believed that the human mission on earth was to love God with all one's heart and mind and to treat one's fellow man with compassion and generosity. Two of Ina's brothers were Methodist ministers, and one of her sisters had married a Methodist parson.

Living their beliefs, America and Fielding Dillard had reared not only their own children, ten of whom reached adulthood, but they had also sheltered eight (some reports claim thirteen) orphans from various families in the district. Some of these were relatives, for several Dillard families had migrated from Virginia at the turn of the century to Oglethorpe County, and the clan had proliferated. Other homeless children were related not by blood but by membership in the Christian brotherhood. Orphaned at age eleven, Fielding Dillard had never shut his door on a homeless child, and the great-hearted America would not have allowed it anyway. For the crowd of male youngsters under their wing, they maintained, next to the main house at Farm Hill, a special log cabin called "the Boys' House." The girls lived in the main house, a solid, heart-pine frame dwelling, with two stories and six rooms. A modest, columned portico on the front was the only concession to ornament.

The Dillard home was open to neighbors and friends alike, especially circuit-riding Methodist parsons. Fielding and America were supporting members of the Cherokee Corner Methodist Chapel, built on an historic spot where an early treaty left to the Creek and Cherokee nations lands to the south and west, and to the colony of Georgia lands to the north. Cherokee Corner was only a few miles from the Dillard farm. It is believed one of their travelling parson friends is responsible for America's choice of the name Blandina for her youngest child.

Devotion to ancient virtues ran deep in the Dillards. Girls were to love and serve. Boys were to be good providers and loving protectors. All must learn to read and write in order to study the Bible. Work out your own salvation in fear and trembling! Almost equally important was the need to stay in touch with each other. James Fielding Dillard, the eldest child, spent four years in the Confederate Army in Virginia. He wrote long letters home and kept a journal. As each child grew up and moved away, letters came back to tell of new homes, and letters responded from those still at Farm Hill. In the Dillard creed, literacy kept close company with godliness.

Willingness to work at whatever task was at hand— usefulness—was another Dillard tenet. To Dillards a useless life was worse than an early death. Energy and industry characterized them, male and female, and lilies of the field they were not. They toiled and spun and whatsoever their hands found to do would be well done. Although pious, they were also good-humored and given to laughing as well as praying over life's little troubles and large ironies. They looked to a better life in the world to come but enjoyed this world to the fullest.

Thus Ina Dillard was a rich heiress in moth- and rust-proof treasure. Early on, she showed her willingness to be a worthy steward of such wealth when she formally joined the church at Cherokee Corner at age nine, promising to live a selfless life. As she grew, she strove to imitate those around her whom she believed exemplified such a life. Her highest example was her mother, whose hearth and heart were freely opened to so many.

Frances America Chaffin Dillard, called "Mec," was famous for her grit as well as her generosity. A favorite family tale related how Mec went one day, accompanied by a servant, to one of the storage sheds near the house, and when she stepped over the threshold, she unknowingly put her foot down on the head of a rattlesnake. While the snake writhed and rattled, she held firm, calling to the servant to fetch an ax. When the snake was dispatched, everyone gathered around, amazed that this diminutive woman had had the nerve to stand on such a creature. "It might have hurt one of the children," she said.

Coming to maturity at the end of her mother's distinguished career, aware of the adulation and respect America had earned from her family and community, Ina Dillard was sure there was no higher calling than that of Christian wife and mother. She longed to find a worthwhile husband to share her dream of an outstanding family, but until he should appear, she had a duty to become well-educated and support herself. She went about this duty with typical Dillard energy and determination. When her lively intelligence outstripped the schools near Farm Hill, her father and mother allowed her to go to Oxford, Georgia, to live with her brother Miles, a Methodist minister, and his wife Lella, in order to attend the Palmer Institute there.

Miles and Lella were a devoted and loving couple with one young child. Ina's affectionate nature thrived in their household where she was a valued helper with the baby and household chores and a cherished companion for Lella. Soon she was beyond what Palmer Institute could offer, and she and Miles made another plan, one that allowed her to go to Lucy Cobb Institute in Athens. It may have been one of Lella's older friends, already living at Cottage Content, who agreed that the young woman could come there to live and study in 1887.

Ina gloried in her studies and walked the long, muddy mile to school and back each day without complaint. She was grateful to be able to take piano lessons and made so much progress that she used her new skills in the summer to help another brother, Walter, who, still studying for the ministry, did home missions work in rural communities.[7] By 1890 she had qualified to teach elementary school and was hired to teach in Athens. She was overjoyed to be able to stay in the Classic City, for she loved the active social and intellectual life of the town and her life at Cottage Content.

When Richard Russell realized he was in love with Ina Dillard, he could not stay away from Cottage Content. In usual precipitous fashion, he courted her ardently, declaring that she was made for him. His feeling of her overwhelming sweetness and the strong tug of physical attraction held. He found her to be all his brothers had said. She was high-minded, amiable, honorable, loyal, pious, and intelligent, a consecrated and virtuous woman to whom duty would be a watchword. In addition, she was pretty.[8] Although he hired a buggy only at rare intervals, he now felt it necessary to have one each morning to pick Ina up and drive her to school. Her school children, particularly the little girls, watched with wide eyes as their teacher arrived with her handsome suitor. The little boys thought he was the meanest man in the world.[9]

The door of Cottage Content stood open to Richard Russell. Although Ina did not know him well, she knew much of him, for once he began to court her, in a town the size of Athens she and her housemates could not have escaped hearing about his first marriage and his long grief after Minnie's death. The role of comforter and lover suited Ina's generous and affectionate nature. It is certain that she fell deeply in love with her take-charge suitor, but certain, too, that she had already formed an idea of what kind of marriage she would make. She now judged Richard indeed the man to make it with.

In 1885, Ina's sister Mattie Dillard Morris, wife of a Methodist minister, had given her a book entitled *Advice to Young Ladies on Their Duties and Conduct in Life* by T. S. Arthur. Ina underlined parts which impressed her about woman's role in marriage and family and the kind of man she would choose to marry. Dates written in the book indicate she received it on July 14, 1885 and read it within three days, then re-read the chapter "Conduct towards Parents" in August 1887. In the latter she underlined several descriptive paragraphs on the nobility and difficulty of a mother's work, ending with the honor and aid due to her.

A chapter entitled "Equality of the Sexes" discusses man's strength of intellect and woman's strength of will and affection. Ina underlined this: "By intellect, do not understand us to say mind: we are only speaking of a faculty of the mind by which man is peculiarly distinguished. Love, the sweeter, purer, stronger quality of mind is woman's...As to which is highest or lowest, superior or inferior, that is another matter. Here we believe woman to be the equal of man; not born to obedience but to be his intelligent and loving companion."

Richard Russell proposed to Ina Dillard on the last day of May 1891, with the assurance that she was made for him. She turned him down. She had bought a piano, she said, and she had not paid for it yet. Richard said if that was the only reason for her refusal, he thought he could make piano payments. Ina changed her no to a yes.[10]

Richard, thirty years old and widowed these five years, was in no mood for a long engagement. Ina, at age twenty-three, was eager to start her career of wife- and motherhood. They went straight to Farm Hill for Richard to request Ina's hand in marriage from her adoring father. Fielding Dillard had been stern about Ina's early beaux, watching

jealously over his baby daughter's welfare. Once he sent a young man
home who had driven his team and wagon with what Fielding judged
was too much haste up the long drive to Farm Hill house.[11] But Fielding
was pleased with her choice of a serious young lawyer, achieving success
in law, politics and journalism. He consented to the marriage, and the
wedding date was set for June 24, at eight o'clock in the morning. The
couple planned to catch an early train to Atlanta, where they would begin
a popular "wedding tour of the North," including Niagara Falls.

Ina announced her engagement to her class as the school term ended
and invited the children to the wedding. They were not surprised by this
announcement, but one little girl burst into tears. "Oh, Miss Dillard," she
sobbed, "please don't marry one of those peculiar Russells."

Ina laughed, but she must have known the child was repeating what
some in the community thought of the Russells. Marriage in the South
was a love-me-love-my-kin affair, and she was prepared to accept
Russell peculiarities. She may not have realized at this early date that as
a politician's wife and an in-law member of an eccentric family, she
would have to ignore more criticism than she was accustomed to. But Ina
was confident. She knew that when a woman has ambition to love and
serve, she has to be tough enough to keep her foot firmly on a
rattlesnake, and nothing in her life had taught her that the power of love
is limited.

Neighbors, friends and family arrived early at Farm Hill on June 24,
1891. The *Athens Banner* declared the June weather was like the coming
Prohibition election: hot and dry. Harriette, William John, Mary, John,
Edward and Lewis arrived with the bridegroom. There was no pouting
from Harriette over this wedding. She had seen her son's misery, and she
welcomed Ina into the family with a warm note that day.[12] Soon the
parlor was thronged.

When the time came for the ceremony, Ina's beloved sister Pipey
could not get into the room. Pipey, who never married, was nearly
twenty years older than Ina, had been her first teacher, and was a model
of loving kindness. Pipey had been frying chicken in the kitchen away
from the house, preparing a country breakfast for the wedding guests, but
seeing the crowded front porch, she hitched up her skirts and crawled

through the living room window. Nothing was going to stop her seeing her brother Walter conduct his first wedding after being ordained a Methodist minister. Pipey did well to be in on the start of this marriage between her dear sister and her Mist-Russell, for it would in many ways be Pipey's life's work as well as Ina's.

The newlyweds spent their first night in Lithia Springs at the Sweetwater Park Hotel. Lithia Springs was a well-known watering place near Atlanta, a short distance from the ruins of the Sweetwater Mill operated thirty years previously by Arnoldus Brumby and William John Russell. The couple were looking forward to the superb hotel, with its deep, cool veranda and grand dining-room finished in cherry and curled pine, where eight large French plate mirrors surmounted handsome sideboards. Then there were the beds of curled hair, with wire mattresses and scrupulously clean linen. Ina had loved fairy tales as a child. Starting her marriage in such elegance and comfort seemed a dream coming true.[13]

The romantic interlude did not unfold to plan. Ina's trunk failed to arrive by bedtime, and she had no nightgown. Richard gallantly offered one of his nightshirts. Not doing anything by halves, he had reserved a room with a bath, and he suggested Ina use the bathroom first. Next Richard went in. Ina, in her husband's night shirt, sat on the bed and listened to him splashing in the bath. Then things went quiet. She waited. No sound from the bathroom. She waited. What should she do?

Finally, she opened the bathroom door softly to find her bridegroom asleep in the tub. She pulled the door closed, and sat down on the bed, prepared to wait longer. Ina sympathized with his fatigue. He had been up well before day in order to get to Farm Hill from Athens before eight o'clock. It was possible that he had not slept at all the night before. She was a maiden, expecting her widower husband to show the way into marital intimacy, but after a few more minutes, she decided it was entirely appropriate to wake him up.[14]

The ruins of the burned mill were a tourist attraction highlighted in the hotel's literature, and Richard and Ina walked out to marvel at the size of the structure and to muse and mourn over the July day Sherman's troops wreaked such havoc with so many lives. The scene was dramatic and romantic: The five-story shell of a brick building stood forlorn, overgrown with vines. The woods had taken over the town site again, and trees grew within the walls of the mill. At the foot of the mill the clear, rushing waters of the creek sang a haunting song. It was the ideal spot for Richard to repeat to his bride his vow to renew the glory of his family name. The title of a book-length poem that he gave her on June 25, 1891, may have expressed the emotions of the moment: *Bittersweet*.[15]

Soon they were off for Chattanooga and Point Lookout Inn before heading north in earnest. Ina had never been out of Georgia, and as their train sped across mountains and rivers, she was enchanted with the scenery and with their love nest, a private cabin that provided seats and a table by day, then turned into berths for sleeping by night. She liked dining on the train and watching other passengers. Best of all she enjoyed being with her husband. She credited her happy honeymoon to her husband's gentle tenderness learned in his marriage to Minnie.[16]

Richard's analysis that they were made for each other may not have been far off. Ina believed "It is the heart and not the brain,/ That to the highest doth attain,/And he who followeth Love's behest,/Far excelleth all the rest." Her ambition was to follow love's behest. Richard, who could and did love deeply, needed first to be loved. "I want to be loved," he said passionately. "I cannot be loved too much."[17]

The *Athens Banner* announced the marriage on June 30, declaring, "Miss Dillard is a lovely and accomplished young lady, quite popular in Athens, while Mr. Russell needs no introduction to the people of this section of Georgia."

The couple were 'at home' after July 8, at 628 Prince Avenue, in a house Richard bought. Richard had court in Watkinsville in late July, and his next stop would be Walton County, where the paper announced, under the heading "The Solicitor's Bride," the hope that the Solicitor would bring the new Mrs. Russell to Monroe for court week. "And no doubt he will, as the session here will be a lengthy one."[18]

Ina did not go with her husband to Watkinsville, thus early in their married life they were separated. During a whirlwind courtship, Ina may not have realized how much time she would have to spend alone as the Solicitor's Bride, and although she felt she was being cowardly, she trembled at the idea of staying by herself. Richard arranged for his father to stay with Ina during his first absence. Ina worried that Father was so deaf he would not be able to hear her even if she called for help, but she early developed affection for this quiet man, recognizing and appreciating his sweet nature.[19]

In August Ina accompanied Richard to the Walton County court in Monroe. Her brother Walter, her closest sibling in age and temperament, was preaching there, and her happiness was complete to be with two men she loved devotedly. Richard and Walter took a liking to each other, and Richard made considerable effort to get to know Ina's large family.[20]

Intense bonding to friends and family was characteristic of Ina. She gloried in the company of those she loved, and her fervent attachments enriched her emotional life and fulfilled her ambition to love. Thus, these separations from Richard were a potential source of serious conflict in the union. Ina, whose parents lived and worked together, expected marriage to give her a companion with whom she would share the work and the play of daily life. Her time with Miles and Lella, a couple who shared the common ambition of serving the Lord, confirmed this expectation. Yet Richard's work and other activities would continue to take him away from home, and these circumstances meant a major adjustment in attitude for Ina.

Richard and Ina loved and longed for children. They dreamed of twin boys to name for their fathers, but no child signaled impending arrival during their first year of marriage. During this time Ina traveled with Richard whenever circumstances permitted, and their bonds of love and friendship deepened. Ina made friends easily in the courthouse towns and enjoyed the social life. She was competent secretarial help, keeping up with correspondence, making notes regarding appointments, arranging meetings, and copying presentments on Richard's behalf. She was satisfied to be of use to her husband, and while she must have found some aspects of politics shocking, her faith in Richard's high ideals was unshakeable. She did try to get him to give up chewing tobacco, a habit she found revolting, but his addiction was too strong for even her loving insistence, and she abandoned the campaign. To be a nagging wife was not one of her ambitions.[21]

Richard, a virile, tender and thoughtful husband, inspired enduring affection in a woman of Ina's loving nature. The couple liked each other in all the rooms of the house. Ina never wanted Richard to leave her, and in spite of the demanding nature of his work and the pleasure of politicking, he found being away from her for more than a few days almost unbearable. At night in his hotel room, he tossed and turned, unable to sleep without her. He longed to enfold her in his arms, know her kisses, her petting, and all the warm caresses he doted on. He wanted to feel her heart beating. Sometimes he missed her so much he confessed he would not even have minded her biting his ears.[22]

His patriarchal role, however, did not allow Richard to stay at home, help Ina plant a vegetable garden and flowers, mend fences, visit the neighbors, raise yard hens.[23] His ambition to achieve greatness and recognition was validated by the biblical injunction that required the husband of a virtuous woman to be known in the gates and sit among the elders of the land. To achieve this in law and politics, he must go where the action was and that necessarily kept him from home.

Although these absences affected their hopes for children and Ina worried each month as her period continued to arrive, Richard enjoyed being the center of her attention. His fear of losing his wife in childbirth loomed large when they discussed pregnancy.[24]

Politics and pregnancies not withstanding, from a practical standpoint, Richard Russell needed to make more money to achieve his ambitions, and this meant working long hours whether in Athens or elsewhere. Times were hard and headed downhill in 1892, yet for many there was nothing to do but borrow more money. Richard and a sometime law partner, F. M. Hughes, had earlier become involved with the Georgia Loan and Trust Company as agents to lend money to farmers or businessmen they considered likely to be able to repay. By early 1892 the firm of Russell and Hughes had been dissolved, and Richard wanted to continue the loan business arrangement. The Georgia Loan and Trust, however, was dissatisfied with the attention given to the business by Russell and Hughes. There were a number of delinquent loans, and they felt that not enough attention was being given to collections, especially in the autumn when the cotton crop was being sold. They advised that "only the best [farm loans] can now be handled" and if Mr. Russell was not disposed to put more effort into the serious business of investment money, they would be loathe to continue the arrangement. Richard suffered to see friends whom he had personally recommended for loans unable to pay, but he succeeded in renewing his contract with the Georgia Loan and Trust.[25]

More money problems arose because the *Ledger* was now in major difficulty. Between matrimony, law and loans Richard did not have time to read a newspaper, much less publish one. His hired hands proved not only disloyal but also incompetent, and by the end of 1891, he was desperate to find someone trustworthy to take over the *Ledger* and make it pay.

He first approached his brother Lewis, a recent University graduate, working for a railroad in Marietta. He wanted Lewis to come back to Athens, run the paper and study law with him. Lewis considered the matter carefully, and although he knew about his brother's money troubles, he had to be sure he could pay his own way. The railroad job might represent only low pay at a dead end, but the salary was sure, and he would have plenty of time to study law in a few years.[26]

Having passed the civil service exam, Edward Gaston had taken off for Washington, DC, and a job with the department of the Navy. So Richard turned to his brother John, who had shown initiative in trying to start a Chamber of Commerce in Athens, and had already helped out on the paper.[27] They both knew John was not interested in newspaper work, but he might keep the *Ledger* afloat until someone else could be found.

John spent the first months of 1892 paddling furiously but to little avail. By March he had determined to go to work for the railroad himself, but not before he had found a family named Shackleford to take over the *Ledger*. As he signed off the job, he advised his brother that he must impress on the Shacklefords the need to work, and he must also put someone in charge of keeping the printers in the office and at work. Clearly, the *Ledger* was suffering from poor management, some might say from no management at all.[28]

As Richard and Ina entered their second year of marriage, Richard learned two things of concern. The first was confirmation of an earlier rumor that he would have opposition in his race for solicitor general in the fall. Charley Brand, a Gwinnett county lawyer and former school mate of Richard's at the university, was testing the waters and looked

ready to jump in.[29] The second was that Ina was quite likely pregnant. He
was in despair over the first news, and perhaps a little anxious about the
second. Because Ina wanted it so bad, he had to be enthusiastic about a
baby, and anyone in public life has to be aware that an elected position is
as fair game for the next fellow as it is for the incumbent. As the summer
wore on, it became apparent that both events would occur.

Brand was snapping at Richard's heels at every court, trying to get
grand juries in Gwinnett and Franklin counties to write endorsements for
him instead of for Russell, endorsements that would be presented to the
legislature in the fall. Judge Hutchins, the superior court judge of the
Western Circuit, seemed to have it in for Russell. He lost cases, he
thought, not only because the judge made fretful and peevish remarks in
the presence of the jury about nearly every question he asked, but also
because when the judge charged the jury, he just "got up in his stirrups"
and knocked Richard's cases out of court. It was hard not to be
discouraged, but the public prosecutor found some comfort in the fact
that other members of the bar complimented his closing speeches.[30]

By late summer the father-to-be, although missing his precious wife,
did not want her to travel over bumpy roads in a surrey to be with him at
court or to travel by train in the oppressive heat. He feared she would
miscarry. Yet he had to stay at court more than ever, not only practicing
law but also campaigning. The long-suffering farmers were in full revolt
at this period, and the Farmers Alliance-Populist Movement was
sweeping the state, making all races from large to small unstable.
Considering Ina's pregnancy and hoping to avoid a fight, Richard had
tried to interest Charley Brand in a deal. He proposed that if Brand would
not run in 1892, Russell would resign in two years to run for judge,
leaving the solicitor post open. The Gwinnett lawyer declined.[31]

At night Richard was compelled to write to legislators in every
district regarding his candidacy, and thus had even less time to write to
Ina. He cherished her letters, which came almost every day, and excused
his own poor correspondence by reminding her that he was a veritable
slave to the court most of the time. In his letters he talked baby talk to
"his boy," and to his darling little wife, his baby girl. He shaved his
moustache and was pleased when his friends said he looked five years

younger. Ina was no doubt pleased that tobacco juice would no longer have such a harbor on his person.[32]

Money woes continued to dog the solicitor. Times were so "awful tight" few could get up money for fines, and thus the solicitor general lost pay. His father took care of his rental property in Athens, but in order to keep the houses rented to reliable tenants, he had had to take reductions in rent, which would mean trouble when loan payments came due. William John needed sixty-five dollars from his son to keep his life insurance policy paid. He had to ask, he said, because it must be paid to make Harriette's and Mary's lives secure. Brother Lewis was out of work with typhoid fever in Marietta where Harriette had gone to nurse him. When the solicitor stopped in Crawford to buy a basket of the scuppernong grapes she liked to take home to Ina, he found he did not have even thirty-five cents in his pocket to pay for them.[33]

By October his campaign was at white heat, with the outcome uncertain. Three men were vying for the job, Russell, Brand and Little. Richard went to Atlanta a week early, ready for a hard fight, leaving Ina peeved at his total distraction.[34] This was her first encounter with an election, and although she wrote to him regularly, she was shocked to see everything else in his life completely eclipsed, including his unborn child. She feared his love was fading, their happiness vanishing. Writing at one o'clock in the morning, he protested his continued love, swearing that her image was never out of his heart. He did not fail to mention that he was suffering from a fearful carbuncle on his left wrist that caused him torturous pain with every step, yet he kept going from six-thirty in the morning until two and three o'clock at night and always on his feet.

Little dropped out, leaving Russell and Brand. Judge Hutchins, of the Western Circuit, not up for re-election, was opposing Russell on the sly. The editor of the *Franklin Chronicle* made vilely false charges that reduced Richard almost to tears. He longed to challenge this editor to a fight of honor, but could not because she was a woman. If Miss Dortch could be a man for three days he would "shoot him if it was the last thing I ever did or make him swallow every word he has said."

On the bright side, these charges energized him and his friends, and as a result, three days before balloting, he had fifty votes more than Brand and expected to surge further ahead. In addition, Judge Hutchins' conduct had not met with approval, and others were promising Russell he could have the judgeship of the Western Circuit in 1894 if he wanted it.

His prediction about the outcome of the race proved accurate, and he was re-elected for four years as solicitor general of the Western Circuit. His fears about his position were laid to rest. His worries for his wife's health and safety did not subside, but the couple looked with optimism toward the spring and the birth of their first child.

7

WE WILL HARDLY CLEAR
THE JAIL THIS WEEK

1893-1897

As the time of Ina's confinement approached, Richard became more and more solicitous, staying at home as much as possible, giving her special attention. She enjoyed being spoiled by her husband. He was hopeful of being present for the birth, but heavy snows fell the last days of February, and he was kept at court in Walton County. On March 1, 1893, Richard was in Monroe when he received the desired and dreaded telegram. Tearing it open, he read: "Mother and daughter doing well come tonight." A pang of disappointment—not a son!—stabbed his ego, followed by floods of relief and joy for a healthy infant and Ina's safe passage through the perilous waters of childbirth. [1]

Ina too had wanted a boy—sons were preferred if Richard preferred them— but as babies do, this one exerted her particular charm, and soon there was no other baby in the world. Making a serious speech before a jury a few days after her arrival, Richard was chagrined to notice they were amused. Soon the entire court room was laughing. A pink baby bootee, gift of a friend, had inched its way out of his coat pocket and was dangling loosely, as if declaring his new status for all to see. [2]

They had difficulty deciding on a name. The first week after her birth, her father sent her a letter addressed to Miss Dixie Russell, but soon thereafter he was addressing her as little Miss Ina. Her mother continued to call her Baby for about a month or six weeks. Southern daughters as well as sons in this era often received names of revered patriarchs, and she was finally named Mary William, after Richard's sister and his father. As time went on, she was called Mary Willie, Mayne, Mamie and other variations.[3]

Parenthood meant adjustments for the loving couple. Ina worried that they would be separated more than ever and had troubling dreams in which Richard had ceased to love her and treated her badly. Although she loved her baby, she mourned the loss of their intimate times together. She especially missed him on Easter Sunday when she took a little walk out in the yard, feeling proud of her slim waist and wanting him to see her. Infamous for careless dress, he wrote that he had new clothes: a blue suit and cravat and a black hat. He was such a "dude," so sweet and charming, that she would have to be introduced to him to know him. Now that she was wearing dresses instead of loose wrappers, he would have to get re-acquainted with her. He was glad she felt like playing the piano again, but how he longed to sit behind her on the bench, hugging her while she played.[4]

Richard had post-partum depression. He was melancholy and "just mad with everybody for no real cause," but he tackled the problem by walking six miles in the moonlight and making the effort to get more sleep. When business carried him to Atlanta, and he had to pass through Athens without stopping because he was due in court in Carnesville, he had never felt "so peculiar." He went out on the rear platform and strained to see anything of his little home as the train passed, but he could not see it. He went back to his seat and offered prayers for the wife and baby his heart was yearning for.[5]

Ina's feelings of neglect did not subside, but she remained faithful in writing loving, usually cheerful letters. When she scolded Richard for treating her letters with "silent contempt," he refused to be apologetic and promised to spank her when he got home for her sarcasm. Saddled with the constant need of a politician to win friends and influence people, he felt he prized more highly than most husbands her unselfish love. There was so little real love in the world, but he knew that she would love him even if he should pass away from her. Correcting this self-indulgence, he quickly added, "[It] was only a passing thought in which no doubt there is mixed some of the sadness which I experience from our present separation, for I hope yet to pass all the happiest years of my life and many of them and all with you. Some day I look for a time when we can be more together than now and therefore happier even (if it be possible) than now."[6]

1893 brought a major economic depression to the country, and southern and western states were particularly hard hit. Richard's financial situation had not improved even before the Panic of 1893. He had shut down the paper at the end of 1892, and although he had more law business than he could readily tackle, his work as solicitor general took most of his time and energy, while producing unpredictable income. In addition, Judge Hutchins remained a source of irritation and enmity, and the solicitor general eyed with a vengeful attitude a run in 1894 for the seat held by his nemesis.[7] When the economy sank to yet more dismal levels, he returned to a plan he had considered since 1892. He determined to move to another area, one not lorded over, in his opinion, by well-entrenched families and businesses. He would leave Clarke County for a little town called Jug Tavern, twenty miles northwest of Athens.

Salty name notwithstanding, Jug Tavern claimed many advantages. The Seaboard Railroad was building a line through the hamlet to connect Atlanta to Athens, and a name change was already in the plans. New railroad towns expected vigorous growth, and growth was a certainty in Jug Tavern because it already had railroad connections to Gainesville, a thriving northeast Georgia agricultural and textile center. Located on a spot that included three counties, Jackson, Walton, and Gwinnett, the tiny municipality generated numerous legal tangles regarding real estate, wills and taxes to provide work for lawyers. Land was cheaper in these counties than in Clarke, and Richard dreamed of owning a farm.

He first considered the change with William Henry Quarterman, husband of his cousin Mamie Brumby. Not only was Quarterman related by marriage, but he was also a member of a prominent family from the old Russell stomping grounds of Walthourville in Liberty County. A graduate of the University of Georgia Law School, Quarterman was ready to make a move to the high country in Georgia. He took up an offer that Richard help him study law in return for his help in Richard's law office at a salary of $37.50 per month.[8]

Ina was devastated at the decision to move. Living in Athens with its lively cultural and social scene made bearable a life laden with Richard's absences. The Classic City had a park-like atmosphere where old trees lined the streets and elegant homes stood on large, shady lots. She did not relish going to a place called Jug Tavern, population two hundred and two in 1892, where streets were newly cut and raw, without trees, where plain new houses sat on small lots. The Quartermans moved to Jug Tavern perhaps as early as July 1893, and Ina visited them to get a feel for the town, where the population was increasing daily. Richard was fond of his cousin, and Mamie and Ina had known each other before Ina met and married Richard, but these circumstances did not make Ina happy about moving to Jug Tavern. Nevertheless, Richard had made up his mind, and she would try to go as cheerfully as possible, perhaps thankful he had not decided to go west as he had imagined in the 1880s.[9]

The autumn legislature of 1893 authorized a name change for Jug Tavern. It was incorporated as the town of Winder, in honor of John H. Winder, a railroad executive. This change may have been some comfort to Ina when they moved into their home there in January 1894. By this time she knew that June would bring another baby to the Russell household, and she was horrified that Dr. C. B. Almond, the only doctor in Winder, was a young man about her age. She made Richard promise that she could return to Athens for the birth of her second child under the ministrations of the venerable Dr. Gerdine.[10]

On June 22, 1894, a second daughter arrived to gladden the Russell hearthstone. This time there was no hesitancy about the choice of a name. While Ina had spoken of the unborn child as 'little Richard,' Richard had been from the beginning certain the baby would be a close sister companion for Mary Willie, and he named her Ina Dillard.[11]

The poor economic picture, their new life in Winder, and an unstable political scene created by the Populist Movement made Richard decide it was unwise to run for the judgeship of the Western Circuit in 1894, no doubt to the great relief of his wife and his mother, not to mention of Judge Hutchins. Her husband stayed away as much as ever, but as time went on, Ina's strong nesting instincts brought her satisfaction in domesticity. Appreciative of Richard's provision and loving him more as time passed, she did not neglect to express her loneliness and to call him lovingly home. He never neglected to tell her how much he missed her and longed to be home, but he knew every successful man must make some great sacrifices and reckoned this was the one he must make.[12]

By late summer of 1895, another Russell baby was on the way. Ina suffered in the early months of her pregnancies, and an ailment which had begun to plague her during her pregnancy with little Ina returned. "Neuralgia," likely trigeminal neuralgia, gave her tooth and face pain far more agonizing than childbirth, and she sometimes felt she would go crazy between that pain and the nausea of early pregnancy. Her mother and Pipey insisted she bring the babies and come to Farm Hill to rest and enjoy the delicious scuppernong grapes, one of her favorite foods, from America's celebrated arbor. Hoping to even her girl-boy ratio, Ina predicted twin boys would make all her trouble worthwhile.[13]

Just before Christmas, someone offered Richard a good price for their home, and he sold it without telling Ina. Then he had to find a house for them by the first of the year. Ina and babies survived the moving, and Richard, pleased with profits, looked more handsome and prosperous than he had in years.[14]

The third baby, born April 11, 1896, was another girl, and again there was initial chagrin, followed by fond acceptance. The baby weighed about ten pounds, and the delivery was difficult. Fearing she would be the last child, Richard requested she be named Dixie. Ina had no objections, but sister Mary, "Auntney" to the children, expressed her opinion that it was a cruel name to give a little girl and questioned whether they were "punishing" the poor little thing. Because the child had not been baptized, Mary hoped for a change of heart and called the baby Marguerite or Frances rather than Dixie. The spelling eventually became Dicksie to further reflect the fact that she was her father's namesake.[15]

Although in later years Richard Russell chose to forget the 1896 Solicitor General campaign, claiming he was never defeated in a race for that post, in fact he was in the race from the start. He found it wearying to

campaign early in the year while carrying on a relentless workload as
public prosecutor. In February he explained to Ina: "It is not from any
lack of affection towards you [that I do not write], for you are still my
sweetheart as in the summer days of 1891. But I have two weeks work
crowded into one this week by starting court Thursday, and in this court
are three men to be tried for their lives besides a jail full for burglary and
assaults with intent to murder. We will hardly clear the jail this week."[16]

The heavy workload was no exaggeration. His grandfather's and
mother's motto of *labor omnia vincit* continued to be one of the most
useful tools in the belief case of Richard Russell. He had early gained a
reputation among his peers as a tireless worker and as a man who studied
in order to become grounded in the fundamental principles of the law. He
was respected because he did not resort to trickery and did not present
his arguments based upon anything other than the facts and the law of the
case. He was adept, however, at using his powerful oratory skills to sway
a jury and could bring an entire courtroom to tears. His friends and
colleagues, aware of his sensitive nature, admired him as an able and
fearless public prosecutor, but judged him sympathetic to the people he
must prosecute. Years of demanding work in the arena had not hardened
him. Prosecutor he was, but he did not wish to be a persecutor. He felt
the flush of victory when a case was won, but then his sympathies went
out to the convicted accused. This duality of emotion was not an easy
one to manage.[17]

The constant travel to the courts, though now usually accomplished
by train, still required physical vigor. If the passenger train schedules
were not adequate, he sometimes caught a freight train to avoid a long
buggy ride through the country over muddy roads. It was impossible to
make much time for his own family, much less for his mother and father.
When he thought of how Harriette had been so supportive of him all his
life, he regretted his inability to spend time with her. He knew he was
fortunate that Ina had such a great heart and would reach out in love to
his mother when he could not.[18]

As the 1896 solicitor's race warmed up and campaigning was added
to his workload, the false sentiments of politics weighed upon Richard.
His opponent Charley Brand was against him with the Grand Jury by day
and writing letters to legislators against him at night. Richard had to

write letters, too, while carrying on the heaviest kind of court to sustain his reputation. Being a candidate for re-election and having opposition meant he had to have a pleasant word for everybody and talk kindly to everybody as long as they wanted to talk. He felt this stressed life was aging him too quickly, but he did not consider giving up politics.[19]

As the opening of the legislature approached, he bought a typewriter and hired a stenographer, Frank Bondurant, to help him write letters to legislators. During the first few days of the session, however, it became clear that he was likely to lose. Brand accused him of having agreed to give up the post in 1896 in return for election to his second term in 1892. Richard declared that he had never made such a promise and if he ever had, he would have lost both arms rather than run.[20] Because this post was one men felt ought to be passed around, Brand gained support especially among new members of the legislature. Richard was forced to withdraw or risk defeat in the vote.

Richard's withdrawal may have also had something to do with the death of Ina's father. Fielding Dillard was called to his heavenly home on October 26, 1896.[21] With Dillard faith and serenity, his wife and children bade him good-bye, but the loss of a parent is difficult at any age, and this was a stressful time in Richard and Ina's household. In spite of Ina's outward peaceful acceptance, she was unable to sympathize with Richard's defeat and to give him her usual attention. She fell ill not long after her father's death, and Richard, in an uncharacteristic ordering of priorities, stayed home a few days to care for her and the children.[22]

As Christmas 1896 approached, Richard considered his options. He would work hard to make more money practicing law. It might be worthwhile to keep Bondurant, who was diligent, did not mind work a bit, and could be hired for twenty-five dollars per month. Recalling Harriette's admonitions about keeping up appearances, Richard hoped that businessmen would think he was something of a lawyer when they saw his business required a stenographer and a typewriter.[23]

His next decision was to aim for a new political office. He toyed with the idea of running for Congress, but decided his chances for the judgeship of the Western Circuit were better. The forces in the legislature that had opposed him this time had promised him support in 1898. He reminded himself that politicians' promises are unreliable, but thought

his position stable. Revenge was not absent as a motivation in the
decision. He wanted to wipe out his defeat in the circuit and beat old
Hutchins. Brand then would have "to crow mighty low" as solicitor
general with Russell as judge over him. He told only his brother Lewis of
these ambitions and swore him to secrecy.[24]

Richard set to work in earnest practicing law out of Winder, and
cases were not lacking. His work kept him travelling, for he was known
throughout the region and had cases in all the counties of the Western
Circuit. Harriette and William John were overjoyed when Richard and
Ina had time to come to Athens for a week-end with them. Ina liked to
dress the girls in white dresses and frilly white caps, and Richard and all
his family showed pride in their development. Little Dicksie was walking
by the time she was a year old and liked her uncle William John, much to
his delight.[25]

William John Jr. had opened a bicycle shop in Athens as the biking
craze hit the community. Wild himself about the new vehicle, he rode his
bicycle everywhere, taking long rides all over north Georgia. Mary
remained at home, teaching in the Athens city schools and struggling
with health problems discreetly referred to as "female." Lewis was again
in Marietta after a brief stint in Knoxville, Tennessee, where he tried to
start a public transport system from the train station into town with a
tally-ho wagon.[26]

On his thirty-sixth birthday, April 27, 1897, Richard was in Atlanta
for a case. Ina was in bed with complications resulting from her fourth
pregnancy. She wrote to Richard that she was much improved, however,
and looking forward to a "bridal tour" with him to Savannah, when she
would leave her three babies at Farm Hill with Sister Pipey and
Grandmother Mec. The new baby was expected in November, and Ina
was again hoping for twin boys.[27]

Richard's law practice was going well and looking ahead to the
judge's race in 1898, he decided he must have an assistant or a partner,
but W. H. Quarterman, who was now practicing law in Winder, did not
meet requirements. As the husband of a Brumby cousin, Quarterman
only semi-qualified as family. Richard wanted someone he could trust to
have his best interests at heart. So he made a proposition to Lewis, who,

somewhat bruised by the failure of his tally-ho project, was reading law while working again for a railroad.

Would Lewis come to work for Richard in his law office for twenty-five dollars per month and legal instruction that Richard valued at one hundred dollars? When Lewis had passed the bar, his pay would increase to fifty dollars per month and board. Richard would expect his brother to remain until January 1899. At which time, if Richard were not elected judge, Lewis could decide if and how he wished to go ahead with a partnership. Lewis' duties would include eight- to-five office hours when Richard was away, and handling all typewriter correspondence, collection of claims and preparation of briefs. Richard added that if his business continued to grow as he believed it would, he would increase compensation. Lewis agreed, and Richard had once more secured a capable and devoted partner, this time in his law practice. Next to marrying Ina Dillard, this would turn out to be the best move he had ever made.

In October William John Russell Sr. decided to undergo throat surgery in an attempt to regain his voice. Harriette's sister Susan was married to Doctor James McFadden Gaston in Marietta, and it was his opinion that William John, a remarkably vigorous man for his age, was able to withstand the operation. It would be performed by Dr. Calhoun, who enjoyed a good reputation in the field, and William John would be cared for in the home of Dr. Gaston. On Sunday morning, October 10, the surgery was performed. Unfortunately, the old warrior did not cope with the ordeal, and "he sank gradually [until]…the angel of death…beckoned him to that home of rest prepared by a Savior's love for the faithful."[28]

Late in the day of October 10, W. H. Quarterman received a telegram from Richard's brother Edward: *Tell Richard father died 4:30. Don't tell Ina.*[29] Edward was concerned that the sad news would be harmful to Ina, who was less than a month from her delivery date.

A brief ceremony was held the next morning in the Gaston home for the Russell and Brumby relatives in Atlanta and Marietta, and then the remains were brought to Athens. The Clarke Superior Court adjourned in order that the bar and officers of the court might be present at the funeral. A concourse of friends met the train at the depot and swelled the cortege to the Oconee Hill Cemetery. Dr. J. W. Walden of the First Presbyterian church conducted the services.

William John Russell had been a serving member of the Presbyterian church for over half a century, and he had occupied the same pew in the Presbyterian church of the city for thirty years. Although he was several times urged to accept offices in the church, he said he preferred to be a private in the ranks of the people of God. At the end he was judged "a successful business man, a consistent follower of his Master, a citizen of exalted character, and a loving husband and father."[30]

The loss of this revered and beloved patriarch was a blow to everyone in the family. All struggled to reshape their lives without their steadying force. Richard had relied on his father for many things, from advice to practical help, and now he felt almost overwhelmed by the loss of the best man he had ever known. Mary, having given all her affection to her father and mother, felt helplessly adrift without her masculine mainstay. Harriette, now dependent on Mary, watched her daughter's agony and felt she experienced a twofold grief, her own and her daughter's.[31]

Then came a comforting, natural emphasis on life. The second of November 1897 was a cold, wet day, and Richard was in court in Jefferson, when a telegram arrived declaring that Ina had given birth to a son. The elated father managed to get the judge to adjourn court, and then he drove to Winder, arriving with horse, buggy and self coated with sleet. Dr. Almond presented Richard Brevard Russell Jr., and the delighted father slapped the doctor so hard on the back that he almost dropped the baby. To express further joy, Richard loaded his shotgun, rushed into the yard, and fired off several rounds. The citizens of Winder guessed the Russell baby was the long-awaited son.[32]

Richard found time to telegraph his grieving mother about this blessed event, and Harriette dispatched a post card to the little boy on the same day, doing what she did best, quoting appropriate Scripture: "Now my son, the Lord be with thee; and prosper thou."[I Chronicles 22:11] She added her own prayer that he would be a source of help and strength for his sisters.[33]

The baby was to be called R. B., and Richard now thought it best to change Dicksie's name. He gave Mary the honor of naming her. She chose the two names she had been using all along, Frances for Ina's mother and Marguerite because she loved daisies and the French language.[34]

A few weeks after R. B.'s arrival, Richard came home to Ina with a proposition. He said he was delighted with his family of three girls and a boy and would not be disappointed if they had no other children. He had in his possession an object that would allow them to limit their family and enjoy their conjugal bliss at the same time. He suggested they use it.

Ina was not impressed. Having produced three healthy, bright and attractive daughters and a vigorous son, she was in her maternal glory. She saw no reason to consider one son or even three daughters enough. Children were gifts from God. She intended, she said, to have all that God would send. Richard could take this object out to the back yard where the hired man had dug several post holes and bury it. Or would she have to do it herself?[35]

8

A TIDE IN THE AFFAIRS OF MEN

1898-1904

The winter of 1898 was bleak for the William John Russell family. Adjusting to life without Father, Mary and Harriette turned to Richard for support, for patriarchal duties passed to the eldest son. Richard was not well, however, having suffered a long and severe bout of flu. Depressed and anxious about the judgeship campaign in the autumn, he needed to be working hard to make money, and not only for his ambition but also for his growing family.[1]

Harriette accused her son of chasing his political dream to the point of folly, putting demands on his health that risked the life of his children's father, not to mention her provider. She urged him to take a month's rest in Sea Breeze, Florida, where William John's sister Euphemia and brother Henry ran a boarding house. "Aunt Pheme" was an extraordinary caretaker on whom the family called sometimes. Although Harriette was willing to go to Pheme's or to keep house herself for her ailing son, she insisted he must have a rest. Relying on her uncomplaining daughter-in-law, Harriette was certain one of Ina's sisters would stay with her to ease her loneliness in his absence and to help care for three children. Harriette wanted to take Mary Willie with them, who at five years old was, in her grandmother's opinion, smarter than Richard had been at that age. In her grief and anxiety, Harriette found the child an indispensable comfort. Daughter Mary, of course, would be part of the family pilgrimage to Florida.

When Richard failed to reply to his mother's exhortations, Harriette urged Lewis to take care of his older brother. She sent medicines from Athens and cautioned that the doctor would not want whiskey given. They must all pray for Richard's restored health. They must not ask God politely. They must importune and beseech Him for blessings.

Lewis was working for Richard in Winder and living with the family but went often to see about his mother and sister in Athens. He was also studying for the bar, and he and Ina seem to have been phlegmatic about this time of family adjustment. Both accepted Richard's determination to push on with his campaign and stood ready to help. Lewis was already writing letters to state representatives and senators as part of his work in Richard's office.[2]

Rob and Edward wrote of their intent to help financially until their father's estate could be settled. Rob, writing from Italy, sent receipts of loans he had made to his father and asked that they be paid to Mary. Rob's life as a naval officer was as cosmopolitan as the lives of his siblings were provincial. He had traveled in numerous European countries and in Asia Minor. He was present at the coronation of the Russian czar in 1896, as part of the official United States military representation. Edward, in Washington, earned a thousand dollars a year in the Post Office Department and spent most of his free time in activities similar to those his brother John pursued in Athens. Both young men were enthusiastic cyclists and liked girls modern enough to ride. Edward had recently completed a law degree at George Washington University but did not appear interested in practicing law.[3]

The William John Russell estate was in disarray. Richard and John Jr. owed their father money, and he had left other debts beside the ones to Rob. All would have to be paid from insurance. No one seemed to think their father died penniless, but the estate was far from large, and it would take time to know how much was there to sustain Harriette and probably Mary, whose health had forced her to take leave of absence from her teaching.[4]

Richard did not take a month off in Florida, and he was well enough in early February to go to New York City on business. While travelling, he skipped lunches to save money and played whist with a Catholic priest. When not playing whist, he read a novel Ina had given him, *Quo*

Vadis. He did not like the novel much.[5] The title may have reminded him too much that he was thirty-seven years old, and did not appear to know where he was going. He had not achieved even one of the ambitions to which he had aspired when he was the youngest man in the Georgia General Assembly, fifteen years earlier. Friends from those assemblies had risen to the executive office or had established more prosperous law practices than his. William J. Northen, with whom Harriette and children had refugeed in Hancock County and with whom Richard had worked on several education bills, rose through the House and Senate to become Governor of Georgia in 1890 and again in 1892. From 1894 to 1898, the governor's chair was held by William Y. Atkinson, Richard's friend who had completed the work he had started on the girls' school established at Milledgeville. Atkinson was not forty years old when he was elected governor the first time.

Other colleagues from Richard's early General Assembly service were Joe Terrell and Tom Watson, men who had established influential positions in Georgia politics and were possible gubernatorial candidates, Terrell through the Democratic party and Watson through the Populist.

Richard must have chaffed under the knowledge that these men, especially the younger ones, had achieved his own goals or looked more likely to achieve them. He felt he must now push on or abandon his dreams forever. Words of Shakespeare's Brutus, learned in boyhood, haunted him: "There is a tide in the affairs of men/Which taken at the flood, leads on to fortune;/Omitted, all the voyage of their life/Is bound in shallows and in miseries." Although he dreaded the thought of defeat, the only tide of the moment appeared to be the Superior Court judgeship that his old nemesis Hutchins had so long occupied.[6]

Hutchins was elderly and had had four terms. He was not particularly popular, and Richard was sure he was vulnerable. The campaign would be less expensive than a Congressional race, which would require newspaper advertising and stumping to crowds. A Superior Court judgeship was a lesser office, but he counted on going into the upper judicial branch at an early date. He admitted a less noble motive for choosing this office: it was his surest way to redeem the 1896 defeat for the solicitor's office.[7] His great ambition remained insistent on the governor's chair, but he apparently took little note of the fact that moving from high judicial office into either the executive chair or the US Senate was rare in Georgia politics of his day.

Family matters remained demanding as Mary and Harriette suffered various illnesses during the spring and summer and ended up in Marietta under the care of Harriette's sister. Rob was home on leave early in the year, but returned to duty, serving on the battleship U.S.S. *New Orleans*, when the Spanish-American War broke out in the spring. While spending long hours working for his brother, Lewis also succeeded in passing the bar in April. Richard's law practice was growing, but he was restless, focused on campaigning for the judgeship, and Lewis' faithful and competent help in daily matters was crucial. Together they wrote several sequences of letters state-wide, Richard dictating, Lewis clacking away at the typewriter. They still wrote some letters by hand, and Lewis' hand was so much like Richard's the younger man could answer for his brother.[8]

On the home front, Ina provided stalwart help, mothering her active brood of four, as well as looking after Lewis and Richard. She sent refreshments to the office when they worked late, and handled the numerous gardening chores on their large lot. Richard wanted her to make him popular in Winder, and although it was not in her nature to court people for votes, she was well-liked in the little town for her good humor and thoughtfulness.[9]

As summer wore on, Ina, like Harriette, grew anxious that Richard put his campaign above all else. A person of peaceful perspectives, Ina failed to see how or why this one thing could deserve such importance. She felt herself and the children neglected, and although it was not like her to nag or criticize, she was hurt that Richard took no notice of how his careless behavior affected those closest to him. Their marital bed had been a place of mutual joy, but now she sensed him indifferent to her feelings in their most intimate moments. She dreaded becoming pregnant in such circumstances. It is not likely that she conveyed her anxiety to her husband.[10]

In September, Richard embarked on person-to-person campaigning, trying to see as many representatives and senators in the state as possible before the legislature convened in October. In spite of a grueling schedule, he wrote to Ina to say how dearly he loved her and to describe at length how he was garnering numerous votes. Never a man to fail to notice female presences, he did not neglect to mention that if the husbands were not at home, he succeeded in getting the wives and daughters to promise to make their husbands and fathers vote for him.[11] Campaigning for a judgeship differed from a legislative campaign because there were no issues to debate. He missed the thrill of oratory, but he enjoyed one-to-one contacts. He was euphoric when near Newnan, a six-mile chase in a buggy, drawn by a fine pair of gray horses, resulted in catching up with the Honorable J. D. Hammett, worth a dozen votes because of his influence. They told jokes and talked general philosophies for an hour by the roadside, and the encounter ended in a handshake and Hammett's vote and influence promised to him.

Richard took time to visit an old friend of Minnie's and regretted that he had not brought pictures of the children to show her. He glowed when he met Mr. William Trimble, who said he would vote for him because he had married such a pretty girl. William had known Ina when she lived with Miles and Lella Dillard in Oxford ten years earlier. Richard declared she was prettier now than when William knew her.

The candidate visited gracious country homes in shady groves and stores and cramped offices in dusty small towns, calling on people at all hours of the day and night. He stayed one night in Lithia Springs at the hotel where he and Ina spent the first night of their honeymoon. Memories of that night and of warm receptions and support encountered during his campaign sent his spirits soaring, but the euphoria was short-lived.

On October 12 he was in Macon for a political gathering, likely a meeting of the state Democratic party. Two years away from the battleground of politics, Richard had forgotten the hostile atmosphere. He was upset, even frightened, to learn that Hutchins' supporters had attacked his character viciously. He believed all his enemies, political and personal, were trying to damn his character, and he feared his children's good name was in question. He was disturbed to the point of considering prayer, for he recalled Harriette's teaching that "the fervent effectual prayer of a righteous man availeth much." Then a better idea came to him. If a righteous man's prayer was worth anything, surely a dear, pure woman's ought to be more valuable. He wrote to Ina, begging her to pray. He knew her well enough to realize she would not be likely to importune the Creator regarding influencing an election outcome, so he added that he was anxious to succeed because without success, he would make paupers of his wife and children. No doubt they had spent a noticeable sum on the campaign, but Ina would only have smiled at the idea that Richard Russell, with all his energy, talent and education, would let his family become paupers.[12]

She sensed, however, that in his obsession with this office he might be tempted to compromise his principles in order to win votes. By the time he and Lewis went down to Atlanta the week before the opening of the Legislature on October 26, she was so concerned about his mental state that, uncharacteristically, she communicated her anxiety to him, begging him not to forget that doing right was more important than winning votes.[13]

Richard heard the good sense in her plea. He believed deep down that the legacy of a good name, especially to the little boy who bore his name, was the only thing worth working for, and he resolved to do nothing to blemish that. He hoped his son would avoid his faults, but he longed to do some good that his child could emulate. Becoming a respected and worthy judge fulfilled this ambition.[14] He campaigned on and his support grew stronger. Lewis worked tirelessly with him, and although word came from John in Athens that an anti-Russell meeting had been held there on October 17, they were not discouraged.[15] By the time the vote was held on October 28, Hutchins had dropped out, knowing he was defeated. One hundred thirty lawmakers voted for Russell, with seventy-nine Hutchins supporters abstaining. Exultant, Richard wired Ina: "Your husband is judge by overwhelming majority."[16]

Harriette, relieved and proud, instructed Lewis to have a new velvet collar put on Richard's old overcoat. He was entirely too careless about his dress, and now that he was judge, he must look the part. She admonished Lewis to tell no one about this, just to do it.[17]

By this time Ina must have suspected she was again pregnant, and as often was her case in the early months, she was not well. Since R. B. was barely a year old, and the three girls ranged between five and two years, they decided she must have help. Hettie Belle Bearden, a white girl of about fifteen from Walton County, came to live with the family and take especial charge of R. B. while Ina was incapacitated. Ina must have grieved at this separation from her son, with whom she had formed an intense bond. She was resigned and cheerful, but she did not forget the uneasy circumstances that had led to her pregnancy.[18]

Miss Hettie, a hard worker with strong maternal instincts, soon became a general favorite in the family, adored by the little girls and R. B. Hettie's large family was so poor she had had to leave school after only three years, and she was gratified for this chance to live and work in a place where she felt she could learn and improve herself. She looked up to Ina as her role model in becoming a homemaker, and Ina valued Hettie's faithful contributions.[19]

In readiness to become Superior Court Judge of the Western Circuit on January 1, 1899, Richard set about clearing his law work. His last days of practicing law in the Circuit were difficult because Hutchins, never anxious to accommodate Mr. Russell, deliberately held off calling his cases until the last minute. These delays meant Richard spent more and more days at court, away from home. Missing his family, he liked to envision them around the supper table: Ina Jr. on her mother's right and Dicksie (he rarely called her Marguerite) on her left, with Mary Willie, their big girl, sitting beside Dicksie, feeding the two-year-old when necessary. He imagined his dear little R. B. crying, off in another room, with Miss Hettie ministering to him. Fortunately, the entire family was able to get away from Winder and enjoy a Thanksgiving feast at Farm Hill with Ina's people.[20]

As Richard Russell began his career as a judge, he was still looking to a future in which he would be a different kind of leader—a governor, a senator, at the very least a congressman. Nevertheless, he poured himself into the work with a will, and he was good at it. Groomed from childhood to preside, his command of the business of the court was so smooth that he received compliments in the local press. Elated, he felt sure he was on his way to further greatness which would make his son proud.[21]

Although a Superior Court judge was not a person likely to become famous, within the judicial system in his circuit he exercised (and still exercises) peculiar power. Lawyers knew this power and had to work within that knowledge. Richard Russell appreciated the importance of his position, and he earned respect as a learned, careful, fair judge. Superior court judges might not have many privileges, but one they did have was to do just as they pleased about calling the courts and adjourning them. Richard enjoyed knowing that in these circumstances his word was a kind of law, but he took into account requests from those affected by his administrative decisions and did not abuse his power. His work ethic well known, no one could have been surprised that he sometimes held court until one in the morning and started up again at 8:00 AM. He was young for a judge, but he showed special consideration to new lawyers, his patriarchal tendencies extending naturally to neophytes. One of his duties was to examine and admit to the bar, and his erudition and patience drew the young men to him.[22]

He was away from home as much as ever, and the early months of 1899 proved challenging for Ina. Mary and Harriette remained ill, and Lewis went to Athens to care for Mary, who was suffering her chronic complaints. Gravely ill, Harriette came to Winder to be under Ina's care. No one expected the old matriarch to make it through the spring, but in April she rallied enough to be moved to her house in Athens where Aunt Pheme and Lewis took over the care of the two ailing women. Ina, by this time eight months pregnant, could not continue to nurse her mother-in-law.

Ina delivered a baby girl on May 16, 1899. They named this daughter Harriette Brumby. Edward thought it was too bad the baby wasn't a boy to be named for brother Rob.[23]

Soon after the birth of this baby, Richard bought or built a house across from the Winder residence on Park Avenue, and Mary, Harriette and Lewis moved into it. The care of Harriette fell to Mary when Mary was well, but to Ina and Lewis when Mary was incapacitated. Harriette continued to admonish her children when she felt they were behaving badly and to praise them for their kindnesses to her.[24]

The tendency to admonish continued through her son Richard, who wrote Ina Jr. on her fifth birthday a letter filled with Harriette-type advice: The most important thing is to be a good girl, for unless we are good, we will not be happy. She must remember that being pretty and rich was not as important as being good. Most of all, she must learn to be satisfied and contented with what she has and where she is.[25] The lesson of St. Paul to be content with whatsoever state one finds oneself was one Harriette Brumby Russell had had to learn over and over in her life, and not naturally a contented person, she preached it constantly. Richard, restless and often dissatisfied, understood the wisdom of the advice and struggled to bring it to mind and heart.

As his work continued to keep him from home, Richard worried more over his children, "the little birds of promise," especially the daughters. He feared he was not doing his duty by them. The theme of their growing up to be good women would return again and again to his mind as he felt keenly the separations from them. He trusted Ina completely as their perfect role model; nevertheless, his years of work in the law courts had taught him by example what his mother's precepts emphasized, namely, that a worthy character was more important than anything else for men and for women. Yet he believed that women without strong characters were, even more so than men, helpless wrecks.[26]

Over the next three years, Richard gave most of his time to his judgeship and his family. He took Ina and one or two of the children with him to court sessions during the summers, wanting his children, especially his son, to understand his work.[27] At other times he managed to write playful and loving letters. In the summer of 1900 he wrote that although Marguerite had offered to marry him the last time he was home, he wanted only Ina and begged her to say yes. As her husband, he could stay at her house and cut some of her weeds, feed her pigs for her and play with the little boy she had done him the honor of naming for him. Ina, though doubting the part about his staying at her house, probably had to say yes, for she was expecting another baby. On August 19, 1900, she gave birth to their second son, who was duly named Robert Lee after the next eldest Russell brother.[28]

Soon after the birth of Robbie, as the baby was called, Ina developed severe mastitis. Burning with fever, she was too weak and sick to care for her children. Cutting the breast was an accepted treatment for mastitis at this period, now frowned upon, but Richard refused outright to consider surgery. After what had happened with William John, the family had great reluctance about going under the knife for any reason.

Miss Hettie could not carry out Ina's work alone. Something had to be done. It was decided that Harriette, only fifteen months old, would go to Farm Hill to stay with Ina's mother and sister Pipey. In the meantime, Mary Willie, now seven years old, was "given" the new baby as her special charge, and the little girl took the charge seriously. She proved excellent help, and she formed a lifelong bond with this brother that would be a joy to both of them.[29]

As Ina recovered, it looked as though family life would return to whatever becomes normal after the birth of any baby. Then Harriette fell ill at Farm Hill, likely with rheumatic fever. After an anxious time, she recovered, but she was weak and needed so much attention that everyone agreed she would have to stay with Grandmother Mec and Sister Pipey in order to have quiet and rest. Ina did not like to separate her family, but this seemed the best way to assure good health for everyone. As time passed, it became harder and harder for Grandmother Mec and Pipey to give up "their" baby, and Harriette did not come home. This meant that Richard saw her even less than the rest of the family, who went to Farm Hill often when he was away at court. He grieved that the little girl his wife felt was more his than hers was a sort of orphan child.[30]

In November 1900 Richard had the opportunity to go to south Georgia and hold court for an absent judge. Wanting to gain state-wide recognition, he chose Valdosta, in spite of the fact that it meant he would miss Thanksgiving dinner at Farm Hill. Sensitive to the fact that she was again left alone with the children, he was touched to receive a tender letter from Ina as soon as he arrived in Valdosta.

Richard found life in the south Georgia town elegant and the citizens well-fixed. Prominent citizens treated him like "a regular lion," and although the era of ardent social activity during court week was fast fading, this experience must have given him a taste of past glories as he was feted at teas, plays, dinners, and parlor musicales. In the Taylor home he was treated to a string ensemble made up of four daughters. One of these had just returned from music study in Germany, and she was the

finest violinist he had ever heard. He managed to attend a Knights of
Pythagorus meeting, where he enjoyed revving up his oratory skills. He
made friends with F. B. Holder, editor of the *Valdosta Sun*—a newspaper
editor is a useful friend for a politician—and was gratified at how old
friends from his days in the legislature welcomed him.

Such a warm reception both fuelled and assuaged Richard's hunger
for recognition, and he longed for Ina to see how he was treated. He
suffered guilt pangs, knowing how much she would have enjoyed the
social life. At these times he recognized how their separations deprived
her of an equal partner's share of the pleasures of their marriage and his
successes, such as they were. As time went on, he became more and
more sensible of the treasure he owned in this noble woman. Knowing
how well she knew and understood him, the fact that she continued to
love and admire him, to think of him as her sweetheart, amazed and
humbled him.[31]

Superior court judges in 1898 made three thousand dollars a year.
Although enough to support his growing family, this salary was hardly
enough to fund the many ambitions of Richard Russell, nor was it
comparable to what he could earn in law practice. Since deciding to run
for the judgeship, Richard had been considering a business venture that
he hoped would earn him the money that giving up his legal practice for
a judgeship had cost him. He was going to open a knitting mill in Winder
to manufacture women's stockings and children's socks. As usual, his
brother Lewis was coming in as a willing partner.

The two men had secured information about cotton factories. As
sons of William John Russell, they were not ignorant of terms referring
to grades of two-ply yarns, spindles, engines, boiler rooms and stacks,
nor to the need for sprinklers and fire equipment. They must have felt
certain they could find skilled labor or train it to knit, top, loop, mend,
press and examine the stockings. Men, women and children from failed
farms in the 1890s were eager to take up paid-by-the-week labor. No
doubt it all sounded familiar, workable. The brothers were advised they
would need $100,000 in capital to start up the plant and to build
tenement houses, but at current prices, they could make a net profit of
sixty-eight dollars per day, a gold-mine profit of $20,400 per annum. If

they chose to run day and night, they could practically double this return.[32]

The Russell men had no cash remotely close to $100,000 to put into such a venture. What little capital they may have accumulated they had spent on land. Rob and Lewis had bought a farm together in Jackson County, and William John had secured several hundred acres in Oconee County. Richard, having spent much of his early savings on campaigns, had also purchased a farm, about two hundred acres, near Winder. His farm was in Jackson and Walton Counties, divided by the railroad running along the county line. It seems certain that they all received a modest settlement from William John's estate, perhaps two thousand dollars each, but as usual, the Russell men were hard up for cash. Winder, however, was a place stirring with people eager to get into the textile business, and the Russells succeeded in getting others interested in their idea.[33]

The Winder Cotton Mills was chartered in the Superior Court of Walton County in 1900, with capital stock of $75,000, divided into shares of one hundred dollars each. Nine Winder businessmen were on the petition for charter, one of whom was Lewis C. Russell. Richard Russell was not on the original charter, perhaps because it was his court to which they petitioned. Nevertheless, he was associated with the cotton mill from the beginning. Brother Edward purchased one share of stock on April 6, 1900. It seems certain that all of the businessmen involved, including Richard Russell, bought considerable shares. In 1901 the name of the mill was changed to the Russell Manufacturing Company. It was located at the edge of town, on Athens Street.[34]

By the spring of 1901, the mill was in operation and Richard went north at the company's expense to find buyers for their hosiery. He wanted to take Ina, but the cost of sending two put this dream out of the question. Writing a steady stream of letters while he was away, he revealed his deep need at this anxious time to share his thoughts and feelings with a trusted partner.[35]

He was on the train on Easter Day, a beautiful, sunny day, and he longed for his family as he looked out at the world speeding by. In Washington he was pleased to have a day to visit with Edward. His brother introduced him to a girlfriend whom Richard found "pretty as a peach but a little stout." When Edward asked what he thought, he said she would be all right if she was heiress to $60,000 as was reputed. "It won't do for all of us to marry for love and be poor. Some of us must have money," he quipped. Edward, however, was like all the Russell men. He was romantic and dreamed only of love in a cottage. Since Richard was still the sole Russell brother to have taken a bride, he must have been referring to his own situation. Ina may not have appreciated hearing herself and the children listed as reasons for poverty.

Richard grew depressed at the reception he received up north regarding the sale of Winder hosiery. He was told that poor economic conditions in Japan and China, the principle markets for cheap Southern goods, had sent prices down; consequently, the Winder plant would have to sell at very low prices. In Philadelphia on a cold and cheerless day, he had trouble finding the men he sought and wished he'd gone to St. Louis or New Orleans instead. When he did catch up with his contacts, they refused to buy, saying they were overstocked and would not buy now anyway because they expected to see all markets in cotton goods fall further. This news made him blue over the mill's prospects.

In New York City he remembered the happy time of his honeymoon with Ina and longed to share again the sights and sounds of the city with her. Suffering more pangs of guilt that she could not enjoy these pleasures (though sightseeing had few charms for him without her), he vowed to bring her back in June, for their tenth anniversary, leaving Winder after June 24, the date they had set to baptize Robert Lee. It was their tradition to baptize the babies on their anniversary when possible.

Unaccustomed to big cities, the would-be Southern businessman felt threatened and alienated, especially in the slum areas, and was homesick for Winder and his little country home. Seduced by low prices, he went into a small café on Fourth Avenue, where he had lunch for fifteen cents—coffee two cents, glass of milk three cents, ham and eggs ten cents, with as much bread and potatoes thrown in as he wanted. His lunch was spoiled when two black men came in and sat at a table next to him and ordered fancier dishes than he could afford. When two nice-looking young couples, white boys and girls, came in and sat down at the same table with the black men, he was astonished.

Talking over the racial situation with his hotel proprietor, he was relieved when the man said he would not hire a Negro, much less allow one to stay in the hotel. All the waiters in the hotel dining room were good-looking white men in full dress suits, and the chambermaids Richard saw on his floor were pretty young girls with fair hair and blue eyes, all neatly dressed. When he saw advertisements for Swedish servants, he thought it a good idea to get Ina a big strong Swede woman who had been trained to work and knew how to work, to come and live with them.

Richard Russell dreaded the lonely hours in his hotel room. His bed reminded him of their tender farewell and the pleasure of nestling against his wife or having her entwine her legs in his, as she liked to do. When he surveyed what he had accomplished while being away, he was sick at heart. He had nearly walked himself to death in Philadelphia and talked himself hoarse seeing hosiery people, yet he had not sold a single pair of socks. In New York, his chief pleasure had been showing off a letter from Mary Willie to two men to whom he was trying to sell socks. As he fell asleep, he found solace in bringing each of his children to his mind: sweet Mary Willie, tender Ina, wise little Marguerite, sturdy R. B. Jr., demure little Harriette and the latest jewel, comely, joyous Rob.

Richard and Ina did not go back to New York City for an anniversary trip, and as the summer wore on, economic conditions did not improve. The mill was not making important profits, if it was making any at all; in addition, he had trouble keeping good employees, especially in positions of management. He feared he would have to shut the mill down completely until he could find someone to run it. Court sessions were long and hot, and being a judge seemed more and more like a poor way to make a living, away from his family.

Another project came to mind. He would start a town of his own on the land he had bought. He had several pieces of property in Winder, and the little town was growing rapidly. Homes increased in value, while town buildings held steady or dropped in price. He had some of both kinds. If he sold these, he'd have money to invest in his own town. [36]

By now they knew Ina was expecting another baby, due on New Year's day 1902. She had spent most of the summer at Farm Hill, where the children could run free on the farm, and she had the help of her mother and sister.

Harriette had not completely recovered from her illness in 1899, and the family had had to make changes to adjust to her frequent need for extended care. With Lewis, Mary and Harriette living in Winder, Ina could help with Harriette's care. Ina's sister Pipcy sometimes filled in as nurse. Harriette, accustomed to being the caretaker, was not an easy invalid. She made gradual improvement until the autumn of 1901 when Mary took her out for a drive. They stopped to visit a friend, and as Mary got down to tie the horse, it became frightened and bolted. Harriette was thrown from the careening buggy. She was never to recover from this accident.[37]

In January 1902, a seventh child and fifth daughter was born to Richard and Ina. She was called Patience Elizabeth after Ina's sisters Pipey (Patience) and Anne Elizabeth (Aunt Annie), who were giving such stalwart care to their younger sister and her burgeoning family.

In 1902 Joe Terrell, Richard's friend of early years in the legislature, ran for governor. Terrell was one month younger than Russell, having usurped him as the youngest member of the Georgia General Assembly in 1884. Terrell, from Greenville, Meriwether County, had enjoyed an enviable career, achieving the record Richard had hoped for. At twenty-nine Terrell had been elected to the Georgia Senate, and at thirty-one he became attorney general of the state, and as such had phenomenal success in trying cases before the United States Supreme Court. Not brilliant, Terrell had a facility for providing solid, conscientious and effective leadership without creating dangerous enemies. Although Richard Russell was good at making friends, his unbending attitudes often also produced enemies afraid of his strength.

In 1902 the governor's race was an open one, and it must have hurt Richard to see his friend enter the race with as good a chance as either of the other candidates, Dupont Guerry, a Macon lawyer, and John H. Estill, a Savannah newspaper editor. Richard had not been able to come up with a race that he had a chance of winning other than re-election to the Superior Court judgeship. 1902 was the first year these judgeships were elected by popular vote, and Richard was re-elected without opposition.

Terrell, Guerry, and Estill waged a hot campaign over the main issue of prohibition. Terrell and Estill advocated local option, the plan that allowed each county to decide for itself whether the sale of alcohol would be allowed. Guerry was a bone-dry prohibitionist. The primary was held on June 5 and in the county unit vote, Terrell came in well ahead of Estill, whose margin over Guerry was slim. In the autumn the state Democratic convention, not surprisingly, endorsed local option.

Although in the autumn the Populist Party ran Judge J. K. Hines, heavily endorsed by Tom Watson, against Terrell, the young Democratic candidate easily defeated the judge. The waning influence of the Populists became more and more apparent, as the Democrats showed the good sense to adopt many Populist reform ideas and thus improve economic conditions and their ability to get votes. Richard Russell, like most other political hopefuls in Georgia, had remained a staunch Democrat.

A great personal grief interrupted the summer campaigns. In early July Harriette Brumby Russell fell ill for the last time. After a prolonged death watch that kept Lewis, Mary and others on constant duty, on July 15, 1902, Harriette crossed over her river Jordan. The funeral was two-fold, with services in Winder at the new Presbyterian Church that Lewis had helped to start, and another in Athens on the pretty rise in Oconee Hill Cemetery, where she was laid to rest beside her beloved John. Many Athens citizens came to meet the train bearing her coffin and followed the cortege to the quiet spot above the river, where they sang "On Jordan's Stormy Banks," to the tune of "Way Down Upon the Suwanee River."[38]

Although they retained the house in Athens and rented it, Lewis and Mary decided to continue living in Winder together, and both were happy with the arrangements. After her father squelched a lowly mill manager's courtship some dozen years earlier, Mary had shown no inclination to marry. Lewis had given up his engagement to a Knoxville girl because of Harriette's chronic illness. He enjoyed the company of attractive women, but he did not seem to find marriage necessary while he had his 'nin tister' [Little Sister] to look after and to look after him.[39]

In 1900 Lewis bought a failing newspaper in Winder called the *Democrat*. He was forced to edit the floundering publication when his editors proved unreliable, which was a frequent occurrence. Lewis was elected mayor of Winder in 1902, and he was also working in his brother's law office and farming at least a hundred acres which he "owed," as he put it, with his brother Rob.[40]

The farm was in peach trees, planted by Uncle Henry Russell, a bachelor brother of their father, who lived with Aunt Pheme. During this period, Southern farmers were encouraged by the Department of Agriculture to try crops other than cotton, and Lewis, Henry and Rob were following this advice. Mary, having given up teaching entirely, helped Lewis with the paper work of his farm business. She may also have helped keep the payroll for the Russell Manufacturing Company. Brother John, whose bicycle shop in Athens had burned, was also farming at this time, on the land he had bought in Oconee County. He called his place New Timothy and planned to make it a farm requiring several tenants. At first, however, he was alone in his work. He could plow a team of four oxen until they tired, when he switched to a team of mules to give the oxen a rest.[41] The energetic Russell brothers had learned well Harriette's lessons about the importance of work.

In August 1902, Associate Supreme Court Justice Henry Thomas Lewis announced that because of ill health, he would resign at the end of the year. Supreme Court justices had been elected by popular vote since 1896, but an election had just been held, so the legislature would elect Judge Lewis' replacement. Richard decided to try for the spot, and during the months of August and September he and Lewis were again writing letters furiously to legislators, extolling his virtues as a jurist. The Athens bar came out with a glowing endorsement, but the post went to John S. Candler, a respected Atlanta lawyer from one of Georgia's most prominent families.[42]

Denied the state-wide office, Richard turned his attention to local affairs. His farm near Winder included a small settlement of several homes, some of these tenant houses. He intended to build others for farm and mill laborers and to incorporate the area as the town of Russell. He had imagined such an achievement since his boyhood days at Princeton.[43]

When he proposed his new town, several Winder citizens took offense because it would shave off a sliver of Winder's territory. Angry at their harsh criticism of his idea and their presumption in telling him what to do with his own land, he was determined to leave Winder as soon as possible. With many friends in the legislature, it was not difficult for him to have the city of Russell chartered.[44]

On December 18, 1902, Dr. Lamartine G. Hardman, the representative from Jackson County, a respected physician, successful textile manufacturer, and future governor, proposed the town, and it was soon legally a reality. All ordinary functions of municipal government were included in the charter, which provided for a mayor and four councilmen. These were named and it was provided that they should hold office for a term of two years or until the election of successors.[45] Richard Russell would remain mayor of the "city" until his death.

Ina, expecting another baby in early summer, was not well enough to move, nor did she think it sensible to ask the children to walk a mile and a half to school in Winder. The issue of their children's schooling vis-à-vis Richard's ambitions was one that frequently came up for avid discussion between Judge and Mrs. Russell. Ina Dillard, compatible, supportive, amiable, was, nevertheless, far from a yes-woman. Where the welfare of the family was concerned, she felt it her duty to speak up. Richard respected her counsel, and, being a fair judge, he must have known that her points were valid.[46]

In spite of these disagreements, he recognized that in his family he had reached a rare plateau of success because of his choice of a wife. Sometimes the knowledge of this success was all that sustained him when he felt disappointed at his lack of political achievement. After a long day in court, alone on the darkened streets of towns like Lawrenceville, Jefferson, or Homer, he fought depression by taking walks. He thought bitterly that he was now past forty and had reached no higher than a judgeship. How had he been so sure he would be, before the age of thirty-five, where Joe Terrell was sitting? These thoughts exacerbated his melancholy.

Then his family came to mind, and his heart felt washed in a great light. He rejoiced in remembering the ten years of privation and hardship that Ina had undergone without complaint to help him succeed. Reflecting on her genuine interest in his successes, on her comfort when he failed, and on the tenderness of their personal relations as husband and wife reminded him that he had chosen a helpmeet without compare. If he had not gained all the jeweled honors he had hoped, he had at least found and won a priceless diamond, and he was resolved to be worthy of her continued love and admiration.[47]

On June 18, 1903, Ina gave birth to a third son, called Walter Dillard, after Ina's brother, who was at that time the preacher at the First Methodist Church in Winder. Walter and his wife Mary were parents of several children, and the two families were close. Although the Russell brothers thought it was Edward's turn to have a boy bear his name, Edward magnanimously gave his approval of the choice, perhaps because he was to take a wife of his own, Susan Buchanan, in November. Susie's father was the owner of a small Washington jewelry store, and so Edward had to decline Lewis' offer of the engagement ring returned by his Knoxville girl during Harriette's long illness.[48]

In July 1903 brother Rob pre-empted Edward and took the giant step of matrimony, marrying Ethel Soley, daughter of a retired naval captain. Although northerners by birth and inclination, the Soleys lived in Talladega, Alabama, where the captain held a high executive position with a railroad. Ethel was a stunningly beautiful young woman with luxuriant dark hair and large, expressive eyes. Although she was good-natured and laughed a lot, there were some misgivings in the family regarding how she would view her Southern relations. Lewis, Mary and Richard attended the wedding, which was held in the elegant parlor of the bride's large and gracious home. Mary Willie, age ten, went as her father's escort because Ina was still recovering from Walter's birth. The Russell representatives thought cutting the wedding cake with the groom's sword dramatic and romantic enough even for Ethel.[49]

On November 28, 1903, with Lewis as a nervous best man, Edward and Susie 'jumped over the broom' in Washington. The Edward Russells, following a wedding trip to Florida, were at home after the second of January in their Washington apartment. Rob and his bride were also living in Washington at this time, while Rob was assigned to the Adjutant General's office, at last having the chance to use a law degree he had earned in 1894.[50]

In the Richard Russell household the issue of moving to Russell appeared to have subsided until one day in early December 1903 when a high-sided wagon pulled by a two-mule team arrived at the door of Ina's house in Winder. The black man driving got out and came to the back door to inform Mrs. Russell that the Judge said for him to start taking furniture out to the Gresham house in Russell. Ina knew that when Richard had made up his mind, nothing would change it. She started loading children and furniture.

Mary Willie would remember all her life that journey in a chair behind the mule driver, holding the baby Walter for dear life, with nearly-two-year-old Patience on the floor beside her.[51] The Gresham house was a frame building with three bedrooms, living room, dining room and kitchen, no different from their Winder house, likely built about the same time. Whether to placate an irate Ina or to show his love, Richard had a large room added to the house, which was called Ina's room, where one door opened into the house and another onto the wide veranda.[52]

By Christmas 1903, the Russells were ensconced at Russell, Georgia. If Ina thought Winder was a cultural wasteland compared to Athens, what must she have thought of Russell, with its few houses and a ramshackle Baptist church built of scrap lumber?[53]

By 1904, Richard Russell was desperate to enter a state-wide election, and he made the office of chief justice of the Supreme Court his choice. Joe Terrell was certain to be re-elected governor, and considering the quiet race, the state Democratic primary had been set for April, rather than the usual summer date that gave long days for campaigning. Richard must have counted on exciting interest in a Chief Justice campaign, in spite of the apathy that usually surrounded state-wide judges' races. People generally felt that sitting justices who were doing their jobs should not be opposed, and upon his early announcement, the general cry of criticism was that Judge Russell was going against precedent.[54]

His opponent, the incumbent Thomas Jefferson Simmons, had served on the court since 1887, and was elected by the legislature in 1894 to succeed the venerated Logan E. Bleckley as Chief Justice. Simmons, characterized as a tall, fine-looking gentleman and a genial person, was re-elected by popular vote in 1896 and 1900. In 1904 he was sixty-seven years old.

Richard launched his campaign by highlighting his own qualifications rather than Simmons' shortcomings, which could only have been related to declining health. Pointing to his eighteen years practicing law before becoming a Superior Court judge, Richard declared he dreamed of winning an enduring reputation by relieving the congested condition of the court.[55] Indeed, the Supreme Court's crowded docket highlighted a need for additional justices or for creating a court of appeals, ideas that were recurring topics in legal circles.

Richard shaved his moustache and the campaign photo showed a straight, handsome man in his prime (he was not quite forty- three years old), with a clear, thoughtful gaze and neatly combed dark hair. Ina was sure to have encouraged the shaved moustache, for she never abandoned her early opinion regarding the evil impression that tobacco stains made.[56]

While hostile papers like the *Augusta Chronicle* complained that Russell was going against the precedent that the Chief Justice should rise from among the Associate Justices, friendly newspapers noted that he was eminently qualified and unanimously endorsed by "the people and Bars of his Circuit." Those in favor of Judge Russell pointed out that Governor Gordon had appointed Logan Bleckley while he was practicing law and that Joseph E. Brown, former Governor, had been appointed while he was superintendent of the Western & Atlantic Railroad. Criticizing Russell for dragging the high office of Chief Justice down to his own political level was unfair. The legislature, by making Supreme court judges elected, had brought about this state of affairs. The argument of elected versus appointed judges was the question in this case, not the character of Judge Russell. The Jackson County *Economist*, perhaps the strongest newspaper in Russell's home county, went so far as to say the people do not believe in the old monarchical idea of succession in office. Electing all officials, whatever the branch, made them the servants of the people, not their masters, which is the American way.[57]

The family pitched in to provide the campaign staff. Lewis typed official letters; Mary helped address and mail them; John traveled state-wide on his bicycle putting up posters and meeting with those rumored to be friendly in each county; Edward, although a new bridegroom, volunteered to come and help with correspondence in the month before the election; Ina also found time from her homemaking and childcare duties to address envelopes for form letters and even to write a few letters by hand.[58]

The candidate embarked on a state-wide tour that kept him away from home almost entirely during the two months before the election, but he comforted himself and Ina that if he won he would have six years of being at home with the family. In early April, two weeks before election day, he was in southwest Georgia, having made a four-day swing through Lee, Macon, Randolph, and Terrell Counties. He went on to Clay and Quitman, trying desperately to cover all parts of the state. Lewis and Ina kept writing letters to influential people or simply to relatives. Richard was heartened by the support he received and felt that if he failed it would be only because he had not had time and money enough to make himself known. Lewis joined him on the tour as election day loomed. Ina, caught up in the excitement of the home run, wrote to encourage them both.[59]

Adjusting to the quieter life outside of Winder, the children and Ina may have found Richard's absences more onerous than ever. Ina often had the children write to Papa as a way of teaching them to write, and so he knew that Uncle Martin's old dog like to have killed kitty Gray, they had a fine garden coming along, they were working on a thousand of his letters, Mama had a new cow and calf, and R. B's old Robinson Crusoe rooster had died. Three-year-old Rob did not neglect to ask: "Papa, have you beat Judge Simmons yet. Papa, I wish you would come home." Written in the hand of his older sister Mary Willie, this letter expresses the feelings of all Russells in the city of Russell.[60]

Although Richard was gratified by the attention he received state-wide in the towns he visited, and was pleased that he was able to find men willing to get up some kind of organization for him, he feared that time would catch him. He wrote an old friend from Georgia legislature days, Steve Clay, Georgia's junior senator in Washington, asking him for help. Clay replied: "The people will pay little attention to the election of Supreme Court Judge. [The way to win this race is] to let your Manager write to the Justices and Notarics in each Militia District in the state asking them to be present at the primary and to see to it that your opponents name is scratched and yours left on the ticket. Write a similar letter to each member of the County Democratic Committee...Another way to succeed is to find out the names of the candidates for county officers, who are the strongest in their counties, and secure their co-operation, if you can." Having given this advice, which clearly involved illegal activities, Clay concluded that he was no longer in favor of the election of Judges by the people.[61]

The hopeful judge either did not see his way to following this advice, or he did not have a support team in each county sufficient to accomplish it. Without a doubt he had no funds with which to "secure the co-operation" of county officials. On April 20, Chief Justice Simmons was soundly re-elected, but Richard Russell carried forty-four counties and polled 68,000 popular votes. The *Atlanta Constitution* praised the dignified way in which the race was conducted by both candidates, and characterized Russell's campaign as brilliant.[62]

There is no evidence that this defeat discouraged Richard Russell. Instead, his good showing encouraged him to look with confidence at the idea of running for governor in 1906.

9

A More Absolute Lie Was Never Told on Any Man

1905-1907

In the spring of 1905 Winder buzzed with gossip about Judge and Mrs. Russell. Ina was expecting her ninth child, and the kind ladies of Winder felt it their duty to go on a mission of mercy. A small group of them arrived at the Russell home one day with a delicate matter to disclose. They wanted Ina to know that there was a way to avoid having so many children. The soul of courtesy, Ina thanked them and then related the shocking news that she knew about that but had rejected it. The ladies went back to town with livelier gossip than they had brought.[1]

In the masculine circles talk was heavy of Richard Russell, and most of it was not so friendly in nature. Richard had stirred up the feud begun in 1902 to such an extent that it was now impossible for Ina or anyone else to make him popular in Winder. A serious move was afoot to form a new county with Winder as the county seat, and Richard Russell was against it.

Almost any town welcomed the chance to become a county seat because a county generated government jobs and local business improved as more people came into town during court week. Winder had more than these usual reasons to aspire to county seatdom. The center of town was situated, literally, on the county lines of three counties, Gwinnett, Walton and Jackson. Winder had the distinction of inclusion in Lucian Lamar Knight's *Georgia's Landmarks and Memorials and*

Legends by virtue of a celebrated case in which two men became embroiled in an argument. One, standing in Gwinnett County, pulled a pistol and shot the other, who was in Jackson County. The victim staggered into Walton County and died there.[2] Proponents of the new county mourned the legal problems arising from this and less dramatic situations in which people lived in one county, had a business in another and, alas, paid taxes to both.

The Constitution of 1877 forbade the formation of new counties, and it was not until 1902 that an amendment was proposed to allow the addition of eight new counties, the first of which were proposed in the 1904 election. In July 1904 Winder advocates envisioned a county to be named for Alexander Stephens. The county committee may have chosen Stephens to honor, knowing of Richard's admiration for the statesman, but to no avail. Russell's influence in the state assembly was good enough to put a stop to that idea in the assembly of 1905, whereupon the town of Toccoa appropriated the cause and became the proud county seat of Stephens County. Winder residents were infuriated.

Why Richard Russell opposed the new county is unclear. The official argument against forming any new county was financial. A new county meant extra tax money would be needed to pay officers. In addition, conservatives opposed new members to the legislature, believing it was large and expensive enough. Although there is no evidence of Richard Russell's harboring personal vendettas aimed at stopping Winder's growth, his strong and continued opposition to something that would benefit the area could indicate he lost sight of the real issues. Eventually his brother Lewis would become part of the committee to form the county, joining their cousin W. H. Quarterman.[3]

The population of the city of Russell increased by one when a daughter was born to Richard and Ina on April 15. She was called Susan Way, in honor of William John Russell's mother. Richard was proud of being a member of the distinguished Way family of Liberty County. The Ways had no Revolutionary skeletons to hide.[4]

Celebrating the birth of the new baby, invigorated by the knowledge that his race for chief justice had brought him state-wide recognition and hopeful that his knitting mill was doing well (it is unlikely that it was), Richard Russell decided that the 1906 gubernatorial race looked open to any candidate with enough energy, time, charm and money to make the fight. Now was the time for him to run for governor of Georgia. His strategy, however, was to "lay low" and let two other candidates, Hoke Smith and Clarke Howell, give each other a bad name.[5]

Smith was a former owner of the *Atlanta Journal* and exercised considerable influence there. Howell's family owned, and he was managing editor of, the *Atlanta Constitution*. These two men, active in state politics for years, were early favorites. It is doubtful that either had more energy, time or charm than Richard Russell, but both had far more money and far fewer children.

Howell had served in the Georgia House from 1885 to 1891, and in the Georgia Senate since 1900. He had been on a first-name basis with Richard Russell since their legislature days, and Clark had recommended prospective editors to his friend for the *Ledger* during Richard's newspaper days in Athens.[6] The Howell family, through the *Atlanta Constitution*, were known for opposing the gold standard and the Watson Populists during the 1890s. Howells also fought lynching, convict leasing, black disfranchisement, and Wall Street plutocrats in the pages of the *Constitution*. Clark Howell supported white migration to the South, railroad development and, in general, ideals of the New South. Henry Grady had been his mentor, and Howell took over the editorship of the *Constitution* when the young Grady died. In addition to his personal fortune, Clark Howell enjoyed financial backing from the railroad lobby.

Hoke Smith, son of a North Carolina academic, had come to Atlanta in the early 1880s and had established a thriving law practice. Investing his fees in profitable business ventures, he was reported to be worth $300,000 by 1885. He bought the *Atlanta Journal* for $10,000 in 1887 and sold it for $300,000 in 1900. In 1892 he supported Grover Cleveland for the presidency and at Cleveland's election was rewarded with the post of secretary of the interior, where he discharged his duties with distinction. Although he left this office in 1896 and had been out of the public eye for nearly ten years, when he decided in 1905 to run for governor, Smith was prepared to do whatever it took to succeed.

Although Richard Russell's candidacy was announced informally in several news articles around the state as early as March,[7] Smith considered him a lightweight with Howell the real threat.[8] With time and money to dominate a long campaign, Smith announced his own candidacy in June 1905, fully one year away from the usual campaign period. In addition, he secured the backing of Tom Watson, a move that, unknown to other candidates at the time, was to assure his victory.

Watson, leader of the Populist Movement in the 1890s, had run as the Populist candidate for vice-president with William Jennings Bryan in 1896, but after this he had retired from politics and had piled up profits from practicing law, writing books and editing his own magazine. Although the Populist movement was virtually defunct by 1904, he ran as the Populist presidential candidate that year and discovered that he still had a considerable following in Georgia. In his early Populist days Watson had liberally included black and white farmers in his crusade, but he had since become a rabid racist. He announced in late 1904 that he would endorse any reform-minded candidate who favored disfranchisement of black voters.

Hoke Smith snatched up Watson's offer, in spite of the fact that Jim Crow laws heavily insured disfranchised black voters. Introducing a racial element was unnecessary in the view of other candidates, as well as of subsequent historians, but Smith was leaving no bases uncovered. Thus began a fifteen-year period in Georgia politics in which Tom Watson became a kingmaker not to be ignored.

Richard Russell had served with Watson in the Georgia legislature, and the two men had roomed together during at least one session. Although Richard did not support Watson's Populist theories, they had remained friendly, and Russell was surprised that Watson would support Smith. He wrote to the Populist leader and Watson replied that he was convinced the battle would be between Hoke and Howell and that he must support Hoke.[9]

Neither Russell nor Howell was rushing out to campaign, thinking the battle would not heat up until the next summer. Smith, on the other hand, put his show on the road, scheduling numerous speaking engagements for the summer of 1905.

Richard's close friend, Walter Brown, a prosperous lawyer in Atlanta, volunteered to help because of his enthusiasm for Richard's abilities. Brown proved a sagacious adviser and a loyal friend. Wise in the ways of politics, without any ambition of his own, he would sustain Richard Russell through many hard times to come.[10]

By the end of June, Richard was concerned that Hoke Smith's campaign circus would steal the show before it opened. Walter Brown thought the Howell camp had it right when they predicted the Smith furor would spend itself during 1905 and have nothing left for 1906. Knowing the slim Russell finances, he was satisfied that Richard could not do better than to hold back his public speaking until late in 1905 or early 1906.[11]

Nevertheless, Richard found opportunities to speak in areas he could reach by short journeys from his home or his courts during the months of July and August, casting himself as a 'prospective' candidate for governor.[12] He waved the "Plain Dick Russell" epithet that a friend had given him when nominating him for judge in 1898.[13] He hoped to convince people that he was the only one in the field free to serve the masses. He called attention to the environment (Atlanta) of the other candidates and claimed that true reformers came most often from the country. "Clark Smith and Hoke Howell will serve the same class after election that they have been serving all their lives," he said.

When he mixed the names of his rivals, his audiences laughed at this clever way of showing they were of the same cloth. They laughed again when he denied reports that he was running for office at someone else's bidding, but could not deny that he had been accused of being ugly. He hoped all the ugly folks would stand together in this campaign so that he would be elected by a fifty thousand majority.

In view of the fortunes arraigned on either side of him, his description of how he was conducting his campaign was touching. A good deal had been said about campaign contributions and buying votes, but he himself didn't have any money to buy votes. He could not afford to hire a campaign manager, and he and his wife attended to all correspondence. Mary Willie, at age thirteen, was pressed into service to address envelopes, and R. B., as Dick Jr. was called, carried them barefoot to the post office in Winder a mile away.[14] He had no campaign headquarters, at the Kimball House or anywhere else. His headquarters were wherever he was.

He might amuse his audiences with references to being ugly, but at forty-four Judge Russell was still a handsome man, straight and lean, his thick dark hair sprinkled with gray. He was at ease with the audiences gathered in courtrooms where candidates for all kinds of offices often took up the lunch hour to speak. Non-partisan newspapers reported that his lively and entertaining speeches increased his following and that he often received sustained applause. He sensed that people were listening and that they liked what he was saying. Recalling that in the 1904 Chief Justice race he had carried every county in which he had spoken, he believed his dreams within grasp if he could make enough personal contacts.

Then tragedy brought the worst pain his family had ever known. Early in August, Susan Way fell ill after being fed canned milk. In spite of Ina's devoted and skilled care through long nights watching by the crib, on August 7 Richard and Ina were required to furnish a jewel in the crown of heaven.[15]

This first loss of a child struck a bludgeoning blow. Their families gathered to mourn, Walter Dillard to preach. Pipey and Annie, as usual, had come during the illness to help care for the other children. Mary, Lewis and John took care of arrangements in Athens at the Oconee Hill Cemetery where the child was to be buried near her grandparents. The oldest children were at Farm Hill with Grandmother America when the death occurred, and they arrived at the cemetery at the same time as the funeral procession. The tiny coffin was opened so that these children could say good-bye to their sister. The morning sun fell onto the pale face of the child with a light so ethereal she looked like a sleeping angel. As the lid was closed, two women, perhaps Pipey and Annie, sang a spontaneous duet: "Safe in the Arms of Jesus."[16]

Ina's health, both physical and emotional, staggered under the dual pain of her baby's death and the prospects of a prolonged political battle. Worried that she might not recover, yet unable to give up his ambition when he had convinced himself the moment was right, Richard persuaded her to go to her Sister Hattie's in Washington, Georgia, for a few days' rest. Hattie, childless, loved to baby sister Ina. Pipey and Grandmother Mec kept the children at Farm Hill so that Ina could rest fully at Hattie's.[17]

After Ina left Hattie's, she went to Oglethorpe County for a time, and Richard came to Farm Hill to take her and the children home. When time came to leave, little Harriette, still living with Pipey and Grandmother Mec, remarked with childish innocence that she was glad they were going. Pipey asked her why. "Because," she answered, "Ina's children make me nervous."[18]

Although this remark brought laughter, the thought that his child did not understand her relationship to her parents and her siblings disturbed Richard. He could not forget that his wife claimed this child was entirely of his making, and he felt his responsibility to her was heavy. Perhaps he believed having Harriette at home again would be a good way to take Ina's mind and heart off the baby who had died. He insisted then and there that Harriette come home to live.[19]

Richard had from boyhood scratched out poems in his school notebooks, and now he tried to assuage his grief by writing poetry about the lost baby girl. When he showed the verses to Ina, they grieved her so that he destroyed them and vowed never to write another word of poetry.[20]

It was Richard Russell's way to deal with grief by working harder than ever and his public image did not reflect his sorrow. An article from the *Atlanta News* reported on September 18, 1905, that he was out talking to people every day and often twice a day. "He can shake hands better than any other politician," the piece declared, "[and] get up sooner . . . and stay up later and be busier all day long than any man who is asking the suffrages of the people."[21]

Richard Russell formally entered the gubernatorial fray when the chance came to speak on October 30 in Monticello on the same platform with Hoke Smith. Smith was unhappy when he heard that Russell had been invited to speak at the same time as he,[22] and in keeping with his determination to leave nothing to chance, he wrote to E. K. Lumpkin, a prominent Athens attorney whom he trusted, asking him first for information regarding Russell's standing in Clarke County and later for anything he might use against Russell.[23] Lumpkin's family, from Oglethorpe County, had held the governor's and the chief justice's posts with distinction. He had numerous important contacts. Lumpkin responded with enthusiasm, advising Smith not to make a big fight in

Clarke County where Richard's support was strong on account of his being "an old Clarke County man" and, in addition, the judge of the Superior Court. Lumpkin thought the lawyers did not wish to antagonize their local judge, especially because he was not modest in asking them how they stood. In the Princeton Factory District he found the Justice of the Peace "for Russell first and all the time."

Two weeks later Lumpkin wrote to Hoke Smith again, alarmed that Russell was challenging Smith to open debates. Lumpkin thought it best to avoid debating, and advised Smith of gossip he had heard that Russell's race was inspired by Howell and his crowd in order to draw votes from Smith's campaign. Lumpkin was inclined to believe this gossip was true because the *Constitution* had been favorable in reporting Russell's candidacy. The lawyer thought Smith should capitalize on the situation by tarring Russell with the 'ring politicians' brush [that is, the railroad ring] they were using to such good effect on Howell. He thought Smith should avoid the joint debate Russell was requesting at all costs because Russell was a happy, catchy, stump speaker, and such debate would only serve to detract attention from the important issues with Howell. "You would be like the Eagle, annoyed and diverted by the attacks of the small bee-martin, or the lion stung by the hornet," Lumpkin flattered the candidate.

Although Lumpkin repeatedly advised Smith not to accuse Russell of purposely being the tool of Howell and to avoid personal attacks of any other kind, Smith wrote asking if Lumpkin knew whether the original charter of the city of Russell included a provision permitting the sale of liquor. He was not going to resort to personalities if the Judge did not, but he wanted to be prepared if necessary.

Lumpkin reported the bitter feelings in Winder towards Judge Russell over his appropriation of part of Winder in forming Russell, an insult he had deepened both by having county hands maintain the streets of the new town and by attempting to establish a dispensary for selling alcoholic beverages there. He admitted that this was all gossip but suggested ways the campaign might verify the rumors.[24]

On October 30, a good crowd gathered at Monticello to hear the two candidates speak. Richard, in spite of his extended speaking experience, was visibly nervous. His hands and voice shook, and it looked as though

Hoke had worried for nothing. But as the judge continued to speak, he gained confidence and the crowd responded with laughter and cheers to what he said. The Monticello paper, clearly favoring Smith, reported that Smith spoke like a veteran and announced many definite points about his platform. Making no mention of the appearance of heavy-set Hoke, the editor belittled Judge Russell's lack of a platform and concluded he would need more than a handsome face, charming manners and ready wit to qualify him for governor.[25]

In early November Russell was to speak in Fulton County, in the metropolitan area of Atlanta, and he invited Smith and Howell to meet him there and participate in a debate. The other candidates turned up, and when the meeting was over, it was clear that Russell's reception was so favorable that the other candidates did not want to continue the forum. Two later debates in Dahlonega and McDonough between Smith and Russell again left Smith looking weak. In Dahlonega the candidates spoke from the back of a wagon in front of the courthouse. Smith emphasized railroad rates and Negro disfranchisement, but Russell made the crowd laugh, mindful that Lumpkin County had no railroad and no Negroes. After this, although Smith continued to ask Howell to debate and Howell continued to refuse to accept the challenge, both tried to avoid situations in which they might have to debate Judge Russell.[26]

Richard set off on a campaign swing that took him from Danielsville in northeast Georgia to Tifton and Waycross in south Georgia, following the county fairs, where he knew he could speak to a big crowd. He was abashed by how much his train tickets cost and discouraged when in Atlanta and Waycross, a popular circus stole the fair crowd, leaving him speaking only to air.

Far from home in a lonely hotel room, recalling the tenderness with which they had comforted each other after the baby's death, he worried about Ina. He asked himself if leaving his quiet, beloved home for such a grueling life was worth the risk to health and to fortune. The answer to that question seemed obvious: it would be far better to stay home. Yet he would not be tempted to give up the ambitions he had cherished all his life. He would ride this tide he felt sure would crest high.[27]

In January 1906, Richard set out on a campaign swing through Calhoun, Bibb, and Miller counties, and by this time he had countered Smith criticism that he had no platform by writing one in rhyme. It was clever and clear.

> 2-cent a mile passenger fares he advocates,
>> Others deal in generalities in railroad rates.
> Favors Child Labor Bill in the interest of education,
>> Do you know of a better plan to enlighten the nation?
> Was for eight hours of labor twenty years ago.
>> Where his opponents stood then their records don't show.
> He advocates removing a tax burden that stings,
>> By exempting three hundred dollars of household things.
> Prohibition will prohibit and never fail,
>> When place of delivery becomes place of sale.
> Build State Road to the Sea to regulate rates,
>> An issue too live for the other candidates.
> He wants a commissioner of Labor by the people elected,
>> That our State may never by strikes be effected[sic].
> From every corporate or ring influence free,
>> He would protect every sort of honest industry.
> You see his platform deals with questions much bigger,
>> While others devote all their time to the nigger.[28]

Richard's contacts assured him that people were listening, and he could not believe that when they realized they had a true candidate of the people that they would fail to vote for him. By this time he knew that Ina was expecting another baby in June, and the coming child must have restored hope. A few papers criticized the judge for his large family, and Ina saved these articles as a matter of pride.[29]

The judge had indicated he would resign from the bench on November 1, 1905, when he formally announced his candidacy for the governorship. He did not, however, resign in 1905 but waited until the spring of 1906, perhaps in order to dispose of work put off while campaigning in the fall.

Smith did not miss the chance to insinuate that the judge was neglecting one office to try for another.[30]

Smith stockpiled some of the rumors heard from Lumpkin as reasons to avoid voting for Russell. In particular, the Smith camp touted the 'fact' that Russell was a Howell candidate, and thus was aligned with, and no doubt financed by, the railroads and big corporations in general, the "ring rule." Howell did have many powerful friends and associates, but Richard Russell, free of such attachments and running as the poor man's candidate, was infuriated to find himself so maligned. He felt he was in a death struggle with the world, the flesh and the devil.

Passionately holding up his lifelong record of independence, he declared Smith's accusations damnable false slander. His current shoe-string campaign was proof enough that a more absolute lie was never told on any man. Powerless to defend himself in the press without newspaper backing or funds to pay for a rebuttal, he fumed at the injustice, the dishonesty. Smith, it seemed to him, was presenting a theory that a poor man had no right to run for governor and that if he did, it was irrefutable proof he was a hireling.

Although Richard had been in politics more than twenty years and understood that he must not be too sensitive, he was shocked and hurt by the success of what he termed Smith's false pretenses, humbug and personal abuse. He felt sure his life was witness to the fact that he would not be a cat's paw for anyone, but it grieved him to think the people of his state might believe the lies. If they believed them, he would have to count his life a failure.[31]

As summer approached, the campaign waxed hotter because five candidates had now entered the fray. The others were John H. Estill, editor of the *Savannah Morning News*, and James M. Smith, an able farmer who owned and worked with great prosperity thirty square miles of land in Oglethorpe County. Estill had lost the governor's race to Terrell in 1902. James Smith, a generous and appealing rich man, was an advocate of agriculture and railroad growth. Both men far outweighed Richard Russell in wealth and fame.

The Russell camp remained under-manned. Although Ina was mothering eight children and expecting another and Lewis had his law practice and a four-hundred-acre farm in peaches and grain to manage, they worked hard in Richard's campaign. They wrote letters, kept up with appointments and speeches, clipped newspaper articles and cheered up the candidate whenever they saw him, which was seldom.[32]

In addition to Miss Hettie, the family now included Miss Nita Stroud, a teacher who helped Ina with the children's schooling. Like Miss Hettie, she had particular charge of R. B., but other white children in Russell went to her school as well, including Miss Hettie. Ina remained the head of this staff, a wizard at organizing her household, assigning specific chores to each child, and she had, quite simply, the ability to inspire cooperation for mutual benefit. In addition, the less money she had, the better she became at economizing. With an artist's touch she kept Richard's home a place of refuge for him and for others.[33]

By summer, Richard had not been home two days in eight weeks and was making from one to three speeches every day. Lewis often worked out this schedule so that the candidate slept on trains at night, changing two or three times, thus avoiding hotel bills. He never allowed himself the luxury of a berth in a sleeper. There were no brass bands, no barbecues, no advertisements to herald the arriving candidate. He spent all he could afford, which was little enough, but every dollar of it was his own money. Friends, aware of his non-existent funds, took care of him. When he arrived in a town looking particularly frazzled, they provided him a meal and a bed. These acts of kindness and caring would be the lasting memories of a rugged campaign.[34]

Ina delivered a son on June 7, 1906. The baby was named Lewis Carolyn Russell, evidence of the gratitude Richard and Ina felt towards their faithful youngest brother. The baby was a beautiful child, robust and lively. Sister Hattie, who had given Ina refuge after the death of Susan Way, came expressly to hold the new baby in her arms and inspect him. She had had a bad dream about a sorrow that was coming to Ina, but she was relieved when she saw Lewis. She had never seen a more nearly perfect baby and was impressed with how the other children were eager to nurse him, even when it meant leaving their meals or play.[35]

By the end of June the campaign was as hot as the weather, which was scorching. Reading the major Atlanta papers, almost any observer would have said the only race was between Hoke Smith and Clark Howell. The *Journal* and the *Constitution* proclaimed their candidate and ignored the others, a fact noted by the struggling *Atlanta News*, which pointed out from time to time the capabilities and true independence of Plain Dick Russell. His virtues of honesty and determination were noted in small papers. He was called the Alexander Stephens and the Abraham Lincoln of Georgia politics because of his ability to work long and hard for the little man. His "staff" of loving family got good publicity. Ina's steadfast support was noted as a sustaining inspiration.[36]

The *Journal* made news of every Hoke Smith Club formed in every county, and they were numerous. It did not miss the one that grew up in Richard's home county of Jackson. Rumors of Richard's debts, loss of credit, and desires to legalize dispensaries because of his own love of drink circulated, reflecting the animosity many Winderites felt towards him.

On the other hand, others in Winder, merchants, bankers, salesmen, mechanics, barbers, lawyers, postal workers, and ministers of the Gospel, got up a petition that condemned the vilifying and abusing of their honored and esteemed neighbor and fellow citizen, Judge Russell. The petition was signed in bold and clear hands by almost forty men, a considerable number of productive citizens for a town the size of Winder. It praised his work as solicitor general and as judge and found him the best-fitted man in the present contest to fulfill the duties of the office of governor. It decried as scandalous and untrue the attacks upon his business ability and his ability and willingness to pay his debts and declared him a "strictly sober man and a man of unusual perseverance, integrity and energy."[37]

On Saturday July 14 a rally in Winder honored the Judge, showing that he had many friends there. Although Richard's rallies never could afford the desired accoutrements of food and music, this one boasted a brass band that came with two hundred people on the train from Lawrenceville, all of whom joined a larger throng in Winder with their own band. When the weather turned stormy, the speech had to be made in the Winder Academy rather than outdoors. Jokes flew about the Judge's oratorical ability to bring down fire and brimstone. Reporter Selene Armstrong spent the day with the judge and came away impressed with his sincerity, energy and faith in himself. When asked if he would run again if defeated, he replied, "I have never considered being defeated."[38]

Armstrong's article featured a photograph of the Russell home and the caption declared, "Though of one story, the house is deep and a side view would show it ample for the task of sheltering so large a family." Someone wanted to assure readers that Richard Russell could support his growing clan with respectability.

Another photograph represented a cottage that, the caption said, Russell had given over to public schooling and noted the cotton bales on the porch had been held over from the Judge's last year's crop. This is certainly the "school" from which Miss Stroud taught.

The *Georgian*, a weekly Atlanta paper, also put in a good word for Richard Russell, perhaps thanks to the influence of Walter Brown. The *Georgian* published an editorial on July 3, 1906, praising the shoe-string campaign of the judge and calling him an "indefatigable man of the people." Making as many as eight speeches per day, he had "prosecuted one of the most vivid, picturesque, and effective campaigns ever made in Georgia." People who had laughed when he entered were not laughing now. A *Georgian* reporter interviewed the judge at home and photographed him with his wife and nine children. Ina was pleased when nine copies of the paper arrived with her family gracing the front page.[39]

In spite of the giants waging war on all sides, the favorable receptions their candidate continued to receive kept hopes high in the Russell camp. The children put up campaign posters along the road into Russell, and the younger ones had no doubt their father was going to be the next governor. They had the idea that the race was a footrace, and when they saw photographs of the portly Hoke Smith and the *Constitution's* cartoons, which showed him cumbersome at best, they knew their lean and lithe daddy, who loved to dig ditches, would beat that big old fat man easy.[40]

Sister Mary was not well during much of the campaign, and found the local acrimony and the jibes from the *Atlanta Journal* hard to take. On July 25 the paper published a front page cartoon showing a Gordian knot of candidates other than Hoke Smith entwined with [railroad] Ring Rule ribbon. Inside, a negative editorial about her brother, insinuating he was a ring-rule-owned "ornament of the bench," horrified Mary and made her wish they were all out of the wretched business of politicking.[41] This issue of the *Journal* also reported informal polls taken at Statesboro and Franklin Springs that showed Hoke Smith well in the lead and Richard Russell ahead of Clark Howell.

The same paper noted that the General Assembly had just passed by 144 to 4 a bill creating the Georgia Court of Appeals. Three judges would have to be elected to man the new court.

Lewis took off from farming and lawyering in early July to go to Macon and man campaign headquarters there until the primary on August 22. Brother John, still riding his bicycle, was putting posters out all over south Georgia. Both men were frustrated that their other work was neglected. John chaffed that two pairs of oxen, a pair of mules and good land were idle, and Lewis mourned that the Elbertas were ripening without his being there to supervise their picking, packing and shipping. Mary helped with Lewis' law and farm correspondence back in Winder.[42]

From Walter Brown's office in Atlanta, Richard sent Lewis seventy-five dollars on July 12 and asked that he make it go as far as he could, but said he hoped to have more soon. With no corporate backing or personal fortune, Richard was eking out loans against his assets. These debts would have to be repaid with interest, but by this time, his continued support from the crowds who came to hear him speak gave him the feeling that he was making great strides and would be nominated.[43]

This optimism was unfounded, but it is easy for a candidate surrounded by eager, encouraging supporters to develop a more favorable view of the situation than is warranted. A blinkered attitude, simple blind hope, may be what keeps minorities risking the unfavorable race in a democratic system.

In spite of Russell gains, the Smith steamroller was pounding forward at high and mighty speed. Backed by plenty of money, enjoying a broad base of support, and offering a platform of reform geared to the progressive spirit of the day, Hoke spoke to huge crowds at barbecues, picnics, and torchlight processions. In courthouses, he was sometimes swept out of the courtroom on the shoulders of supporters so that he could speak to larger crowds outside. Trains hired at the campaign's expense carried people from one rally to another, establishing the idea that he had strong backing in every county. Hoke Smith was a powerful man with popular ideas and proven ability in statecraft. More and more voters lined up behind a sure winner.[44]

Before the primary dust had cleared on August 22, Hoke Smith emerged the overwhelming choice of Georgians for governor, walking away with 104,796 votes, to the combined total of 79,477 of the other four candidates. To the surprise of everyone outside the Russell camp, Richard Russell had persuaded almost 24,000 Georgians that he was their man, thus coming in second, with Howell a close third.

Richard had existed for months on the adrenaline rush of stump speaking and the elixir that hope and courage create in a man sure of his own abilities and ideals. The letdown was bound to be painful. The day after the election the atmosphere in Russell was glum. Ina, seeing her dispirited husband, broke down and wept. Any grief to his mother distressed little R. B. deeply, but her eldest son comforted her by saying, "When I am grown up, Mother, I will be governor and you can live in the Governor's Mansion with me."[45]

Ina would not have been weeping over the Governor's Mansion. Her broken heart came from seeing her husband, whom she believed in as much as he believed in himself, crushed by defeat.

Their mutual heartache was, tragically, soon eclipsed by one still greater. Richard was in Macon for the Democratic Convention that nominated Hoke Smith by acclamation on September 4. When he returned home a day later, he found little Lewis ill with what was likely an intestinal blockage.[46] Medical attention was insufficient to save the three-month-old boy. On September 9, Richard and Ina saw their little one slip away, leaving them with empty arms and aching hearts.

The day they laid the baby boy beside his sister in Oconee Hill Cemetery was one of the bleakest of Richard's life. In addition to the loss of his child, which must have brought feelings of failure as a father, he felt bereft of his dreams, his hopes, his ambitions. In burying his child, was he burying everything he had lived for?

Distraught and depressed, Richard looked at his other sons and tried to take comfort in them. R. B., an active, sturdy child at age nine, enjoyed reading history and newspapers, but that day after Lewis's funeral he was playing war games with a stick longer than he was. His father followed him from the back yard into a little wood behind the house, where Richard sat down on a log, mesmerized by his barefoot boy. Again his failures welled up and overwhelmed him, and he despaired. He called R. B. over to him.

"Son," he said, "I have failed in my dream of becoming governor. You are not only my boy, but you bear my name. It is my prayer that you will one day do what I failed to do."

R. B. was good at comforting his parents. "I will run for governor and I will be elected," he assured his downcast father.[47]

The boy's simple faith was scant comfort at the time. Richard's depression deepened. Ina's faith in a creator who was too wise to err and too good to be unkind sustained her, and she felt His loving hand holding her fast. The path was dark but she had been taught to look for the light. Family and friends sent letters of loving sympathy, and she took strength from these, treasuring them. In characteristic fashion, Ina turned her attentions to her husband and went away with him for a few days' rest.[48]

In the meantime, Walter Brown, deeply worried about his friend's downhearted turn, had a brilliant idea. The judges to the new Court of Appeals were to be elected in the November election, and Brown thought Richard could easily win a post. The Atlanta lawyer managed to get a telephone message to Richard that he wanted to enter his name as a candidate. Richard had no money with which to pay a fee, and if his name were to go on the ballot he had no money, energy or heart to campaign. He would not answer Brown's message. Ina's reply was straightforward. Her husband had offered to serve and had been turned down and beat up into the bargain. She did not want him running for any other political office at all.[49]

Brown, a favorite visitor in the Russell household, sympathetic to Ina Russell's feelings, aware of the risks to his invitations to share her turnip greens and cornbread, was not deterred.[50] He knew Richard needed a boost badly and that Georgia needed good judges on the new court. He and other friends paid the nominating fee, one hundred dollars, and Richard Russell's name went on the ballot with fifteen other judicial hopefuls. In light of the uniqueness of the event, the election would be decided according to the popular vote, with no consideration of the county units.

Richard agreed to leave his name on the ballot, but only if his friends understood that he would not campaign for the post at all. His brother Lewis wrote a few letters to friends, asking for their support. When campaign expenses were disclosed, Richard listed expenses of $4.70, the cost of a train ticket to Atlanta to find out if his name was indeed on the ballot.[51]

This gesture of friendship and faith from his friends, together with assurances that he would win the post, cheered Richard Russell as Walter Brown had hoped it would. When in November his name led the votes for all candidates, he was pleased that in spite of his reticence, the people of Georgia had called him back to service. In later years he would point with pride to the fact that he had not solicited one vote in this victory, a rare occurrence in politics.[52]

In January 1907 he met in Atlanta with the other newly-elected justices, Benjamin H. Hill and Arthur Powell, to begin work. The Appeals Court met in the same rooms that the Supreme Court used, but at different times of the day. Richard Russell had dreamed more of the governor's chair than of the judge's bench, but residing on one of the top rungs of the judicial ladder could not have displeased him. In the first session he showed his independence and dissented. A woman stenographer had applied for a post on the court, and it was the opinion of Powell that under the Civil Code women were not eligible for such work. Hill looked set to agree. Harriette Brumby Russell's son could not be persuaded. He argued his case so well that Hill was soon agreeing with him and Powell also changed his opinion. Miss Marion Bloodworth was hired, making headlines in the Atlanta papers, the first woman to work for a court of last resort in Georgia. The early record of the Court proves these three men were excellent choices for establishing Georgia's Court of Appeals.[53]

At first, there could be no question of moving the family to Atlanta, and so Richard commuted by train, taking a room in the Kimball House on weekdays. The Court worked six days a week, but having Papa home regularly on Sundays was a treat for the family. Because the court had breaks between sessions, he was able to be at Russell, managing the knitting mill and digging ditches and leveling banks to improve the street system of the tiny community. He had, over recent years, earned a reputation as an addicted dirt digger. His farming activities increased as he hired more tenants for his land. He admitted only to making enough from his farming to pay his taxes, but he continued to invest in it. He had acquired perhaps another two hundred acres by this time.[54]

Ina was not idle in her sphere. Those closest to her, her sisters and sisters-in-law, marveled at how she ran her home. Looking well to the ways of her household, she managed her eight living children with gentle aplomb while going on to produce her long-awaited and longed-for twin boys.[55]

The twins arrived early in the morning on August 21, 1907. Delivering the first boy, Dr. Almond beamed as a lusty cry came from the baby. When the second son put in his appearance, the doctor looked grave. This baby seemed weak and fragile. "Mrs. Russell, I'm afraid this little fellow won't make it," he said. "Let's be thankful for the strong one."

"You get to work on that baby right this minute, or I'll get out of this bed and do it myself," Ina ordered her doctor and friend. "I've wanted twin boys all my life and now I've got them, I'm not going to give up on one of them."

Dr. Almond did as he was told, and by morning both babies were thriving.[56]

Little Patience Elizabeth, at age five, was accustomed to coming downstairs each morning and crawling into bed with her mother. That morning she found the room governed by a bossy nurse who sent her away with a sharp word before she got her nose in the door. A little while later the nurse came to find her and lead her into her mother's room where she saw to her amazement that her mother held a baby in each arm.

"Look what Dr. Almond brought us last night," her mother said, smiling like a queen.

Patience climbed onto the bed and carefully surveyed each baby. She knew this delivery was pleasing to her mother, but for herself, she wondered why Dr. Almond had so many babies to give away at their house.[57]

The boys were called, as planned, William John and Fielding Dillard, in honor of Richard's and Ina's respective fathers. Their arrival was announced as a judiciary wonder in the Atlanta papers.

Ina, basking in her crowning moment, saw the twins as replacements for the children she had lost and admitted she hoped her family was complete. Richard, his manhood an object of state-wide admiration, accepted with bemused pride his congratulations.

Richard contemplated the responsibilities of fatherhood and the magnitude of his family. One day while they were gathered at the dining table, he casually remarked that he had been thinking about the age differences between the twins and Mary Willie, and how old he would be when they were grown. "We will probably have grandchildren who won't know each other," he concluded.

Ina, who sat at the head of the table, with Richard on her right in the place of an honored guest, burst into tears. The children sat horrified to see their serene mother weeping. So did their father.

"Whatever is wrong?" he asked.

Unable to hold back the tears, she said, "I can not bear the thought that we would have grandchildren who won't know each other."[58]

10

Perplexing Points of Law on My Mind

1908–1910

Richard Russell turned his considerable legal abilities to his court work with a will and skill reflected in the high reputation the court earned from the beginning. In his early opinions he gave the text a literary flair, using a battle metaphor throughout, or writing the decision in verse in response to the lawyer's argument in the same medium. He admitted his poetry might not be better than the lawyer's, but he believed his interpretation of the law was nearer the mark.[1]

In cases regarding liability for baggage left overnight, bankruptcy, fraud, cows and mules, child abandonment, watermelons, wife-beating, perjury, wanton and malicious killing of dogs by trains, sheep-killing dogs, men playing cards at night in the cemetery, assault with intent to murder, manslaughter, insurance disputes, and myriad other subjects, he mused over the daily life the law was required to regulate. His knowledge of the law was already deep and thorough, but now he must train it to encyclopedic proportion as he struggled with the nitty-gritty of civilized living, not as a lawyer or a trial judge, but as the judge charged with correcting errors.[2]

This life of studying and reading, the constant struggle with the immensity of the law, the impossibility of always reconciling principle with precedence, and the basic evasiveness of justice yielded a lonely existence compared to his former work. Appellate court judges are not in the limelight. Not for them the tumult and the shouting, the thunder of political guns. Little about sitting on a court of review, listening to others talk, or laboring behind closed doors over confused transcripts catches the imagination. Tedium must often be the appropriate word to describe their labors. They could not have the social contacts, the local importance and power of superior court judges. Life is much the same day after day in office or conference, at the same site. They have nothing to do with writing or enforcing laws. They only administer and in rare cases decide what the law is. They are few in number. Yet if the people have not confidence in the law, law and order stand in jeopardy, and thus what the judiciary contributes to social security is vastly immeasurable. Richard Russell knew this, but the general public took little heed.[3]

This work would not bring the fame or fortune Richard had dreamed, but his keen mind and his great heart were suited to it. At first he made Powell and Hill nervous because he held onto troubling cases for months without writing an opinion. Then two weeks before the end of term, he would hire extra stenographic help and begin dictating at seven in the morning, carrying on until two or three o'clock the next morning with relays of stenographers. After a few hours sleep on the couch in his office, he would continue, working in this way for a week at a time if necessary. Naturally the other two justices were apprehensive about the quality of this work, but when they read these opinions, they were reassured. Here was a great lawyer and a great judge, whose opinions were never swayed by anything but his honest, unbiased conviction of the law of the case. As they watched him dissent when to concur would have been politically expedient or concur when to dissent might have served a friend, their respect and confidence in his basic honesty of mind and soul grew.[4]

In spite of the long hours and slight recognition of judges' work, an office in the Capitol had the advantage of a ringside view of the legislative and executive branches. Judges on both courts of last resort had complimentary membership in the Atlanta Athletic and Peachtree Driving Clubs, and he occasionally attended functions at these elite venues. He was honored at dinners in homes in Atlanta, for he was good company, and these broke the loneliness of life away from his family. There were times when he would have preferred to stay in Atlanta for social gatherings, but his sense of duty drove him home on the weekends.[5]

His surprising second in the governor's race encouraged Richard to reconsider the executive situation.[6] A wide-spread panic in 1907 and a quarrel with Joseph M. Brown, a railroad commissioner he had fired, caused major problems for Governor Smith. Richard watched these developments closely, and living all week in Atlanta, more exposed than ever to the titillation of political intrigue, his enchantment with politics was by no means finished. No doubt many who saw him as a political threat breathed a sigh of relief that he had a good job, but it would have been unwise to take bets that the judge would stay on the bench.

His priorities of the moment, however, were repayment of debts made in the 1906 campaign and educating the children. At fifteen Mary Willie was in need of more important schooling than she could get in Russell or even in Winder. Since her father now worked in Atlanta, he decided to send her to Agnes Scott College in Decatur. Ina Jr. would require a similar move within a year, closely followed by Margo, R. B., Harriette and Rob. Tuition fees for as many as half a dozen children at one time loomed large beside campaign debts. The Court of Appeals salary of four thousand dollars per annum may have looked like ready money at the end of the governor's campaign, but it was clearly not enough to fund political dreams, past or future, and educate ten children.

The judge figured up his assets and his debts. Assets included lots in Athens, Winder and Russell, his farm and tenant houses in Russell, several notes owed to him worth about fifteen hundred dollars, a brick yard in Winder and the knitting mill, of which he claimed 14/16 ownership. Debts included a loan from the Athens Savings Bank and one from the Winder Savings Bank that together totaled nearly five thousand dollars, likely the money borrowed during the governor's campaign. Other debt was for clothing, groceries, taxes and small personal loans. Assets he counted as worth about thirty-five thousand dollars, against which he calculated he owed seven thousand four hundred and three dollars, leaving him in the black by nearly twenty-eight thousand dollars.[7]

Although the asset column looked good on paper, there was little in it that was producing disposable income. The knitting mill hummed low-key, able to pay salaries for the workers but not to pay dividends to the stockholders. The only one in the family who profited from the mill was R. B., who occasionally earned small sums for hauling firewood.[8]

The founder of Russell tried hard to keep the several houses he owned in the settlement rented, but these often went as trades to tenant farmers or to his teachers. The feud with Winder meant he now refused to let his children go to school there and so was faced with the expense of keeping a teacher in Russell. As a chartered town Russell was eligible for state funds to pay a teacher, and these were granted, but the money was not always forthcoming.[9] Ina and Pipey, both experienced teachers, took up the slack when other teachers grew faint-hearted. Already overloaded with general childcare and housekeeping duties, these most intelligent, longsuffering and persevering of women knew this way would not educate the children to demanding Brumby and Dillard standards. Ina was patient and understanding with her husband's political ambitions, but she insisted he provide school funds.

Like every other farmer and planter in the state, Richard's farm income depended on the weather and markets, both highly variable and unpredictable. Providing groceries and farming supplies for his tenants, also dependant on these forces, increased his risk. The farm produced cotton each year, but when accounts were summed up, the bales sometimes did not bring hoped-for prices. Mules were expensive, and keeping them working instead of eating worried him. Ina kept careful books of both farm and home expenses, and it was her skilled management that often saved him. There is no record of her having asked for information regarding income. She simply took what he gave her and made it go as far as she could. She did, however, record when he had to borrow small sums from her household purse.[10]

Their relationship as full partners operating in different spheres held up well, thanks to Ina's ability and cheerful willingness to handle multiple interests, and Richard's ability to admit his mistakes and to express deep affection and appreciation. He mourned his separations from Ina and worried that the little ones would have no fond memories of their father, yet his financial condition and his desire to leave a name that would be valuable to all of them, but especially the boys, bound him to his work in Atlanta. When he consulted his own happiness, he felt he would resign tomorrow.[11]

Richard Russell felt keenly the responsibility of his early court decisions. Always prone to pre-occupation, he became more absent-minded, his head filled with opinions he must write and perplexing points of law. Visions of his five sons reading his work years hence in the *Georgia Reports* spurred him to do well. As he adjusted to this more contemplative life, he remained his wife's devoted and vocal admirer, ready to admit his dependency on her, unashamed to tell her how much she meant to him.[12]

Although the court work was demanding—they were trying between fifteen hundred and two thousand cases a year—it was more regular than Superior Court work and certainly than political campaigning. He was home week-ends, arriving late on Saturday. The children looked forward to his arrivals because he brought a big sack of goodies, boiled peanuts, for example, or pigs' feet. Best of all, he brought a heart glad to be home. The older girls loved to dance with their handsome daddy, and all admired his clog dancing as Mary Willie or Ina played the piano.

Ina and her sisters encouraged the children to be happy when Papa came home and to make his home a pleasant place. The women washed and dressed the children, and they were allowed to walk the quarter-mile down to a crossroads where the train slowed down enough to let the judge swing off. The engineer could not legally stop, but the judge preferred to jump from the moving train rather than use the Winder station.[13]

On Sundays he loved to walk about his farm and to dig and move dirt on the roads of Russell. Local citizenry in Winder thought he deliberately dug up the road so that it would become muddy and impassable and then the county road crews would have to repair it.[14]

In spite of having trouble keeping his dues paid, Richard continued to assuage his desire for adulation with memberships in fraternal organizations, particularly Royal Arcanum, where he frequently assumed titles like Grand Regent, Supreme Commander or Deputy Supreme Commander. This organization sold life insurance, and although Richard was not involved in selling, he sometimes served as legal adviser. In return, the order sent him, expenses paid, to the national meetings, and these otherwise unaffordable trips became the delight of the family. Ina had loved to travel with Richard from the time of their honeymoon, and thanks to Sisters Annie, Pipey, and Hattie's excellent care of the brood of ten, she enjoyed a trip with the Grand Regent to the Supreme Council whenever possible.[15]

In the spring of 1908 they went to Chicago on the "Dixie Flyer," enjoying the luxury of a Pullman Imperial, remembering their honeymoon and marveling at their brood, especially the twin boys. They were still deeply in love, each aware of the other whether together or apart.[16] At the convention, Richard regaled the crowds with his jokes and speeches, and Ina charmed the cream of the Supremes as she made friends with successful businessmen and their wives from all over the United States.[17]

The state political scene in the summer of 1908 was so bleak that even Richard was not tempted to get involved. The Recession of 1907 coupled with Smith's reform legislation gave Joseph M. Brown, who represented conservative and railroad interests, the ammunition to label Smith with the blame for Georgia's economic woes. Although tradition allowed the governor a second term unopposed, Brown decided to run against Smith.

Joseph M. Brown was the son of Georgia's wartime governor, Joseph E. Brown, who had increased his fortunes after the war through railroad syndicates. Little Joe, as the younger Brown was called, had no political experience, having worked for the railroads in Atlanta for over twenty-five years, serving in such varied positions as conductor, claims clerk, claims agent, timekeeper, accountant, freight agent and traffic manager. He had retired from his railroad work, and in 1904 Governor Terrell appointed him to the Railroad Commission.[18]

In the campaign of 1906, Brown had written highly critical articles against Hoke Smith's proposed reforms, especially those intended to restrict the power of the railroads. Smith promised if elected he would fire Brown, a campaign promise he kept. Inexplicably, he waited until three days after the legislature had adjourned to give Brown his notice, thereby preventing Brown's answering the charges brought against him. This seemed unfair to many, and Brown became a martyr deserving vindication.

Many powerful interests, including the liquor interest and the railroads, had been antagonized by Smith's reform legislation, and it was easy for these through Brown to demonstrate that Hoke Smith caused the panic of 1907. The campaign slogan became "Brown and Bread: Hoke and Hunger." Almost everyone who had opposed Smith in the 1906 race jumped on this bandwagon, but the Brown supporter who made the real difference was Tom Watson.

That Watson, champion of the poor, the small farmers, and enemy of big business, could support someone of Brown's persuasions seemed inconceivable. The reason was personal. Watson and Smith had disagreed over the pardon of a condemned prisoner, a friend of Watson's. When Smith refused the man a stay of execution, he made an arch enemy of Tom Watson, who became determined to oust Smith from office. Watson issued an invitation to discuss how he and Little Joe might cooperate in their mutual goal, and following their secret meeting, Brown announced he would run. At first Watson did not announce his support but asserted he wasn't for either man. Gradually he began to criticize Smith, to the bewilderment of his followers. In spite of their misgivings about voting for anyone as conservative as Joe Brown, enough of the old Populists voted for Brown to turn around the Smith landslide of 1906. Joseph M. Brown was nominated by a small majority of 12,000 at the June primary.

Richard Russell took no part in this campaign except to make no secret of the fact that he supported Brown. He had never forgiven Smith for the lies his camp spread about Russell as a railroad ring candidate and could not respect him as a man or as a politician.[19]

Ina celebrated her fortieth birthday on February 18, 1908, and Richard surprised everyone by coming home in the evening bearing a prodigious box of candy for his sweetheart and her children. A week later Ina bought a ham from a travelling butcher, and after he weighed her selection, someone suggested weighing the six-month old twins on his scales. First William, who was feared much smaller, was put in a market basket and placed on the scales. William weighed exactly as much as the ham. Fielding then went into the basket and to everyone's surprise, he pulled the scale less than an inch more than had William. Cries of "hooray for little William!" went up from the crowd of children watching the process. Richard had Ina bring the twins to Atlanta to have them photographed, and he enjoyed showing them to friends in the Capitol.[20]

In the autumn of 1908 Richard fell ill with pneumonia and was so sick that Ina had to come to Atlanta to care for him. Mary Willie began her studies at Agnes Scott at the same time. Ina knew she would miss her big girl's help, but she insisted that nothing should inhibit her children's education, whether girls or boys. While nursing her husband back to health, Ina suffered a miscarriage of another set of twins and was ill herself for a few days. Margo had a serious throat infection and was also brought to Atlanta from Farm Hill for treatment while her mother was recovering.[21]

Richard went back to his court work as soon as possible and worked hard until the court adjourned just before Christmas. On Christmas Eve he shopped in Atlanta, choosing small gifts for all the children. He grieved that his limited finances made him appear mean. When he and Ina had placed the gifts under the tree after the children were in bed, he wept because he had no gift for his beloved wife. Ina assured him only the children mattered and what he had provided for them was generous. Tenderly she took him to bed.[22]

On September 26, 1909, Ina gave birth to her thirteenth child, a delayed but cherished Christmas present. He was named Henry Edward for brother Edward and uncle Henry Russell. His birth made front page headlines in Atlanta, as the state's prolific judge again fathered a son, and this one had the distinction of being the thirteenth child of a thirteenth child on his mother side. The next day New York and Washington papers picked up this human interest story, and Richard Russell achieved through his family what he had not achieved through his political aspirations: He made national headlines. He received letters of congratulations from men all over the country, some of them perhaps Royal Arcanum friends.[23]

Mary Willie's schooling at Russell had not prepared her to do well in the rigorous academic program at Agnes Scott, and her father found the tuition fees rigorous as well. Thus, in the autumn of 1909 Mary Willie and Ina Jr. were off to school at the Georgia Normal and Industrial

College in Milledgeville. This was the girls' school Richard's inspiration had helped to bring into existence while in the Georgia legislature, and he had watched its progress during the following twenty years with pleasure. As his daughters enrolled there in the autumn of 1909, he began a close association with the school that would last nearly three decades and make a significant contribution to Georgia education.

The academic demands at G.N.& I.C. proved as demanding as those at Agnes Scott, and Mary Willie, learning discipline, set to work determined to succeed. She placed in the freshman class, and Ina Jr. placed in the sub-freshman group, and they believed this a fair assessment of their levels. In addition to keeping up studies, all girls had to help with chores in the dining hall and in the dormitories, and daughters of Ina Dillard did not find this demeaning or unexpected. Ina Jr. struggled with asthma, inherited from her Brumby grandfather, and lacking physical stamina, she spent many days in the infirmary. One night an attack so terrified Mary Willie that she called a doctor, fearful her sister was dying. The school made clear from the beginning that it was "no place for weakly or sickly girls," but Ina was sometimes given a few days respite from table chores. Richard worried about her constantly. She struggled to stay with Mary Willie, but by the end of the year was unable to return.[24]

The 1910 governor's campaign loomed like a thundercloud on the political horizon as Hoke Smith geared up to wrest his governor's seat back from Joe Brown. Brown, shy and taciturn, had promised in 1908 that if elected he would attend to the duties of the office without running all over the state for weeks at a time, allowing state business to take care of itself, and had kept this campaign promise. A fiscal conservative, he sought no major legislative innovations and supported economy in government, strict enforcement of prohibition laws, lower taxes and limits on the powers of labor unions.

The 1910 campaign seemed sure to be a reworking of the old issues, with Smith seeking further reforms such as strengthening the Railroad Commission, establishing juvenile courts and a parole system, increasing money to public schools, and enacting anti-lobbying measures. He proposed shortening the maximum workweek for textile workers to sixty hours.

It was rumored that Joe Brown might not run again, and Tom Watson kept quiet, waiting for the decision. Almost obsessed with stifling Smith, and aware that his tour de force in bringing Smith down in 1908 had cost him heavily among his supporters, Watson looked around for someone besides Brown.

Richard Russell was undecided about whether he had a chance in this dangerous field, but his 1906 supporters wrote letters, urging him to run. He tested the ground, writing to various friends all over the state for their opinions or in answer to their queries about his intentions. Some urged him to run; others warned him not to get smeared in a hopeless battle.[25]

In April 1910 he received a petition from Bullock County, signed by 2700 voters, asking him to be a candidate. About the same time he received a letter from Tom Watson, expressing esteem for his old friend and suggesting they develop closer relations. This must have been tempting, but Richard looked at it with a cautious eye. Watson suggested the judge pay him a visit, and Richard countered that as Sunday was his only day off and sacred to his family, he must invite Tom to visit him in Russell, where he could offer him a sincere and warm welcome. He was sure when it was known that Tom Watson was visiting Dick Russell, many would come to pay their respects. Watson did not visit his old friend.[26]

One person who had decided Richard should not run was Ina. She did not want him in that fight. Although women without the vote often maintained a certain political naivete, Ina had a keen sense of what was possible and what was not. She let it be known that she did not advise his running and hoped he would not run. Richard knew that his races cost her dearly in emotional capital, that she often cared more for his success, almost, than he did. He worried when she grew thin and tired during campaigns. However much he regretted the concern they caused her, he could not give up his ambitions.[27]

In the spring of 1910 while Richard was yet questioning his decision, he was surprisingly elected to represent the Royal Arcanum again as representative of the Georgia Grand Council to the national convention in Montreal. Having been given this honor and financial advantage frequently in previous years, he did not expect it again so soon. The meeting at which he was elected was a stirring one, where candidates appeared and disappeared with the same excitement as in a political scene. Some thought this was a sign that he was definitely the man of the hour for the governor's race as well, so that as he set off for Canada about May 15, flushed with his local victory, he seemed ready to enter the race.[28]

Richard chose this time to give his eldest sons a trip abroad, and Ina, expecting another baby in October, was delighted with the prospect of such a trip. They went northward with R. B. and Rob, stopping in Washington to visit Uncle Ed and Aunt Susie overnight. Edward was still in the Post Office department and finding raises hard to come by. Susie ran a boarding house to make their finances more comfortable. They had a daughter, born in 1905, and a son, born only a few months before Richard and Ina's Edward.

Richard and Ina spent a night in New York City to give the boys a chance to see the great metropolis. The time in Montreal thrilled Ina and the boys as the death and funeral of King Edward suspended Royal Arcanum business and gave them all the chance to see military parades and attend stirring ceremonies that included 101-gun salutes. Catholic priests wearing skirts like women and institutions where nuns gave their lives to caring for orphaned children and pitiful old people made the familiarity of home more cherished.[29]

While Richard and Ina were enjoying life outside Georgia, the governor's campaign blazed into a fury of abuse such as the state had seldom seen.[30] By the time they returned, Richard realized that such crossfire would be deadly for him, and he withdrew, no doubt to Ina's great relief. Either of the other candidates might have feared or wished his entering the race because votes would surely have been affected, but Richard Russell had no motive to enter a race other than the intense desire to be elected.[31]

Tom Watson kept a low profile, preferring to give his time to other projects,[32] and when the primary was held the last week in August, Hoke Smith received 96,638 popular votes to Brown's 92,469, with the county unit vote more heavily in favor of Smith. This result precipitated another bout of Hoke Smith mania in Watson, who persuaded Brown to allow his name on the November ballot as an independent candidate. Seventeen thousand Watson/Brown supporters voted for Brown, but Smith walked away with 95,000 votes and was governor-elect again.

Brother Lewis ran for the judgeship of the Western Circuit, Richard's old bench, at this election. Although as a judge Richard could take no active part in a campaign, Lewis' race became his main concern as he quietly wrote to friends asking for their support. Lewis was not elected.[33]

In the meantime, Richard's old friend Senator Alexander Clay died in Washington in the autumn, and Joe Brown as governor appointed Joseph M. Terrell to succeed him. The legislature would not elect a successor until the following summer. This appointment unsettled the troubled political waters for many months because rumors were rife that Hoke Smith would run, leaving the governorship open again.

Richard Russell kept his eye on the scene, but turned the bulk of his attentions to his family. The house in Russell was bulging. Mary Willie had gone back to G.N.& I.C., and Ina Jr. and Margo had gone to live with Aunt Hattie in Washington, Georgia, to attend school there. Hattie's husband, James Wylie Arnold, a prosperous merchant in Washington, had died in 1907, and she rejoiced to have Ina's children in her home to ease her loneliness. Richard and Ina appreciated what the peaceful life with Aunt Hattie, a prominent matron in an established community, meant for the girls, and held her in high esteem.[34] That left eight children and a live-in teacher at home, and another baby arriving any day. The six boys slept together and Harriette and Patience roomed with the teacher. Although while Papa was away, it was not unusual for a child or two or three to end up with Mama for the night, it was an unquestioned rule that when Papa was at home, no one slept in Mama's bed but him. Something had to be done about their crowded quarters.[35]

Richard bought a house in Atlanta with more bedrooms than their house in Russell, and Ina went to see it. The house was somewhat larger than the one she had, but the lot was so small she could not see how she would have a garden, much less give up to twelve children, used to more than three hundred acres, space to play. She thought it would be better if they all stayed in the country until he could afford a stunning mansion she particularly liked on Peachtree Street.[36]

Richard knew that his wife was teasing about a mansion on Peachtree Street and that she was right about not having twelve children spilling over into neighbors' yards. Yet when he visited friends and associates whose families were much smaller than his, who lived in elegant Atlanta homes, padded with studies, sitting rooms and bedrooms, he grieved that his numerous brood was crowded into so few rooms. He dreamed of building a big house and thought he could see his way to doing that in about two years.[37]

On October 19, 1910, Ina presented Richard with another son. He was a big baby, the biggest since Marguerite, and Papa wrote to his girls, Ina Jr. and Margo, in Washington that the child weighed more than ten pounds, probably a proud papa's exaggeration.[38] Possible names included Alexander Lawrence, but in the meantime Richard called him Dickson—Dick's son. Edward, not yet thirteen months old, was barely walking, and so Pipey stepped in to save the day again. She took Edward and Harriette to Farm Hill to stay until Christmas. Margo and Ina had been given the twins, and Harriette was promised the next baby. She claimed Edward before he was a week old. Ina watched these two leave with mixed feelings. The age difference between Edward and Dickson made them almost another pair of twins, and she felt Edward too young to be no longer the baby.[39]

Change was afoot on the Oglethorpe County farm. Grandmother Mec had gone to meet her Maker only a few months before, and Pipey and Sister Annie were thinking of moving nearer their little sister. Richard offered them a house in Russell, and they moved into it near the end of 1910 or in early 1911.

For the rest of the family, Richard bought a large house in Russell, called the Jackson house. The two-story house boasted front porches upstairs and down and had three more rooms than the "Gresham house" but was in bad repair. He wanted to move before Christmas, but Ina, nursing a six-weeks-old baby, found this impossible, and with the girls home from school the family crowded in together for the holidays.

After Christmas the Russells moved into the Jackson house, where Ina tried to patch things up as best she could, painting floors herself. Her help situation was critical. Miss Hettie had married in 1908 and moved to Atlanta, and with no older girls at home, Ina's work load became more than she could keep up, in spite of her reputation for energy and efficiency. She sent out her washing to a black woman in the community, and she had domestic help from time to time, but not surprisingly, keeping servants was a perennial problem. No one could blame them for shying off to other homes where even if the pay were no better, the numbers were smaller. [40]

In the winter of 1911, as if in answer to a prayer, Ina found an excellent cook who was not afraid to work for a family with twelve children. Laura Glenn came to Ina just in time to save a woman growing desperate. This black woman won high praise from her employer for her kindness to the children and her efficiency in getting Papa's breakfast in time for the early train. Laura's cakes became the delight of the entire family, and nothing pleased the girls away from home more than receiving one of Laura's cakes in the mail. The two women became good friends as Laura added her talents to Ina's in the important work of homemaking. Ina was appreciative and said so to the family. Ina taught her children to be courteous and appreciative of all servants, but her feelings of affection and respect for Laura went deep.[41]

11

IN THE HOUR OF
MY KEEN HUMILIATION

1911

In the spring of 1911 rumors swirled regarding the highest political offices in the state. Hoke Smith seemed certain to seek the senatorial toga, and the legislature looked disposed to drape him with it. Joe Terrell, serving as appointed senator, had indicated an interest in the seat, but he suffered a stroke in the early part of the new year, and his health remained precarious. If Hoke became the senator-elect, what would Georgia do for a governor?

As he had since youth, Richard Russell stood ready to offer his services, but when articles in the *Atlanta Constitution*, the *Atlanta News*, and the *Georgian* stated that he could be positively counted upon as a candidate and was at the moment quietly conducting his campaign, he remonstrated. He had never hidden his ambition to be governor, he wrote to each paper, in denial of the articles, because he believed he could serve his fellow citizens well in that capacity. It was, however, unfair to say he was engaged in a campaign when in fact his court duties kept him so busy he did not even have time to reply to the many letters he was receiving urging him to run. If he decided to run, the people as a whole would be the first to know, not a coterie of politicians or other leaders.[1]

On April 27, 1911, Richard Russell turned fifty. In early May, Walter Brown and other Atlanta friends gave a big bash for him at Cafe Durand. Influential Atlantans heard the judge lavishly lauded before being invited to support him in a bid for the governorship. About the same time a special Atlanta "tabloid" highlighting prominent Atlantans of the bench and bar gave Judge Richard Russell a favorable write-up.[2]

In July the Georgia Senate elected Hoke Smith as United States senator to fill the unexpired term of Alexander Clay, and everyone expected an announcement of a special election for governor. Smith had other ideas. The U.S. Senate was adjourned until the autumn, and Smith decided to stay on as governor and push through more of his reforms, then resign and go to Washington in November. Terrell was outraged at this assumption of dual mantles and resigned his Senate seat, saying Hoke now had to fill it. Hoke, unruffled, continued to work as governor and managed to pass laws for reforms in education and the textile industry.

Richard Russell did not argue with Governor Smith over his right to hold both positions. He announced his candidacy for governor as soon as Hoke was elected senator and went right to work. The Appeals Court was in recess until October, and the judge intended to make the most of this time. He opened his campaign in Dublin, where he took Ina with him for his first speech. One of only two women present in the packed courtroom, she felt a little like a Peerless Mamie in a carnival, but judged that her husband made a good impression. She liked to hear him speak, even for an hour and twenty minutes, taking pride in his clear voice that was never harsh or too loud.[3]

Richard was the only formally announced candidate at this time, although Pope Brown, an Atlanta lawyer and businessman, was a sure candidate. Pope Brown had earlier been pegged to run as Watson's man before Hoke Smith got into the 1906 race, but withdrew when Watson wanted him to do so. Now he hoped to benefit from the Smith factions. Joe Brown had not declared at all and was not giving interviews. Richard Russell made seven speeches the first week of his campaign, four of them by appointment and three impromptu.[4] Richard's confidence grew as response to his speeches remained enthusiastic. The Russell train was gathering speed, headed for the Governor's Mansion.

Ina was determined to travel with her husband as much as possible. It was a pleasure to both to share a feeling of fulfillment when a friend introduced him at a rally as "the friend of the poor but the peer of the mighty." Richard whispered to her that if he ever had a tombstone, he wanted that put on it.[5]   She was fortunate in being able to be with him as he wished because of Laura's help and because Pipey and Annie were nearby. The two older sisters had also now the care of three children who belonged to their brother Ben, a travelling salesman whose wife had died in a tragic buggy accident in 1908.

Richard's patriarchal responsibilities became vastly more complicated at this period. Ina wanted to help her husband win his heart's desire, but she knew it was time for their children to have the advantages of better schooling, and she would not allow the expenses of a political campaign to take precedence over education. In the autumn of 1911, four Russell children were going off to school. Mary Willie and Margo would be students at G.N.& I. C; Ina Jr. was enrolled at Lucy Cobb Institute in Athens so that she would be close to home in the event of illness; and R. B., not quite fourteen, was going to Gordon Military Institute in Barnesville, Minnie's hometown. These schools would cost Judge Russell between thirty and forty dollars a month for tuition and board alone. Uniforms, books, spending money would come on top of that. The father of twelve saw his salary of less than four hundred dollars a month easily disappearing in schooling for the first four.[6]

The farm helped to sustain them, thanks to Ina. She raised a successful garden each year and taught her boys to grow vegetables and to raise chickens and hogs. The children showed a lively interest in the farm, especially young Rob, and all were proud of contributing to the family table. Richard had groceries sent out from a wholesaler in Atlanta, both for his family and for tenants, who bought them from Ina. R. B. and Rob early became managers of these stores when Ina and Richard were away. Pipey and Annie were also good managers, growing prolific gardens and preserving fruits and vegetables. Apple and peach trees on the Jackson place provided bounty. For "cash money" the little boys picked cotton in the autumn, on their father's and surrounding farms, starting at an early age.[7]

The knitting mill continued operation, and Richard also opened a bottling works in Russell during this period, to produce a drink healthier than Coca-Cola. He turned down the chance to buy stock in the Atlanta soft drink company on the recommendation of his old friend Joe Jacobs, the druggist. Jacobs had seen what Coca-Cola did to the metal work in his soda fountains and was sure it was bad for the stomach. This was probably the extent of Richard Russell's knowledge of soft drinks.[8] His bottling works became known only to locals in Russell. Winderites no doubt thought it was a dispensary.

To finance his campaign, Richard may have sold some of his lots in Winder, and he must have borrowed a larger sum than for the 1906 race. A group of friends formed a Russell Club in Fulton County and helped him open headquarters in Atlanta at the Kimball House. He had an official campaign manager, James B. Nevin, and Russell stationery. The candidate kept up a busy autumn schedule of speaking, and he bought a new suit and hat. Seeing him so dressed up and neat, Ina was not sure he was her husband.[9]

By the end of September Joe Brown had announced he would run. In the minds of many Georgians he deserved his second term, and realists thought he was sure to win. The Russells, caught up in their dream, were not realists. Ina believed her husband's head start and superior speaking ability put him in good shape to win. Joe Brown had never made a political speech in any campaign before this one and made only one ten-minute speech in 1911. Richard knew people were tired of the Smith-Brown feud. Surely they would welcome a candidate of his caliber, under no obligation to anyone.[10]

Eager for the whole family to support the effort, Ina wrote to her children that they had a heavy responsibility to keep up their father's name. Joe Brown's daughter Cora was in school at Lucy Cobb Institute with Ina Jr. Ina Sr. worried particularly that this situation would be stressful, but she urged her daughter to remain pleasant, sweet, charming, composed, sympathetic, fair and square at all times. She instructed R. B. to stand up for their side with great composure and not to be upset when he heard criticisms of his father, which he was sure to hear. She feared the fight would become bitter, but she advised her children to keep their heads and never forget whose children they were. In spite of being incredibly busy, Richard also found time to write a few letters to his children, especially when they needed money. He urged them to study hard and make good records so that his name and theirs would be honored.[11]

Whether Richard Russell's candidacy had a chance against the popular Brown support, the big business interests behind him, and Brown's personal fortune is doubtful. It may have been possible for public sentiment to swing his way in spite of Brown's advantages, but Richard became embroiled in an issue that would bring him down as surely as if he had declared himself an atheist. That issue was prohibition.

In 1906 the state Democratic Party had adopted the platform of local option, allowing each county to vote for itself whether it would sell alcohol. Brown, however, was a strict prohibitionist, as were many others, especially in the religious community. By 1910, Georgia had gone the way of total prohibition. Most of Richard's friends begged him to stay away from this issue because it was emotional and volatile. His brother-in-law Walter Dillard, a Methodist minister and himself a prohibitionist, advised him not to wreck himself on the rock of local option, but to come out for the law as it stood. At first, Richard seemed inclined to take this advice, and he denied all reports that he was a local option candidate. However, by the autumn, he had come out for what he saw as the good sense of local option.[12]

There were many who saw the folly of making a law that could not be enforced, and thus there was support for the idea of local option. Under prohibition in Georgia Richard saw the tax money that would have been generated by Georgia liquor sales going to Florida and Tennessee, money Georgia could sorely use in schools especially, and he thought people could be brought to see the reason of his argument. He pointed out that before prohibition, there were some illegal liquor sales in dry counties, but since prohibition, the illegal places of sales had quadrupled. He also felt pressured to keep quiet about the issue, and the mere idea that he could not express honest sentiments he had adhered to for twenty-five years drove him to speak out.[13]

No matter how reasoned the argument, the forces against moral corruption were outraged at any suggestion of going back on prohibition. They came out against Richard Russell wearing the armor of righteous indignation. The Women's Christian Temperance Union attacked him like a setting hen on a June bug. Mary Harris Armour, a passionate

WCTU speaker, often followed him on speaking tours and stood on the courthouse steps decrying his stand.

Worse, this position caused a rift in his own family. Ina's sister-in-law Lella Dillard, widow of her brother Miles, was an avid WCTU member, prominent in the work of the organization. Lella had begged Richard not to come out for local option, but when he did, she had no choice but to oppose him. Ina and Lella remained close friends, a relationship developed from girlhood, but Ina found it difficult to visit Lella's home with her husband. Walter Dillard and his family also chose to oppose their brother-in-law's candidacy on these grounds.[14]

The Methodists and the Baptists protested particularly vehemently. Preachers in these denominations railed against the evils of drink and extolled the wisdom of prohibition. A Methodist bishop was reported to have said from the pulpit that Richard Russell ought to be tied to a whipping post and every church-going citizen in the state be allowed to strike a blow at him. The Winder Methodist Church, where Richard and Ina were members, planned to ask him to leave the congregation. Hearing this, Richard left without being asked, and Ina followed. She could not go to a church that refused to receive her husband.[15]

Richard disputed that he was a whiskey candidate. If he could get the votes of all the people who drank more than he did, he said, he would win by a majority of a hundred thousand. To him this was not an issue that deserved much attention. He was surprised that prohibition had become a powerful crusade and seems not to have suspected that social pressure could cause men to vote differently from the way they drank. The continued criticism from the pulpit puzzled him because he believed this an illegal if not downright immoral mixture of church and state. His sincere admiration for true men of the cloth made the attacks from this quarter hard to rebut.[16]

The slings and arrows of outrageous fortune bombarding the Russells were not all political. On October 15, Pipey's house, which had cost him eight hundred dollars, burned to the ground. She barely escaped with her life and those of Ben's children and Ina's thirteenth child. Edward, who was now two years old, slept with Pipey many nights. When the fire broke out, he woke her up, pointing to the flames coming from the closet, patting her face, saying, "Hot burny hand, hot burny hand."

Neighbors and Ina and the children gathered and stood helplessly watching as walls of flame revealed the piano disintegrating inside the burning house. Ina mourned over the loss of Sister Annie's trunk, destroyed with her photographs of her dead husband and daughter. Tears running down her face, Laura gave Pipey a dollar. Winder friends brought clothes for the children, and there was nothing to do but move Pipey and Ben's children in with the Russells.[17]

Campaign exigencies took no notice whatsoever of this domestic setback. A couple of weeks later Ina and Richard were in Milledgeville for a Royal Arcanum convention and Richard used the time to mingle. Ina, however, used it to attend a Halloween party at G.N.& I.C. with Mary Willie and Margo. Ina cherished these opportunities to be with her husband and some of her children at the same time.[18]

Richard gained a certain national attention during the race from the size of his family. The November *Cosmopolitan* magazine printed a story that had gone the rounds in Georgia at the birth of Dickson. This tale reported that the Judge had taken his brood to the fair to see a two-headed calf. When he requested twelve half-fare tickets, the ticket agent asked him if those were all his children. When the reply came in the affirmative, the agent said, "Wait right here a minute. I'm goin' get my calf so he can take a look at *you*."[19]

While that story is most likely apocryphal, there is no doubt that in Georgia Richard Russell's paternity was legendary. Another well-known state judge, Judge Bell, took his Sunday school class to the state fair, and when he asked for a dozen child's tickets, the agent asked him if he was Judge Russell.[20]

On November 4 Richard made an epic speech in Atlanta, and the *Atlanta Journal* printed the speech in full. Russell's picture and his name were prominent for several days as campaign posters went up all over town. Ina grew excited by all this attention. Richard had never been satisfied with any speech he made, but he knew that this one had had a lively response from a big crowd, and he listened happily to people who praised it as the greatest speech ever given in Atlanta.[21]

Hoke Smith resigned on November 6 and at last left for Washington. The special election was set for December 7. Throughout the autumn Richard had struggled to keep up his court work in Atlanta, but he now set out on a thirty-day speaking tour of Georgia. The dramatic change in travel since 1906 meant he often rented not a horse and buggy but an automobile. He spent at least one night in a cotton patch in Pike County in a broken-down auto, with rain pouring for three hours. Veteran that he was, he did not mourn or bemoan the trials of campaigning. Generally pleased with the receptions he received, he admitted disappointment in his old hometown of Athens when only about three hundred men turned out. Carloads of Athenians had gone to Atlanta for the Georgia-Georgia Tech football game, and the trains did not return until after his speech. It was a sign of the times that politics was losing its place as prime entertainment.[22]

Long hours, long distances, short nights, short funds, he campaigned on. His old friend Emory Speer saw him whiz by in an auto late one evening on his way to a speech in Macon. Although a Joe Brown supporter for personal and family reasons, Speer's heart went out to his old friend for the brave and manful way he was making his fight. Speer, a federal judge since 1885, did not have time to hear Richard speak, but he sent his messenger, a mountain boy, and the youngster said it was the finest stump speech he had ever heard.[23]

As the day of the election neared, excitement was high in Russell's Atlanta headquarters. Nevin, studying the map of Georgia, predicted that Richard Russell would carry one hundred and four counties. Walter Brown said not less than eighty-seven. Either figure would elect him governor.[24]

Although Richard tried to be at home on Sundays, during these last tense days he could not get to Russell, so he sent for Ina to join him at the Kimball House. He told her to come alone. Suspecting what he had in mind, she brought Walter and Rob. She did not want to be alone with her husband that day because she feared becoming pregnant.

Richard gave the boys money for ice cream and sent them out to a restaurant at some distance from the hotel. The next governor of Georgia wanted his wife, and he meant to have her.[25]

Georgians went to the polls on December 7 and elected Joe Brown. As if that were not blow enough, Pope Brown came second. Richard Russell was the third choice, the last man. Joe Brown received 43,395 popular votes and 198 county units. Pope Brown received 38,024 popular votes and 114 county units. Richard had made no appreciable gains since his 1906 campaign. He received 28,362 popular votes and 56 county units. He could find no explanation for this loss of votes but the stand the clergy had taken against him and local option.

When results were assured on December 8, Richard Russell sat down and wrote to his children away at school. Out of the winepress of a great grief and disappointment and in the hour of his keen humiliation, he begged them to take heart. To the girls he wrote of his pride in and love for them and of the importance of love when all else fails.[26]

To R. B. he reiterated his 1906 theme:

> I know that before this, you know the sad, sad news. I write to say that I have lost all except my manhood and my manly honor. These are still unimpaired and will sustain me as I sink into forgetfulness. You will never be a Governor's son, but you can be a man and a gentleman and after I am dead and gone you can carry on my fight against dirty and hypocritical politicians and unchristian churchmen. The same old fight that has been going on since the world began of poverty against wealth and privilege must be fought . . . [a]nd above everything we must fight against the control of our rights by those who use the pulpit of our Holy Savior for dirty politics. Keep this letter and read it often after I am dead. I did all I could to give you a better chance than I had... I failed and now you must fight for yourself. Be a man and you can be a Governor, but if you never are a Governor be a man dear boy...I know you will not let my loss dishearten you, for you can think about the fact that no boy has a father who loves him better than yours loves you. Be cheerful and work hard for the sake of Your loving father Rich. B. Russell.[27]

On Saturday he went home to Russell. The children had prepared a bonfire and fireworks and horns for celebration, but the horns and the fireworks went unused. Richard broke down in tears at the sight of his chicks lined up to comfort him. They wept at the sight of their downcast dad.[28]

R. B. wrote the day after the election and complimented his father on the heavy vote he had received in most counties. With the confidence and practicality of a fourteen-year-old he said it was too bad to get beat but they could run again next time. He also advised him not to sell his cotton yet. Margo and Mary Willie wrote loving letters the day they received theirs, protesting their love. They admitted to pain and embarrassment but felt they had conducted themselves in ways that would make him proud. Above all, they urged him not to despair and not to worry about taking them along the path of fame. Margo assured him she would rather have his love than all of the fame in the world, and Mary Willie declared that "you have not failed, and I believe some day you will be repaid even if it is only in the comfort of your children."[29]

Ina, although grieving for her wounded husband, for the sake of her children turned her thoughts to a joyful Christmas celebration. Yes, the defeat was awful, she told them, but they must all be game.[30]

12

THE TORTURE OF MY DEBTS

1912-1916

His gubernatorial dreams buried with the onset of winter, Richard Russell felt his life passing swiftly and the close of all things human looming near. Fighting his depression with the habits of a lifetime, he turned his attention to other projects, determined to concentrate on his family and town. He told his children that he could give them everything but money. They had a strong and respected family background, and with that and education, they could do anything. He would provide educational opportunities, and they must look to family precepts and examples and help each other. He urged them "to strain every nerve and muscle to succeed in their studies."[1]

His hurt over the election persisted. The ache festered as he recalled the virulent criticisms of the clergy and others in a land legally dedicated to separation of church and state. More than the legal question, ingratitude hurt him. He had attended Methodist churches with two devout Methodist wives and supported their churches gladly. In Russell in 1907 he had built and donated a four-room cottage as refined as the house his own family lived in—which is not to say overly refined—for the use of a superannuated Methodist preacher. The house was at the moment inhabited by such a one and his wife, Preacher and Mrs. N. E. McBreyer. Richard had also given a lot and a hundred and twenty-five dollars towards the construction of a Baptist church in Russell. He could not have been blind to the advantage of a Georgia politician's having a reputation as a supporter of churches, but given his limited income,

Harriette's teachings, and his wife's sincere piety, his desire to be helpful and generous is certain. His inability to be more generous to charitable causes genuinely embarrassed him. As a politician he was often called on to donate to worthy causes from all corners of the state, and knowing the wealth of his opponents, he blushed to be thought mean. He believed a man had to pay his just debts before he could be generous, but he had tried to give what he could with a joyful spirit.[2]

Thus what he saw as the hypocrisy of churches in attacking him wounded him deeply. He said he would not go to church again. Ina followed his suit, at considerable sacrifice, for she had enjoyed church life since the age of nine. They could have their own church, she said, with hymn singing around the piano and the children reciting Bible verses on Sunday. This state of affairs was to endure several years. Lewis could not believe that Ina would let Richard lead her from church, and he often asked the children to go to the Presbyterian Sunday school with him, and they did.[3]

Anger at the Dillard stand on prohibition drove Richard to change eight-year-old Walter's name from Walter Dillard to Walter Brown. However much this hurt Ina, she maintained her priority of easing her husband's pain and did not object. Walter Brown was the good name of a good man. Richard's home must remain a haven, a place where he was safe from jibes, criticisms, and petty stresses. As for Walter, he was too young to dare to object in a climate where Papa could do no wrong.[4]

Dragging their feet at the thought of leaving home, the older children went back to school. In spite of their crowded conditions, their mother's skill at homemaking made home a longed-for place, and bouts of homesickness were common. Ina missed each child, but encouraged all to fight the feeling and make the most of their educational opportunities. Mary Willie and Margo were eager students, striving to achieve and please, while Ina Jr. and R. B. showed a mild indifference to scholarship that worried their parents.[5]

Richard encouraged Ina Jr. at Lucy Cobb to work harder because he had no money to buy her way into polite society, the society she deserved. She must arrive there by her own abilities, and this meant getting a good education. To R. B. he constantly repeated his theme of

his namesake's fulfilling his own unfulfilled ambitions. In his hurt over
the election loss, nursing feelings of rejection, he harped on the subject.
R. B. lost little sleep over such admonitions and continued to socialize
rather than study.[6]

The winter of 1912 was severe, with temperatures plunging to
record lows and heavy snows falling.[7] Richard worked hard in Atlanta all
week, and the contrast of a warm hotel room with a drafty, frigid house
on the week-ends may have finally convinced him to build a suitable
house for his family. More likely, he dreamed of development in Russell
and had the idea of getting a train station established with a hotel near the
station as a good business investment. He sketched hotel plans.

Such fantasies were short-lived. Ina, learning of this proposition,
made it clear that if he was going to build anything as large as the
intended hotel, she and their children were going to live in it. The judge
could not dispute the fairness of her argument.[8]

Another matter between them made him reluctant to refuse Ina
anything. By early spring, they knew that she was again pregnant, the
baby expected in August.

Ina spent the winter and early spring adjusting to the idea of yet
another Russell but kept her secret from the children away at school until
she was sure she would have the good news about the new house to tell
them. Even then she wrote to Mary Willie and Margo only, afraid that
Ina Jr. and R. B. were less able to take the news. She regretted they
would not be able to have their usual house parties, picnics and other
summer social activities, but she must count on the girls to help cook and
clean so that she could save money for Papa to put on the house.[9]

Mary Willie, who now liked to be called Bill, wrote immediately of
their delight in the prospects of a new house and a new baby. Bill was at
a loss for words to express her feelings for her beloved mother in this
time of change and adjustment, but she made a good try:

> My heart was almost *melted* when I read your letter. You
> brought it all in in such a sweet way and the sentence, 'I've
> thought of the effect on my big children more than on myself,'
> was almost more than I could stand. I don't see how you *could*
> think of *us first*, for to *me*, the *real* effect would be on Mother,

and on *no* body else. What is a *little* pleasure that we would be denied compared with what *you* will be denied and the danger thru which you must pass?

At nineteen, Bill understood the perils of childbirth. She knew the struggles her mother had with pregnancy and was acquainted with the anxieties attendant at the actual birth. She had more than once been the child sent to town for the doctor as birth of a sister or brother was imminent.[10]

Ina had well-honed skill in negotiating these dangerous waters and keeping quiet about the difficulties, but she rarely had an easy time with pregnancy or with childbirth.[11] Aware of her problems and never forgetting that he had lost one wife to childbearing, Richard was not casual about birth. The circumstances of this pregnancy especially worried him as he set out building the new house. As the time for Ina's confinement neared, he and she liked to walk to the building site and admire the rising structure. The house was on the opposite side of the railroad tracks from the old dwelling and across the still-unpaved highway.

It was a simple, large clapboard house. A deep one-story veranda stretched across the front and around one side. Downstairs it contained a parlor, a separate sitting room, a comfortable dining room, a kitchen, a pantry and a large bedroom. Upstairs six further bedrooms occupied the floor space. One bedroom upstairs opened onto the second story of the two-story back porch. There were spacious hallways upstairs and down. The house would have plaster walls and modern gas lighting.

One day when the house was almost finished, Richard and Ina walked over to see it. Patience, at age ten and Walter, who had just turned nine, went along. Walter raced around the big, empty house, excited, delighted. He crashed out the front door in his glee and ran smack into his mother, nearly knocking her down the front steps. Richard just managed to catch her and prevent the fall. Terrified that his pregnant wife could have been critically injured, Richard whipped the little boy so hard that Patience, fearing for his life, wept as brokenheartedly as her brother. Richard had a reputation for leniency in matters of discipline. It was Ina they feared for their misbehavior. When their father did have one of his rare descents into corporal punishment, it was usually in a fit of temper, and his children did not view these as just.[12]

The family moved into the new house in early August. On August 19, 1912, two days before the twins' birthday and on the birthday of Robert Lee, a little girl put in her appearance. Richard and Ina were parents of a baker's dozen of living children. The baby's name, Carolyn Lewis, honored brother Lewis, whose first namesake had died in 1906. Because she was born on his birthday, she was called "Rob's baby," but she in fact had five older sisters standing ready to step in if needed.

Ina did not welcome every pregnancy, but she welcomed every baby. Carolyn was soon the smartest little one she had ever seen, and she bragged on her growth and development and enjoyed her as she had the others.[13]

Richard had spent the good part of the year trying to build up the town of Russell, both as an idea and as a fact. As Christmas approached, he thought he was doing pretty well except that he could not borrow money anywhere to go on with some of his projects, much less to begin new ones. He had found it easier to get money back in 1881 when he first set out in tough economic times. Perhaps lenders had learned that the judge would over-extend himself, and that he could be slow about repayment. He repaid, but he was hard work. His philosophy was that no debt should be paid before its time, but not being able to pay on time troubled and embarrassed him. So many debts came in for school, household and farm expenses that he lost track. He became suspicious of all to whom he owed lesser amounts and had to be reminded constantly when a debt was due. With large items such as interest on property loans or his yearly insurance premiums, he had no trouble keeping up with due dates. He maintained a varied stable of insurance policies to provide for his family in case of his death and these cost him as much as a thousand dollars a year. As his anxieties increased, he took to prophesying his demise in the near future.[14]

School expenses came in with deadly regularity and infinite variety. R. B. needed money for uniforms, encampment, books. Ina Jr., developing her seamstress skills, bought cloth, ribbon and threads in Athens stores. Bill and Margo were talented in frugality, but they too had to buy books, paper, uniforms, material for a hat. Music lessons, which all the girls were taking, cost extra. Their father hated for these children not to have a little spending money, but sometimes he could not even send their board money on time, much less extra money for treats. They dreaded to write him for money, but he repeatedly told them not to be afraid to ask for what they needed. Their letters were filled with careful accounts.[15]

Just before Christmas R. B. wrote that he wanted to drop out of school. He was failing Latin, not doing well in math, and lagged even in a favorite subject, history. He had turned fifteen, an age when young men who were not already working would be going to work. Discouraged with school, aware that his father was eternally "hard run" financially, he thought this was time for him to try running a store in an empty building in Russell.

His mother responded emphatically that he would never be allowed to drop out of school by her consent. He must make the necessary effort to be competent and educated and achieve a high mark in the world. She ridiculed his idea of keeping a store: "I can see you with your case of soda water & jar of red candy & box of chewing gum & you, R. B. Russell Jr. sitting on the 'small of your back' waiting for a customer to come along with his pennies to trade with you...No, boy, I didn't bring you into this world to be a failure or to ever fail in anything you might undertake. So *rub up* that 'block head' [his term] & get good marks from now on." She closed with tender expressions of her love and pride in all her children.[16]

Richard took a different tack. Ignoring his son's plea to drop out of school, he gave a detailed run-down of how well things were going in Russell. He mentioned that the brick store house had been rented to someone who was going to stock it with farming materials worth four thousand dollars. According to his account, all the houses in Russell were rented. Richard had rented not only his houses but also his blacksmith shop, his mill machinery, and the brick storehouse. In order to rent the storehouse, he was having to build a four-room house for the merchant to live in. All this was in addition to putting in the train station for a flag stop he had arranged with two rail lines. Russell was on a little boom.[17]

Farming, however, was not profitable, and the debts Richard owed for farming may have been another reason he had trouble borrowing money. He had not even made enough cotton to pay for the guano on three black tenant farmers' land and barely enough from two white tenants' land to pay guano and supplies. He had four words of advice: "Work *hard* my boy."[18]

Richard was also farming the Dillard farm in Oglethorpe. Fielding Dillard had made gifts to all his other children before his death, and Ina, Pipey and Walter had inherited the farm when America died in 1909. Richard bought out Walter's part, with a down payment and the rest paid in installments that came with an irregularity to tax even Walter Dillard's Christian forbearance. Ina and Pipey were to have shares of the farm's profits. Unfortunately, in 1912, its tenants had not made a profit at all.[19]

Brother William John had at last given up his farm, and he and his wife Addie, whom he married in 1907, had moved to Washington, DC, where John took up two jobs, one with the Census Bureau from seven until four and another with the Post Office from four until eleven. He was not sure he would be allowed to keep both places, since it took him a little time to get from one place to the other. Even at that, a double shift at a government job was easier than farming. Although John had farmed fulltime, Richard thought his own problems were related to the fact that he did not give his farm enough attention.[20]

The Russell knitting mill was not on a boom. Richard had borrowed a thousand dollars against the mill in 1906 to be repaid at eight per cent interest in payments of two hundred and fifty dollars a year. As he struggled to meet payments, the mill shut down operation several times. Richard could not manage the labor situation or find anyone with skill enough to do this at the salary he would pay. The site was also used to mill flour and corn, but that, too, had failed to turn a profit. Renting mill machinery that cost nearly eight thousand dollars in 1900 for one dollar a month in 1913 was a serious business reverse.[21]

In January 1913 the biggest excitement in town was the opening of a new school. Richard had secured state funds to pay a teacher and to buy desks. The school opened the first week in January with forty pupils in attendance, proof that the population of the area was growing. The

school building was a former hopstand. The desks did not arrive on time
and when they did they were damaged. The teacher was Mrs. Pearl
McBreyer, wife of the superannuated preacher. Ina went over twice to
look at the school, trying to convince herself it was in fact a reality. She
sent all her children except Edward, Dick and Carolyn out each morning.
When she noted that almost all the school children had pennies, she
urged Richard to send stick candy and attractive penny candy from
Atlanta for her storehouse.[22]

   While Richard worked on Russell as a town and kept up a grueling
schedule of Appeals Court work in Atlanta, Ina continued her written
instruction to her children away from home. She was as dismayed as
parents always are when bright, adoring little ones turn into recalcitrant,
crabby teenagers. She could not help comparing these difficult
adolescents to little Carolyn, who was the smartest baby she had ever
seen for her age. "All of you were such smart babies," she wrote to Ina
Jr., "it's a wonder to me you are not more wonderful now. What's the
matter? You, especially was a perfect wonder. It's too bad that we so
soon out-grow so much notoriety."[23]

   Although Ina's reign in the home was incontestable, she knew when
to call on Richard to help her make decisions, and he delivered learned
opinions that backed her proposals. The ethics of the culture did not
permit a father's authority to be questioned, but this patriarch was so
reasonable, loving and wise that his children valued his contributions.
Although they rarely did exactly as he wished or instructed, being
independent spirits themselves, they showed no signs of resentment or
rebellion. He seemed to have total confidence in their ability to do the
right thing once they had thought a situation through. Ina venerated him
as father and provider, never letting the children forget how hard he
worked for their sake.[24]

By 1913, Powell and Hill had left the Court of Appeals. Richard
threatened to leave from time to time, but he clung to the salary and the
life close to the corridors of power. [25] In salary and official life, if not in
title, Appeals justices enjoyed the same rank as the justices of the
Supreme Court. When former President Teddy Roosevelt came to town,

all these justices were invited to sit on the platform as dignitaries of the state. None of this kind of attention was wasted on Judge Russell.[26]

A big day of celebration came in 1913 when Bill graduated from G.N.& I.C. She would continue her studies in domestic science for another year on scholarship. She was pleased to be almost off Papa's payroll. That summer Ina Jr. fell ill with typhoid fever. An anxious time followed when they despaired for her life. Dr. Almond spent a long night with the Russells and on his way home next morning met the Winder undertaker on the street. "Don't leave town," he told the man. "Judge Russell is likely to have to bury his daughter before the week is out."[27] Thankfully, the doctor's prognosis was wrong, and she was on her way to a slow recovery when the autumn term began. Her mother thought she would not be able to return to Lucy Cobb Institute before Christmas.[28]

R. B. did not return to Gordon Military Institute, for, to his father's deep disappointment, he had failed Latin. He was now sent to the Seventh District Powder Springs Agricultural and Mechanical School in Cobb County. Rob, having outstripped the Russell school, was sent to the Monroe Agricultural and Mechanical, about fifteen miles from home. Ina Sr. knew she was going to miss her second son because he was her main helper on the farm and in the store that served the tenant farmers. It was Rob who kept the apparatus for the gas lamps filled and working. A serious lad, caring and thoughtful of his mother, but sometimes sharp with the younger children, he was too old for his age, according to sisters Bill and Margo.[29]

The agricultural and mechanical schools were a far cry from the military institute. At the latter the boys roomed in homes where mothers gave their laundry and meals the same attention they received at home. At A & M schools, the students lived in dormitories and had to work on the attached farms nine hours per week in addition to keeping up their studies. Monroe was more modern than Powder Springs, with electricity, better bathrooms and better food. R. B. was not enchanted by his new surroundings, in spite of the fact that a few girls also attended these schools. Rob, homesick, was abashed that his professor's daughter had better grades than he did and led his class. Richard was pleased that the sum of both lads' fees was less than R. B.'s fees the year before.[30]

Bill and Margo were still together at G.N.& I.C., and another scholar had left home. Harriette was in Washington, Georgia, with Aunt Hattie. Harriette made glad the heart of her father by excelling in Latin, and he did not neglect to brag on her to R. B., who was still struggling with the elusive language his father so loved and insisted would be necessary in law practice. R. B. had dreamed of going into the navy like Uncle Rob, but his weak math grades meant he would never gain an Academy appointment, so he turned his thoughts more and more to the law.[31]

It was during this period that Richard began to serve on the Board of Trustees at G.N.& I.C.[32] He became a close friend and avid supporter of Marvin Parks, head of the school. The Russell daughters enjoyed frequent visits from their father, and as an important personage to the school, he often was asked to speak at Chapel. He was not displeased to do so.

While Richard struggled to promote Russell, he continued to oppose the formation of a new county. In 1911 a bill was introduced at the end of the legislative session proposing the county, and in 1912 it looked as though it would get a favorable reception. However, in the house it never left committee because of an adverse report. Richard Russell spoke against the county at this meeting and must have gotten the ear of its members.[33]

By this time his brother Lewis and his cousin William H. Quarterman were on the committee to form the county. Lewis promised Richard that if he would support the county, they would name it for him. This was a tempting offer to a man with Richard's appetite for fame and recognition, but Richard likely suspected Lewis would not be able to deliver on that promise because of the enmity towards him in Winder.[34] He continued his opposition.

By 1913, the bill was set to be signed into law by the governor the next year. Nevertheless, Richard still hoped to waylay it, and hired J. R. Pottle, an Albany lawyer who had served on the Court of Appeals for two years. People in Winder were furious that he refused to let the matter drop. One day Richard's train arrived at the Winder station, and he made the mistake of sticking his head out the window to speak to someone.

Mrs. Laveda Holsenbeck, an avid new county advocate, jumped onto a loading trolley, grabbed his head and began pulling his hair, screaming imprecations against him for his new county opposition. It was only as the train pulled away that she was persuaded to let go. The judge did not appreciate the indignity of this event. He warned his children not to get off the train in Winder but to come on to the flag stop at Russell.[35]

The flag stop station made getting to Russell safer than in the days when Richard had to jump off the moving train. The station was a small white building to provide shelter in inclement weather, and outside stood a flagpole where a flag was displayed to indicate that there were passengers to get on the train. During these years, the little station could be busy as guests came to visit the Russells or children returned from school. Richard loved to invite Atlanta friends home for Saturday night and Sunday dinner, and the children were constantly having guests, whether from nearby Winder or school friends from farther afield.

Although he could not be persuaded to give up activities that kept him from home, Richard cherished his time there. Proud of his larger house and the flag stop station, he invited people to visit, and they accepted. Ina never knew whom he might bring home unless he phoned, which he did occasionally. During these years he started a phone company with the Braselton brothers in nearby Braselton, so this modern convenience had come to Russell. Between Papa's procrastination and his absent-mindedness, everyone learned to live with the unexpected, and the little children looked forward to his homecomings as much as had the older ones. A favorite friend who often came was Walter Brown, bringing presents of oranges, nuts and candy for the children. Brown sometimes wrote up these visits for the *Fulton County Daily Report*, a newspaper devoted to the courts and business interest of the county.[36]

Guests felt as if they had come to the right place, and they recalled with glowing words their pleasure at being in the Russell home. Friends of Mary Willie, Margo and Ina confessed that they fell in love with Judge Russell. Young men called Ina's home "a haven of joy long to be remembered." The patriarch of this vaunted hearthside continued his dirt digging and bank leveling activities to beautify the grounds of his home, all the while concentrating on knotty problems of law. He and Ina planted trees and shrubs all around the house together. Ina loved flowers and each year added more roses, gardenias, pinks, violas, pansies, cornflowers, snapdragons, sweet peas, and hydrangeas. She chose many different varieties of roses, Paul Neyron, Arch Duke Charles, Polyantha, sweetheart, Mamon Cochet, Silver Moon, and filled the house with vases of roses. Their young magnolias beside the house perfumed the spring air, and honeysuckle added its fragrance. Richard basked in praise of his home and thanked God over and over for his Ina.[37]

Papa's homecomings were not more memorable than his leave-takings. He was incapable of eating fast and no matter how near it was to train time, he would sit long at the table. Sometimes he had not finished his toilet, his collar was unbuttoned, his shoes untied. He liked to hold little Carolyn on his lap and feed her sugared coffee as the clocked ticked towards train time. When the train whistle sounded, there would be a great rush to get him out the door.

To lessen the tension of these mornings, the children set up a system. One of the boys would stand at the station after he had raised the flag, or, in winter, hung a lantern, and he would watch for the train to come around a far bend. When this sentry spotted the train, he would call out to another son standing about halfway between the station and the house. "'Round the bend!" came the first cry, and the relay would take it up, so that it reached the house loud and clear: "'Round the bend!" At this Papa must finish his coffee, tie his shoes and button his collar. He more often than not went down the porch steps pulling on his jacket, his collar still unbuttoned, a child or Laura the cook beside him with a cup of coffee for him to have a last swallow. More than once he reached the station only in time to wave at the engineer as the train sailed past, but then the driver would slow down and back the train up for the judge. The little boys found this duty so thrilling that they would fight for it.[38]

Richard's fight against the new county continued but it was another losing battle. On July 7, 1914, Governor John Slaton signed the Constitutional Amendment creating the new county of Barrow, named for David Crenshaw Barrow, Chancellor of the University of Georgia. The Barrow family were old neighbors of Ina's in Oglethorpe County, and Richard had known them, especially Pope and Dave Barrow, since his student days at the university.

When the news of the new county reached Winder, many citizens could not contain their joy. Youngsters came out to Russell and painted the flag station with huge letters declaring BARROW COUNTY. As night was falling, adults, men and women, came in automobiles and buggies and drove around and around the house, throwing rotten tomatoes at the house and singing, "Let's Hang Dick Russell from a Sour Apple Tree." Richard was not at home, but his two eldest sons were. They loaded a rifle and watched the parade from the second story of the darkened house. R. B. was inclined to fire a shot to scare the crowd. Rob talked him out of it. The children old enough to remember this event never forgot their fright on this momentous night. Patience, Walter and the twins, trailed by Edward and Dick, got up early next day and washed BARROW COUNTY off the station wall.[39]

1914 was a year rife with opposition for many state offices, and during the summer it was rumored that Robert Hodges, a Macon city judge, would run for Richard's seat on the Court of Appeals. There was a good show of support for Judge Russell from newspapers all over the state when this story got into print. The *Americus Recorder* reported that "Judge Russell works long hours yet works rapidly and has the reputation of being able to turn out more volume of work than any other judge in the state." Richard had talked of leaving the court, but he did not want to be defeated in an election. Many wrote to assure him he could not be beat, including Pope Brown, one of his 1911 rivals. He had been friends with Robert Hodges for nearly twenty-five years and felt he was worthy of the post. Having been disappointed so many times, he composed his heart for any fate, but he was relieved and happy when his friend wrote that he had no intention of running against Judge Russell.[40]

Free from this worry, Richard and Ina took a Royal Arcanum trip, this time to New York, and Ina Jr. went with them. Richard continued to need these gatherings where he was "the lion of the hour." In addition, as a representative he was paid about five dollars a day over and above his expenses, which helped him give his wife and children chances to see more of the world outside Georgia.[41]

R. B. graduated from Powder Springs A&M in the spring of 1914 and spent most of the summer at the University of Georgia taking Latin so that he could enter Gordon Military Institute again. His father wanted him to have a diploma from there as well as from Powder Springs. Bill, whom her father still called Mary, finished her scholarship year and took a job teaching Domestic Science in Sandersville, Georgia. When the 1914-1915 school year opened, Harriette was a freshman at G.N.&I.C. with Margo a senior, and Rob was at Monroe A & M. Bill insisted on paying his tuition and when her father remonstrated, she had the school principal send her the bills. She knew her father would not think to pay a bill he did not receive.[42]

Ina Jr. did not go back to Lucy Cobb but stayed home to help her mother and to take occasional work in a rural school not far from home. She hated teaching, her health problems continued to make life anxious, and she was unhappy living in such a hole as Winder. Her mother advised her to do her best to be interested in life, however dull it seemed. Ina Jr. did her best to follow her mother's advice, but some evenings she sat in the porch swing, crying because she lived in Winder.[43]

In March 1915 a heavy and unexpected blow to their family life fell. Laura Glenn, who had ably assisted Ina in so much of her work as homemaker since the birth of Dickson in 1910, died of a brain hemorrhage. Ina was devastated at the loss of this faithful friend and servant. Richard and Ina were to leave for a Royal Arcanum trip to Tennessee when Laura died, but Ina was too upset to consider leaving home. Even Richard at his most persuasive and demanding could not change her mind.

She helped prepare Laura's body for burial, and her children made wreaths. They all went to the funeral, except Ina Jr. and little Carolyn. Ina wept as the coffin was lowered into the grave. In the weeks following Laura's death, she mourned her friend, remembering her ways about the house, her fine character and her affection.[44]

Spring brought commencements for Margo at G.N. & I.C. and for R. B. at Gordon. Margo was overjoyed that she at last would be able to teach. She had longed for this time since her sophomore year.[45] R. B. was accepted for law school at the University of Georgia. His father was more than pleased with his second diploma and the prospect of law school. He was thinking again of leaving the court to practice law and to have a son as a partner would make that venture more palatable. The Russell boom had petered out, and the farm struggled. He had borrowed and borrowed, keeping his children in school, while trying to repay campaign debts. He was even reduced to borrowing fifty dollars from Ina Jr., who made so little teaching school. He had been forced to sell valuable property purchased back in the 1890s, but he hoped to hold on to some assets. The war in Europe was playing havoc with his plans as interest rates went up. Soon he would have to do something to make more money.[46]

Not forgetting his now-Barrow County neighbors' fierce criticisms, he considered moving to St. Marys in deep South Georgia, where his Russell ancestors had come from. He and Ina traveled there in the spring of 1915. Ina, at least, was briefly tempted by the serene, out-of-the-way town where gracious ante-bellum homes gleamed in the shade of live oak trees. She sent postcards to the children asking them how they would like to live in one of these fine homes. Richard quickly realized St. Marys was too far from Atlanta, and this plan was abandoned.[47]

Money problems surfaced in another way in the summer of 1915. A circular written by W. E. Moyers appeared in Atlanta, charging that Judge Russell had misappropriated funds owed to a stenographer of the court. Newspapers took up this story, and after thirty-three years in public life, with honesty as his flag, Richard Russell found himself accused of petty theft. When friends and associates read the pamphlet, they were sure there was nothing to it and advised ignoring the whole thing. Richard would not hear of this tactic. He demanded a full legislative investigation of the matter, and, in addition, of his conduct not only on the court but in all aspects of public service. [48]

The charges were related to seventy-five dollars that Richard had drawn from the treasury and paid to a stenographer in October 1910, a Mr. Shelton, who was substituting for Miss Bloodworth. It was not unusual for judges to draw the salaries of stenographers directly and pay them in cash or by check. Although Richard put on a calm, assured face before reporters and the legislature, in his heart he trembled over the possibility that this was an attack by enemies contriving to bring him down. He saw the worst happening: impeachment and shame to the children and the precious wife who bore his name, the name he had worked so hard to raise so that they would be honored and proud.

Walter Brown was a steadying hand during the initial hullabaloo and helped Richard prepare for the legislative committee hearing. It turned out to be an unnecessary defense. When Moyers had presented his "case" to the committee, Richard's legal adviser stood up and said he could see in no way how Mr. Moyers' presentation had proved the accusations. Indeed, he believed the committee would agree that he had proved the opposite. Therefore, he felt it unnecessary to waste further time and asked that the judge be exonerated and fully cleared. The Committee unanimously agreed to this proposal. Richard then asked that the entire matter be expunged from the record and this was done. The *Atlanta Constitution* reported the full story over two days.

In the autumn Papa enjoyed a slight respite from school fees because Bill was paying Rob's fees and only Harriette and R. B. needed tuition money. Ina Jr. and Marguerite were at home, working in local rural schools. Ina Jr. still hated teaching, but Margo found the challenge invigorating. Bill had taken a job at Roanoke Institute in Virginia. She liked this quiet, private school, but found life so far from Georgia painful.

Everyone looked forward to Christmas, but it was not to be a happy time. R. B. came home from the university with a severe cold and wracking cough. He was suffering from an acute case of pneumonia, which escalated, and on Christmas Day he nearly died. Even the little children tiptoed about the house, seeing their mother and father strained and anxious as the doctor came and went, his face grave. The sick boy did not want his mother out of his sight nor did she want to leave him. Richard stood long by the bed, willing him to live to fulfill the dream of working together that had seemed to flower in son as in father when he began his law studies.[49]

Dr. Almond recommended a private nurse from the Atlanta Registered Nurses' Club. Miss Dovie came on December 27 to take over the boy's care and assure his recovery. He had come through the worst phase, but he suffered intensely as he improved. He coughed blood and phlegm and vomited his food. His limbs wasted away to nothing. He had recurring abscesses in the groin. Pains in his chest and sides left him in agony. For weeks they could hardly get him to take a step, and he complained about everything. By the end of March he was able to go to Sea Breeze, Florida, to be under the care of Aunt Pheme in her boarding house. He was unable to go back to school and would have to start over in the autumn term.

During this time of his son's nearly fatal illness, Richard became more depressed than Ina had ever seen him. His financial situation tortured him, but he could decide on no course of action. Some dissatisfied voters were urging him to run for Congress in the Ninth District against Tom Bell, who had served six terms. Tempted by this idea, Richard could not make up his mind, and indecision added to his depression. When he surveyed his financial situation, it seemed that for the honor of wearing judicial robes he had had to sell, to support his family, everything he had accumulated. At his age, he feared that he might not be able to support his family while getting established in a legal practice. His choices were bleak: continued poverty on the bench, terrible risk if he quit.[50]

Richard was utterly worn out by the arduous court work. They were trying up to 1600 cases a year, yet always falling behind. The entire legal community urged that something be done to change this stressful situation and an amendment to the Constitution was proposed to change the jurisdictions of the Appeals and the Supreme courts and to add three judges to the Appeals. Whether this amendment would pass was uncertain in the spring of 1916. Weary of courts and cases and people, he longed for peace and quiet, for rest. How he could have worked so hard and gained so little mystified him. Had he been born under an unlucky star? As always he turned to Ina for comfort, deploring that his failures made her life as well as his nothing but work, work, work to the end of the chapter.[51]

New medical bills and unpaid old campaign debt notwithstanding, Richard Russell decided in April to leave the Court of Appeals in June and run for Congress in the summer, while opening his law practice, which would then be under way if he did not win. He considered how a

Congressional salary would not settle his debts, but he was lured by the thought that the next five years would be a vastly important epoch in national affairs. He was tempted to write part of his own history in the nation's eyes.[52]

His announcement that he was leaving the court brought expressions of regret in the press. His reputation for gargantuan quantity and excellent quality of work was the continuing astonishment of the Georgia bar. His numerous family was a fascinating subject, and reporters were delighted to write about the respected judge who was also a proud father, genuinely fond of each child.[53]

Ina was pleased that her husband's work was acclaimed, however mildly, but she was sick about this decision to run for Congress. She had urged him in 1910 to put aside everything but getting the children educated, and she had been comfortable and happy with his position on the court. She viewed the prospect of another campaign with dread.[54]

One thing made this situation tolerable. As his major campaign expense, Richard was thinking of buying a car. By mid-April he had announced his resignation from the Court, to become effective in June, and he had rented a car to begin his campaign with a tour through the mountains. Ina went with him and was enchanted by the journey. They spent nights in Blairsville, Blue Ridge, and Jasper, but one evening their ambition got them stuck on the mountain, unable to continue safely on the rough mountain road. Ina thought it grand that they had to sleep in the car until daybreak.[55]

The driver on this first trip was Mr. Crooks, Richard's stenographer. The plan was for him to continue driving until R. B. came home from Florida to take over chauffering. Richard was in high spirits as he met men who remembered him, laughed at his jokes, and said they would support him. Ina was proud of his wit and quick speech.[56]

The convenience of a car caught on quickly in the Russell household. A couple of weeks after this trip, Ina hired two autos from Mr. Mathews in Winder so that she could take her entire family to Lexington, Georgia, where there was to be an unveiling of the Confederate monument on Southern Memorial Day. She transported sixteen people to Lexington in two five-passenger cars without anyone's being squashed. These included Pipey, Annie, Auntney [Mary], R. B.,

Margo, Ina Jr., Carolyn, Dick, Edward, the twins, Walter, Patience, Ina herself and the two drivers. It was an unforgettable day out, where Ina saw many of her relatives at the picnic following the unveiling, and Carolyn and little Dick were able to eat all the cake they wanted. Ina enjoyed showing off her brood.[57]

Knowing that his wife approved wholeheartedly of the purchase, Richard bought a new Ford in May. R. B. and Rob were wild to drive, and so were Ina Jr. and Margo. Richard had no intention of learning to drive. He knew he had drivers in reserve for years to come.

On the campaign trail again, Richard Russell's mood lifted. At chatauquas, Sunday school associations, fiddlers' conventions, court sessions, commencement exercises, Oddfellows meetings, and reunions of Confederate veterans, he received warm applause and laughter, and his ego revived and thrived. When he was not making a formal speech, he was on the streets, shaking hands, mixing, telling the voters how eager he was to serve in Congress. He had preferred to serve on the state level before now, he said, but with the Great War bringing massive and far-reaching changes, important laws affecting the country for one hundred years would need to be made. He wanted to be a part of that, and as the campaign moved on, he believed more and more strongly that his long years of service had uniquely prepared him to make a lasting contribution. The only other reason he could give people to vote for him was that Tom Bell had served six terms and it was someone else's turn. He reasoned that a public office is never one man's property but is the property of the people.[58]

Bell had been a successful Congressman, defeating opposition in each of his six previous races. A veteran campaigner who had brought federal dollars to his district, he was not believed vulnerable. Richard himself analyzed the situation clearly, but failed to understand that his race was therefore doomed. When his friend W. C. Edwards of Toccoa wrote urging him not to run, saying he underestimated Bell's strength, Richard replied:

I do not...under-estimate Mr. Bell's strength, because I consider him not only a very clever gentleman, but by all odds the smoothest politician in the State. I know that he has a magnificent political machine while I have none; I know that, in the past, he has been lavish with his campaign expenditures while I shall make none, but the race is not always to the swift, nor the battle to the strong.[59]

That the race usually *is* to the swift and the battle to the strong was a fact that, under the effects of political inebriation again, Richard overlooked. A political cartoon commented on his candidacy by showing a strong, vigorous horse named Bell crossing a deep stream with a voter on board, while behind on the bank, a pitiful, thin, plaintive horse named Russell begs, "Try me." The cartoonist advised: Don't Swap Horses in the Middle of the Stream.[60] When the white male Georgians of the Ninth District went to the polls on September 12, 1916, they confirmed that they wanted to ride the Bell horse.

Richard Russell had gone deeper into debt for another unsuccessful attempt to break into the legislative or executive branch of government. Having given up his rank as high court judge, he was now, for the first time since 1896, just a lawyer. His three oldest children had finished school and were self-supporting, but he had ten children left to educate. Even if he managed to stay out of political campaigns, that was a tall order for a fifty-five-year-old lawyer without a practice.

13

SOMETIMES I FEEL LIKE
RUNNING AWAY

1917-1921

Richard Russell set up his law office in Atlanta, where he could attract a broad range of clients. His reputation as a highly respected judge of the Court of Appeals meant clients were not long in showing up. If he needed to work from Winder, he used his brother Lewis' office, and his attitude towards Winder began to soften. Lewis and Mary threatened periodically to move back to Athens into their old house, which Mary had inherited, and at some point during this period they did that, but Lewis continued to practice in Winder. Richard may have been at home a little more than he had been as a judge, but the difference would be hard to measure. His cases came from people all over the state, and he went where the work was.[1]

R. B. had been back at law school since the fall of 1916, and he early showed aptitude and pleasure in these studies. His father's dream of having a son in practice with him grew closer to reality. Bill was teaching in Columbus, Georgia, a lively military town in the lead-up to America's entry into the great war in Europe. Margo, too, left home, to teach in a rural school near Eastman, Georgia. She roomed with a friend, also a teacher, in conditions that must have improved her view of Russell and Winder. Hers was not an easy life, and she was often blue, but she kept at her teaching dream.[2]

Ina Jr. tried to leave home and teaching by accepting a job in south Georgia near Thomasville, as a companion for an elderly couple, friends of Richard's. Richard was not happy about this plan, and the day his Ina Jr. left was one of the hardest in fatherhood for him. They sat on the front steps together, silent, unable to speak their emotions. Ina Sr. hoped the climate change would help her daughter's asthma and the change of scene her attitude.[3]

Ina Jr. lasted only a few weeks in this situation, unable to rejoice in the speeds she was required to drive her employers' Ford, the cold water she had to wash dishes in, the clothes she was expected to wear or not wear, and the books she was expected to read or not read. A former stenographer of her father's, W.E. Perry, and his young family lived in Valdosta, and they took her in. Soon her father sent her enough money to come home and she went back to her teaching job in rural Barrow County.

Rob had graduated at Monroe Agricultural and Mechanical in the spring of 1916, winning prizes in debating and "ready writing" essay contests. He had not yet decided what he wanted to do in life, and Richard was not able to send him to the University with R. B. at law school. Ina wanted him to go to Georgia Tech but that proved too expensive. Bill stepped in again and offered to pay his fees at Gordon Military Institute, so he followed his brother's lead in earning two diplomas. Harriette was back at G.N.& I.C., the happiest she had ever been there, for this was her final year. In the autumn of 1917 when Richard had paid school fees, train fares and spending money for Rob, Harriette and R. B., he told his wife he had one dollar left.[4]

Lack of money is probably why the other children were doing the unthinkable. They were in school in Winder. The Russell school project had fizzled, and Richard, besieged with financial worries, gave up the school battle. With a flivver, Ina knew she could get her children to school in bad weather. In good weather they walked a mile into town. Patience was entrusted to drive the car. Walter and Patience were in high school, and the twins, Edward and Dick were in grammar school. Only Carolyn was left at home.

In law school, R. B. became enthusiastic about practicing law with his father and also about entering the political arena. He early recognized that the name Dick Russell carried a familiar and respected ring, and he decided he wanted to be Dick Russell Jr., to be called no longer R. B., but Dick. This desire presented a problem in the family because there was little Dickson, at age six, another Dick Russell. Richard, eager to support his eldest son's ambitions, agreed to change his youngest son's name to Alexander Brevard. Years earlier Richard had thought of naming this child Alexander Lawrence. Now he chose Alexander Brevard in honor of their distinguished Revolutionary War ancestor. By choosing this name, he also gave his Benjamin, as he liked to call this son, part of his father's name as he took away another part.

Patience protested. Little Dick had been given to her at birth, and she, as his special sister, was horrified that his name would be changed at this date. She hoped her mother would object, but Ina respected the wishes of her husband and eldest son, and the youngest son became Alexander Brevard, called Alex.[5]

When America entered the war in Europe in the spring of 1917, the Russell household experienced the anxieties common to homes with young men of draft age. Dick Jr. was of age, and Rob only a year away. Ina trembled. Richard took cases of people willing to pay a high price to try to keep their young men out of the war, but the idea of draft dodging was not one Russells could adopt. He and Ina knew that their sons would want to serve and would serve.[6] They did not imagine the war was to take their eldest girls, not their boys.

Working in Columbus, near Fort Benning, Bill met a tall, robust young soldier, Lieutenant Samuel Gordon Green, a Georgia Tech-trained engineer, from Gray, Georgia. After a few months of casual dating, Bill decided Gordon was a good prospect for matrimony, even though she occasionally had to correct his English. Gordon knew she was the woman he had dreamed of winning when, through the years, he had had to remind himself to keep high ideals. In early 1918 Gordon looked sure to be ordered to France, so the couple decided to marry.[7]

The announcement that his precious first-born would marry shocked Richard Russell. He had hoped she would remain single and take care of him in his old age. That he did not know her sweetheart and, therefore, could not say whether he was worthy of his daughter bothered him. He spoke his fears but assured her he had confidence in her judgment and would give the marriage his blessing. He could not resist adding how it hurt to know that he was replaced in her affections.

Bill was not put off by this pitiful approach. She was young and in love, and her heart was big enough to love her husband while she loved and would always love her dad. She thanked him for his check and to his promise to send more money, said she would not need it. She had resigned from her teaching post and could collect her remaining pay because marrying or dying did not require the teacher to give a month's notice. Gordon, stationed in Springfield, Massachusetts, would have only two days' leave. They would meet in Washington and marry at Uncle Ed and Aunt Susie's house.[8]

Near the end of February the date was hurriedly set for March 1, Bill's birthday. Gordon thought he would be shipped out on March 4. Richard and Ina came to Washington on the train with Billie, Carolyn and Ina Jr., who was maid of honor. Miss Hettie also came with them. In contrast to the festive air of the women, Richard looked rather downcast. It grieved Billie to see him so, but not for long.[9]

The morning of the wedding Richard could not bear to go down for the nine o'clock ceremony. Susie had decorated the parlor with ferns and other pretty plants, and Ina brought a wealth of pink carnations. When all was ready, Gordon arrived, radiantly happy, with his brother Maddox as best man. Upstairs, Richard sat on the edge of the bed, weeping, with one shoe on and one off. Billie sat down beside him and held his hand, then helped him put the second shoe on. At last he dried his tears and escorted his daughter to her wedding.[10]

Patience had been sent to Lucy Cobb Institute in January of 1918, and Richard had grumbled at this separation. Almost as soon as he could become a little reconciled to losing Pat and Billie, Ina Jr. announced she was leaving home again. Never happy with living in Winder or with teaching, while in Washington she had heard that government jobs were going to women in order to free men for military service. She decided to take the Civil Service examination and try for such a place. She told no one about this plan until she had sat the exam and received word that she had passed. A job was waiting for her in Washington, DC, as a clerk in the Bureau of War Risk Insurance (later the Veterans Administration). The post paid one thousand dollars a year, more than twice what she could make teaching. Excited, if a little scared, she was determined to take it.

Richard and Ina were at first appalled by the idea of their unmarried daughter going off to Washington, but when Ina Sr. realized she could live with Ed and Susie, she approved of this plan for her dissatisfied daughter. Richard could hardly be consoled on any account, but Ina Jr., nearly twenty-four years old, was ready to fly. Her father made it clear that he would come to see her soon, and if he was not satisfied with her situation, he would bring her home. He could not bear the thought of his daughter wild and unreasonable in Washington, DC.

The father was good to his word. About a month after Ina Jr. arrived in Washington, he went to see her. He was worried about the number of soldiers in town, the long work week of six full days, and her health. Ina Jr. assured him she was happy and well. She had found the adjustment to city life and the long working hours difficult at first and had looked with some longing towards home. If her father had come a couple of weeks earlier, she might have been tempted to go back with him. As it was, he came a few days too late. She was not going home on any account. She had just received her first paycheck.[11]

In the spring of 1918, Dick Jr. finished law school, while Rob graduated from Gordon Military Institute. Dick Jr. went immediately into the Navy, and Rob joined the Army. Dick Jr. had idolized his Uncle Rob and had dreamed of going to Annapolis until his math grades burst that bubble. The navy was the logical place for him. Fortunately, he was stationed at the Naval Supply School in Athens. Rob's Army training was taking place at a camp on the university campus. Richard went to Athens whenever he could and had to be content with speaking to his sons through the fence.[12]

Harriette, graduating the spring of 1918 from G.N.& I.C., saw an amazing thing happen: Young men arrived in droves on the campus of the all-girl school. Senior girls were asked to show visiting soldiers in Milledgeville around campus. Harriette felt it bad luck that her soldier was a married man, but she enjoyed being part of this social scene. After graduation, she came home to help her mother. Harriette had never shown interest in teaching, and because she was a good cook, Ina was glad to have her at home while she looked for other work.[13]

Harriette also wanted to spend some time with her second mother, Pipey, who had been ill. Richard and Ina had sent Pipey to a hospital in Atlanta and paid for treatment and a special nurse, and Pipey was soon well enough to come home. Richard's patriarchal duties continued to extend as naturally to Ina's spinster or widowed sisters as their homemaking skills extended to his family. Pipey and Annie were on hand in Russell and visits to and from Aunt Hattie were still encouraged.[14]

Dick Jr. was not happy in the navy. There was no water deeper than the Oconee River to be seen, and no ships at all. Camp life was confining, especially when the flu epidemic of 1918 broke out and all were quarantined. He hated scrubbing barracks floors, and the courses in mathematics, physics and navigation that he had to take did not speak to his strengths. He spent many hours in study hall, and questioned whether he had made a mistake by going into the navy.[15] When the war ended in November 1918, he was delighted to be released. It does not appear that he considered going anywhere but to the farm at Russell. At twenty-one, having been away for nearly seven years, Dick Russell Jr. was glad to be returning to his mother's home circle.

Leaving home to find work did occur to young Rob. Upon leaving the Army, he went to Atlanta. His first job was selling tombstones.

Gordon Green did not go to France. Instead he was transferred to Washington, DC, to work in small-arms development. He decided to stay in the Army and was to earn recognition for invention of firearms.[16]

Ina Jr. moved in with Billie and Gordon, so that all saved on rent money. The three spent their first Christmas away from home, cheering each other up. Ina Sr. sent a roast turkey and their favorite cake in a surprise box on Christmas Eve. Gordon's people, farmers in Jones County, sent butter, eggs, ham, dried apples, canned peaches and potatoes. Gordon's brother was on hand, so the four had a Georgia Christmas feast in Washington.[17]

When R. B. Russell Jr. came into his father's law practice in 1919, business was going well. Richard opened an office in Winder, in the most imposing structure in town, so that he could practice out of Atlanta and Dick Jr. out of Winder. Richard Sr. continued to travel statewide in his practice. He had succeeded in paying off some of his debts and easing the family finances considerably. He needed another man, and although Dick Jr. had a chance to go with other firms, the son agreed wholeheartedly with the idea of fulfilling Dad's dream of partnership.[18]

Lewis was living in Athens with Mary, but he worked in Winder and now shared the same office. Richard and Ina's house was like his own, and he stayed with them frequently. Harriette was called in to perform secretarial duties at the office, and Lewis, at least, sometimes remembered to pay her.[19] Another young lawyer in town, Joe Quillian, a distant cousin of Ina's, worked with the three Russells, also sharing the office. Before 1919 was out, Rob left what Ina called his "hark from the tomb a doleful sound" business and joined the team, reading law and preparing for the bar. Rob was admitted to the bar before he was twenty years old, and Richard had doubly fulfilled his dream of filial partnership. They had enough business to keep five men working.[20]

Harriette talked of studying law and sometimes read the code when she was supposed to be typing. Working for five demanding male lawyers kin to her may have put her off reading law, but she managed to learn to drive in spite of their ridicule. They were niggardly in giving instructions and made excuses about the worthiness of the car to avoid letting her drive.

One afternoon she announced she was going to drive home and slid behind the wheel of Rob's car to show she meant business. He smirked as he got in the passenger seat and then refused to give her any instructions. He should have remembered whom she was named for. Harriette got the car into gear some way and started off. She knew the gas pedal had a tendency to get stuck, but she did not know what to do if speed became a problem. When she noticed she was gaining speed at an uncomfortable rate, she took her foot off the gas, but the animal did not slow up. They careened around the corner at the cotton mills, crossed the railroad tracks at thirty miles per hour and hit a curve, skidding towards the railroad cut and a telephone post. Rob was not saying anything.

Harriette did not lose her nerve, and managed to get the car under control. By the time she got home, she knew how to work the brakes.[21]

Having a car was an accepted necessity. Rob and Dick each had one, and Ina insisted Dad keep one for family use. Richard still counted on his children to drive for him, and like Harriette, all were determined to learn to drive. The twins, both small for their age, were driving at the age of thirteen because the older boys were often too busy to take their mother places.

In December death brought dramatic change to the family. Richard's cherished sister Mary, age fifty-three, died unexpectedly of pneumonia. The loss of his Nin Tister, his homemaker, devastated Lewis, and in an effort to comfort him, Richard and Ina asked him to live with their family. Lewis accepted this offer. A few months later, Joe Quillian's wife died from influenza, as she gave birth to her third child. The child succumbed within twenty-four hours and was buried with its mother. Shocked and grieving, Joe was completely unable to cope with the older children, and so his wife's people took them. Richard and Ina offered again their home, and Joe moved in to share a room with Lewis.[22] With Rob and Dick Jr. in their old room, the house at Russell was in no danger of emptying.

One room was soon to be vacated, however, and that was Margo's. Margo had given up teaching in 1919, to work for the Federal Reserve Bank in Atlanta. Her father had approved of this change because she lived with Miss Hettie and her husband Jim Langley. Margo had flirted with the idea of marriage to Ralph Sharpton, a local man, for several years, but she had not been able to make up her mind. In addition to the disadvantage of being from Winder, Ralph did not have a profession, and Richard feared he might not have a steady income. Richard urged his daughter to take her time and wait for someone who would be more likely to give her a high standard of living. He was emphatic that all his daughters choose men with intellects and education worthy of them.[23]

In Atlanta Margo met and fell wildly in love with Jim Bowden, who also worked at the Federal Reserve Bank. Margo and Jim wanted to marry immediately, but Auntney's death caused them to put the wedding off for six months. They would marry on Richard and Ina's anniversary, June 24, 1920.

This wedding would cost Richard more than had Billie's. Ina planned to fix up her house, and Margo wanted a traditional bride's dress and an informal reception following the home ceremony. Richard again reluctantly agreed to give his blessing and his money to a daughter's marriage. His relationship with Gordon Green had developed into genuine affection, and he looked forward to other sons-in-law with confidence.[24]

Ina's sister Hattie had died in March, leaving Ina two thousand dollars, and Ina told Richard in no uncertain terms that this money was not going into political debt. She would buy a nice car, have her house painted, and perhaps even put in electric lights. Richard, embroiled in an important case with Georgia Power, would not hear of a power pole going on his land. After buying a second-hand Chalmers, Ina settled for remodeling the front part of the house so that the entrance hall and sitting room became one large room, a perfect place for the wedding altar to be set up in front of the fireplace. They would decorate the house with daisies, in memory of Auntney, who had chosen the name Marguerite for her little niece, now a bride.[25]

Richard was making more money than he had ever made, but expenses for his large family kept pace with his income. Patience, who wanted to teach, had transferred to G.N.& I.C. in the fall of 1919. Walter, an exuberant athlete and a capable farm worker who could pick cotton like an adult, was bored in Winder, and so Richard agreed to send him to Monroe A & M where he could play on the baseball team and burn up other energy in farm work. The lad excelled on the ball team, but his scholarship suffered from lack of attention. He too was homesick and begged his mother to be allowed to come home often.[26]

In July 1920, Dick Jr. announced that he was a candidate for the Barrow County seat in the Georgia General Assembly. His goal was to use this race to become better known and thus bring in more clients. He was twenty-two years old, and no one thought he had a chance against the opposition, an elderly and well-liked newspaper editor, Albert Lamar. As Dick Jr. met and talked with people, he became convinced he could win. He followed his father's example of working hard, going from house to house soliciting votes. He had inherited a wealth of his father's and his mother's charisma, and his youth, good manners, sincerity and friendliness pleased people. On September 9, he was chosen over Lamar by a vote of nearly two to one.[27]

Richard and Ina were proud of this successful race. Women were on the brink of getting the vote, and this situation may have encouraged Ina to try something she had not dreamed of doing for Richard's many contests. Billie and Gordon were visiting at home on election day, and Ina asked that Billie take her to the courthouse to hear the voting results. In town they saw men staggering drunk on the streets around the courthouse, shouting and cursing. As Billie parked their car and they were getting out, a man on the sidewalk beside them pulled a pistol and threatened to shoot another man. They got back in the car and returned home as quickly as possible. Ina vowed she never wanted to see another election night courthouse scene.[28]

It was rare that Ina admitted to being upset by the exigencies of living with five lawyers, any of whom might break out in politics. Yet sometimes she felt like running away. She had often to repeat a favorite motto to herself: "Be not weary in well doing." She and Richard shared these feelings and laughed about them as they worked to provide for their family.[29]

In the autumn Edward was hit by a car as he was trying to cross the road in front of the house late in the evening. Richard, sitting on the front porch, went to pieces when he saw Ina, Alex, William, Fielding and Carolyn running down the driveway behind their neighbor Mr. Florence Bell, who was carrying Edward. The little children were sobbing and terrified at their brother's bloody face, but Ina urged calm and hot water. When Dr. Almond arrived, he stitched up the wounded boy, and the prognosis was good that he would recover. Richard's panicked predictions that his boy might die or be paralyzed proved that he was no better at caring for a wounded child than he was at disciplining his children dispassionately.[30]

1921 was the year that Ina and Richard had their first grandchildren. Margo and Billie presented them with a granddaughter and a grandson respectively. Margo's daughter was called Marguerite Russell Bowden. Named in the fashion of the Old South, as Richard himself had been named, after the wife's father, Billie and Gordon's first son was called Richard Russell Green.

Economic woes still plagued rural and small town Georgia, but Richard Russell made enough money to keep two sons and himself solvent. He had enough to lend Billie and Gordon five hundred dollars to buy furniture, money they paid back over several years.[31]

By the autumn of 1921 two children, Patience and Walter, were causing anxiety. Both had finished school in the spring, but neither was settled. Patience had gone to Washington to help Billie and Gordon with their newborn son and was considering looking for work in the nation's capital, but she worried that her father preferred that she come home. While he joked that she was to take music and learn to play and sing to amuse him in his old age, he would not say what she should do.[32]

Walter enrolled at Oglethorpe University on the advice of his brother Dick, but did not like it because the athletic program was limited and few boys were interested in athletics. He left the school after only two days, embarrassing his parents. Richard, serving on the Board of Trustees at the University of Georgia, showed faith in the boy's character and hoped to enroll him in Athens. Walter, however, decided to go to Washington and find a job. He would live with his sister Ina until he could get settled. Three daughters and one son were now in Washington. Patience came home around Christmastime, but the others spent another cold holiday away from home. Ina Jr. was particularly depressed, likely over a love affair, and she and Walter, who may have been working in a candy factory, agreed not to think about its being Christmas.[33]

14

ALL THIS HAPPENED ON OUR PORCH

1922

In the winter of 1922 Richard Russell found even hard work could not dispel his depression and lethargy. He suffered constantly from an ailing digestive tract, but disliked seeking medical help. His friend Henry Braselton of Braselton, a prospering farm town between Winder and Gainesville, wanted to go to Hot Springs, Arkansas, for a cure, but he feared going alone. He begged the judge to go with him. Dick Jr. and Ina Sr., concerned that Dad remained blue and weary, encouraged him.[1]

He went, wishing he could have Ina with him instead of Braselton. He had taken a little law work along, to help Rob with a case, and once he had finished that, he made a business of feeling better by taking the hot baths and massages, no matter how useless he felt.

The room and board at the Lamar Hotel cost ten dollars a week. Richard thought a man as rich as Braselton would want to stay at a finer hotel, but Henry was content to room with his friend.

Almost as soon as he arrived, Richard wrote cards or letters to all his grown children and felt ashamed when he had to request that Ina send addresses. He was particularly disturbed that he did not know Ina Jr.'s address in Washington. Harriette had taken a job in a bookstore in Atlanta, and he wanted to send her a pair of Indian-made beaded moccasins but didn't know the name or address of her boarding house. He longed to see the grandchildren, and his heart warmed to overflowing as he thought of his two namesakes, Dick Jr. and Richard Russell Green.

In this time of retrospection he realized he would soon be sixty-one years old. Although he had not achieved his political goals, he had accomplished the monumental task of educating eight children who were now in the world earning their way and serving their fellow men. Most men would consider this a life's work, but he had five others to provide for and he intended to do that. He gave himself little credit for doing what a father was supposed to do. When he received five letters from these children that he and Ina called their second set, he was pleased and satisfied.

Richard hoped Walter would get more schooling and was willing to pay for it, but the father wanted the son to make up his own mind. Richard continued to give thanks for the joy of working with his two eldest sons. He had dreamed and expected R. B. would be his partner, and now he added the unexpected delight of his second son, Rob. When he compared Rob to other young men he knew, the more satisfied he was.

The patriarch watched eagerly for letters from Ina and was jealous when Braselton got more from his wife. Ina still wrote an affectionate letter, and so when one did arrive, Richard was cheered, soothed and sweetened. He continued to find deep satisfaction in his marriage and to recognize how much his wife meant to his happiness and to the success of their family.

Richard especially missed Ina's home cooking because one of the reasons for his poor health was that he had lost almost all his teeth. He would eat nothing but soft foods, which Ina prepared as he liked them, rice, grits, potatoes, turnip greens, eggs, dumplings. As he began to feel better by taking the baths, he decided to have a set of false teeth made. Patience had given him twenty dollars for that project, and he found he could have them made for less than that amount.

Letters from Rob and Dick Jr. cheered their father. Rob wrote affectionately, while Dick Jr. gave news of the death of one of Russell's important farmers, Leet [Leak?] Smith. Richard's eldest son was sure Mr. Smith had succumbed because he gave up his determination to live. The unspoken and worried message to Dad was obvious.[2]

Richard returned from Hot Springs determined to live and live well. He went back to work with vigor and the family breathed easier. Ina may have thought the only politics she would have to deal with was Dick Jr.'s re-election to the House, and opposition looked doubtful. Papa had not mentioned running for any office in several years, and because his practice was lucrative and interesting, she may have dared to dream that he was through with politics.

On the last day in June, in the evening, Richard was in his office in Atlanta with Walter Brown and other friends, discussing the summer political scene. The primary was set for September 9, and June 30 was the last day to qualify. The current governor, Thomas Hardwick, had been elected in 1920 over Clifford Walker. In that election Hardwick had supported the revived Ku Klux Klan while Walker opposed it. Klan support carried the day. In 1922 the tables were turned. As governor, Hardwick had denounced the Klan's activities and in 1922 faced opposition from Walker again, now an avowed Klan fan. It looked like a hard and bitter fight.

Perhaps Walter Brown, remembering Richard's courage at stepping into a campaign against two strong adversaries in 1906, regretted that there was no office open to him. But wait. There was an office for which Richard was eminently qualified, which should by rights be his some day. It seemed unfair that in all likelihood its current holder would live long enough to be re-elected, then die in office. Then the governor would appoint the chief justice of the Supreme Court of the state of Georgia, as he had when Richard ran and lost against a failing Simmons in 1904. Simmons died shortly after his re-election, and William Fish was appointed. Eighteen years later Chief Justice Fish was elderly and in frail health, but it was not custom to run against a sitting justice. Thus, Richard would again miss his chance.

As Richard and Walter talked, the old passion stirred. Could he convince the people of Georgia that electing him chief justice was in the interest of democracy? Could we say that when the chief justice is appointed, the people are denied their right to elect him? And if the General Assembly has decreed that judges should be elected, well, let's elect them. Why shouldn't everyone have the right to run for any office at any time? It would not do to criticize Fish. Keeping the argument clearly in favor of younger blood and democracy would be a challenge in persuasion. Election would cost money, if it was even possible. But if elected, he would have achieved at least one of the dreams he had dreamed as a young man who wanted to serve his state and gain personal glory.

Richard got out a map of Georgia and considered how many friends he could count on to help in each county. He had been more than ten years out of state-wide races, but he knew his friends were steadfast. One thing he had wanted from youth was to make good friends, and he was satisfied that even if he had not been elected to high executive office, no man, governor or not, had better friends than he had. He also had money in the bank and had paid off the old political debts. He could afford to finance the campaign without borrowing.[3]

The idea produced instant intoxication. With Walter Brown urging him on, he paid his one hundred and fifty dollar qualifying fee shortly before the midnight deadline.

The sudden decision took everyone by surprise, not least his family. Ina dreaded another defeat, but the young men did not question their father's decision. They set up campaign headquarters in Atlanta and went to work to elect Papa. About the only thing Ina could rejoice in was that they bought two new cars, and Richard promised they would keep one after the election. Lewis, as surprised as anyone, took over managing the campaign, with Rob and Dick Jr. as first assistants.[4]

Richard made his formal announcement on July 4. In a carefully prepared statement he addressed the criticisms he was certain would come.

It had already been said by this time that "the Judge" was coming back to the public trough. Critics liked to show how many public offices he had held, encouraging the idea that he was sponging, and occasionally Lewis was brought in as sidekick sucker.[5] Richard pointed out that if it was money he was after, he would stay with his law practice, which was much more remunerative than the seven thousand per annum judge's salary. He was running for this office because he wanted to serve. From his Court of Appeals experience, he knew the hard labor involved, but it was a burden he was willing to shoulder because he knew he was qualified and could serve well.

Against the argument that removing a sitting justice who was doing a satisfactory job was unfair, Richard Russell brought measured democratic vocabulary. Any office within the gift of the people to confer must be open to any one at any time. To deny that a sitting justice could be challenged was to withdraw hope from aspiring youth. It was to check the stream of democratic principles and close the door of hope upon those who, no matter how worthy, are unfortunately not possessed of either prestige, influence or money.

There was the perpetual argument to address that the people are not qualified to elect judges. Advocates of this view recommended judges be appointed by the governor or perhaps by a board of lawyers appointed by the governor. To this argument Russell said simply that if the people were not qualified to select a chief justice, how could they be qualified to elect a governor who would then select the judge?

Conscious that all the associates justices had come out for Chief Justice Fish and that they were canvassing the legal community for support, Richard trod that narrow ledge with care:

> I appreciate beyond my powers of expression many old and written evidences of the confidence and affection of hundreds of my friends among the lawyers of this State. I am proud to be a member of the profession. I have been glad to be at many times of service to my younger brethren of the bar, but I am far too much interested in the old land marks and in the future safety of democratic institutions and of popular democratic government to make an appeal merely to the lawyers of the State, or to fail to deny that the question is one for their sole determination. Every clean, honest and fair-minded voter of this State, man or woman, has the same right to pass judgment upon me as has any other.[6]

As the campaign geared up, the men realized there was a new element in it. For the first time in statewide election, the women of Georgia would have the chance to vote. No one knew how many would vote, but estimates of up to 60,000 women voters meant it was risky to ignore them. Examining Richard's life and work, they found they had a candidate who ought to appeal to women, and they lost no time in publicizing his sponsorship of the girls' school in Milledgeville, his appointment of the first woman to the staff of the Court of Appeals, and his early support of women's suffrage, claimed to go as far back as the gubernatorial campaign of 1906.[7]

Harriette Brumby Russell and Ina Dillard Russell, key women in Richard's life, were promoted as exemplary women of intellect, making their contributions to the good of the future through their influence over their children. No less a personage than Rebecca Felton, Georgia's distinguished and long-time "woman in politics," came out for Richard partly on the grounds of his mother and his wife. Felton, whose husband, Congressman William Felton, had been the leader of the Independent Democrats during the late 1870s and early 1880s, had continued an active political life even after the Independents waned and her husband left politics. Eighty-seven years old, she wrote a popular column for the Atlanta papers.

That Richard Russell was eminently qualified in his knowledge and experience of the law, Rebecca Felton had no doubt. Yet more important to her were the excellent qualities that undergirded his qualifications, and these she attributed to the work of his mother: his interest in mankind; his integrity and honest purpose; his brotherly kindness; and his resolve to deal justly with the poor and the ignorant as well as the opulent and the influential. Felton quoted Richard with great approval: "I owe everything to my mother. She made me what I am. I ask nothing better for my own children than for them to be such characters as my honored wife and my blessed Mother."[8]

Although some of the campaign claims regarding his support of the Equal Rights Amendment and votes for women seem a little far-fetched, it is certain that Richard Russell had genuine respect for women. Once they received the vote, he was willing to appeal to them as he did to the men, with intelligent arguments and the force of his character.

The family rallied as the summer rolled on, and with several grown children on hand, the workload could be spread a little thinner than in campaigns past. Billie and Gordon were stationed at Fort Benning, so they worked hard in Muskogee County, strong Fish territory. Pat, Margo, and Harriette worked in Atlanta in the campaign headquarters. They wrote to former schoolmates at G.N.&I.C. as well as helping with the general campaign mailings. Busy in the legislature, Dick Jr. nevertheless spent hours at his father's campaign headquarters, writing his friends and helping with strategy. Rob drove all over the state with his father as he made speeches. Lewis continued his indefatigable work writing and typing. In addition, they hired several part-time stenographers. The money spent on this campaign proves that Richard Russell had done well in his law practice. The law practices of all the lawyers suffered, but this development would have to be counted an expense of the campaign.[9]

Walter was spending the summer working on a freighter out of Philadelphia, bound for Brazil, scheduled to return in the autumn. He found life on the freighter, where everyone else spoke Portuguese, less romantic than he had imagined. Home looked better than ever. When he learned of his dad's campaign, he wrote telling of his unhappiness and asking if he was needed at home. Richard's brother Rob had arranged Walter's job, and Richard wanted Walter to stick out that contract. He wrote a brief reply that concluded: "When you come to the end of a rope, son, tie a knot and hang on."[10]

Later in the summer Dick Jr. went as his father's driver on speech-making tours. He was up for re-election himself, but no one in Barrow County had come forward to challenge him. One of the most important outcomes of the campaign would be the friendships young Dick made with his father's friends all over the state. Richard had said for years that he wanted his political career to serve his son, and although he was not perhaps thinking at this moment of helping Dick Jr., in fact, he was helping him build his own career.

Rumblings that the Women's Christian Temperance Union was coming out actively against Richard reached the Russell headquarters. Because of what had happened in 1911, this news sickened Richard, Rob and Dick Jr. Prohibition was the law of the land by this time, and the issue of local option was as dead as slavery, but they feared an emotional appeal against Judge Russell, however illogical, could be successful.

When the W.C.T.U. came out endorsing Justice Fish, there was nothing to do but write Aunt Lella for help. An eloquent and diplomatic woman, Lella had, with her family grown, turned more and more to her crusade. Her influence in the W.C.T.U. had increased with the advent of prohibition. Surely she could talk some sense into these women who were trying to make an issue of nothing.

Dick Jr. and Rob, who had held Lella responsible in some vague way for their father's defeat in 1911, were loathe to make this appeal. Dick Jr. asked his mother to write but said that she must not in any way humble herself. Ina wrote to Lella, but she also wrote back to Dick and Rob telling them how hard they made things for her. For once, the pain politics brought to her life was showing. She wrote: "I have grieved over Rob's hostility and haughty spirit and fierce criticisms—just because somebody didn't think as he did. Papa has been harsh & hurt me so, in things he would say about aunt Lella. Aunt Lella gave papa the opportunity of running on her ticket. He didn't believe that way. I don't see that she could well be for him. But I don't believe she ever said one ugly thing about him & many men did, that you all are friendly with now."[11]

Richard himself wrote a sensible letter to Lella, and he wrote to Walter Dillard, appealing to common sense. This was a dead issue, but even if it were not, a judge does not make law. He is bound to uphold the laws that there are, and this is what Richard had always done and would continue to do. Not only that, but the Supreme Court did not deal with liquor questions. That was the prerogative of the Court of Appeals. There was no sense whatsoever in failing to elect him because he had favored local option ten years ago.[12]

Although he had heard the associate justices and their stenographers were furiously writing to people all over the state to support Fish, Richard felt confident as the election neared. They had worked hard, and the mood of the people seemed to be to listen to what he had to say and to consider that he was younger and more vigorous than Fish. He pointed out that even in six years, he would not be considered, at sixty-seven, an old man. The best thing was to give Fish a much-needed and deserved vacation and put Russell to work instead.[13]

On September 9 every adult in the family except Ina went to the Atlanta headquarters. She stayed home with the younger children, feeling a little pitiful. William was away at Monroe A & M. Thus she had only four children at home: Fielding, Edward, Alex and Carolyn. Pat might have come to stay with her on election night, but she had taken a job teaching in Cochran, Georgia.

The night before the election, with the children asleep, Ina sat upstairs writing, near the sleepers, because she did not like to stay downstairs alone. She thought of all the hard work her husband and sons had put in. She trembled to think they might again be disappointed. She did not see how any of them would stand it if Richard were not elected.[14]

At the end of election day Ina went to prayer meeting at the Presbyterian Church, accompanied by Alice and Jack Stickney, distant Brumby cousins and friends of Lewis. Coming home through town, they stopped for the local news, in spite of Ina's fear of election night antics. Jack phoned the *Athens Banner* and received word from the Associated Press that "Russell was sweeping the state." Ina arrived home feeling hopeful and happy.

The papers next morning verified her hopes, and spirits soared in Winder and in Russell. It was eleven at night before some of her family showed up from the Atlanta office. Richard, Harriette and Walter, just home from Brazil, came in, and Ina was no doubt kissed by the chief justice-elect. She was reserved with Richard before the children, but he tended to search her out when he first got home for a hug and a kiss, wherever she was in the house. That evening he would not have to search far or show too much restraint. They stayed up talking until one o'clock.[15]

The next morning word came to Ina that the people of Winder were planning an ovation to honor Richard in the evening and could she be sure he was there and perhaps not digging dirt? Ina expected a few ladies and at most fifty men. About seven o'clock more family came in from Atlanta: Jim, Marguerite and baby, Rob, Lewis, and Walter Brown. Within an hour ladies from Winder, headed by Ina's friend Sunie Johns, descended on her kitchen and ran her out. She was to go to the front of the house and greet guests and not worry about a thing. She did as she was told, delighted, walking on air.[16]

The crowds came pouring in. One hundred ladies congratulated Ina, and four times that many men stood in the yard and on the porch, eager to shake hands with the new judge. Richard beamed as his friends rejoiced over his success. The old feud was shelved as Winder and

Barrow County took pride in their native son. Truckloads of refreshments arrived—tubs of lemonade and punch, boxes of cakes and cookies. Soon trays laden with drink and food were going the rounds, and Ina had as much fun as she would have had at someone else's home, where she would have had no responsibility for the crowd.

Before long the governor-elect, Clifford Walker, from nearby Walton County, arrived to congratulate his friend, and this distinguished arrival pleased the crowd. Ina graciously welcomed Mrs. Walker, and Richard and Ina were overjoyed that the governor-elect had thought to bring William. Walker's brother, the head of Monroe A & M, had been glad to release the boy for this celebration.

One hundred ladies in her house did not bother Ina so much, but when she looked outside and saw a sea of faces in the yard, all turned towards her husband on the porch, one hundred and fifty cars parked along the road and in the fields, she gasped. The crowd was called to order by G. A. Johns. The judge was going to speak.

G. A. Johns was Ina's friend Sunie's husband. Richard, as a judge, had married them in 1900.[17] Johns, a successful businessman, had opposed Richard on the forming of the county, and his presence as master of ceremonies was a clear indicator of the improvement of relations between Winder and Russell.

Johns hailed the chief justice-elect and Richard began to speak, animated by victory, not hopes of success. The response of the crowd was thrilling. They clapped, laughed—the judge could always make them laugh—cheered and threw hats into the air, celebrating the triumph of their friend and neighbor.

Sitting just inside the front door, listening and rejoicing, Ina marveled that her Richard was at last getting the recognition he craved and she believed he deserved. That it was all happening on their front porch gave her a feeling of being a part of history.

It was a special pleasure to hear Johns note, after Richard's speech, that on this porch there were representatives from all three branches of state government. They had heard from the judicial. From the executive he introduced Governor-elect Walker, who spoke briefly, since, he said, it was Richard's ovation. He was only a guest come to pay his respects to the chief justice-elect. Then Johns introduced the representative of the legislative branch, Dick Russell Jr., who also made a lively speech. One thousand two hundred and forty-seven Barrow Countians, the total vote, had approved his re-election. His father got eleven hundred votes, and Ina said she did not want to know the one hundred and forty-seven who voted against him.

Walter Brown, devoted friend, spoke last, happy and proud over this successful end to years of arduous struggle. It was fitting that he have the last word on such a triumphant evening.

Richard now turned his attention to closing down his law practice in time for the January 1923 court term. Family responsibilities and interests did not abate. Walter wanted to return to the University and did. Marguerite and Billie were both expecting babies again.

Rob was courting a popular Barrow County woman, Sybil Millsaps, a grade-school teacher who had been Pat's roommate at G.N.&I.C. When Richard met Sybil, he said, "I want Dick or Rob to marry that girl. I don't care which one marries her, but we've got to have her in the family." Rob looked set to make this happen in June of 1923.

Frightful news came about three weeks after the election when an *Atlanta Constitution* front page story reported that Patience Russell had been injured in a car accident near Macon. Ina and Richard took this news hard, especially coming from the papers, instead of first-hand. They had only the day before heard that Walter was among the students who climbed the water tower in Athens to paint "[Class of] 26" on it, and had been giving thanks that he was safe. They wondered what Patience was doing in Macon, a long way from Cochran, but were afraid to ask. Later they learned that Pat had gone with a date and another couple to a concert in Macon. They had properly invited a chaperone who, having been thrown from the car, was the worst hurt in the accident. Pat suffered a broken arm, the first broken bone among Richard and Ina's numerous chicks.[18]

Lewis received a unique opportunity at this time. Tom Watson, serving in the U. S. Senate from Georgia, died on September 26, and in a special election, Walter George was elected to replace him. Lewis was employed by George to be his Executive Secretary and went to Washington in

November. Governor Hardwick appointed the first woman U. S. Senator, Georgia's Rebecca Felton, prior to George's taking his seat. Felton served two days in the U. S. Senate before George was sworn in. Lewis was present at this historic occasion and enjoyed recounting the scene to his brothers. The picture of a grand old Southern dame receiving her due had to be pleasing to sons of Harriette Brumby Russell. Lewis enjoyed going to dinner with Georgia's Senators George and Harris. When he felt he had to attend a United Daughters of the Confederacy dance, he took his niece Ina, proud that she was a good-looking, diminutive young woman of wit and fine spirits.[19]

When he took office in January, Richard Russell would be facing five associate justices who had hoped to prevent his election. If he was nervous or anxious at all, he did not show it. He dug dirt avidly in December, but no one could say if it was an unusual amount. He was likely more worried about Marguerite's' confinement and was relieved when on December 22, 1922, she gave him, without complications or dangerous passage, another granddaughter, Jane Mayo Bowden.[20]

15

IN THE SIXTY-FIFTH YEAR
OF MY LIFE

1923-1926

When Richard Russell went to Atlanta to assume the mantle of chief justice of the Georgia Supreme Court, he was the first man ever elected to that office without previous appointment. His predecessor was an able and illustrious jurist, and the five associate justices, Marcus W. Beck, Samuel Atkinson, H. Warner Hill, S. Price Gilbert, and James K. Hines, had not hesitated to support William Fish in the election. Hines was Fish's brother-in-law. Yet there was no hint of trouble as the new chief justice took office. The other justices had confidence in Russell's ability because of his excellent service on the Court of Appeals. Like many others in the state, they admired his spirited ambition and determination to succeed in the campaign. His treatment of his opponent had been exemplary in the judicial tradition of honoring fellow judges. They soon learned that his reputation for courtesy, kindness and harmonious dealing was well-deserved. He became an admirer of Justice Hines, who was a soul-mate in many ways. Hines had also been disappointed in gubernatorial aspirations, and they discovered they were kin through William John Russell's grandmother, Druscilla Hines. Russell believed Hines knew the law better than anyone he had ever known.[1]

Richard continued commuting to Atlanta, usually staying the week at the Kimball Hotel, although sometimes he took the train each day. His son Rob became his stenographer, and the two men worked well together. It was not easy for Rob, working for his father in these circumstances, but he was determined to broaden his knowledge of the law and knew there was no better school than this one.[2]

Rob also had another reason for taking a job in Atlanta. When Sybil Millsaps became his bride on June 27, 1923, he became the first son to marry. The wedding was the social event of Winder's spring season as two of the county's prominent families joined forces. Lewis lent the young couple his car for a honeymoon to Asheville, North Carolina, and they were delighted to report they did not have a flat tire during the entire trip. They moved into a small house in Atlanta, on Glen Iris Drive, opposite Marguerite and Jim Bowden. The young couple enjoyed such conveniences as electricity and running water, and Rob was not going to follow Dad's example of leaving home all week. Richard glowed approval of this match and thereafter called Sybil his daughter, rarely his daughter-in-law.[3]

Governor Clifford Walker appointed Lewis Russell the first judge of the new Piedmont Superior Court Circuit in 1923, and Lewis left his work with Senator George to take the place. Both brothers seemed pleased with another Judge Russell.

In the autumn of 1923, Richard and his brothers were reunited in Russell. It was the first time in twenty years that they had been together, and they used the time to take a sentimental journey to Princeton. The *Athens Banner* ran an article on the reunion and listed their accomplishments as a patriarchal tribute to William John Russell, whose one hundredth anniversary was part of the celebration.[4]

In 1924 Richard toyed briefly with the idea of running for the US Senate, perhaps dreaming that the strength of his broad electoral base in the chief justice campaign would elect him. Political and family reasons constrained him. He might have ignored the fact that William J. Harris, elected in 1918, seemed scarcely vulnerable, but Lewis was up for election to an endorsement term, and W. W. Stark, a friend of Richard's since 1888, was opposing him. The campaign was certain to be rigorous. Ina may have threatened him with breach of promise if he got into another campaign so soon after telling everyone he wanted to be chief justice as the capstone of his career.[5]

Richard could not campaign for his brother beyond asking friends to vote for him, but the rest of the family worked hard for Lewis. Rob, Dick and Joe Quillian all got involved, and by the end of the summer they were looking haggard and discouraged. A political cartoon showed five Russells at the public trough, with Little Lewis standing by. Greedily gobbling government gold are Plain Dick, his brother John, his sons Dick and Robert, and "Major" Russell— an erroneous reference to naval captain brother Rob. Just how John is "drawing government pay" is not clear. Rob is labeled "secretary to Papa Dick at large salary." Why "Major" Russell does not deserve a retirement pension after forty years in the navy is not explained.[6] Inaccurate and unfair as such material could be, the figure of fun it made of the younger brother and of the family must have been hurtful. Stark defeated Lewis and became the new judge of the Piedmont Circuit.

Crushed by this defeat, sensitive to being dubbed a "little" Russell (he was fifty-two), Lewis left Georgia. Suffering financial difficulties, he hoped to make more money by going to Florida to sell insurance and real estate. At about the same time, Joe Quillian remarried and moved back into Winder.

The only other lawyer left in Richard's home was his son Dick Jr., who was gaining a reputation as an effective criminal lawyer. He was not making much money at this work in a small rural community, though some of the cases filled the town with excitement as people interested in the verdicts poured into town during court week.[7] He had also been elected Speaker Pro Tem of the Georgia House in 1923, and this chance to preside over the House from time to time increased his popularity. He enjoyed law and politics as much as his father had, and, gifted with an abundance of talent in both fields, through heredity and environment, he was a political force to watch in Georgia.[8]

School expenses had let up a little for Richard Sr. until Walter enrolled at the University of Georgia in 1923-1924. After a year, however, his third son decided to go to work fulltime in the Washington, DC area. He found work that interested him through Brumby relatives associated with the A&P Company. Walter lived with his sister Ina and tried going to school at George Washington University at night, but soon his ambition to excel in business took him out of school. Richard did not get along as well with Walter as he did with his two older sons. Walter was more rebellious, high-tempered and adventurous. To his contemporaries he referred to his father as "the old man." Richard remained affectionate in spite of disagreements with this son, and after Walter went to work fulltime, his father agreed to help him pay tuition if he wanted to go back to school. Richard backed his belief in the importance of education with genuine offers of help. He repeatedly told his children that he did not want them, whether dependents or adults, to want for anything as long as he had anything they truly needed.[9]

Fielding, Edward, Alex and Carolyn were doing well in high school, definitely college bound. Richard Russell was going to need plenty of tuition money.

Only one of Richard and Ina's children showed no interest in school. William struggled with academics, falling behind his twin brother in school promotions so that as Fielding was starting the tenth grade, William was determined to finish the eighth.[10] He was a bright lad, hard-working and good-humored, but he had inherited no intellectual bent. He enjoyed farming and got along especially well with the black people who worked his father's land. He was a favorite of his siblings for his quick wit and his generous spirit. In 1924 he went to Florida with his uncle Lewis and took a job in a café in St. Petersburg. He was only seventeen. His parents accepted his different way of looking at life, but dedicated to education as they were, they worried about his ability to provide for himself. Richard wrote affectionate letters to William, reminding him frequently that he was named for the dearest, best man in the world, William John Russell, his grandfather. He sometimes called William his "daddy," which he may have thought would give the lad a feeling of being needed and of being a provider.[11]

The patriarch enjoyed his older daughters as they matured into responsible and successful women. Billie gave him another granddaughter Mary Nancy in 1923, and as the decade wore on, it became one of his great pleasures to go to Washington each year in May to the American Law Institute meetings, when he reveled in time with Billie and Gordon's family. He sometimes had lunch with Marguerite and Sybil in Atlanta. Harriette and Pat took an apartment together in Atlanta where Pat was teaching and Harriette working at Coles Book

Store. Richard eyed this venture of two young, unmarried and attractive women with a patriarch's watchful eye. He volunteered to help pay the rent, and after he had paid, he let them know this meant he was part lessor and could show up at their door at anytime, day or night.[12]

When he thought about these beautiful young women he called his daughters, he was surprised to feel that he loved them perhaps more than he loved his sons, for whom he had longed. He felt close kinship with his daughters and was delighted that they had pluck, ingenuity and ambition, and were not at all dependent and weak. Yet they possessed traits of modesty, affection, and tenderness, as much as any woman should. He felt puzzled yet pleased that he could think that they no longer depended on him and that he could lean on them when the shadows lengthened.[13]

Richard still enjoyed the social events of the Atlanta Athletic and Piedmont Driving clubs, where he spent time with people of wealth and influence that his limited income would not otherwise have afforded him. He became active in the Burns Club, a group to celebrate the Scottish poet Robert Burns, sponsored by his friend Joe Jacobs. Jacobs built a replica of the poet's humble home, where the meetings took place, as well as gala dinners.[14] Richard had dropped his Royal Arcanum and other fraternal activities while he was practicing law, and these new clubs gave him another sphere in which to shine. He was at ease with people from all social strata, and lack of money had never made him feel inferior. Ina found it difficult to leave home with her teenage boys and girl active in the local high school, so sometimes Marguerite, Pat or Harriette, or all three, accompanied Richard to dinners and dances at the Driving or Athletic Club.[15]

Another development important to his family during the Twenties was that Richard Russell began to go back to church. Not long after the 1911 election, when Richard was embittered by the stand churchmen had taken against him, particularly the Methodists, Ina had encouraged her older children to go to the Presbyterian church if they could do so in good conscience. She hoped some day Richard would be persuaded to join the family. Her dream came true in 1923.[16]

The younger children had become active in the Presbyterian church, and the young bachelor preacher there, Taylor Morton, was a family favorite. It was rare for a Sunday dinner to take place in the Russell house without Morton. He further endeared himself as leader of an active Scout group in which Fielding, William, Alex and Edward gloried. When the five younger children and Ina joined the Presbyterian church at a revival meeting, even though he refused Ina's request that he join then, Richard must have felt an old tug.[17]

Morton may have sensed this, and the young preacher asked the venerable judge to speak at a union service of all Winder churches held to welcome a new minister at the Christian church. Ina rejoiced that the church was full and silence reigned while Richard was talking. She glowed with pleasure as her husband spoke eloquently and sincerely. After the service he was surrounded by his friends, and warm words flowed. His brothers Rob and Lewis were there to share in this long-desired return of a slightly lost lamb. This attention and the forgiveness of old Winder wounds warmed his heart. Before long Taylor Morton and Lewis had persuaded Richard to teach the Presbyterian men's Sunday school class. These activities endeared him more than ever to Ina. She was never happier than when they sat in church together, holding hands.[18]

Richard Russell had not ceased to be a believer in Christ as the Savior of mankind, and his grandfather's and his mother's early training in biblical scholarship and 'awful truth' stayed with him. He surprised contemporaries with his knowledge of the Bible and his skill in teaching. No doubt he wanted to serve as a better example to his children by returning to church, and long years of judicial service had convinced him that religious training was an important part of the solution of crime problems. Nevertheless, in his deepest heart, he never forgave the church as an organization for meddling in politics, particularly his own.[19]

On December 7, 1924, a disaster struck one of Richard Russell's favorite children, his beloved Georgia Normal and Industrial College, renamed the Georgia State College for Women in 1922 when it gained four-year college status. A horrific fire destroyed the main building, where the blaze was so intense that for fear other buildings would catch eight hundred girls housed in nearby dormitories had to be marched out in the winter night. The fire destroyed twenty-one classrooms, the auditorium and the administrative offices. They lost all official papers, including student records.[20] When the word reached Richard Russell early next morning, he sent Rob to telegraph President Marvin Parks that he was on his way. He caught the first train to Milledgeville.[21]

Richard began serving on the board of directors of the school about 1915.[22] In 1918, he became chairman, following a bitter political battle in which President Parks was so severely criticized by state-wide forces that the educator felt it necessary to make a protest resignation. The response of friends from all over the state persuaded him to withdraw it. People in middle Georgia feared University of Georgia board members, who by law served on the G.N.&I.C. board of directors, would take control of state school funds and channel most to the Athens and Atlanta area. Mourning the election of Richard Russell as Chair in 1918, the *Macon Telegraph* declared he was a "dyed in the wool [University of] Georgia man."[23]

Richard Russell loved the university as his alma mater and served willingly and ably on its Board of Trustees, but the girls school was his particular pride. Its protector, he trusted no one else to look after her interests as he would, and he used all his political skills to bring harmony to this situation. When he addressed the student body at the 1919 graduation exercises, his speech praising Dr. Parks brought down the house and reassured students, faculty and the public. He promised to win funds for a new dorm and a large auditorium, a promise he and Parks would make good in three years.[24]

Richard Russell had great respect for the ability and character of Marvin Parks and enjoyed his company as a friend. He loved to go to Milledgeville to visit "the bevy of beauties" there, and to have dinner with Dr. and Mrs. Parks. He said he hoped his association with Parks and his work would be in later years a claim to fame. He praised Parks as the only man in Georgia who could "get $1.50 out of every $1.00 placed in his trust."[25] Examination of the records of school finances and advancement under Parks prove this statement is hardly an exaggeration.

When Russell arrived in Milledgeville on December 8, the two leaders so devoted to the college may have wept, but they were determined to apply the phoenix principle to the situation. Russell called a meeting of the board of directors for December 10 at the Piedmont

Hotel. At this meeting, Parks pledged one thousand dollars of his own money and Russell pledged four hundred to a recovery fund. Following the example of these two men, who were in nowise wealthy, other citizens soon contributed enough to establish the fund with ten thousand dollars. Local leaders offered churches, the courthouse and nearby buildings for temporary classrooms.[26]

Richard Russell continued to chair the board of directors of the school, to feel strong paternal pride in its growth and accomplishments, and to cherish his friendship with Parks. A new auditorium had been completed in the autumn of 1926 but not yet named when another tragedy occurred. Marvin Parks was struck and killed by a car on the streets of Tampa, Florida. The death of this leader had a profound effect on the small, closely knit campus. Richard Russell shared the grief, mourning the loss of a great educator and friend. In the memorial edition of the school paper, *The Colonnade*, he wrote of Parks as an outstanding educator of the South, who was perhaps better known in more homes in Georgia "than any man who lived in this commonwealth. Dr. Parks possessed to an unexampled degree the heart touch of sweet sentiment which makes the whole world kin. He was the most manifold man I have ever met. He was an intense student, a great scholar, a profound philosopher, a splendid teacher, yet at home in important matters of financial business." One of the most eloquent tributes came from Marguerite Russell Bowden, President of the Atlanta Alumnae Club: "There is not a member of our club who does not realize her life is bigger and better because he lived."[27]

Richard Russell lent a strong helping hand to the new president, J. Luther Beeson, and soon developed an effective working relationship with him.[28] The students voted to raise money for a much-needed infirmary to be named for Dr. Parks (there was already a classroom building named for him), and by May 1927 alumnae contributions proved sufficient for construction preparations to begin. The Parks Memorial Infirmary was dedicated at the 1928 commencement exercises. In the meantime, the new auditorium was named for Richard Russell. It is hard to imagine anything that could have pleased him more.

Russell family life continued with its boisterous catalog of perils and pleasures. In early 1925 the family trembled as Rob nearly succumbed to pneumonia. On February 25, he was recovering as his wife Sybil presented him with Robert Lee Russell Jr. Fielding entered the University of Georgia in the autumn of 1925, and Richard carried him to Athens to begin his studies. He was to room with a Brumby cousin, Bell Brumby, who ran a boarding house. Young Fielding was chagrined when his father introduced him around campus as "his Phi Beta Kappa son." He had not realized that to be the son of the chairman of the board of trustees carried a heavy weight of expectation. Fielding idolized his father, and looked to him as a role model for grit and determination. Richard, however, did not think Fielding was cut out for the law and hoped that he would become a doctor. Fielding thus began his collegiate career as a science major.[29]

The judge continued to dig dirt with vigor. With the proliferation of automobile travel, he became a familiar sight in Barrow County along the roadsides in Russell. Friends shouted hellos to him and he might hear them or not. Sometimes they stopped to chat and tease him about being preoccupied "mulling over cases," and he did not take this as a joke. He said that was exactly what he was doing.[30] He frequently now noted his advancing age and would announce at Christmas and birthdays that he likely would not see another year. Fielding, Edward and Alex thought this a huge joke from a vigorous dirt shoveler. He had tried to inspire all his sons with love of this work, but he could not get them to do it without pay. His solution was to make cash for trips, dances and gifts depend on how much dirt they had dug to help Papa's projects. They groaned over the areas he marked out to be leveled before money was forthcoming.[31]

In the spring of 1926, Richard Russell received a singular honor. At the request of his friend the pharmacist Joe Jacobs, he was the featured speaker at the dedication of the statue of Crawford W. Long in the nation's Statuary Hall. Each state chose two representatives and Georgians had chosen Long and Alexander H. Stephens, but no statue had been set for either man. The state itself could not spend money on anything outside government, and so Jacobs spearheaded a drive for funds to provide a statue of Long. Jacobs had worked for Long in the

Athens of his and Richard's youth, and his veneration of the physician bordered on adoration. Because he was the instigator of and inspiration for the statue and because of his wealth and influence, he was the first choice to be the principal speaker, but he asked Dick Russell to take his place. He knew how much it would mean to his friend to give such a speech, and he knew that the speech would be elegant and appropriate.[32]

As Richard Russell studied those heroes whom other states had chosen, he noted that most were statesmen or military leaders. As the life of Marvin Parks had shown him, he saw that Long's contribution to mankind, though it had not brought wealth or fame in the conventional sense, was the most outstanding kind of contribution. He concluded that contributions that cross boundaries of state or nation and answer to needs of all the world are indeed the highest worship of Almighty God.[33]

In June Richard Russell surprised everyone by announcing that he would run for the Senate seat held by Walter George. In examining George's record, Richard Russell became enraged over issues of the World Court and relief to farmers. He believed that George had made a perfidious compromise in fostering an agreement that the United States would join the Court under certain circumstances, and the judge did not care that they were about as likely to occur as King George V was to become President of the United States. He saw the Court as a treacherous rearranging of the League of Nations. In addition, it seemed to him that George, a senator from an agricultural state, had done nothing to help the farmer, and he feared he would do nothing because of his associations with business interests such as railroads, power companies and banks. He pleaded with four other politicians to oppose the senator, but all declined to run. So intense were his feelings that on the last day to qualify, he stepped into a fight in which he was bound to get beat up pretty bad.[34]

The judge's announcement may have caused consternation in George's camp, which was not expecting opposition.[35] In the judge's family it was met with dark despair. Dick Jr. and Rob, who would be expected to run the campaign, were embarrassed to be going against a man whose popularity was on the rise and whose record they did not criticize. Lewis was grateful to be in Florida, unavailable to wage political battles against his former employer. Ina, after nearly a dozen

campaigns, was wearied to the bone. She said little, but she lobbied for
all the children to come home for the last days of the campaign so that
there could be a joyous family reunion to offset what was almost certain
defeat. She particularly wanted to try for a complete family photo.

In the Russell family, arguments with patriarchal decisions did not
last long. By July 4, when Richard formally announced his candidacy,
they had rallied, and a long hot summer of campaigning ensued. [36]

The Senate Campaign of 1926 was not as well financed as the
earlier chief justice race. By 1922 Richard had paid off old debts from
his lucrative years of law practice, but in the years since, he had
continued to buy land and family expenses remained demanding.[37] On a
judge's salary of seven thousand dollars per annum, not much was left
for a campaign fund. Rob and Dick ran a tight ship from an office in
Atlanta, where Alex and Walter also worked. One "lady stenographer"
was hired for this office.

Fielding, nearly nineteen, and Jeb, only sixteen, took the job of
driving Dad through Georgia to speaking engagements. Richard had lent
William eight hundred dollars to open a café in St. Petersburg, so there
was no question that he could leave this business. Richard was proud to
point out that he had little money, but that his six sons were forming a
capable staff, without pay. In Washington, Gordon Green took time to go
to the Senate and listen to George's speeches and report anything he
thought might be helpful. Billie wrote letters to GSCW alumnae, and
Marguerite, Harriette and Pat must have done the same. Once again
family formed the fortress from which he fought.[38]

Although ready to serve Papa, Fielding and Edward, now called Jeb
by everyone but his mother and father, were not political enthusiasts.
Fielding thought it prudent to devise an elaborate code for telegramming
news from where Dad was speaking, aimed at preventing anyone's
figuring out whether the crowd was good, enthusiastic, or abusive, and
whether Dad was well or sick. Usually, however, Fielding found politics
boring.[39] Jeb, who thought he might become a Presbyterian minister,
observed the scene with an honest eye. He judged George well-organized
and powerful, but took heart in his father's wealth of friends. Listening to
his father's tales of previous campaigns, he suggested what might be
done in this one to avoid the pitfall of newspaper articles predicting

victory for George. Richard Sr. had seen in 1911 how newspaper accounts of victory for Joe Brown had swung undecided votes in the last days of the race. Jeb wrote that they must be sure to give out positive statements about how the race was going. He did not use the code but wrote a personal letter, sitting under a tree in the car, listening to other political candidates "cuss" each other.[40]

Dick and Rob, on the other hand, were soon caught up in the kind of fight they relished. They had never taken intimate part in a campaign in which their father or Dick Jr. had been defeated, so the euphoria of remembered victory spurred them. Nevertheless, family history assured they knew that in politics, the specter of defeat haunts every race. As the summer wore on, it must have become apparent that their father did not have a whisper of a chance, yet they followed Jeb's advice and proclaimed loudly their confidence of winning in all official statements from the campaign headquarters and in correspondence to others who confessed fear of defeat.[41]

Dick Jr. had no opposition for re-election to his house seat, but he was campaigning to become Speaker of the House in the 1927 legislature. His mother worried that his race might suffer because of Papa's, but in fact, the young man found time, as he accompanied his father on speaking engagements or went places to speak for him, to campaign in his own behalf for the Speaker post. He had many friends who were supporting him in this goal, and he made new friends among his father's acquaintances, all of whom were quietly gathering support to elect him to one of the state's most powerful positions.[42]

The negative response in newspapers all over the state to Richard Sr.'s candidacy had to be discouraging, even painful, to a family who respected and loved their father. Editorial comment was often brutal, presenting the judge as a laughingstock. He was criticized everywhere for being a perpetual office seeker, for feeding at the public trough for nearly fifty years, for not resigning his judgeship before running, for having a boozy reputation. The *Macon Telegraph*, fond of attacking the judge because of differences of opinion with him on the college at Milledgeville, now attacked him in favor of Walter George, declaring Russell was a misfit as chief justice and would be a tragedy as senator. A few papers defended him as a credit to the bench, and it was noted that if he should resign to run, so should everyone else who was running for different offices than ones they already held.[43]

He had learned to turn a thick skin to such charges, but he was hurt when he heard that the George camp was circulating rumors that he was such a buffoon and so uncultured and ignoble that he was incapable of moving in Washington society. He wrote to a few women friends asking them to assure their friends that this was not true. Although he could not resist adding that "Me Too George" could not come up to his class for blood or culture, he did not want a word said against him.[44]

Russell invited George repeatedly to debate him, but like Smith, Brown and Bell, George avoided debate. He was not a lively speaker and knew that he would not come out ahead if he went one-to-one with Russell. He wrote an open letter declaring that there were really no issues to debate. George enjoyed warm support from newspapers statewide.[45]

Russell hit hard at George's big business backers, hoping farmers and working class people would resent these connections. There was one pro-George group, however, that the Russell camp did not criticize on the outside chance that its support might swing to them: the Ku Klux Klan. The Klan remained such a force in state politics that many believed one could not be elected to state-wide office without it. The Russells were not comfortable courting the Klan, but they did not come out against it. They were careful to point out that they did not oppose it and were sure many Klansmen would find their candidate acceptable. Nevertheless, they also took pains to deny at every chance that Richard Russell was a Klan member or ever had been. Although one of his objections to the World Court was that justices would be "mongrels, Japanese, Chinese, etc.," Richard was against violence and could not support lawbreaking. He thought it unwise to join any organization whose members would not show their faces. Dick Jr. almost certainly flirted with the idea of joining the Klan—he already had his eye on state-wide office—but his father advised him against such a move.[46]

George's contention that there were really no issues in the race is the one the vast majority of voters adopted. The *Atlanta Constitution* editorialized that it was the opinion of the people that change was unnecessary. George should remain senator, and Russell should remain chief justice. On September 8, the voters agreed, giving George a vote of 128,179 to 61,911 for Russell.[47]

Although Richard Russell had exhibited symptoms of an insatiable desire to run for public office, this race does not appear to have been part of that old malaise. He repeatedly stated that he did not want to run, but when he felt that no one else would take up the banner, he stepped willingly in to fight. It is a basic but easily overlooked principle of democracy that the minority must have its candidate, else how can it influence the actions of the majority? Nineteenth-century statesman John C. Calhoun eloquently explained the principle of the importance of the minority voice: "The necessary consequence of taking the sense of the community by the concurrent majority is...to give to each interest or portion of the community a negative on the others."[48]

Richard Russell knew that he had little chance of winning, but he wanted to give the people who thought as he did an opportunity to have someone they could vote for, and he was comforted to think that he gave 61,000 Georgians a voice. This understanding of how democracy works was an old theme with him. Although in the past he had clearly thought he had a chance, this time he seems to have fought solely for the sake of a cause that he saw as a danger to his state and his country. However much he wanted to achieve glory in his youth, age had tempered his desires, and he genuinely felt winning this race might help the people of Georgia who had done so much for him. He had gained in wisdom, but he had not lost courage. He returned home, satisfied that in the sixty-fifth year of his life he had been unafraid to make a stand on questions he believed to be critical.[49]

The family had their reunion and Ina was proud to have family photos made. Everyone is dressed in proper attire. The young women have all bobbed their hair, even Carolyn, and they are wearing the loose, silky, soft dresses of the Twenties. The men are in suits. Alex and Jeb, ages sixteen and seventeen, look like they are growing too fast for their clothes, the Judge's suit is old and rumpled, and Dick Jr.'s bow tie is askew, but on the whole the family looks civilized.

In a way not likely appreciated at the time, this much-maligned and regretted Senate campaign was a decided success. Dick Jr.'s bid for

Speaker of the House, contrary to his mother's fears of its being hurt by
Papa's race, grew stronger by the week, and he and Rob had learned
much that would help them to conduct their next state-wide campaign.[50]
Their father would have little to do with that coming battle. The most
significant fact of 1926 for Richard Russell was that the spotlight on
Russell achievement shifted forever from father to son.

16

I AT LEAST FURNISHED
THE CANDIDATE

1927-1930

The first day of 1927 a surprise family wedding disconcerted Richard and Ina. Walter, true to his reputation for doing the unexpected, married his third cousin, Dorothea Bealer, daughter of an A&P executive. They were married on short notice at the bride's home, but Ina was grateful they had not run away to marry, a plan they had considered. In spite of Richard's history with Minnie, it was no secret that Ina took a dim view of runaway marriages. Ina Jr. talked the couple out of that, insisting their families must be told, and the home ceremony resulted. The Bealers, wanting to do the right thing, invited the Russells to come to Washington, but there was no money to travel. Richard struggled to pay tuition for Edward, now at Davidson College, and Fielding at Georgia. Taxes, insurance and bills that continued to come in from the Senate campaign took every dollar he had. At Christmas he had not had money to buy even one present.[1]

Another family change occurred at the beginning of the year when Jim Bowden was transferred to Savannah. Marguerite did not want to leave north Georgia, but she and the two little girls soon took up residence on the coast with Jim.

On March 1, Billie's birthday, Rob and Sybil welcomed a daughter to join Robert Lee Jr. She was named Sybil Elizabeth. Richard sometimes spent the night with this little family in Atlanta. Having his beloved Rob and his dear ones nearby gave Richard the feeling of a home away from home.

In June Richard Brevard Russell Jr. was elected Speaker of the Georgia House of Representatives without opposition. His friends had cleared the way by garnering enough support to make opposition futile, and other hopefuls dropped out. He asked a friend he had won over in recent years, Hugh Peterson, representative from Montgomery County, to place his name in nomination. Although the election was not in question, Peterson took this opportunity to praise Russell as a man of superior abilities, a natural young leader—judicious, conservative and fair—who would make a presiding officer of unsurpassed excellence.[2]

Russell was twenty-nine and E. B. Dykes, president of the Senate, was thirty-three. The in-coming governor, L. G. Hardman, was seventy-one. Richard Russell Sr., chief justice, was sixty-six. At the inauguration ceremonies on June 25, when the leaders of each legislative body, the governor-elect, and the chief justice sat on the platform together, the contrast between the aged and the young leaders was apparent. Many felt that this vigorous young legislature was a much-needed change and that the forthcoming session would be a fortunate one.[3]

The legislative session of 1927 tested young Dick Russell to the extreme. He emerged as a consensus leader, able to encourage acceptable compromises, an ability inherited from his mother, and it was obvious he had a generous share of his father's political industry and verve. He worked people hard, calling Saturday and night sessions and sometimes started the legislative day an hour early. When it was obvious the necessary bills could not be passed by midnight of adjournment hour, officials covered the clocks so business could proceed. Nevertheless, much necessary legislation surrounding taxes and other budget measures was postponed.

Dick Russell Jr. returned to Winder in late August, exhausted, to find his personal finances in about as poor condition as he felt the state's were. He had lost half a year of law practice in 1926, thanks to his dad's and his own campaigns. Nevertheless, he took time off to go hunting with Hugh Peterson on his plantation near Ailey, Georgia, and on September 10, 1927, he left on the *Leviathan* for France, where he attended a meeting of the American Legion in Paris and then toured some of Europe. His mother and father were happy to see him broadening his horizons.[4]

Dick Jr., an adult child living at home, continued to attract parental attention, while the younger children also kept the couple well-occupied. Edward had entered Davidson College in the autumn of 1926, just before his seventeenth birthday. During his sophomore year in 1927, his father wrote him fairly frequently to arrange finances, to advise him on studies and to praise his successes or caution him about weaknesses. He reminded him that he was kin to the Davidsons, for whom his college was named, and he sometimes described outstanding performances of preachers at weddings or funerals. Both Richard and Ina hoped to see Edward solidify his idea of becoming a Presbyterian minister.[5]

Fielding, a junior at the University, had not done well in his science courses. He was not likely to earn a Phi Beta Kappa key, and he knew he was not cut out to be a doctor. He dreaded telling his father that his dream was to teach English literature. A skilled boxer in the collegiate featherweight division, he had won all his matches, but the family expected Dad to frown on such frivolity. Richard surprised them by taking pride in his son's pugilistic prowess. When the boxing team, expenses paid, traveled to Charlottesville, Virginia, Richard lent Fielding cash to carry on to Washington to visit family there and see the capital city. He said he would not have to dig dirt for it if he won. Walter, who also enjoyed the sport and had tried it professionally in his earliest days in Washington, planned to be in Charlottesville to see his brother box.[6]

Alex, in his last year of high school, sympathized with his older brother's school problems. He told Fielding to study his real love, and he would take up the doctor standard to placate Dad. A strong student, Alex was undaunted by the idea of pre-med courses.[7]

Carolyn did not have an easy life with four older brothers who enjoyed tormenting her. A pretty, petite blonde, she had a sunny nature, and a sincere desire to please. Not surprisingly, she was known as "the universal favorite." Her father, referring to the circumstances of her birth, called her "his" baby and would have spoiled her if his finances and his wife would have allowed it.[8]

Finances remained a source of stress. The burden of repaying the money he borrowed for the Senate campaign made him groan as bills continued to come in, and Ina could not remember his having been lower financially. He was making interest payments for William on the eight hundred dollars they had borrowed for the café. Brother John was unable to pay a note on which Richard had stood as security, and so Richard paid it. Lewis had lost heavily in real estate, and Richard's love of land made him take up payments on at least one piece of land Lewis was in danger of losing.[9]

Ina cautioned the children not to ask their father for money. Edward took a part-time job at school, assuring his father that it was "like recreation," perhaps worried because Davidson was more expensive than the University. His father continued, as he had with all the others, to assure him that he must put studies first and let Dad worry about paying the bills. Providence had always been kind in allowing him to borrow what he needed and to repay it.[10]

Richard was unable to be at home for Ina's fifty-ninth birthday on February 18, 1927, but he wrote a tender and loving letter and sent a check for thirty-six dollars, one dollar for each year of their married life. Some of the poetry may have been spoiled when he had to caution her not to cash the check until March 10.[11]

On September 23, 1927, Walter and Dolly entered a daughter in the family annals, Emily Ellen. The grandchild count stood at two males, five females. Richard kept count of the genders, but his main concern was that the labors and deliveries were passed safely.[12]

Ina Jr. remained unmarried, satisfied with single life in Washington, where she had made many friends, both male and female. Although the family watched and wondered as various suitors tried their luck, she said she had never met a man she liked as much as her job and her name.[13] During this period, she decided to go to law school at night in order to qualify for promotion in her job with the Veterans Administration.

In October 1927 daughter Harriette married her long-time sweetheart Ralph Sharpton, Margo's former beau. Harriette comforted Ralph when Margo fell in love with Jim Bowden, and over the years friendship deepened into love. Richard approved of Ralph Sharpton for the support

Sharptons had showed him through the years, but the fact remained that he never considered a Winder man good enough for one of his girls.[14]

Ralph's main drawback was unsteady employment. He worked for the railroad and had been out of work from time to time. He and Harriette had longed to marry since 1924, but Richard and Ina had not been happy to think their daughter in a precarious financial situation. When Ralph had been employed several years with a railroad in Florida, the reluctant parents gave their consent to the wedding.

October 5, the day of the wedding, Richard lay in his bed feeling the day dawning with the poignant fullness that is often October's gift. A breeze murmured through the pine trees near the house, and a mockingbird outside his window began to sing a melody as sweetly intense as the day. After listening for awhile, he got up and went into Harriette's room to tell her he thought it was an omen for her future happiness. He thought her happiness shone in her face like the sunshine of the day itself.

Taylor Morton read the simple wedding ceremony in the living room of the home where they had now lived for fifteen years, and the young preacher's remarks about the marital relationship gave Richard deep satisfaction. Pat was her sister's maid of honor, and the father thought both daughters beautiful. Although the flag stop was going out of use by this time, Richard flagged the train that day so that the couple could leave for a honeymoon to Havana before returning to their home in Florida. As the guests showered the couple with rice, Pat and a girlfriend got on the train and went up and down the cars, ringing a loud bell, declaring the new state of wedded bliss of Harriette and Ralph.

In the joy of the marriage moment, Ina and Richard walked back to the house, satisfied that everything was going to be all right for Harriette. They grieved, however, that more than half of their children had been absent for this important family occasion. Pat and Carolyn were the only sisters present, and Rob, Fielding and Alex the only brothers. They felt especially sorry that Edward, who had been given to Harriette at birth, had not been able to leave school at Davidson and come for the mid-week wedding. Richard wrote Edward a long, descriptive letter to include him as much as possible in the festivities.[15]

The year brought other reasons to celebrate because it turned out to be a good year for Richard's tenant farmers and he cleared about twelve hundred dollars in cash, with hay, corn and peas into the bargain. The corn and hay made feeding mules through the winter less expensive.[16]

In 1928, Rob decided it was time to go back into law practice. He and Sybil planned to move to Russell, into a cottage next door to the main house. The little house was in poor shape, but Rob and Dad went in together to pay for repairs and to build a garage-wagon shed with an office upstairs nearby. Rob made a startling announcement as the moving day neared. He intended to have electricity brought to his house. Ina thought this was the best idea her progressive son had ever had, and she asked Richard to have the line brought over to their house. Alex was a freshman at the University, and Richard said he would have to take one of their three boys out of college in order to pay for electricity. Ina said she would burn pine knots before she would allow that.[17]

No doubt Richard Russell was, as usual, "hard run" financially, but there was another reason he did not want to pay for lights to his house. He had fought a long and unsuccessful court case against the Georgia Power Company while he was practicing law in 1917-1922, and he carried a grudge about it.[18] Knowing his stubborn nature, Dick Jr. volunteered to pay for electric lights to the house. At first Richard objected, declaring the power company would never put a post on his land, but Rob talked his father around the question until he agreed to put the post right where the company had asked to put it. His daughter Ina wrote to scold him for not thinking of his wife, and this letter shamed him. By Christmas of 1928, the house was ablaze with light. Papa sulked awhile, then began to enjoy the luxury as did everyone else.[19]

William, following Walter's lead, had moved to Marshall, North Carolina, and taken a job with the A&P Company, managing a small grocery store. He was able to join his twin brother at Christmas at home when the college boys came roaring in, leaving socks, shirts and ties everywhere. Ina gloried in her lively group. Dad was home almost the entire month, to his wife's delight, even if he did dig too much dirt and then complain his legs pained him.[20]

Other lights were added to the family when on November 26, 1928, Billie gave birth to Samuel Gordon Green Jr., and on January 26, 1929, Margo gave birth to James Harris Bowden Jr. The Walter Russells added Walter Brown Russell Jr. on July 24, 1929.

On January 11, 1929, David Barrow, Chancellor of the University of Georgia, died. Dave Barrow and Richard Russell, friends since their youth in Athens, had worked together in the common cause of university education for many, many years. The disputed county Richard now lived in was named for Barrow. He was also an old friend of Ina's, their families having worked together to provide education for the children of Oglethorpe County when Ina was a girl. His funeral was a solemn and moving occasion in the University Chapel, for Dave Barrow's lifework and his character had earned love and honor.

Pat chauffeured her mother and father to Athens, and the two women sat with the Barrow County delegation and had good seats to view the stage where Richard, Chairman of the Board of Trustees, would sit. As the Board and other dignitaries marched in, Richard came in beside Hoke Smith. Their old adversary looked good, but when Ina spoke to him afterwards, she realized he had become senile, his decayed mind useless. She pitied him but rejoiced that Richard's mind remained sharp, that he spoke with a clear, firm voice. It did not matter that they had never become governor, senator or millionaire. They had the most important things in life.[21]

A year later, on January 11, 1930, the Board of Trustees gave a special memorial service for Barrow and for Richard's old friend Sylvanus Morris, dean of the law school, who had died soon after Barrow. Richard Russell gave an oration for Barrow, his long associate in the work of education, that glowed with the beauty of friendship and the poetry of sincere admiration for work well done. The judge praised the "grandeur of the humble life of a great soul." As he had done with Crawford W. Long, he highlighted, "the pure gold of consecrated service to the best needs of humanity." When the book of life must be closed, "no yearning for the pomp and circumstance attendant upon the tenure of great office, but faithfulness in the performance of the little things in life…at last constitutes the summary of true greatness."[22]

In his own work on the Supreme Court he performed his daily duties faithfully and well although no pomp or circumstance attends the work of judges. It was here as the years wore on that he fulfilled, perhaps without realizing it, his ambition to serve the poor and the oppressed as well as the rich and the mighty. He was merely doing what his heart and his mind led him to do. The other justices learned that sometimes his decisions were swayed from the straight and narrow course of cold judicial logic by his ideology of mercy and of sympathy for the poor, the helpless, the unprotected and the underprivileged. He tried never to forget that the law had its origin in the necessity of protecting the weak against the strong. Although his associates sometimes felt he was a pesky dissenter, they knew no judge works without making errors. Because they never questioned his honesty of mind and soul, they believed what they considered errors in his opinions to be errors on the side of mercy.

His powerful intellect had by this time developed a depth of knowledge of the law seldom seen, and he inspired associate justices and advocates before the Court. He retained his classical and biblical knowledge and his speech glowed with poetry and unpretentious learning. His colleagues felt he was as much a scholar of English literature and Latin as he was of the principles of law. In casual conversation he still claimed that he was happier in political activity than judicial, but his friends, evaluating his judicial career as remarkable, were never sure that this sentiment was serious. His close friend, associate justice Price Gilbert, would then remind him that although he coveted political office, the people had elected him to judicial posts, compelling him to build a life if not wiser than he knew, then wiser than he wished.[23]

His life was necessarily one of contemplation and study, and his keen mind honed by years of such work served well. Yet his sociable nature meant his office in the Capitol was open to those who wanted to discuss politics, law, or life in general. An outstanding conversationalist of appealing wisdom, he spent office hours talking with old friends or young lawmakers and others sent to him by friends or admiring associates. The other justices gathered there to discuss cases bothering them. Thus he was often late at night working on cases he had not had time to get to during the day. Careless from youth of his need to eat and rest, he was prone to skip meals to save money, but his old energy endured.[24]

His interest in justice, in law, in equity, endured as well, and his work on the court was gratifying. He needed other activities, however; he had always been many-sided. He became the first President of the American Agricultural Society and was active in promoting it. He was pleased to have the chance to make a radio address when the group met in Atlanta. Ina went to a friend's house in Winder to hear him on the radio. He continued his work on the Boards of Trustees of the University of Georgia and Georgia State College for Women. His spirits stayed buoyant when he had this other work to do in addition to his demanding court work.[25]

Life in Russell revolved now around youngsters at school and problems of the elderly. In her junior and senior years in high school, Carolyn became a champion orator, surprising her father and mother with her confidence and talent. Could this be their baby? Alex made such high marks in college that Ina felt she had at last produced a child who could make grades good enough to please Dad.[26] Fielding finished his studies at the University of Georgia and went back to graduate school. Fortunately for Richard, he won a teaching assistantship and was off the payroll, but Richard did not complain about school expenses. He told his children that it was his duty and his pleasure to furnish the money for their necessary expenses, and they, recognizing the efforts he made, were in turn diligent about keeping these to a minimum.[27]

Pipey and Annie grew more feeble daily, and they had been joined by their brother Ben, utterly destitute and losing his mind. Ina and the children at home shouldered the burdens of caring for these kin who had cared for them, and the family spent anxious times over their health and welfare. The older children sent money so that electric lights could be added to Pipey's house. In the summer of 1929 Ben Dillard, who had lived the final six or seven years of his life without a penny to call his own, died, leaving Pipey and Annie to care for each other.[28]

It was apparent as 1930 loomed into view that Richard Russell Jr. was going to make a run for the governor's office. There was never any doubt in Georgia politics that he had his eye on the governor's chair, but at

thirty-two, he was young to be entering the fray. It is not known whether
he ever discussed his plans with his father, and it seems likely that he did
not. He had appeared neither burdened nor inspired by his father's earlier
exhortations to him to make good the name the father thought he had
failed to elevate. A lively and capable politician, the son had his father's
ambition and nerve. He also had his father's political machine, that is, a
web of good friends throughout the state, ready to assist a young Russell
in whom they had faith, a man from proven stock. Heir to his mother's
and his father's genius for friendship, he had many friends of his own.

Before he could announce his candidacy in April 1930, several of
his siblings upstaged him and gave the family reasons for joy and
sorrow. Pat was hinting at an engagement to Hugh Peterson, Dick Jr.'s
good friend and political ally. Richard Sr. had introduced his daughter to
the rising young politician and lawyer, asking her to attend a dinner at
the Piedmont Driving Club where he knew Hugh would also be in
attendance. Pat did not want to go because she had a date for that
evening with another man named Hugh. She brought this Hugh to the
dinner and dance, but he turned out to be a wallflower. He would not or
could not dance. Hugh Peterson, on the other hand, invited Pat to dance
repeatedly, and romance blossomed.[29]

On January 31, Rob and Sybil added another son and grandson to
the family tally. He was named Richard Brevard Russell III for his
grandfather. Could Papa have been more pleased?

Then on February 4 an alarming call came from Raleigh, North
Carolina. Edward, an avid wrestler on the Davidson team, had been
injured in a match. Details were sketchy, but the anxious parents heard
with dismay that he was paralyzed.

Dick Jr. drove with his mother to Raleigh immediately. Richard Sr.,
never one to take charge when the children were sick or hurt, took
instead refuge in his work and waited with deep dread for his wife and
son to report. They found Edward in poor shape, unable to move his head
or his arms, but the prognosis was that he would regain use of his limbs
gradually and completely.

Richard wrote his love and anxiety and sent money, but he did not
go to Raleigh, pleading that this was his busy time of year. His greatest
fear was that the boy's mind would be affected, but Ina assured him that

Edward's mind was as bright as ever. He was the pet of the hospital, thanks to his cheerful disposition and quick humor that won over doctors and nurses alike. The stream of flowers from girlfriends, as well as from girls he had never met, was sure to prove effective tonic.[30]

Dick Jr. insisted his mother stay in Raleigh with Edward, no matter the cost. They were spared most expense because Edward's roommate had a sister there, Katherine Coker Cannon, who welcomed Ina warmly into her home. Katherine and her husband took care of her, Ina reported, as Billie and Gordon would have. Someone notified the Supreme Court of North Carolina, and Mrs. Stacy, wife of the North Carolina chief justice, with two other wives of justices, called on Mrs. Chief Justice of Georgia at the Cannon home. Ina was pleased to report these kindnesses and many others to the family. While her mother was away, Carolyn did a superior job keeping the ship on course at Russell. In her final year of high school, she looked after Pipey and Annie with patience, compassion and good-humor, and she cooked Dad and Dick's grits, too.

By the beginning of March, Edward was improved enough for Ina to come home, and about two weeks later, he came home in a body cast. He was weak and in pain, but he longed to go back to school. His greatest worry was that he would not be able to graduate with his class. He felt God's hand in his recovery and believed the entire experience had called him irrevocably to preach the Gospel. Richard and Ina rejoiced with him. His brother Dick called him aside and asked him if he was absolutely sure. "We don't want any hypocrites in this family," he said.[31]

On April 5, Dick Jr. announced that he was a candidate for governor of Georgia. No one who knew anything about Georgia politics was surprised, but many believed he did not expect to win, that this was simply a trial run to get his name before the public. Those of such opinion did not know Dick Russell Jr. He had a keen sense of political timing and was determined to work hard enough to win. At first there was not much public notice of his candidacy, but he set off on speaking engagements all over the state.[32]

While his eldest son was stirring the political pot, Richard found his youngest daughter and child making a noticeable splash as an orator. Carolyn won a state-wide oratorical contest, bringing home one hundred and fifteen dollars in gold. On the night of the finals in Atlanta, Richard sat in the audience astonished at his daughter's knowledge of the Constitutional Convention and its authors, as evidenced in her extemporaneous speech. Doing his best to bar a father's natural prejudices, he judged she spoke like a well-seasoned lawyer of long experience.[33]

Edward went back to Davidson in April, and with the support of his professors a plan was drawn by which he would complete his studies by the end of summer but be allowed to sit with the spring graduating class.

No one in the family besides Dick Jr. and Rob took much notice of politics until after June 24, 1930, when Patience Elizabeth Russell married Hugh Peterson in the Winder First Presbyterian Church, on a day so hot the candles melted in the candelabra. It was Richard and Ina's thirty-ninth wedding anniversary.

There were five candidates in the field for governor in 1930, and three had potential to be stronger contenders than young Dick Russell. George H. Carswell, a former state representative, senator and secretary of state, had wide support, as did E. D. Rivers, who was aligned with Gene Talmadge, the powerful Commissioner of Agriculture. Rivers had lost to Hardman in 1928, and many thought it was Rivers' turn. John N. Holder had been a strong contender for several years and once had actually won the popular vote but lost the county unit vote. He was chairman of the highway commission and had the support of legislators who wanted highways in their districts. Russell, a popular Speaker of the House, was a threat to these three. The fifth candidate, James Perry, head of the Public Service Commission, was not considered a serious contender.

As his father before him, Dick Russell Jr. pitched his campaign on the premise that he was the people's candidate. He used the same arguments that his father had used; that he was not associated with any big interests or any political faction and that he would bring a clean slate to government. He planned to run a person-to-person campaign, seeing as many individuals as he could. In the spring he kept up a busy speaking schedule, talking with hundreds of people statewide, getting mechanics out from under cars, chatting with farmers along the roadsides in their fields, and going up and down the main streets of small towns introducing himself and asking for support. Sometimes he woke people up late at night out in the country to pitch his speech to them. He had inherited his father's phenomenal memory and from childhood had witnessed his ability to talk with anyone about anything with ease. Thus he turned these individual encounters into powerful assets. People recognized his sincerity and liked the fact that he did not promise things he could not deliver. They liked his clear explanations of issues, his apparent integrity.

He set up his headquarters in Winder, making a point of withdrawing from Atlanta, while also saving money. His uncle Lewis came in to head up the campaign, with brother Rob a stout second. Alex, Edward and Fielding were at home for the summer, and they helped in the office, as did Carolyn. The youngsters marveled that Uncle Ed, who came from Washington to help, could sit for eight hours at a desk without a break.[34]

The active young men preferred speeding along in a car from spot to spot, jumping out to hammer up campaign posters. They were all at ease meeting people, talking and socializing, so Lewis sent them out to various counties on what he called "missionary trips." Their evangelizing for brother Dick wore out their uncle's car.[35] The sisters wrote letters and came to help in the office from time to time. Richard had enjoyed family support when he ran for office, and now his family had grown to a larger labor force for his son. The whirling activity of the house bewildered the judge when he was home, and he sometimes withdrew from the table, wearied of talking that often ignored him.[36]

Some editors took aim at young Dick with the old criticism of Russells feeding at the public trough. They thought to make being the chief justice's son a liability. Dick Jr. diffused this charge of nepotism by naming it a false issue. If the children of successful fathers could not hold public office, they were condemned to oblivion, he claimed. He believed the voters would recognize this accusation as unfair and senseless. He said he was proud of his father and he wanted his father to be proud of him.[37]

Dick Jr. was purported to be too young to be governor, and in addition, said critics, he wasn't married. Who would take care of the duties of First Lady? He answered these criticisms with humor and mystery. As to being too young, he declared he was growing older as fast as he could, and he pointed to his experience, his youth, and his energy as assets. When the age criticism continued, he offered to debate his opponents so that voters could compare the candidates. They all backed away from such a challenge. Like his father's opponents before him, no one wanted to meet Dick Russell on the platform, where his sharp mind, his skill in turning a phrase, his store of facts, and his effective sarcasm would bring down anyone.[38]

As for being unmarried and having someone to perform the duties of First Lady, he declared that he had been a candidate for matrimony long before he became a candidate for governor, and he promised that when he was elected governor, there would be a Mrs. Russell to greet them at the governor's Mansion. This remark about a Mrs. Russell was intriguing to those who did not know young Dick Russell well, for he was a popular bachelor with numerous women friends, at least one or two of whom may have been considered serious candidates for the title of Mrs. Dick Russell. Nevertheless, at this period it is sure that when he spoke of a Mrs. Russell in the governor's Mansion, he had in mind only one person. He intended for Ina, his life-long "dear," to take up residence in Atlanta and keep his home life happy as she always had done.

Did anyone think this strange that he blithely borrowed his father's wife? It is not likely that either Ina or Richard found the assumption unusual. Richard had early advised his son not to marry, believing he would have more political success if he "traveled light." Whether by design or accident, his son took this advice. Dick Jr. may have modeled his associations with women more on those of his bachelor uncle Lewis than on his father's example of patriarchal fecundity with attendant responsibilities. Lewis was a bachelor whose company women sought without the prerequisite of marriage. Another factor is almost certainly that young Dick Russell could not find a woman who measured up to his ideal, Ina Dillard Russell. Women like Ina, women to whom husband and home were a high calling, had always been in short supply, even when the culture promoted them. By Dick Jr.'s day, they were scarce indeed.[39]

The summer of 1930 unfolded with classic hot weather and steaming politics. When the primary was over on September 10, white Georgians had put Dick Russell and George Carswell into a run-off.

Russell received 56,177 popular votes and 132 county unit votes to Carswell's 51,851 popular votes and 126 county unit votes. Russell carried forty-nine counties and Carswell forty-seven. Rivers ran third.

Dick Jr. was pleased with this result and with how little he had spent. Following his father's example again, he had spent only three thousand eight hundred and eighty-eight dollars, all of it his own money except about six hundred dollars donated by relatives. Rivers and Carswell had spent a good deal more. Thus when speculation arose over what political alignments might develop during the run-off, Dick Russell was able to maintain his position of "no trades or combinations" and to ask for support from all the people who wanted "clean, honest and progressive government."

Rivers tried to swing his support to Carswell, fearing, he said, a Russell-Holder alliance. Holder had, indeed, declared for Russell, but Russell hotly denied any alliance, and as the heated campaign continued, it became apparent that Rivers could not deliver his support to Carswell. The voters believed Dick Russell and they liked him. Heir to his father's energy and love of a fight, he spoke at rallies two and three times a day. Lewis and the younger brothers, Alex, Fielding, and Edward, were tireless in taking campaign literature to all locales. Rob held down the Winder fort and ferried between there and Atlanta, effectively running the entire show when school terms began and the others had to go back to school. A radio address was arranged, sponsored by Dick's friends, one of the first ever used in a Georgia election.

The ground swell of Russell support grew to such an extent that nothing Carswell did or said could stop it. Richard Sr. could not remain entirely serene and above the excitement. More and more men came by his office to talk politics and predict success. The phone rang with callers forecasting victory. Hopes ran high.[40]

Young Dick Russell was elected governor of Georgia on October 1 by the largest majority in any gubernatorial race in the state's history. He carried 126 of the 161 counties and 330 of the 414 county unit votes. In the popular vote, he took 99,505 to Carswell's 47,157. Richard and Ina had acquired a radio for their home, and the night of the election, they and numerous family members sat by it, listening intently as the results poured in, showing a victory that was judged not a landslide, but a political earthquake.

During the campaign, Richard Sr.'s position as chief justice dictated that he keep a low profile. Thus the old fighter had had to sit by, quiet, waiting, watching, and he did not find this inactivity easy. He dug a lot of dirt that summer. When the race was over, he and Ina enjoyed the taste of victory denied them so many times before. Letters poured in from friends of many years, rejoicing with them and expressing satisfaction that in some way, the old dream had finally come true.[41]

If local response to her husband's election as chief justice had surprised Ina eight years earlier, she was stunned speechless at the mammoth victory celebration Winder held on October 3 to honor her son. Between five and ten thousand people converged on the little town, starting early in the afternoon. Among the throng, friends put up a platform in the center of town, readied microphones, set up chairs, strung flags and buntings from housetop to housetop, lettered signs that said "Hello Dick," "Welcome Home Dick" "Hurrah for Dick!" News reporters noted the absence of the word "Governor" as proof that Dick Russell's claim to being a plain country boy was legitimate.

When the governor-elect arrived near dusk at the head of a cavalcade that had an impromptu start in Gwinnett County, he was swamped with well-wishers. After shaking a few hundred hands, he managed to slip away home to hug his mother. Asked the secret of his success, he gave her credit, much in the same way his father had given Harriette credit.[42]

In the evening, when the family took places on the platform for the speaking exercises, the crowd cheered wildly. Richard's brother John and his wife Addie were there, as well as many of the governor-elect's siblings: Ina Jr., Fielding, Alex, Edward, Carolyn, Pat and her husband Hugh, Rob and Sybil. Cheers went up especially strong for Chief Justice and Mrs. Russell, and also for Lewis and Rob, spearheads of the campaign. Bands from schools in Monroe, Gainesville, Jefferson and Athens played stirring patriotic songs. This was victory wine at its finest. When the governor-elect stood to accept his ovation, he introduced his mother to the crowd as "the best sweetheart I ever had." Shouts and cheers demanded she speak, but she would not.

Then the judge was brought to the microphone amid lavish cheering. The crowd quieted, waited expectantly for a memorable accolade. The moment was fraught with too much feeling for him to speak at first, and when he did, his voice broke. The crowd was sympathetic as he tried to express his pride and joy in the fact that his son had done what he could not do, but only Winder citizens understood the full meaning when he said, "No tribute could come to me from anywhere or from any people that would equal. . .the devotion you have given to young Dick Russell." In his old oratorical style, he inserted a little humor to temper the great emotion. "I was unable, on account of my position," he noted, "to contribute to his election, but I at least furnished the candidate."[43]

He finished with the now-familiar reference to his own death, but his sincerity and his sensitivity to his diminished role were not in question: "I have only a short time before I shall meet my Maker. God knows I appreciate what you have done for Georgia, for as God is my judge, I believe Georgia has put into the executive office to rule over the people who need help a pure, a brave, an honest boy." Whatever his longing for recognition, Richard Russell first required that he and his serve well.

Uncle Lewis was not too overcome with emotion to express his joy in the election of a candidate, "born on this soil," who would go into office with no promises to big interests. For once, the office had not been bought. He had taken up his job on the staff for love of the boy, he said, but as the race wore on, he saw the value of the man with a more objective eye.[44] Lewis, too, was seeing an old dream fulfilled after years of grueling labor.

The crowd cheered brother Rob, a favorite in Winder, but he declared he was too happy to speak. "No man ever had more loyal friends and neighbors than we have had," was all he could say. Rob may have been too tired to speak. Photos of the campaign staff show him thin and drawn. It was Rob who suffered most from his brother's races.

Bands played, the crowd cheered, cannon fired a salute, and after the governor-elect had spoken, he jumped down from the platform into the crowd and shook hands for hours.

The new governor's term did not begin until June 1931 so there was time for the family to prepare for the move to Atlanta. Carolyn entered Agnes Scott College during the thick of the run-off fight, and Edward entered Columbia Theological Seminary, both schools located in Decatur. Alex, studying hard, was in his final year at Georgia. By doubling up, he would finish four years in three. Fielding, enjoying his work as teacher and student, fell in love with Virginia Wilson, a physical education major from Duluth. Marriage plans lay not far ahead.

On November 1, 1930, for the first time since their home was built in 1912, Richard and Ina found themselves in the house alone. Richard had never stopped rejoicing in this wife who was made for him. He still called her the idol of his heart, his soul's desire. That night they sat by the fire awhile, talking over the events they had lived through in their home. Then, since the moon was shining, Richard went out to dig dirt awhile. At midnight, when Ina went to bed, he was still digging.[45]

SEARCHING FOR PAVED SIDEWALKS IN RUSSELL

1931-1936

Richard Russell went to work in Atlanta in January 1931 with a heavy heart. At Christmas word had come that Billie was gravely ill. Expecting her fourth child, she faced life-threatening difficulties. Richard and Ina tried during the holidays to keep up their spirits for the sakes of their other children and grandchildren, but as the holiday wore on and the news did not improve, they grew tense and anxious. Recalling that Minnie had been taken ill at Christmas and had died twelve days later drove Richard to distraction. Ina, outwardly pursuing her usual mode of cheering everyone up, secretly dreaded for the phone to ring.

On Christmas Eve, near midnight, in an agony of anxiety about her eldest daughter, Ina tenderly displayed on the dining room mantel photos of their absent children: Pat and Hugh, the newlyweds, in Ailey, Harriette, Marguerite and Billie with husbands and families, all were displayed. She put out a favorite of her and Richard and Billie, when Billie was their only child. She could not find one of Walter and his family. He was the only son absent.

Richard was sure that bad news would come on January 6. He watched the approach of this day with terror. Billie's baby, a boy, was born dead on January 5. Richard grew wild with fear, and Ina went to Atlanta to be with him. He could not be comforted until they called Ina Jr., and she assured them that Billie was receiving good care. Thanks to blood transfusions and improved maternity care in general, she would not suffer Minnie's fate. Like her father and mother, Billie was not one to give up. Two years later, on January 2, 1933, she gave birth to a healthy boy, William Benjamin.[1]

Governor Hardman called a special session of the General Assembly on January 6, 1931, to deal with the state's worsening financial plight. The Great Depression was creating havoc even in a state where extreme poverty had been the norm for sixty-five years, and the governor and the legislature could not agree on how to meet financial crises. As Speaker of the House, Dick Russell Jr. managed to hold a neutral position and so avoid the acrimony that had developed between the legislative and the executive branches.[2]

With her home empty of husband and children, Ina came into Atlanta frequently to stay with Richard, though she felt it a queer life for her, living in Atlanta during the week, going home on week-ends. With no children, house or farm to tend to, she rested. Once or twice she slept until nearly lunchtime. The Kimball did not charge extra for her, so she felt Dad could stand the expense of feeding her. The Hugh Petersons were in town for Hugh's legislative duties, and Ina and Pat enjoyed spending the day together, window shopping. They had no money, but they liked dreaming of the things they would buy if they had it.[3]

Important events occurred in the family with regularity as the June inauguration date approached. In February Pipey went to her well-earned rest, leaving Aunt Annie watching feebly at the gate. With Ina moving to Atlanta, Annie's future was a worrying concern until another Dillard niece, Mary Pope Moseman, daughter of Ina's sister Tabitha Morris, took Annie in. Ina Jr. graduated from law school and passed the bars in Georgia, Virginia, and the District of Columbia. She planned to come home for her brother's inauguration and for her father to swear her in to the Georgia bar before the Supreme Court. She would come by a new mode of transport: an airplane. Fielding announced his engagement to Virginia Wilson. In spite of the Depression, the couple planned to marry in August. Alex graduated from the University of Georgia, pleasing his father with high marks and acceptance to Emory University's School of Medicine, but not with fast driving and wrecking borrowed cars.[4]

As the excitement and hype of the inauguration increased, Richard Sr. gained a fair share of fame as the patriarch of this numerous clan that the young, unmarried governor proudly claimed as his family. Such a functional family made appealing fodder for newspaper reporters in an era that emphasized families. Although Ina was the adored heroine of the story, Richard's place as faithful provider, prominent judge, honored patriarchal figure, was not overlooked. This publicity may have resulted in an invitation to debate the nation's most famous and effective birth-control advocate, Margaret Sanger, in Atlanta on May 14. A two hundred and fifty dollar fee was offered.

Financial consideration was the major reason for his acceptance, but Richard did not mind debating this subject. He and Ina spent two days and nights reading up on Sanger-proposed legislation that would allow doctors to send birth control information and devices through the mail. They felt this harmless opening would be the beginning of unspeakable evils.[5] There can be no question that the pair realized this was not the central issue and that they were on the losing side of the argument, but Richard Russell was no stranger to the role of minority voice.

Sanger, a slim, attractive woman in her early fifties, was a formidable debater with right on her side. She had heard that Judge Russell was a legal and literary scholar who could use sarcasm and ridicule with effect. It was her policy to control the debate, and more than ever she felt this must be so with Judge Russell. He would have the home field advantage and his numerous successful children would make it difficult for her to point out that five of his boasted eighteen children had died at birth or in infancy. Thus she insisted on having the opening and the closing remarks.[6] A debater of experience who must have known the advantage this gave her, Richard, the gentleman, accepted these terms.

Ina protested vigorously the mention of eighteen children on publicity posters. She made Richard promise he would debate as if he had no children. Nevertheless, pre-debate publicity emphasized the size of his family, often including recent photographs of the thirteen living children. Richard was hailed as a leading opponent of birth control, but he had no prior public record on the issue. Sanger was presented as the leader of the birth control movement in the US, and readers were reminded of her frequent arrests and her books on the subject.[7]

Sanger was pleased when scouts sent to Atlanta reported Richard Russell had the reputation of chewing tobacco during debates and kept a cuspidor on the stage, for it seemed to her he was the kind of traditionalist she felt was easy prey. Although Richard's life-long addiction to tobacco had not lessened, his sense of propriety did not allow him to chew during a formal debate, especially with a woman opponent. Tobacco in courtrooms, even the Supreme Courtroom, was the accepted custom. On stage he did without it.[8]

The publicity posters claimed birth control was a "timely question" but the debate, held at the Erlanger Theatre, attracted a small crowd. It was an entertaining evening nonetheless. Coverage in the *Atlanta Constitution* next day likened Russell's old-fashioned arguments to an unsuspecting Roman phalanx going grandly into a nest of machine guns. He used the biblical injunction "to increase and multiply" and clung to other Catholic arguments to such an extent that Sanger suspected him of being a papist. Her statistics, logic and modern ideas brought down the old warrior with rapid fire.

Sanger made no reference to the size of Russell's family, and Russell did not use sarcasm and ridicule on her. Sitting in the audience, Ina watched with pride as her husband conducted himself in such a way that most of the audience appreciated him if not his arguments. When he painted a glowing picture of happy family life, emphasizing the feelings of satisfaction in mother and father as they sacrificed for their children, he could have been speaking directly to her and for her as well.

Women sitting behind Ina called him an old fool who did not know what he was talking about, and she may have smiled to herself at the irony of the situation. Then one of them said, "I'd like to see his poor wife." Moved by his glowing defense of big families and grateful for his continuing sacrifices, Ina was unable to stand this. She turned to the women and said, "Well, here she is."[9]

Dick Jr. was horrified by his father's participation in this debate. He said he would gladly have given his father the money rather than see the

family exploited in this manner.[10] Such harsh judgement may have
opened a rift between father and son, for about this time Richard
withdrew into a sulk. Why should he move to the Mansion? He would
continue living at the Kimball, doing his court work, bothering nobody.
Ina could run the governor's Mansion without him.

These threats of non-participation hurt Ina. After all his years of
yearning to see her mistress at the governor's Mansion, he should not be
making trouble. Nevertheless, she went on arranging her home in Winder
so that she could leave it, planning a huge reception (punch for three
thousand!) at the Mansion following the inauguration, and organizing a
family reunion for the next day. All their children were coming home,
including Harriette and Ralph, who had moved to Washington state the
year before when Ralph took a new job with an oil company.

On inauguration morning, Richard Russell Sr. took a long time
getting ready, going to great lengths with his toilet. He trimmed and
washed his moustache so that no tobacco stains showed. He consulted
with Pat about his tie.[11] Before the ceremony he swore his daughter Ina
Jr. to the Georgia bar in the presence of the Supreme Court. When a little
later he swore in his own son as governor of the state of which he was
chief justice, photographers went wild. Both men felt their bond increase
in that moment. The photos made appeared in newspapers all over the
country. On June 27, 1931, Richard Russell Sr. joined his wife and son in
taking up residence in the governor's Mansion, greeting more than a
thousand well-wishers at the inaugural reception. Family unity would not
be spoiled by petty hurts.[12]

By autumn Dick Jr. had his mother and father almost to himself. Alex
was a freshman at Emory University Medical School, and thus he,
Edward, and Carolyn were in the area but lived on campus at their
schools. Fielding and Virginia married on August 3, 1931, and the family
enjoyed prenuptial celebrations at the governor's Mansion. Twin
William lent the young couple his car for their honeymoon, but when
they returned to Fielding's teaching job at Monroe High School, they
were without a car. Richard developed a close bond with his new
daughter, who "fell in love with him" at their first meeting, in spite of the

fact that her sweetheart had tried to frighten her with reports that his father was a gruff old fellow.[13]

Richard Russell Sr. had celebrated his seventieth birthday on April 27, 1931. As a twenty-year-old youth he had dreamed of residing in the governor's Mansion before the age of forty. Fifty years and seventeen political campaigns later, courtesy of a son reared to take his place, he occupied a quieter role there with a certain grace. Age had brought him a noticeable wisdom and tempered his ego. Stepping out of the political arena, he refused from the beginning of the governor's election to allow friends to ask him to intercede for them with his son. His standard answer to such a request was this: "If it isn't a family matter, your argument is as good as mine." Some of his old friends took offense at this stance, but his son appreciated beyond telling how it eased his position. He felt his father as an understanding friend more than ever.[14]

The unusual occurrence of the chiefs of two branches of government housed in one household continued to attract attention. Richard's position as chief justice was hailed with honor and his dignity in the role noted. When asked whether he was not a little regretful that his son had done so much better than his own ambitions, he answered: "If our sons go no farther than the marks we set, the world stands still!"[15] It was pleasant to have a chauffeur to drive him to the Capitol if he wished it, but he could and did still take the tram. Plain Dick Russell had not changed.

His family, hailed in articles as 'remarkable,' felt a certain sadness at the way the dream had come true. To declare their continued love and admiration for their father, they commissioned a portrait that they presented to him at Christmas of 1931, to hang in the Mansion while he and Ina lived there. Memories as well as tears flowed as Richard and Lewis gathered with the family around a little Christmas tree in the parlor of the Mansion and spoke of their long-ago family, of Harriette and William John's dreams for their sons.[16]

Life in the longed-for Mansion with Ina Dillard Russell at the helm turned out to be as pleasant as life had always been with her, whatever structure they called home. Their financial situation had not changed, but they were reaping rich rewards for their perseverance to their ideals. Dick Jr. enjoyed success as chief executive, and his general popularity increased. They could look forward to his winning another term, at the end of which their younger children would be out of school. Retiring quietly back to Winder would then be a welcome move. On April 18, 1932, any dreams of a respite were shattered when Georgia's Senator William Harris died in Washington, DC

Ina described political life as one in which a person was more than usual "a victim of the unexpected." With the death of Senator Harris, all Georgians wondered what to expect. Pleased with their young governor, they had counted on him for another two-year term. He, however, might want to go to Washington where his tenure would likely last as long as he wanted to serve. What would he do?

The old guard statewide knew exactly what he ought to do. He ought to appoint his father to the post. Letters poured in, urging him to take this step. Glenn Giles entreated: "Let me earnestly beg you, early in the morning on the day following burial of Senator Harris, that you walk into your father's office, lay on his desk the Senatorial toga and say: 'Dad, here it is—without any strings—without any conditions—and without any apologies.'" Another letter invoked the fifth commandment. Copies of some of these letters arrived at the chief justice's office as well as at the governor's.[17]

It is impossible to say whether Richard Sr. ever thought there was a chance of this appointment or whether, in fact, he wanted it. There was tension in the governor's Mansion during this time, but little was said about the situation.[18] Certainly to appoint his father to the post would mean that Dick Jr. was not interested in it, for he would never be elected in that scenario. Perhaps the pleasure of handing his father a life-long dream tempted him slightly, but it is unlikely that he seriously considered that alternative. He wanted to serve his state on the national political scene, and he knew he could serve well. Although this vacancy had occurred at a time he would not have chosen, it was the ultimate opportunity. He would have to run the race as it was dealt.

On April 21, Senator Harris was buried with full honors at Cedartown, his funeral attended by three thousand mourners, including Governor Russell. On April 25, Dick Russell Jr. announced that he was appointing John S. Cohen, Democratic national committeeman from Georgia and publisher of the *Atlanta Journal*, to serve as interim senator. He announced also that he would seek the unexpired senatorial term in an election set for September 14, the regular Democratic primary. Cohen declared he would not seek election to the office.[19]

On April 26, Charles R. Crisp of Americus, the dean of Georgia's Congressional delegation, announced he would also seek the Senate seat. Crisp's father had been a successful Congressman, Speaker of the House in the second Cleveland administration, and the younger Crisp was a well-known and respected House member. Many considered he would be an easy winner, that this promotion to the Senate was the logical conclusion of a life of distinguished service. Having made his announcement, he boarded the train for Washington, to give the impression that he was a hard-working and conscientious public servant and a man used to dealing with large and important issues.

Dick Russell Jr. set out campaigning with characteristic energy and determination, and he had no trouble getting speaking engagements. He appointed Frank Scarlett, a close friend and supporter from Brunswick, as campaign manager and set up headquarters at the Ansley Hotel in Atlanta. The day-to-day running of the campaign, however, was again done by Rob and Uncle Lewis. The family was once more embroiled in a political campaign that took over their lives. In addition, Hugh Peterson, Pat's husband, was running for Congress in the First District. Tensions ran high all summer.

Richard Sr. may have been relieved that he was exempt from this work. He was seventy-two, and although he still dug dirt when home at Russell, his judicial duties largely took up his energies. He felt a deeper understanding of and commitment to the work to which he had given so many years of his life. In June he attended the Georgia State Bar Association meeting in Albany to hear a report on the need for judiciary reform in Georgia. The report revived the old issue of whether judges should be elected and urged drastic overhauling in the Georgia system. The plan of the lawyers was to empower the governor to appoint judges selected from three candidates chosen in an election among the members of the bar. The report was receiving favorable comments until unexpectedly, the white-haired chief justice rose and asked permission to speak on a point of personal privilege.

In a voice that shook with emotion, the old judge made a passionate defense of Georgia's judiciary. He did not believe popular election had been a failure, and unless popular education had been, the people would not sit quietly back and see their judges selected by a few men. "The selection of judges is not a new problem in Georgia," he said, "and we will always have some poor judges, but I deny in toto the allegations of some inferior persons that the judiciary of the state is weak, inefficient or time-serving."

This attack by the chief justice on the recommendations took the convention by surprise and was heard in and followed by dramatic silence. The presiding officer called a recess, and many lawyers crowded around the old judge to agree with him and thank him for his remarks. His place as capable judicial leader, a man respected for his wisdom, honor, and service, was once more confirmed. His own son was among the members, and he was struck with admiration at his father's ability to command such a situation on the spur of the moment.[20]

One of the goals of Dick Jr.'s governorship had been to reorganize the university system so that the state's schools would be overseen more efficiently by one board. Success in this goal meant the formation of the University System of Georgia Board of Regents, and Richard Russell Sr. lost his position as Chairman of the Boards of Trustees at the University and the Georgia State College for Women. He was in agreement with these changes, but he was worried that no one suitable would be on the new board to guard and protect his girls' school. Although he never liked to question his son about any of his appointments, he dared to ask him if he had considered the girls' school in his composition of the board. It was only then that he learned he would be asked to serve on the Board of Regents, and only then that his son told him he was specifically considered the girls' champion. The father's relief and gratitude for this move brought him to tears.[21]

For Dick Jr., the summer unfolded with campaign events while the usual duties of the governor continued. By the end of the summer he was

making fourteen to sixteen speeches a week. He invited Crisp to a series
of debates, but as others before him, Crisp judged a Russell too
formidable to fight face to face on the platform.

Once more Dick Jr. had to rely on his family to help. Fielding, out
of school for the summer, helped in the Atlanta office. Alex, having
finished his first year at medical school, worked until July. He could not
pass up a chance to serve as driver across country to Taylor Morton and
his mother and aunt to see the Los Angeles Olympics. Edward was
engaged in a rural student pastorate preceding his senior year at
Columbia Theological Seminary. Pipey, who had scarcely had two
pennies to rub together, had left him a few hundred dollars out of her
own inheritance from her father, and thus he was able to buy a car and
increase his efficiency as a country pastor.[22]

In August Dick Jr. was involved in a frightening head-on collision
while dashing from one campaign speaking engagement to another. Ina
and Richard heard about it first when the newspaper extras hit the streets
of Atlanta. Their son lost four front teeth, but after a local dentist
repaired the damage, he went on with his campaigning.[23]

The majority of large newspaper support in the campaign went to
Crisp, including several national papers, with the *Augusta Chronicle*, the
Atlanta Journal and the *Columbus Ledger* the only major dailies to
support Russell. Unfazed, Dick Jr. took out ads in numerous local
weeklies, and many of these publications backed the young politician
unreservedly. They pictured him as a man of the people who kept his
promises. A healthy campaign fund of twelve thousand dollars had been
garnered to pay for this kind of publicity.

As the election neared, the big papers predicted a Crisp victory, but
the Russell camp had the pulse of the people. The clubs from 1930, many
based on Richard Sr.'s old friends, had been revived in every county, and
reports from these indicated strong Russell support across the state. Dick
Russell Jr. was a skillful politician, and, in addition, he had a reputation
for sincerity, honesty and integrity that came across when he spoke. No
criticisms in the opposing camp had been able to sully this reputation. On
September 14, Dick Russell Jr. was elected United States Senator by a
large majority. 162,745 popular votes, representing 296 county unit votes
went to Russell, with 119,193 popular votes and 114 county unit votes

for Crisp. Winder again put on a gala party celebrating the success of its native son, and Richard Sr. once again found the moment too emotional for him to make a speech of any great length.

The only bad news on election day was that Hugh Peterson did not win in his bid for Congress in the First District.

Eugene Talmadge was elected governor in this election, to begin his first term in January 1933. Dick Jr.'s state government re-organization had included legislation to change the governor's inauguration from June to January, thus shortening his own term as governor. Ina and Richard would leave the governor's mansion after only a year and a half.

Ina felt a pang over this shortened tenure. She wanted to be sure Dick Jr. had fulfilled his obligations. She went to the person she most respected for giving fair and impartial judgements. She asked Richard, "Has Dick been a good governor?" Richard took a long time to reply, as he thought over their son's work. Then he said, "Yes, I think he has been one of the best governors Georgia has ever had." Ina did not go to any other authority. She was satisfied.[24]

History would agree with the judge. In spite of a shortened term, Dick Russell Jr. had left his state in much better shape than he found it. In state government for thirteen years, Speaker of the House for two terms before being elected chief executive, gifted in the art of compromise and trusted as a man of his word, he operated from a strong base. Government reorganization was implemented, the state was operating within its income, and state agencies were meeting minimum demand. The young senator-elect continued to emphasize the need for strict economy in perilous times as he prepared to go to Washington.

The family had suffered a deep worry as the campaign progressed because Ralph Sharpton, like so many others in these depressed times, had lost his job. From Washington state he and Harriette moved to California, but found no work. The way Harriette's siblings rallied for her must have made Richard and Ina proud. Ina Jr. moved into a larger but cheaper apartment so that they could come back East and live with her while Ralph looked for work. Others in the family contributed to buy the steamboat tickets to bring them back to the eastern seaboard. Ralph found employment in the Washington area after a few months.

Virginia and Fielding moved to Statesboro, where Fielding took up a teaching post at the Georgia Teachers' College. Fielding Dillard Russell Jr. was born there on October 14. Edward, elected president of the student body at Columbia Theological Seminary, was causing no worry, but Alex, now in his second year of medical school at Emory, caused some concern as the family turned towards a new life. Alex had a wild streak wider than most of the other boys, and to steady him, Ina asked if he would like to live with them in the Mansion for the remainder of the governor's term, then move with them into an apartment or house. She and Richard had decided that taking a house temporarily in Atlanta, which Ina could make a home, was the best way to try to see Edward, Carolyn and Alex through their studies. Alex agreed with this idea and moved in as the autumn term began. He was up late and early to study. His sister Carolyn, happily pursuing her studies at Agnes Scott, thought he slept with his anatomy book.

Alex's serious study did not stop his getting into a shooting scrape at a house of prostitution in Atlanta, where he and two friends had gone on a dare, none having had experience in such places. When a story describing the fracas appeared the next morning in an Atlanta paper, Alex had to face his mother and his father at the breakfast table, knowing they would have seen the piece. The judge did not neglect his parental responsibilities.

"I see in the paper that you've been somewhere you ought not to have been," he said to his youngest son.

"Yes, sir, I'm guilty."

"Are you going to go back?"

"No, sir. I learned enough from that experience to know I'll never go back to a place like that again in my life."

"All right, then."

At the next family gathering, Alex's brothers Dick Jr. and Rob ragged him about this embarrassment and tried to get him to reveal further details.

"There's no more to say about it," he declared and concluded, "That case has been tried before the chief justice and dismissed."[25]

Ina and Pat set out to find a house for the Russells to live in after January 10, when the new governor was inaugurated. They settled on 1198 Piedmont Avenue, a furnished house across from the Piedmont Driving Club. Ina declared it as nice as the Mansion. They moved the afternoon of the inauguration. Ina had had everything cleaned at the Mansion before leaving and tried to be helpful to Mrs. Talmadge, but she could not accommodate the Talmadges when Mrs. Talmadge wanted to send things over a few days prior to the inauguration. Carolyn was holding a reception for Agnes Scott students at the weekend.[26]

Richard was not bothered by any of these domestic upheavals, nor apparently by the fact that he would now have to pay rent to keep his family in Atlanta and pay for Ina to have a servant to clean and cook. He rode serenely over to 1198 Piedmont Avenue in his eldest son's car. Ina did not mourn leaving the state's Packard and chauffeur, which she had greatly relished, because Dick Jr.'s car was safely locked in the garage of the new domicile. With Carolyn, Alex and Edward in town, there would be someone to drive them places when needed. For getting to work, Richard had only to step out the front door for a tram.[27]

When Dick Russell Jr. was sworn in on January 12, 1933, as Georgia's junior senator, he had just passed his thirty-fifth birthday. He was the youngest man in the Senate by three years. He expressed deep humility that he had come to the greatest deliberative body in the world, from the greatest state and people in the world. He was grateful that, having left home for the first time in his life since his student days, he had supportive family nearby. Ina Jr., Billie and Harriette were all present for his swearing in. Ina and Richard were unable to go, although he had offered to pay their way. Richard's work, always heavy in January, and Ina's conscientious efforts to establish the new home as a warm, loving place caused them to forego this great pleasure. It was also the case that both were worn down by the final months of life in the governor's Mansion.[28]

On April 11, 1933, Edward was ordained a Presbyterian minister in a ceremony at the Athens Presbytery meeting at the old Hebron Church in rural Banks County. He and his roommate of three years, Alton Glozier, had done their student preaching in this Presbytery, and the two were ordained together.

Alex drove his parents and his sister Carolyn to the church, set deep in the country, in a grove of lovely old trees that the four took time to admire before entering the sanctuary, where gas lights hanging from the ceiling illuminated the church. They listened with pride as Edward and his friend each preached a literate, ordered, inspiring and short sermon. When the two young men knelt, and the elders of the Presbytery came and laid hands on them and the moderator prayed an earnest prayer, Richard and Ina were deeply moved. Visions of his mother and her high hopes for a son in the ministry came to Richard, and he had to wipe away tears. As much as had been Dick Jr.'s inauguration, this simple ceremony in a backwoods church was a crowning moment of their lives.[29]

In June Ina moved back to her home in Russell. The expense of living in Atlanta seemed unnecessary, and to all the family the old homeplace was in a class by itself when it came to the production of human happiness and contentment. Living in a hotel in Washington, Dick Jr. longed to come home to Russell when he had time off, and his mother and father were happy to provide his home. The burgeoning grandchild population (there were now eleven) needed room indoors and out during summer visits. Richard would have to go back to his old way of being at home only on weekends. Ina had loved living in the city, but she did not go back to Atlanta for nearly a year. Sometimes she felt homesick for the easier city life, but she kept her feelings hidden from Richard.[30]

Rob and Sybil had built a house nearby large enough to house their three children comfortably. With Rob's guiding, bathrooms were at last put into the homeplace at the same time. Following in Dad's footsteps, Rob was doing a little farming on the side. Richard wanted to step up his farming activities as well, but for five years he had done little on the two farms he owned. They had even sold the milkcow when Alex went away to school. Richard viewed with despair the work needed to put the land back into production. Nevertheless, when a neighboring farm, the Bell place, came up for sale, he scraped together money to pay down and got a loan for the rest.[31]

On April 10, 1934, he and Ina welcomed Cecil Bealer into the Walter Russell family, their sixth granddaughter.

Richard's brother Rob died on May 8, 1934, while Richard was en route to Washington, hoping to see him and attend the Law Institute. Shocked and heartbroken, the old judge stayed for the funeral in Arlington National Cemetery, then rushed back to Georgia where the family was gathering for an important event honoring Ina. The library built in 1931 at the Georgia State College for Women had been named for Ina Dillard Russell, and a portrait to hang in the building had been commissioned. Now it was time for the unveiling, and the family traveled to Milledgeville.[32]

The hasty trips and deep grief over his brother's death may have brought about a physical breakdown. Richard Russell's body had been a strong machine, able to take all kinds of demands, many of them unreasonable, but when his associate, Justice R.C. Bell, found him in agony in his office one afternoon, suffering from an inguinal hernia, there was nothing to do but go into hospital. They made every effort to keep the hospitalization quiet and managed for four days to succeed. Then the news broke and articles appeared all over the state. This kind of publicity embarrassed and frustrated Richard. His recovery was slow, and he was not an easy patient. His almost-doctor son Alex got good practice going to see his father and checking up, under orders from Dad, on what was being done and why.

Although Richard was able to go home after a few days, he remained a demanding patient for Ina for several weeks. He was unable to go to Carolyn's graduation from Agnes Scott College. Ina was grateful for the new bathrooms in these trying circumstances. Richard's loving and all-patient wife learned to fit his truss long before he did, and she allowed him a medicinal toddy each evening, preparing it herself with whiskey supplied by their eldest son. She could not have managed that if she had not loved him so much.[33]

Carolyn began her first job teaching in Blakely, Georgia, three hundred miles from Winder. Richard and Ina found themselves amazed to be talking of their youngest attending faculty meetings. Hugh Peterson ran for Congress again in Georgia's First District and was elected in the autumn of 1934. In the new year, he and Pat joined her brother and sisters in Washington to swell the numbers of the Russell colony there. Ralph and Harriette, however, had moved to Knoxville, Tennessee, where Ralph had taken a job with the Reconstruction Finance Corporation.[34]

In June 1935 Alex graduated from Emory University Medical School. His brother Dick made the graduating address. At last there were no more tuition fees to pay. Alex visited his father a few days after the graduation, his mission to thank him for his education. The old man, his desk piled with cases, his office littered with work-related papers, was moved by his son's recognition of provision. For a moment he could not speak and as was often the case these days, he shed a few tears. Then he said, "Son, if you want to do further study, just say so. I'll do my best to send you anywhere you want to go."[35]

Richard had no worries about any of his sons in their chosen livelihoods except William. In 1935, Papa was aware that William was unhappy in his work, and with the same patriarchal fervor that had made him offer Alex more education, he turned his thoughts to helping William. He felt his son was a competent and trustworthy storekeeper and recognized that after success at Marshall, North Carolina, he had been given a larger store to manage by the A&P Company, in Sylva, North Carolina. Nevertheless, Richard and Ina both may have worried that William drank too much because of his dissatisfaction and loneliness so far from home and family. Richard came up with a couple of plans he thought might be workable for his light-hearted and hard-working son.[36]

By this time Richard Russell owned nearly a thousand acres in Barrow County, the majority surrounding the homeplace. He figured it would take several thousand dollars to repair terraces, put up new fences and re-seed pastures, before an initial crop could be sown. There would also be the matter of buying mules. Richard confessed to being unable to help in the latter.[37]

Where money was concerned, he was willing to go on a loan with William if William felt he could pay the interest and eventually the principal. It was important to note that farming was a high-risk employment, and that this would not be an easy road. Another possibility, which Richard was also willing to help finance, was to build a fireproof bonded warehouse, equipped with a sprinkler system, for cotton storage. The Winder area in the autumn of 1935 had quickly exhausted its cotton storage, and Richard Sr. believed there were profits in this endeavor, especially if coupled with selling fire insurance. He was willing to take any risks to open these businesses or to begin a serious farming operation because he felt that William must make a change, and he had confidence that his son, "his Daddy," would do his whole duty.[38]

1935 saw his grandson total increase by three. In May he had the double thrill of Virginia and Fielding's William Don, their second son, and Marguerite and Jim's Richard Russell Bowden, the third grandchild to be named for Richard. In July Pat and Hugh Peterson became parents of Hugh Peterson Jr. The next year Walter and Dolly added Ina Dillard III to their family. The grandchild count stood at eighteen, equal at last to the number of children.

On June 24, 1936, Richard took an early train from Atlanta to his home in Russell, hoping to surprise his bride of forty-five years. She was looking for him, had felt sure that he would come. They found pleasure in talking over their wedding day and the years since then. They walked over to see Rob, who was recovering from an automobile accident. A heavy storm swept in with rain, lightning and hail, but when that had passed, they welcomed impromptu guests throughout the afternoon who came by to congratulate them. Next morning they had to get up at three so that Richard could catch a train back to Atlanta in time for a long day at the office.

The day would be long for Ina, as well, for Dick Jr. had come in the day before, and he was gearing up for the toughest political battle of his life. On June 25 Ina began answering phone calls at 8:00 a.m., and soon people were coming by, hoping to see the Senator to discuss the looming campaign against Georgia's Governor Eugene Talmadge.[39]

In the four years since his election to the Senate, Dick Jr. had for the most part supported President Roosevelt's New Deal policies, believing narrow views of government functions and responsibilities were counterproductive. He spoke in Georgia frequently and eloquently about the benefits resulting from New Deal legislation. In the Senate, he gained a reputation as a quiet, unobtrusive young man who could get things done. Never a publicity hound, he preferred to work behind the scenes and seemed indifferent to who received credit, as long as the necessary legislation passed. His pleasing personality continued to stand him in good stead, and back home in Georgia he remained popular. Yet anyone could see the re-election campaign would not be for the fainthearted.

Eugene Talmadge had been re-elected governor in 1934, and he was enormously popular. Although well-educated and from a cultured background, Talmadge chose to play the role of the demagogue, and he had gained popularity by proclaiming, in extravagantly poor English, that he was the champion of the common man. As such, he had license to run roughshod over the legislature and many state agencies. Several times he called out the National Guard to enforce his will. He was an open and avowed racist. At the 1934 Democratic National Convention he tried to organize Southern Democrats to block Roosevelt's renomination. While he was popular with tens of thousands of rural Georgians who considered him their 'beloved governor', many other Georgians were aghast at his behavior.

Eugene Talmadge launched his campaign for the US Senate at McRae, Georgia, on July 4, 1936. He held a huge barbecue that brought thousands of people to enjoy barbecued pork, beef, lamb, and chicken and Brunswick stew in massive quantities. The crowd roared its support as Talmadge attacked Roosevelt and the New Deal and promised he would prevent national debt, reduce the federal budget and defend states' rights. He left no doubt that Gene Talmadge was the most dangerous political rival Dick Russell Jr. had yet faced.

Senator Russell had a different feel for what the people wanted. He sensed that the President maintained an almost blind devotion from the electorate and sought to identify himself closely with Roosevelt and the New Deal. His record in the Senate proved that he believed in most of the New Deal policies and had supported them. While Talmadge tried to label him as a stooge and rubber stamp for Roosevelt, Russell said he took pride in his support of the President. He emphasized how important New Deal agricultural policies were to Georgia farmers and said they should vote for him if they wanted a senator who would keep on trying to give the farmer and his family a fighting chance in the future.

Russell was not as flamboyant a speaker as Talmadge, but he was far from boring. He could make his audience laugh and think. He had also the advantage of being able to stress what he had done for senior citizens, labor, veterans and others. He pointed out how much federal money had been spent in Georgia, in particular counties, with resulting benefits. His speeches had substance. By August he was making six, seven, or eight speeches each week, travelling hundreds of miles. Most of his main talks were broadcast over the radio, as were Talmadge's. The 1936 campaign was the first political contest in Georgia to use the radio extensively. Richard and Ina did not attend many of the rallies for their son, but they listened by the radio intently all summer. By the end of the summer, eight grandchildren were staying at the homeplace, and Richard, though growing frail, sometimes still went out to dig dirt when the crowd around the radio was too noisy or boisterous.[40]

Ina noticed the difference in behavior of Russell crowds and Talmadge crowds. She was proud of the orderly responses to her courtly son. Nevertheless, the campaign was the bitterest Dick Jr. had ever encountered, and he needed all his parents' good examples to keep up his gentlemanly demeanor. As Talmadge attracted large crowds to more and more barbecues, often set up with the aid of state workers and state equipment, news from around the state was not encouraging to Senator Russell. News of Talmadge gains made the Russell forces battle all the harder and keep up an optimistic front.

Rob was once again managing the main campaign quarters and keeping his older brother on schedule. The rest of the family was in and out of the homeplace or the campaign headquarters in Atlanta all summer for stints of duty. The bachelor younger brothers, Edward, Alex and William, worked hard when they had time off. Jim and Marguerite canvassed tirelessly in Savannah and Chatham County. Pat and Hugh were caught up in their own race in the First District. The network of non-family state-wide support was as resilient and loyal as it had been since 1930. Everywhere Russell supporters sent out letters, gave out flicrs, put up posters, and attended rallies. Talmadge might be able to use state workers, but they did not work as hard as Russell volunteers.

Talmadge supporters dragged out the old charge of too many Russells at the public trough. According to a document purportedly circulated by Barrow and Jackson county residents, the Russells had a total of 219 years on government payrolls, fifty-six years assigned to

Judge Russell. The Russell reputation for hard work turned this kind of charge into praise. When Talmadge himself accused young Dick Russell of paving sidewalks in the tiny community of Russell at the expense of Georgia taxpayers, the irony was too heavy for Russell humorists to ignore. Someone, perhaps William and Alex, still digging dirt for Dad and trying to persuade him to stop digging, put up a large poster on the highway that declared a ten-dollar reward to anyone who could find paved sidewalks in Russell. Sidewalk search parties arrived from time to time, but not one paved sidewalk was ever found.[41]

This was the first time Dick Russell Jr. had needed a large campaign chest, and he was humbled when voters began to send steady contributions, many of them from one to five dollars. He saw that they were acknowledged promptly, with his sincere thanks, and he closed the letter by saying that although the fight would be hard, the outcome was not in doubt. Some supporters donated bales of cotton, one of which was ginned the year Dick Russell Jr. was born.[42]

On August 26, Russell and Talmadge met almost face to face at a large political gathering in Griffin, Georgia. Although Gene Talmadge did not agree to debate Russell, he did agree to their meeting on the same platform, at separate times, among other candidates for other offices. As the speaking schedule developed, Russell would speak just before lunch, then Talmadge after lunch, giving him the advantage. In what would be his finest campaign speech, Dick Russell Jr. rose to the challenge. Using a combination of humor, sarcasm and hard facts, he ripped the governor's platform to shreds and soon had him on the political ropes. His fatal punch was to tack to the podium fifteen questions that he expected the governor to answer. He told the cheering crowd to demand answers. The questions included how Talmadge proposed to help farmers by cutting their federal payments, how he could reduce the national budget to one billion dollars, and how government could be funded if the income tax were eliminated as Talmadge insisted.

When Talmadge took the floor after lunch, he ignored the questions, but the crowd's insistence that he respond to them neutralized his bombastic form and his performance was weak and disjointed. The governor "had been drawn and quartered—his style and stomping, his demagoguery and showmanship all pared away."[43]

Predictions were that the race would be close, but the votes on September 9 created another Russell landslide. Dick Russell received 256,154 popular votes to Talmadge's 134,695. The county unit tally was even more lopsided. Talmadge received a mere thirty-two county unit votes to Russell's three hundred and seventy-eight. Georgians had eaten Gene's barbecue, but they had voted for Dick Russell Jr.

On September 10, Winder staged another gargantuan victory celebration. A violent thunderstorm held up the party by knocking out the electricity for half an hour. Dick Russell Jr. introduced his mother this time as the only sweetheart he had ever had. Richard Sr. could not find words to express the joy that all were feeling. Besting an opponent of the strength of Gene Talmadge was the headiest victory wine any of them had ever tasted. Even being elected governor did not come up to this. To the crowd that evening, Richard Sr. judged it the happiest moment of his life because he felt that dignity and democracy for Georgia had been saved. A photograph made the next day shows the judge frail but happy, with the senator, robust and relaxed, sitting on the arm of his father's chair.[44]

As the dust settled over the campaign, Alex stirred up a little of his own when on September 28, he married Sarah Eaton, a nurse he had been courting for two years. They moved into the homeplace with Richard and Ina as they set out to establish a medical practice in Barrow County.

Not long after the election, Richard experienced a peculiar physical weakness. Hardly able to walk to the Capitol, he told no one of this except Ina. Insurance premiums and loan repayments were relentless, and his work ethic would not allow him to take time off. He would rather die than draw a state salary without earning it. He resolved to hold a stiff upper lip and backbone. His mind was as clear as it ever had been in his life and his current decisions measured up to any he had ever written. With quiet pride, he noted to his wife that counting his Appeals and Supreme Court decisions, he had written a greater number of decisions than any other man before him in Georgia.[45]

The story of a junior following in his father's footsteps and far beyond again attracted attention nation-wide, and it was hoped Richard B. Russell Jr.'s success in the Georgia Senate campaign signaled a change from Southern emphasis on demagoguery. Reporters who came to question Richard Sr. would begin by asking him, as a politician, about his pride in his senator son. He did not deny that he was proud of Dick Jr.'s accomplishments, but he preferred to highlight Edward's success. He believed that Edward, in his sacred duties as a minister charged to preach Jesus Christ and Him crucified, had fulfilled an ambition more important than politics, one Richard had been unable to achieve in spite of his blessed mother's guidance and hope.[46]

18

HE HAS FINISHED HIS WORK
AND SLIPPED AWAY

1937-1938

January 1, 1937— "Another year! It seems only a very short time since my 1936 diary was started. Heavenly Father, may I not have any heart breaking experience to record in this book. If I should have, help me to say, Thy Will Be Done. May we go on gladly, joyfully, and cautiously into the days that are before us."[1]

New Year's Day evening 1937 Ina and Richard sat by the fire in their living room, keeping an ear open for two small grandsons asleep upstairs, while their parents, Virginia and Fielding, were at a movie in Winder with Alex and Sarah. William was now living at home, determined to farm, but he was out as well. The two old folks sat quietly, Ina writing in her diary while her husband of forty-six years read aloud the familiar and well-loved words of Gray's "Elegy Written in a Country Churchyard." Both had ever honored the short and simple annals of the poor, and Richard, with all his Ambition and dreams of Grandeur, knew too well the madding crowd's ignoble strife. In old age, he saw clearly the paths of glory are no different from any other. All lead but to the grave. The worm that eats the pauper eats the prince.

At the Christmas family gatherings, Richard had not neglected to predict his own demise. Physical frailty had almost eliminated his dirt digging, but he continued to do his court work, and his mind kept its edge and its depth. He was alert, too, to the success of his many offspring.

The Russell home remained a center of activity, reflecting the creative, productive lives of the Russell children. Alex and Sarah were busy night and day with Alex's medical practice, and the medical needs of the small community emerged in a strong light. Automobile accident victims, children with diphtheria, and mothers traumatized by difficult births became reasons to dream of building a hospital. William worked occasional jobs with the sheriff's department, transporting prisoners to state facilities, while getting his farm operation going. Farm laborers ate their dinners on the back porch of the homeplace.

Dick Jr., earning a reputation as one of Washington's hardest-working senators, was home seldom, but when he was, the house buzzed with telephone calls and visitors. Sometimes he brought staff from his Washington office to help with work and they shared in family life. Rob and Sybil's three active children from next door were in and out constantly. The other family members were home often, hungry for a taste of that old-time, homey feeling that being in their parents' house gave them.

Richard wanted his wife to come to Atlanta and spend time with him, but life at home kept her attention. She had soon recovered from any homesickness for Atlanta. Sitting in a hotel room, never knowing when Richard would finish his work at the Capitol, could not compete with the active days in Russell. Working in Atlanta was becoming more and more difficult for Richard, for the train schedules were not as convenient as they had been in years past. Now he sometimes had to take the bus.[2]

On his seventy-sixth birthday, April 27, 1937, they had a special family celebration. Alex drove him to Braselton in a new car, to pay off an old, old debt to the Braselton brothers, freeing another of his farms from debt. The loan was for five thousand dollars, and the Braselton brothers refused to take the final interest payment, sending the judge home with money in his pocket. A happy family gathered around the table that night. Rob and Sybil and children came over to join Alex, Sarah, William and Mother and Dad. Sybil, an excellent cook, brought the cake.[3]

In May Ina and Richard were overjoyed to be invited to Washington for a time with Billie and all the other family. Dad would, of course, attend the Law Institute. Then all the family would travel to Camden, New Jersey, for the christening of the USS *Savannah*. Thanks to her parents' active life in the Savannah community and her senator uncle, Jane Mayo Bowden was chosen ship's sponsor.

Ina and Richard had an elegant room in the Washington Hotel for their stay in the capital city. Richard paid cheerfully for this extravagance and also for cab rides to the Law Institute meetings. Ina attended a White House reception in the Rose Garden with Ina Jr., Pat and Billie. The Chief Justice of the Georgia Supreme Court was interviewed by the *Washington Post* regarding his opinion on the President's attempts to change the national Supreme Court. Although Richard Jr. wanted to keep a low profile on this question because it was one in which he disagreed with Roosevelt, the old judge was in favor of the changes. His son found their differences trying when his father made them public because his father never seemed to consider how his remarks might stir up trouble. He had always spoken his mind frankly.[4]

The night before the launching, the shipbuilders entertained at a gala dinner. Richard had for years been negligent about his false teeth, keeping them more often in his pocket than in his mouth, and this night he had failed to wear them. Trying to chew a piece of steak, he swallowed it prematurely and began to choke. He continued to cough so much that he left the table. Before long, his sons Dick and Rob had followed him, and soon he was in hospital, where the meat had to be removed surgically. The entire family spent an anxious night, but joy came in the morning with Richard's complete recovery. Ina's children convinced her it was safe for her to attend the launching, but she found the pomp and circumstance disquieting. She was grateful to have escaped recording a tragic event in her diary.[5]

In June, the unthinkable happened. The entire family had been aware of their father's growing feebleness and watched his health anxiously, but they were taken by complete surprise when their mother fell ill with a debilitating malady. They may have thought of a world in which Ina had to exist without Richard, but one in which Richard had to exist without Ina was unimaginable. Ina spent a week in the hospital, and although nothing definitive was discovered, she remained weak and as she put it, 'too good-for-nothing.' She was assigned to bed rest and forced limited activity. As the year wore on, she had other attacks and had to return to long days and weeks in bed. Unable as ever to cope with the illness of loved ones, Richard gave over her care to Alex, Sarah and William, a capable trio, and kept up his court work. Sometimes he stayed as many as ten days in Atlanta without coming home. When he did come home, he insisted on carrying water to young trees he had planted. He could no longer dig dirt, but he watched over William and his laborers at it.[6]

William's farm work brought another blessing to this situation. One of his laborers was a young black man named Grant Thomas. Thomas's wife, Modine, came to work in the house and proved a reliable cook and housekeeper. Not given to subservience in any form, she was a capable worker and fierce in her loves and loyalties. She came to love Ina Russell and would remain a formidable force in any question of Ina's welfare for the rest of her life.

Another family development that pleased Richard and Ina was Fielding's decision to continue his studies towards a doctorate. He was accepted as a student at George Washington University, and the family moved to Virginia in the autumn. They lived for several months with Billie and Gordon before a part time job in the Post Office Department allowed them to rent an apartment. Mutual support was a family tradition.

Although travel was more and more difficult for Richard and Ina, by going to Washington, they could now see five of their children in one place: Billie, Ina Jr., Dick Jr., Pat, and Fielding. Harriette and Ralph were in Tennessee, Walter and Dolly in North Carolina, Marguerite and Jim in Savannah. Carolyn was teaching in Fort Valley, Georgia, and Edward preaching at McDonough. Alex, William and Rob were on the homeplace, all three trying to farm while engaged in other work, as their dad had done. Alex bought a hundred acres from his father at the beginning of the new year and planned to build a tenant house on it. The farm was priced at five dollars per acre, and Dick Jr. thought this extravagant proof that doctors had money to pour down rat holes.[7]

Edward was engaged to Ala Joanna Brewton, Hugh Peterson's cousin, whom he met when helping out with a Peterson campaign. She was only seventeen when they met, and Edward had to wait patiently for her to finish college at GSCW, but he was willing because he had proof she would be an understanding wife. When she and Edward took Ina and Richard for a drive to Oglethorpe County, Richard sat in the front seat. He spit tobacco juice out the window, causing no small anxiety in the women in the back seat, but Ala Jo had not cancelled the engagement. A June wedding was still planned.[8]

The biggest announcement of the new year 1938 came from Ina Jr. who at last had found a man she liked enough to give up her name. She was engaged to Captain Jean Killough Stacy, United States Army. Captain Stacy, a World War I veteran like Gordon Green, was stationed in Pennsylvania and was hoping for a transfer to the Washington area because Ina was not going to give up her job. They would also be married in June.

Ina Sr. fell ill again in February, and the family spent an anxious month praying for her to be well enough to leave Emory Hospital. Alex and Sarah presented her with Alexander Brevard Russell Jr. on March 16, born at the same hospital, and Ina wondered if she would live to see his first birthday. His father predicted she would live to see his sixteenth birthday. She took heart, especially when on April 20 Rob and Sybil added another daughter, Mary Ina, to the grandchild ranks.[9]

Richard and Ina traveled to Washington for Ina Jr.'s wedding to Jean Stacy on June 4. Richard was so feeble that he could not escort his daughter down the aisle, and Dick Jr. gave his sister away. It was, nevertheless, a happy family gathering, followed by another in Vidalia, Georgia, on June 15 for the nuptials of Edward and Ala Jo. A big family reunion had been planned in Winder for June 24, Richard and Ina's forty-seventh wedding anniversary, but the date was moved to July 3 to allow honeymooners to attend.

After fried chicken and trimmings, the family was herded to the front porch for a photograph, with Ina and Richard in the center of forty-three other members of their family, all children, spouses of children, or grandchildren. "Just look what Papa and I started," Ina said.[10]

The judge tried to hold Mary Ina, his newest grandchild, but she had to be passed to Dick Jr. for the photo. Ina held Alex Jr. The judge leaned on his cane and against his daughter-in-law Sarah as the picture was snapped. A report that had to please the progenitors of this clan accompanied the photograph when it appeared in the Sunday Atlanta paper, bringing letters of congratulations from other patriarchs in the state. Could any other family have a stronger claim to First Family of Georgia?[11]

Immediately following the reunion, it looked as though the wedding craze would continue. New marriages of siblings and remembrance of one of the finest of all times may have stirred Dick Jr. to propose marriage to his sweetheart, Pat Collins, whom he had met in Washington three years previously. Pat, a dark-haired Georgia beauty ten years his junior, was a graduate of Agnes Scott College and Emory University Law School. Pat was Catholic, but the couple had not felt a difference in religion would be a problem. Dick brought Pat home to meet his mother and father following the family reunion, and a late July wedding seemed likely as Pat returned to Washington.

When the question of marriage and children came up, however, so did problems. Pat visited her priest in Washington, and she felt bound by the Catholic ruling that all children of mixed marriages had to be brought up as Catholics. Dick Jr. wanted his children to be able to make up their own minds about their religion. He also assumed that his brother Edward would perform the wedding ceremony, while Pat wanted a Catholic priest to officiate.

These differences revealed deep-seated beliefs that made marriage an unwise risk. Deeply in love, the pair experienced enormous pain in breaking their engagement. Some thought Dick Jr. would be wary of marrying a Catholic as a political liability in the Georgia of the 1930s, but he had had Catholics on his staff since his days as governor and refused to base his judgment of a man on religion. It is not likely that this fear would have prevented his marrying a woman he loved. The fear that she could not be satisfied outside her own spiritual realm was enough to make him pause. Such a union might be like a broken arm that would not heal. The family sympathized with both people in this emotional turmoil, but Dick Jr. had always been intensely private about his romantic life. Little was said about it after the engagement was broken.[12]

In the autumn of 1938, bent and infirm, the judge was at his desk daily. His colleagues and friends still enjoyed going in to talk with him throughout the day, and he never refused to see anyone. Sometimes his stenographer, Claude Houser, drove him home and stayed there several days with him so that they could work undisturbed. Although the judge was eligible for a state pension, he showed no inclination to retire. "The people have put me into office," he liked to say, "and they will have to put me out."[13]

No one noticed that as November drew on the judge seemed more determined than usual to clear his desk, not only of cases but of all other administrative questions. One of his colleagues did comment to Justice Bell that in round table discussions, the Chief, as they affectionately called Richard, had grown quiet, more dignified and serene than usual. Possessed by an increasing calmness, he listened alertly but left debate to others. In retrospect his colleagues understood that the spirit had simply poised for its long and momentous flight.[14]

In late November Richard gave Rob instructions to write a will. Writing a will was natural to anyone of seventy-seven, but Richard had in the past feared the act was a portent of death.[15] He had kept his numerous insurance policies carefully labeled to indicate how his estate would be distributed to pay debts and provide for Ina, but now he must consider what to do with his property.[16] On December 1, 1938, he signed a simple will leaving everything to his wife. His son Rob, as executor, was to pay all debts before turning the estate over to Ina. Witnesses were his sons Edward and William and the daughter-in-law whom he called his daughter, Sybil Millsaps Russell.

On Saturday, December 3, Richard Russell finished the last of his court work for the autumn term 1938. His consulting partner, Justice R.C. Bell, came into his office for a final discussion of a case. Judge Bell noticed that the chief's desk was entirely cleared, but he thought little of it. When Richard arrived home, he told Ina that he was tired and his chest hurt. The old pair were home alone, Sarah and Alex having moved next door to the Weaning Cottage where Rob and Sybil had first lived. William was out.

Ina prepared her husband's simple supper, grits and a piece of tender steak. While he was eating, his son Rob came in, having walked over to check on his parents as was his habit. With Rob was his son Richard Brevard Russell III, now eight years old. The lad was a favorite of his grandfather, who gave him his yearly copies of the *Georgia Reports*, inscribed with hopes and gentle exhortations. That evening the judge asked the boy to sit next to him, and gave him an especially tender bite of steak, which he relished. This attention made him feel important because usually the children were sent away from the table when adults were talking. Richard III went home alone and was preparing for bed when the telephone rang. He heard his mother talking in a serious tone to his father, but when she came into his room, she said only that she had to go over to Grandmother's house.

Richard Sr., Ina and Rob had talked a little while, then Richard said he would go to bed. Ina followed him into the bedroom and helped him undress and lie down. Then she went out for a last word with Rob before he went home. As Rob was leaving, they heard Richard coughing, then silence. Uneasy, Rob looked back into the room. He understood immediately that his father had stopped breathing.

Rob phoned Alex first, but he was not home. Sarah called around in the county to try to find him, but she could not say why she needed to speak to him. There was no trusting the Winder phone exchange to hold the news of the judge's death for long. In the meantime, Rob called Dr. W. L. Matthews, another Winder doctor, who came straight away but found there was nothing anyone could do in this world for the old judge.

"He has gone away," Ina said. Her beloved had left her for the last time.

It fell to Sybil to phone the other children with the sad news.[17]

Dick Jr. was at a banquet in Coral Gables, Florida, part of a Congressional delegation touring Florida. When the news reached him, a train in West Palm Beach bound for Atlanta was held for him. As they rushed towards West Palm Beach, the car left the road and turned over. The senator crawled out, refused treatment for an injured knee, and got into another car that reached the train safely.

The next morning the news of the chief justice's death was emblazoned on the front pages of papers statewide,[18] and the story remained front page material until after the funeral on December 6. The commanding headlines, the thorough history of his life in the articles, and the public recognition of his distinctive service would have astonished and gratified Richard Russell. As he had noted so eloquently when speaking of the lives and work of Crawford W. Long, Marvin Parks and Dave Barrow, the record of his own life glowed with faithfulness to unsung work. Its success in the highest values to which humans aspire was clear. To his family, gathering for the sad task of burying their patriarch, it seemed fitting that he was eulogized as an honored father-figure of the state of Georgia.

The rainy morning of December 4, Rob and Alex walked the farm Richard had bought and clung to through so many changes of fortune. Their purpose was to choose a site for his grave. They settled on a spot on a little rise that could be seen across the fields from the kitchen window of the house.[19] The fields would soon become woods as pine trees took the place of cotton, and the spot would not long be visible from the back porch. Yet as the years passed, it would become known and loved as a place of solitude and peace. His grandchildren christened it Papa's Hill.

The body of the Chief Justice of the Georgia Supreme Court lay in state at the Capitol on Monday December 5. His colleagues, who knew him as a man of great heart and brilliant intellect, classically educated, deeply learned and gracefully civil, were somehow astonished at the long lines of common people who came to pay their respects to this able public servant. They knew he treasured his title as the Great Commoner, but he was so far from common that they had ceased to think of his years of close contact with the man in the road, as newspaper reporter, solicitor general, superior court judge, country lawyer, and farmer. They realized that he had achieved a rare balance. In his inimitable way, he regarded every man as his equal and none as his superior, and thus counted all as friends. So they came to the Capitol, from all over the state, to say a last farewell, men and women, old and young, rich and poor, some clothed in finery, and many in their everyday work clothes, filing by his bier, in an unparalleled manifestation of affectionate esteem.[20]

As the magnitude of his life's work emerged, the respect and admiration of those he served poured out. Newspaper reports of his genius, his brilliant mind and his caring heart painted a proud portrait of a useful and illustrious life.

The funeral services were conducted at the First Baptist Church, the largest church in Winder, by three Presbyterian ministers. John Smith, pastor of the Winder Presbyterian Church, led the services. A close minister friend of Ina's, McLeod Frampton, offered the opening prayer. Taylor Morton, whose influence had helped bring Richard back to church, read the Scripture and pronounced the benediction.

So varied were Richard Russell's accomplishments that two eulogies were requested. Justice R.C. Bell, Richard's consulting partner for more than six years, gave the address for the Court. T. W. Reed, a long-time friend from Athens, a man Richard had worked with for fifty years in law, newspaper editing, and education, would give an address on other aspects of his life. In 1938 Reed was in his twenty-ninth year as registrar of the University of Georgia and along with the judge was known as one of the last of the old-time orators.

Neither of the speakers felt it necessary to list Richard Russell's many official accomplishments. They spoke of his brilliant intellect, his rugged individualism, his lofty and inspiring conception of life's duties, his determination to succeed, his unquenchable energy, his courage to stand for his deepest convictions. Above all, they pointed to a life record starred with family and friends in astonishing numbers. Both speakers closed with reference to worldly ambition eclipsed by enduring service. Christ's enigmatic directive had been wonderfully worked out. He who had wished to be chief among his people had been the servant of all.[21]

The *Winder News* of December 8 described the last rites of Judge Russell with tenderness that proved the old feud was finished. "On a pine-studded knoll overlooking his home, Chief Justice Richard B. Russell Sr. was laid to rest Tuesday, borne there by his sons, joined in their mourning by other members of the Russell family, a host of state dignitaries and hundreds of 'just folks.' . . . The church was filled to overflowing. . . . Winder ceased business activity in tribute to the jurist's memory and scores of farmers and mill workers in overalls mingled with the great men of the state in paying their last respects. The body was removed to the church several hours before the funeral and hundreds who realized that they must wait outside during the services viewed the bier before services began…Messages of sympathy were received from all over the nation, President Roosevelt…leading in the tributes."

The family gathering was a sorrowful, yet rich in sentiment. Awareness of the incorruptible wealth he had left them gave them cause to rejoice. Their concern was, as they knew he intended, for their mother, and there was no doubt that she would be well cared for. He had left debts of about twelve thousand dollars, half of which would be paid for by life insurance. The remaining debts were paid for by sale of land. All the children offered help of all kinds until debts were cleared. Dick Jr. never failed to send his mother a generous check each month as long as she lived.[22]

Ina bore up well in the early days after Richard's death, her habit of serenity and dignity in all circumstances not failing her. Granddaughter Betty came at night to sleep with her. In January Ina succumbed to another attack, and for nearly thirty days she lay in a coma in Emory Hospital. By March she was home, determined to face life without the cherished partner with whom she had ridden so many years in tandem. This scene was not different, after all. He had completely entrusted the home fires to her during his absences over forty-seven years. She loved life and rejoiced in the continued successes of their children, but she never lost her sense that she and Richard would be reunited beyond the grave.[23]

In September 1939, the traditional memorial service for justices was held at the Supreme Court of Georgia to honor Richard Russell Sr. Even nine months after his death, so many in the legal and judicial communities wanted to speak that all had to be asked to limit their remarks to three minutes. The Court-appointed committee's report was deliberately shortened to give time for volunteers to speak. Forty men, lawyers and judges and friends, were asked to serve on the committee, with Arthur Powell, from the early Court of Appeals days, as Chairman. They noted their difficulties: "The pride that the members of this committee feel in having been selected to present this memorial is overshadowed by the feeling that in none of us nor in all of us is there the skill and competency to pay adequate tribute to him whom we are this day called upon to memorialize...We may be able to commit to writing some of his achievements which give testimony to his greatness, but there was in him and in his life a vastness that evades definition and defeats delineation—vastness of heart and of mind and of personality."[24]

The tributes from this unique jury of his peers overflowed with praise for a brilliant legal mind, but greatest emphasis fell on the life of a good husband, father and friend. The breadth of historical and literary comparisons would have warmed his heart. He was compared to Benjamin Franklin and John Adams for his family background, to Thomas Jefferson as a man who chose to be remembered for his contributions to education and as author of the Declaration of Independence, to Alexander Stephens and Robert Toombs as men young lawyers could emulate, and to Odysseus, for there was none left in Ithaca who could draw his bow. Lines from Homer, Shakespeare, Bryant, Rossetti, Wordsworth, Stevenson, and Kipling added music he loved to the prose.

Justice Bell's response for the Court summed up the vast subject as perhaps only a superior jurist could. "His passing brought to a close a truly remarkable life, one full of years and full of usefulness. For more than half a century he served the people of his State in responsible position; and considering what was done by him directly, together with the forces he influenced, few, if any other men have left or will ever leave such in imprint on the life of this State . . . . He was genuinely human and could not have been immune from the frailties of flesh and blood, or of passion and sentiment. Any man is good whose virtues outweigh his faults. Character is determined by the good that remains after a balance has been struck. As in other matters, take into account assets and liabilities in determining value or insolvency. By this standard Judge Russell was indeed a great and a good man."[25]

His family went forward in the knowledge of his character, courage and achievements, aware that life bestows no richer heritage than such a father.[26]

EPILOGUE

The records of the lives of the thirteen children of Ina Dillard and Richard Russell provide reliable witness to support the claim that their joint ambition to found a worthy family was fulfilled in stunning fashion. These descendants were human beings with all the frailties that flesh is heir to, but in trying to live according to the lights their parents had instilled, through precept and example, they represent a strong argument for the plain wisdom that children learn what they live. These children had lived ambition, industry, loyalty, honor, integrity, deep emotional attachments, respect for spiritual life, courage but not intolerance in conviction, and selfless community service. While struggling with whatever demons they had, they continued to live these ideals. They produced thirty-nine grandchildren, thirty-eight of whom reached maturity. One of these was invalided at an early age with severe asthma, but thirty-seven others went into various careers of service and maintained as well the Russell-Dillard tradition of strong family ties.

Richard Russell's ambition to leave behind a name associated with service and achievement was also fulfilled beyond his wildest hopes. At the girls' school he helped to establish and to which he gave decades of loyal service (now Georgia College and State University), the auditorium bears his name, and a bust of the chief justice adorns the foyer. The bronze bust has a shiny nose because it is campus custom that before examinations, students go by to touch the nose for good luck. All over Georgia the names of public buildings, parks, schools, lakes, libraries, and forests carry the name of Richard B. Russell through his son. In a thirty-seven-year career in the US Senate Richard Russell Jr. became one of the most powerful and respected men in Washington. When the Senate was instructed to choose a name for the Old Senate Office Building in 1972, a year after the death of Richard Russell Jr., they named it the Russell Office Building.

One family of the clan has followed closely in the judge's legal footsteps. Not surprisingly, it is that of Robert Lee Russell Sr. In 1940, President Franklin Roosevelt appointed Robert Lee Russell Sr. to the Federal Court of the Northern District of Georgia. For the confirmation of this appointment in the US Senate, Senator Walter George sponsored the new Judge Russell. Richard Russell Jr. wanted no charge of nepotism to taint Rob's appointment and so did not even vote during the confirmation process. President Harry Truman appointed Robert Lee Russell Sr. to the Fifth Circuit Court of Appeals in 1949, where he served until his death in 1955.

When he died of cancer in 1965, Robert Lee Russell Jr. was a judge of the Georgia Court of Appeals.

Rob's daughter Betty married Ernest Vandiver, who became Governor of Georgia in 1960. As governor, Vandiver had the honor of appointing seven judges to the Court of Appeals and one to the Supreme Court. One of these appellate judges, Robert H. Jordan, was elevated to the Supreme Court and became Chief Justice.

In 1964 Richard Brevard Russell III, Rob's second son and Richard Sr.'s namesake, was elected judge of the Piedmont Judicial Circuit and served one term. Later two of his law partners, Robert Adamson and Penn McWhorter, also served as judges of this circuit. It is rare for one law firm to produce three judges.

Robert Lee Russell Sr.'s grandson and Richard Russell's great-grandson, Robert Lee Russell III, is currently (2003) a superior court judge in Georgia's Atlantic Judicial Circuit.

Rob Sr.'s second daughter, Mary Ina, married a Virginia lawyer, James Franklin Ingram. Jim Ingram served twenty-five years as a Circuit Court Judge in the Twenty-second Judicial Circuit, Commonwealth of Virginia.

Another of Richard Russell's protégés, Joe Quillian, who lived with the family in the early 1920s and practiced law with the Russells, served on the Court of Appeals from 1953-1960 and was an Associate Justice on the State Supreme Court from 1960-1966.

One son, Alexander Brevard Russell Sr. and three grandsons, Robert Lee Russell, Jr., Walter Brown Russell Jr. and John Davidson Russell have served in the Georgia General Assembly. Walter Brown

Russell Jr. was also elected Chairman of the Dekalb County Board of Commissioners.

Richard Russell's emphasis on education continues to be a strong family tradition. Indeed, it can be argued that it is in the field of education that Richard Russell's legacy is strongest. His son Fielding became a distinguished professor at Georgia Southern College, now Georgia Southern University, where he taught for forty-three years. The student union there bears his name. The Russell daughters tallied up many years of teaching. Marguerite Russell Bowden taught in elementary school for more than thirty years. Carolyn Russell Nelson taught history and political science in Georgia's high schools for seventeen years. Patience Elizabeth Russell Peterson taught in elementary school for eight years before her marriage. Later she served on the Board of Regents of the University System of Georgia, the third woman to be given the job. During her tenure (1967-1972) several of her colleagues claimed she was the best man on the Board.

Grandson Hugh Peterson Jr. serves today on the Board of Trustees at Georgia College/State University, keeping up Richard's tradition of service to his favorite school. Of the numerous Russell grandchildren, great-grandchildren and spouses, nearly sixty have been involved in teaching, most for lengthy careers in grade and high schools or in colleges. Others have taught as second jobs, on a long-term basis, skills as varied as flying, school bus driving, horseback riding, tennis, writing, religious education, and acting.

Henry Edward "Jeb" Russell became a successful and beloved minister in the Southern Presbyterian Church. He preached evangelical missions world-wide and earned the love and admiration of his congregations in Georgia, Alabama and Tennessee. It is difficult to quantify the success of those whose distinguishing mark is largeness of soul, but it has been said that within his profession Jeb Russell achieved as much success as Dick Jr. achieved in politics.

Carolyn Russell married a Presbyterian minister, Raymond Lee Nelson, in 1942. They served churches from Arkansas to Florida for more than forty years.

Four grandchildren became ministers. Fielding Dillard Russell Jr. and his brother William Don Russell followed the Presbyterian path, as did Richard Montgomery Nelson. William Don played the opposite role of his grandfather. Bill planned to practice law and be a politician, but after a couple of years in law school decided the world needed more ministers than lawyers. The fourth minister in the family was a woman and a Methodist, Nancy Green Carmichael, only daughter of Mary Willie Russell and Gordon Green. Like her great-grandfather Brumby, Nancy, a brilliant scientist, with degrees in chemistry, illustrated in her ministry that science and religion can be reconciled.

Richard B, Russell Jr. never married, yet he carried on as patriarch in his father's footsteps. The ruling elder of the Russell clan for thirty years, he insisted on family reunions each year, paying the bills himself for the gala weekend gatherings. He bought the homeplace from his siblings after his mother's death in 1953 and kept it open for all the family.

When Richard Russell Jr. died in 1971, he left the homeplace in trust to all his brothers and sisters, nieces and nephews, and great-nieces and great-nephews. Thirty-two years later it remains a place of shelter for family members who need to retreat there or who want to share a celebration. The Russell Reunion still takes place there the week-end in June closest to June 24. In 1991, the one hundredth anniversary of the wedding of Ina Dillard and Richard Russell, all thirty-five of their surviving grandchildren and their four surviving children were there. We all knew each other and each other's children. We are struggling to keep up with great-great-grandchildren, but no one has surrendered the fight.

Richard Russell and Ina Dillard began their marriage with a determined desire to build a strong family, and both had in early youth formed the dream of leaving a lasting influence for good on their world through their work. It is fortunate that Richard recognized that Ina was made for him and that she took his word for it. Together they fulfilled their lofty ambitions. Ina had all the children God intended her to have with the assurance that their father could and would provide for them. Secure in the steadfast love of a good woman, Richard was free to take or make any challenge in his chosen profession and ride it out to defeat or victory.

Richard Russell repeatedly said that he wanted to serve his day and his generation in such a way that his name would be blessed and honored long after his body had molded in the dust. He hungered for recognition, but only as a result of faithful service that would inspire his children and other youth after them. His talented life given to work and service may not prove conclusively that *labor omnia vincit*, but it goes a long way in that direction. In addition, it constitutes substantial evidence that when joined with high ideals and sustained love, persistent work in the face of overwhelming odds, and even in failure, will reveal a noble spirit.

BIBLIOGRAPHY

Boatwright, Eleanor B. *Status of Women in Georgia, 1783-1860*. Brooklyn NY:
Carlson Publishing, 1994.

Bryan, Ferald J. *Henry Grady or Tom Watson? The Rhetorical Struggle for the New South, 1880-1890*. Macon GA: Mercer University Press, 1994.

Chestnut, Mary Boykin. *Diary from Dixie*, Editor Ben Ames Williams. Boston MA: Houghton Mifflin, 1949.

Coleman, Kenneth and Numan V. Bartley, William F. Holmes, F. N. Boney, Phinizy Spalding, Charles E. Wynes. *A History of Georgia*, Second Edition. Athens: The University of Georgia Press, 1977, 1991.

Coleman, Kenneth and Steve Gurr, editors. *Dictionary of Georgia Biography*, 2 volumes. Athens: University of Georgia Press, 1983.

Cook, James F. *The Governors of Georgia, 1754-1995*. Macon GA: Mercer University Press, 1995.

Cook, Ruth Beaumont. *North across the River: A Civil War Trail of Tears*.:Crane Hill Publishers, 1999.

Cooper, Walter G. *The Story of Georgia*, 4 volumes. New York: American Historical Society, 1938.

Deen, Braswell D. and W. S. Henwood. *Georgia's Appellate Judiciary, Profiles and History*. Norcross GA: The Harrison Company, 1987.

Dittmer, John. *Black Georgia in the Progressive Era, 1900–1920*. Urbana: University of Illinois Press, 1977, 1980.

Edwards, Laura. *Gendered Strife and Confusion: The Political Culture of Reconstruction*. Urbana and Chicago: University of Illinois Press, 1997.

Fite, Gilbert C. *Richard B. Russell Jr., Senator from Georgia*. Chapel Hill: The University of North Carolina Press, 1991.

Friedman, Jean E. *The Enclosed Garden: Women and Community in the Evangelical South, 1830-1900*. Chapel Hill and London: University of North Carolina Press, 1985.

Gilbert, Sterling Price. *A Georgia Lawyer*. Athens and London: U. of Georgia Press, 1946.

Glover, James B. V. *Colonel Joseph Glover (1719-1783) and His Descendants*. Privately published, 1997.

Grantham, Dewey W. Jr. *Hoke Smith and the Politics of the New South*. Baton Rouge: Louisiana State University Press, [1967, c. 1958].

Grice, Warren. *The Georgia Bench and Bar: The Development of Georgia's Judicial System*, Vol. 1. Macon GA: J. W. Burke Company, 1931.

Hahn, Steven Howard. *The Roots of Southern Populism: Yeoman Farmers and the Transformation of Georgia's Upper Piedmont, 1850-1890*. Yale University Ph.D. 1979.

Hair, William Ivy, with James C. Bonner, Edward B. Dawson and Robert J. Wilson III. *A Centennial History of Georgia College*. Milledgeville: Georgia College, 1979.

Hall, Jacquelyn Dowd. *Revolt Against Chivalry: Jessie Daniel Ames and the Women's Campaign against Lynching*. New York: Columbia University Press, 1974, 1979.

Harris, Nathaniel E. *Autobiography: The Story of An Old Man's Life with Reminiscences of Seventy-five Years*. Macon GA: J. W. Burke Company, 1925.

Hitt, Michael D. *Charged with Treason: Ordeal of Four Hundred Mill Workers during Military Operations in Roswell, Georgia, 1864-1865*. Monroe NY: Library Research Association, 1992.

Hoeling, A. A. *Last Train from Atlanta*. New York and London: Thomas Yoseloff, 1958.

Ingram, C. Fred, editor. *Beadland to Barrow A History of Barrow County, Georgia from the Earliest Times to the Present*. Atlanta: Cherokee Publishing, 1978.

Jones, Thoms P. [Commissioner of Agriculture] *A Manual of Georgia for the Use of Immigrants and Capitalists*. Atlanta, 1878.

Kloeppel, James E. *Georgia Snapshots: Glances at the Past*. Union City GA: Adele Enterprises.

Kousser, J. Morgan and McPherson, James M., editors. *Region, Race and Reconstruction: Essays in Honor of C. Vann Woodward*. New York, Oxford: Oxford University Press, 1982.

Lumpkin, Katharine Du Pre. *The Making of a Southerner*. Athens, London: Brown Thrasher Books, University of Georgia Press, 1991.

Martin, Harold M. *Georgia: A Bicentennial History*. New York and Nashville: W. W. Norton, American Association for State and Local History, 1977.

Northen, William J. *Men of Mark in Georgia*. 1907-1912. 1974.

Ownby, Ted. *Subduing Satan Religion, Recreation and Manhood in the Rural South 1865-1920*. Chapel Hill and London: University of North Carolina, 1990.

Powell, Arthur G. *I Can Go Home Again*. Spartanburg SC: The Reprint Company, 1984.

Rogers, Berto. *Opinions and Stories of and from the Georgia Courts and Bar*. Oxford NH: Equity Publishing, 1973.

Rozier, John. *The Houses of Hancock, 1785-1865*. Decatur GA: Distributed by Auldfarran Books, no date.

Sellers, James B. *History of the University of Alabama*. Tuscaloosa: University of Alabama Press, 1953.

Shivers, Forrest. *The Land Between: A History of Hancock County*, Spartanburg SC: The Reprint Company, 1990.

Smith, Elizabeth Wiley and Sara S. Carnes. *A History of Hancock County, Georgia*. Washington GA: Wilkes Publishing, 1974.

Stegeman, John F. *These Men She Gave: Civil War Diary of Athens, Georgia*. Athens: University of Georgia Press, 1964.

Surrency, Erwin C. *The Creation of a Judicial System: The History of Georgia Courts, 1733–Present*. Athens: 1999, privately published.

Temple, Sarah Blackwell Gober. *The First One Hundred Years: A Short History of Cobb County in Georgia*. Atlanta: Walter W. Brown, 1935.

Thomas, Frances T. *A Portrait of Historic Athens and Clarke County*. Athens and London: University of Georgia Press, 1992.

Thompson, C. Mildred. *Reconstruction in Georgia: Economic, Social, Political 1865-1872*. Savannah: Beehive Press, 1972.

Tindall, George Brown. *The Emergence of the New South 1913-1945, A History of the South Series, Volume 10*, Editors, Wendell Holmes Stephenson and E. Merton Coulter. Louisiana State University Press, The Littlefield Fund for Southern History of the University of Texas, 1967.

Turbeville, Robert P., editor. *Eminent Georgians*. Atlanta: Southern Society for Research and History, 1937.

Ward, Geoffrey C. and Ric Burns and Ken Burns. *The Civil War: An Illustrated History of the War Between the States*. American Documentaries, Inc. 1991.

White, John E., D. D. *Prohibition: The New Task and Opportunity of the South*, Pamphlet reprinted from South Atlantic Quarterly, April 1908.

Wilson, G. J. N. *The Early History of Jackson County Georgia*. [edited and published by W. E. White] Atlanta: Foote & Davies, 1914.

Woodward, C. Vann. *Origins of the New South 1877-1913*. A History of the South Series. Volume 9. Editors, Wendell Holmes Stephenson and E. Merton Coulter. Louisiana State University Press, The Littlefield Fund for Southern History of the University of Texas, 1951.

Woodward, C. Vann. *Tom Watson Agrarian Rebel*. New York: Oxford University Press, 1963.

Wright, Gavin. *Old South, New South Revolutions in the Southern Economy since the Civil War*. New York: Basic Books, 1986.

FAMILY TREES

THE WILLIAM JOHN RUSSELL FAMILY
Rebecca Harriette Brumby (1829-1902)
William John Russell (1825-1897)
    married December 30, 1859
Cobb County, Georgia
To Whom Were Born

> RICHARD BRUMBY [Brevard] 1861-1938
> WILLIAM EDWARD 1863-1865
> ROBERT LEE 1864-1934 [Rob]
> MARY BREVARD 1866-1919 [Auntney]
> WILLIAM JOHN 1868-1960 [John]
> EDWARD GASTON 1869-1962 [Ed]
> LEWIS CAROLYN 1871-1950 [Lewis]

THE RICHARD BREVARD RUSSELL FAMILY
Ina Dillard (1868-1953)
Richard Brevard[Brumby] Russell (1861-1938)
    married June 24, 1891
Oglethorpe County, Georgia
To Whom Were Born:

> MARY WILLIE [Billie, Bill] March 1, 1893-May
>   16, 1983
> m. Samuel Gordon Green, March 1, 1918
>
> INA DILLARD [Ina Jr.] June 22, 1894-May 13,
>   1991
> m. Jean Killough Stacy June 4, 1938
>
> FRANCES MARGUERITE ["Dicksie," Margo]
>   April 11, 1896-August 30, 1967
> m. James Harris Bowden, June 24, 1920
>
> RICHARD BREVARD, JR.([R.B., Dick] November
>   2, 1897-January 21, 1971

HARRIETTE BRUMBY May 16, 1899-January 20,
1959
m. Samuel Ralph Sharpton, October 5, 1927

ROBERT LEE [Rob] August 19, 1900-January
18, 1955
m. Sybil Nannette Millsaps June 27, 1923

PATIENCE ELIZABETH [Pat] January 4, 1902-
August 8, 2002
m. Hugh Peterson June 24, 1930

WALTER BROWN [Dillard] June 18, 1903-
December 17, 1986
m. Dorothea Bealer [Dolly] January 1, 1927

SUSAN WAY April 15, 1905-August 7, 1905

LEWIS CAROLYN June 7, 1906-September 9,
1906

WILLIAM JOHN [William, Bill] August 21,
1907-June 7, 1971 twin
m. Ethlene Huff Booth March 10, 1948

FIELDING DILLARD August 21, 1907-February
15, 1993 twin
m. Virginia Boyce Wilson, August 3, 1931

HENRY EDWARD [Jeb] September 26, 1909-
March 26, 1979
m. Ala Joanna Brewton June 15, 1938

ALEXANDER BREVARD [Dickson/Dick/Alex]
October 19, 1910-February 10, 1995
m. Sarah [Sara] Eaton, September 28, 1936,
divorced 1957
m. Kate H. Roberts, April 15, 1958

CAROLYN LEWIS August 19, 1912-
m. Raymond Lee Nelson, February 18, 1942

NOTE ON THE NOTES

In mid-eighteenth century Samuel Johnson observed that a man will turn over half a library to make one book. In the early twenty-first century, an age of information overload, we have not, men or women, that luxury. It has been my goal not to bog down in researching others' comments on this era but rather to add something from original sources. I have had an archival library and a homeplace stuffed with papers to turn over. I had to let the regular libraries go, so I have kept to primary sources as much as possible. The select bibliography lists some of the volumes I consulted but is in no way exhaustive.

My primary source for this biography of a family man has been the extensive Russell family archives, which come in various categories, as noted in the Preface. First there are the blessedly inventoried collections at the Russell Library for Political Research and Studies (abbreviated as RLPRS). These are noted using the Library's system.

Next there are what I elect to call the Russell Family Papers (RFP), some of which are at the RLPRS, but uninventoried, and some of which are at the Russell homeplace. Russells are notorious packrats and the possibilities of where information might turn up were close to infinite. I have used letters, diaries, bills, receipts, scrapbooks, ledgers, daybooks, school assignments, telegrams, items scribbled on the backs of envelopes and notes on calendars. The fly leaves of books have yielded a couple of gems. I try to indicate these sources as clearly as possible. If I know that the source is located at the RLPRS but uninventoried at this writing, it is noted as RFP, RLPRS. If it is located at the homeplace or I cannot recall whether I found it at the homeplace or at the RLPRS, I classify it RFP. Other sources were from private collections of letters belonging to family members and these are so noted. It is my hope that all will eventually end up at the RLPRS. Collections that chronicle one family for over one hundred and fifty years are extremely rare. Being a packrat might turn out to be worth something.

Having been brought up in the Russell family, which adores to tell its stories and to which I adored to listen from an early age, I am heir to a colossal fund of tribal memory. Where I note something as Family History, or with a comment on the storyteller, you will have to take my word for it. My belief in the reliability of oral history has been strengthened throughout this work because research has verified most of what I have heard told.

Since beginning my work on Ina Dillard Russell's letters in 1994, I have interviewed the surviving children or in-laws of Ina Dillard and Richard Russell Sr. several times. Sometimes these were formal interviews, sometimes they were not. I have dated specific interviews made for this book or for Ina's. Patience Elizabeth Russell Peterson before her death in 2002, and Carolyn Russell Nelson, the sole surviving child, have been constant sources of help and inspiration. The last surviving in-laws, Virginia Wilson Russell and Ala Jo Brewton Russell, have also been supportive and encouraging. Many family oral histories are available at the Russell Library and other material of this type has been recorded at our family reunions over the years. These tapes could be made available to researchers.

Several family members wrote their memories or answered specific questions by mail. Where it is impossible to say when I came by information, I use this form: Memory of ____.From 1991-2000, I edited the family newsletter, which we call the *Russell Family Herald*. I used many documents from the family papers in various articles and so I cite these volumes as sources to avoid guessing where the originals are. The *Heralds* are available at the RLPRS. These may also serve as a source regarding the growth and continued success of the family Richard Russell and Ina Dillard founded.

For the numerous people prominent in Georgia politics, I have used two main sources: James Cook's, *The Governors of Georgia* and Coleman and Gurr's *Dictionary of Georgia Biography*. I do not indicate these sources with notes. I here declare that everything I say about people like Charles McDonald, Joe Brown, Jonathan Northen, Alexander Stephens, Nat Harris, and others is taken from one or both of these two sources unless otherwise noted. Anyone can easily look them up. (The *Dictionary* is, to my mind, the best Georgia history in existence. I hope it will soon be updated.)

Wherever possible, I tried to use Ina Dillard Russell's book, *Roots and Ever Green*, because as her amanuensis I am deeply familiar with this source. Letters or parts of letters that had to be omitted from her book have been used, documented according to collection.

In the notes I have abbreviated family names for simplicity's sake. See the family trees to match initials to names. Richard had four brothers, a sister, two wives, and thirteen children, and several of them had the same names, a situation bound to be confusing. Into each life a little rain must fall. If it seems necessary, I indicate in parentheses which relative is writing, for example, RLR (brother). Sources from grandchildren indicate the person's name because when relative numbers have risen to over fifty, initials cease to be useful.

Finally, I note that all emphases are from the originals.

NOTES

Chaper 1

[1] Family history. Oral history of Patience Russell Peterson, and her interview with Karen Kelly, RLPRS; Sarah B.G. Temple, *The First Hundred Years: A Short History of Cobb County, in Georgia* (Atlanta: Agee, 1935) 130-31. Ruth Beaumont Cook, *North Across the River, A Civil War Trail of Tears* (Crane Hill, 1999)47.

[2] Harriette Brumby's character is based on reports from Mary Willie Russell Green, Ina Dillard Russell Stacy, Richard Brevard Russell Jr., Patience Elizabeth Russell Peterson, and Carolyn Russell Nelson. Brumby actions and letters bear out the truth of those reports. See all letters between Harriette and John in the 1996 and 1997 Russell Family *Heralds*, RLPRS.

[3] James B. Glover V, *Colonel Joseph Glover (1719—1783) and His Descendants* (privately published, 1996)195-202.

[4] Ibid., 202. Geoffrey C. Ward, with Ric Burns and Ken Burns, *The Civil War, An Illustrated History* (American Documentaries, Inc., 1990) 320.

[5] Robert P. Turbeville, editor, *Eminent Georgians* (Atlanta: Southern Society for Research and History, 1937) 12-16; sketch of life of William John Russell, RBR Sr. Collection, III, Personal, Memorial Folder, RLPRS.

[6] Cook, *North Across the River,* 11-14; James E. Kloeppel, *Georgia Snapshots—Glances at the Past* (Union City, Georgia, Adele Enterprises) 80-81.

[7] Charles Campbell to H.W. Brown, April 10 1970; RBR Jr. Collection, V, Personal, Family Genealogy, RLPRS; Deposition of Henry Lovern, provided by the Sweetwater Factory Museum.

[8] Ward, *The Civil War*; all direct quotations in following paragraphs are from this work, 320-25.

[9] A. A. Hoeling, *Last Train from Atlanta* (New York, London: Thomas Yoseloff, 1958) 30,60-61,102-105.

[10] Michael D. Hitt, *Charged With Treason: Ordeal of 400 Mill Workers during Military Operations in Roswell, Georgia, 1864-1865* (Monroe, New York: Library Research Association, Inc., 1992) 21.

[11] Ward, *The Civil War*, 324; Hitt, *Charged With Treason*, 21.

[12] Glover, *Colonel Joseph Glover (1719—1783) and His Descendants*, 196-97, 204; See also Mary Boykin Chestnut's *Diary from Dixie*, Ed. Ben Ames Williams (Boston: Houghton Mifflin Co., 1949) 487-88, 497-98. This most famous of Southern diarists bought supplies from the Brumbys.

[13]Glover, *Colonel Joseph Glover (1719—1783) and His Descendants*, 204; *RFC*, 1996, 37-41; memory of Patience Russell Peterson.

[14]Family history; author interviews with Patience Russell Peterson; Karen Kelly's interview with PRP, RLPRS.

[15] Patience Russell Peterson recounted William John Russell's history many times at various family gatherings; see Karen Kelly interview with Patience Russell Peterson and Kelly's dissertation on Richard B. Russell Jr., RLPRS.

[16] C. Mildred Thompson, *Reconstruction in Georgia* (Savannah GA: Beehive Press, 1972) 90; *RFC*, 1996, 37-41.

[17]Ibid., 37-41; Cook, *North Across the River,* 210; Lewis C. Russell interview with survivor from the mill, *Atlanta Journal*, April 28, 1932.

[18] Hitt, *Charged With Treason,* 22; Cook, *North Across the River,* 80-81.

[19] Ward, 322.

[20] Hitt, *Charged With Treason,* 22; Cook, *North Across the River,* 69.

[21] Webb Garrison article on Sweetwater Mill, *Atlanta Journal-Constitution*, 30 December 1984; Charles Campbell to H.W. Brown, 10 April 1970, RBR Jr. Collection V, Family Genealogy, RLPRS; Patience Russell Peterson interviews with author and oral history at the Russell Library; Cook, *North Across the River,* 64-118.

[22] Glover, *Colonel Joseph Glover,* 198; Cook, *North Across the River,* 98-99; Lewis Russell interview with mill survivor, Atlanta *Journal*, April 28, 1932.

[23] *Russell Family Herald,* 1996, 37.

[24] Glover, *Colonel Joseph Glover,* 196-97 and 204; see also Temple, 373.

[25] Ward, *The Civil War*, 329.

[26] *RFH*, 1996, 38.

[27] Ibid., 39.

[28] Virginia Russell Black, granddaughter of Richard Brevard Russell and daughter of Fielding Dillard Russell Sr., reports that during her childhood on their frequent trips from Statesboro to Winder, Georgia, her father rarely failed to stop and show his children the once-elegant, then-abandoned Northen home on Highway 15 where he said his grandmother had taken refuge during the Civil War with her three little ones. The house is no longer standing. See also John Rozier, *The Houses of Hancock, 1785-1865* (Decatur GA: distributed by Auldfarran Books)121-22 and Elizabeth Wiley Smith, assisted by Sara S. Carnes, *A History of Hancock County, Georgia,* (Washington GA: Wilkes Publishing, 1974) 23; also William John Northen, *Men of Mark in Georgia*, vol. 4, 287; FDR Sr. Oral History, RLPRS.

[29] *RFH*, 1996, 40-42, 122.

[30] Ibid., 40-41.

[31] Ibid., 41.

[32] Ibid., insert.

[33] Turbeville, *Eminent Georgians*, 12-16.

[34] Glover, *Colonel Joseph Glover,* 199.

[35] Ibid., 199; life sketch of WJR, RBR Sr. Collection, III, Memorial Folder, RLPRS.

Chapter 2

[1] Information filed in the Clark County Library, sent by Richard N. Fickett III on January 15, 1965. Luke F. Ferguson, "The Old Princeton Mill," *Athens Magazine*, April 1990. Vertical File, Georgia Room, UGA Library: "Princeton Factory." Louis De Vorsey Jr., "Early Water-Powered Industries in Athens and Clarke County" (Papers of the Athens Historical Society, Volume 2, 1979) 39-51. F. T. Thomas, *A Portrait of Historic Athens* (Athens: UGA Press, 1992) 48-50. Although several works from the period and later mention the Princeton Factory, anything specific on life at the mill and its environs is lacking. Family material has not uncovered anyone identifiably connected with the village. A family photograph shows the manager's house.

[2] James B. Glover V, *Colonel Joseph Glover (1719—1783) and His Descendants* (privately published, 1996) 202-204. James B. Sellers, *History of the University of Alabama* (Tuscaloosa: University of Alabama, 1953)68-69, 72, 76-78, 163, 203-204. M. Laborde, *History of the South Carolina College* (Columbia: Peter B. Glass, 1859) 389-94. Daniel W. Hollis, *South Carolina College*, vol. 1 (Columbia: University of South Carolina, 1951) 155-57, 174, 190. Edwin Green, *A History of the University of South Carolina* (Columbia: The State Company, 1916) 52-54, 62. See also the diary and other papers of John Matthews Winslow Davidson, MD: Southern Historical Collection, University of North Carolina, Chapel Hill) 13-16 and 73-76.

[3] Information filed in the Clarke County Library, sent by Richard N. Fickett III on January 15, 1965, gives an unfavorable quote from the Athens *Banner/Watchman* in the early days of the factory. Augustus Longstreet Hull, *Annals of Athens, 1801-1901*, (Athens: Banner Job Office, 1906. Reprinted 1978, Mary B. Warren, Heritage Papers, Danielsville GA) 390-91.

[4] HBR to [Sister] Sissie Glover, January 21, 1898, RBR Jr. Collection, V., I, Personal, Family; HBR to LCR, [tentatively dated 1898], LCR Collection, Family Correspondence, RLPRS.

[5] A famous family story, used for generations to encourage girls in scholastic endeavor. Frederick A. P. Barnard, a Yale graduate and later President of Columbia University (1865-1889), taught at Alabama with Richard Brumby. Professor Barnard reserved seats in his lecture rooms for the young ladies of the Tuscaloosa Female Institute (Sellers, *History of the University of Alabama,* 73). Harriette almost certainly attended TFI. There is no record of her attending Barnard's classes, but his example may have prompted her request of the faculty at the University of South Carolina. See also Rebecca Felton's article on RBR's mother, RBR Sr. Collection, IV, Political, 1922 Chief Justice Campaign, RLPRS.

[6] IDR Scrapbooks, Box 2 of 5, 1931-1940. IDR Collection. RBR Jr. to RBR Sr., March 9, 1935, RBR Sr. Collection, III, Personal, Family, RLPRS.

[7] HBR to Mrs. Bolan Glover (sister), series of three letters, including the note on back from Sissie to RBR, RBR Sr. Collection, III, Family, 1872-1899. HBR to LCR, August 3, 1896 and HBR to LCR, May 25, 1897, LCR Collection, RLPRS.

[8] Family history. See also HBR to RBR, September 26, 1893, RBR Sr. Collection, III, Personal, Family Correspondence; RBR to IDR Jr., February 20, 1912, IDRS Collection, RLPRS.

[9] Deposition of Henry Lovern, provided by the Sweetwater Factory Museum.

[10] Robert S. Gamble, "Athens: the Study of a Georgia Town During Reconstruction 1865-1872" Masters Thesis, University of Georgia, 1967, 101-102, 108-110.

[11] RFH, 1997, 136-137.

[12] Family history. See also OH of PRP, RLPRS. Richard Brevard Russell Jr. told me the snakebite story in 1965. Ina Russell Stacy verified that they heard this story often as they were growing up.

[13] For the fascinating details of the career and character of Richard Brumby, see the early histories of the University of Alabama and of South Carolina as given in note 2 above. All descriptions of Brumby are based on this information unless otherwise noted. See also Sarah Hansell Cousar to Richard B. Russell Jr., "A History of My Great-Grandfather, Richard Trapier Brumby." RBR Jr. Collection, V, I, Family Genealogy, RLPRS.

[14] RBR Sr. to RBR Jr., April 8, 1914, RBR Jr. Collection, School Years File. Barnesville Speech, 1884, RBR Sr. Collection, III, RLPRS.

[15] In later years Richard Russell rarely mentioned his grandfather as teacher, although he told his children stories of how his childhood had been spent in arduous study. He preferred to give his mother credit for his education.

[16] Family history. Written notes to author from Virginia Wilson Russell, undated. Author interview with Patience Elizabeth Russell Peterson, November 28, 1998. Author interview with Carolyn Russell Nelson, February 10, 2001. Chancellor Dave Barrow to RBR, July 22, 1902, RBR Sr. Collection, III, RLPRS.

[17] Way genealogical information sent to RBR Jr., May 5, 1965, RBR Jr. Collection, V, I, Family Genealogy. RLPRS.

[18] Rebecca McDowell to Richard B. Russell Jr., undated, "A Short Sketch of Alexander Brevard and Other Brevards," RBR Jr. Collection, V, I, Family Genealogy. RLPRS.

[19] RBR Sr. to son William John Russell, October 27, 1931. RFP, RLPRS.

[20] Sketch of WJR's life, RBR Sr. Collection, III, Memorial Folder. ABR, youngest son of RBR, told me the story of the whispering Mr. Russell, which his father told him. Other character traits of William John Russell are based on interviews with PRP and CRN, and from impressions gleaned from numerous letters of his children in the Lewis Russell Collection and from William John's own letters. See also RBR to his son William John Russell, October 27, 1931 and RBR Sr. to son RLR, November 5, 1913, RFP, RLPRS.

[21] Speech of RBR, RBR Sr. Collection, IV, Political, 1922; Athens histories in general note that factory owners in the post-war period had such gatherings.

[22] Richard T. Brumby to RBR, August 14, 1872, RBR Jr. Collection, V, Personal, Relatives.

[23] Sarah Hansell Cousar to Richard B. Russell Jr., see note 13 above. Richard T. Brumby to RBR, ibid.

[24] Richard B. Russell Diary, RBR Sr. Collection, III, Diary, Exercise Book, RLPRS.

[25] Walter Cooper, *The Story of Georgia, Biographical Volume* (New York: The American Historical Soc., 1938) 227-28. RBR Jr. to Sarah Hansell Cousar, December 16, 1968, RBR Jr. Collection, V, I, Family Genealogy, RLPRS.

[26] See copy of this letter of introduction, June 3, 1872, RBR Jr. Collection, V, Personal, Family, Parents Correspondence, pre-1932, RLPRS.

[27] Richard T. Brumby to RBR, August 14, 1872, see note 22.

[28] Ibid.

Chapter 3

[1] RBR Diary, January 1, 1878, RBR Sr. Collection III. RLR (brother) to HBR, March 1896, LCR Collection, Family Correspondence. HBR to RBR Sr., undated, RBR Jr. Collection, V, Personal, Family, Pre-1932, RLPRS. Richard's children often testified to their father's love of the Longfellow poem. Many of them could also recite it with gusto—and did so, sometimes in chorus.

[2] Family history. See also *Georgia Reports* 188, 887-90.

[3] In addition to the excellent entry by James Z. Rabun in the *Dictionary of Georgia Biography*, see Lucian Lamar Knight, *Georgia's Landmarks and Memorials and Legends*, vol. 2 (Atlanta: Byrd Printing, 1914) 144-53.

[4] Stephens' work, with WJR's inscription, extant in the library at the Russell homeplace.

[5] John F. Stegeman, *These Men She Gave, Civil War Diary of Athens, Georgia* (Athens: University of Georgia, 1964) 17.

[6] RBR to Charle G. Balmann, April 14, 1914, RBR Sr. Collection, III, Misc., RLPRS.

[7] ABR told me this story numerous times. See also *Georgia Reports* 188, 887-90.

[8] Memory of ABR.

[9] Sarah Hansell Coursar, "Life of Richard T. Brumby," RBR Jr. Collection, V, Family Genealogy. RLPRS. Reminiscences of Hugh Peterson Jr.

[10] *Georgia Reports*,188, 887-90.

[11] Ibid., 887-90. Virginia Boyce Wilson, "The Russell Boys at Georgia." *Atlanta Journal* June 6, 1931. Oral History of PRP, RLPRS.

[12] Author interview with PRP, November 21, 1998. See also family letters in the LCR Collection, RLPRS. These repeatedly witness to Harriette's high standing with her children.

[13] Laura Edwards, *Gendered Strife and Confusion: The Political Culture of Reconstruction* (Urbana and Chicago:University of Illinois Press, 1997) 108-110

[14] Eleanor M. Boatwright, *Status of Women in Georgia, 1783-1860* (Brooklyn: Carlson, 1994) 16. RLR to LCR, March 9, 1896, HBR to LCR, January 19, 1896, LCR Collection, Personal, Family, RLPRS.

[15] Friendship Book page in Nancy Green Carmichael private collection. RFH 1994, 65.

[16] RBR to Frank T. Pentecost, February 2, 1916, RBR Sr. Collection, IV, Campaign 1916, RLPRS.

[17] E. Merton Coulter, *College Life in the Old South* (Athens: University of Georgia, 1928, 1979) 266-67.

[18] Henry Tuck, *Four Years at the University of Georgia, 1877-1881* (Athens: published by the author, 1938) 8, 16, 17, 30-31.

[19] Diary of RBR, January 1-8, 1878; Mamie Glover to RBR, September 24, 1881, RBR Sr. Collection III, Diary and Exercise Book and Family, Relatives, RLPRS.

[20] Ferald J. Bryan, *Henry Grady or Tom Watson? The Rhetorical Struggle for the New South, 1880-1890* (Macon GA: Mercer University Press, 1994) 9-10; C.Vann Woodward, *Tom Watson, Agrarian Rebel* (New York: Oxford University Press, 1963) 28.

[21] Tuck, *Four Years at the University of Georgia, 1877-1881,* 158-161; Henry Grady, quoted in Bryan, *Henry Grady or Tom Watson?,* 32; see also Coulter, *College Life in the Old South,* 268-72.

[22] RBR to RBR Jr., April 8, 1914, RBR Jr. Collection, V, School Years, RLPRS.

[23]Tuck, *Four Years at the University of Georgia, 1877-1881,* 180-181.

[24] Ibid., 16.

[25] Ibid., 17-18.

[26] Ibid., 26.

[27] Ibid., 184.

[28] *Notable Men of Georgia*, RBR Sr. Collection, IV, January 1913, RLPRS.

[29] Tuck, *Four Years at the University of Georgia, 1877-1881,* 36-38.

[30] Ibid., 38.

[31] Ibid., 39, 167.

[32] RBR to M.G.Michael, May 13, 1910, RBR Sr. Collection, III, Personal, Fraternal Organization (Royal Arcanum), 1909-1910, RLPRS.

[33] Exact date of change is unknown, but family history is united in placing it at the time he started his law practice.

Chapter 4

[1] See card to brother Robert, at Annapolis, 1881, RBR Sr. Collection, III, Family, 1872-1899. RLPRS

[2] RLR to HBR, April 13, 1899, LCR Collection, Family Correspondence, RLPRS.

[3] James Reap, *Athens, A Pictorial History* (Norfolk: Donning Co., 1982) 60, 64. Julia P. Moss to Lewis Russell, Program of Closing Exercises, June 12, 1885, LCR Collection, Miscellaneous, RLPRS. Diary entries of RBR, 1878, RBR Sr. Collection, III, RLPRS.

[4] Sterling Price Gilbert, *A Georgia Lawyer* (Athens GA: UGA Press, 1946) 48.

[5] RBR to Frank Pentecost, Feb. 2, 1916 and RBR Diary, RBR Sr. Collection, III and IV, Campaigns, 1916, RLPRS; Thomas P. James, *A Manual of Georgia for the Use of Immigrants and Capitalists* (Atlanta: 1878) 68-69. W. J. Ham, *Representative Georgians, Biographical Sketches of Men Now In Public Life with Portraits* (Savannah GA: Savannah Morning News Print, 1887) 145.

[6] RBR Diary entries, 1880, RBR Sr. Collection, III; RLR to HBR April 13, 1899, LCR Collection, Family Correspondence, RLPRS.

[7] RFH, 1996, 122, RLPRS.

[8] See diary and speech made in Barnesville in 1884 for young RBR's attitude towards women, RBR Sr. Collection, III. Harriette's hopes for her sons are noted in David Barrow to RBR, July 22, 1902, RBR Sr. Collection, III, RLPRS.

[9] All details of courtships, unless otherwise noted, are taken from the diaries, RBR Sr. Collection, III, RLPRS

[10] Although Richard never writes Lily's full name (a reluctance to name a lady in written accounts was common at the time), she was almost surely the daughter of R. L. Moss, whom he does name, and whom Sylvanus Morris cites as prominent in the history of Athens. See Sylvanus Morris, *Strolls About Athens during the 1870s* (Athens GA: Athens Historical Society Reprint, 1969) 32.

[11] Mamie Glover to RBR, September 24, 1881, RBR Sr. Collection, III, Family, RLPRS.

[12] Morris, *Strolls About Athens during the 1870s*, 17.

[13] RLR to LCR, March 9, 1896, LCR Collection, Family Correspondence; RBR Diary, October 28, 1881, RBR Sr. Collection, III, RLPRS.

[14] Ibid., RLR to LCR.

[15] Numerous diary entries in 1881 refer to his frustrations with lack of standing in Athens. This is a long-established family reason given for why he eventually left Athens.

[16] *Georgia Reports* 188, 885.

[17] ABR, eighth son of RBR, said his father told him of this multiple ambition many times.

[18] RBR Diary, October 28, 1881, RBR Sr. Collection, III, RLPRS.

[19] James P. Davis to RBR, April 10, 1930, RBR Sr. Collection, IV, 1930 Governor's Campaign, RLPRS.

[20] *Athens Banner Watchman*, November 7, 1882

[21] Frank G. Lumpkin to RBR Sr., 21 Dec. 1932, RBR Sr. Collection, IV, RBR Jr. 1932 Senate Campaign, RLPRS.

[22] Gilbert, *A Georgia Lawyer,* 66-67.

[23] John T. Boifouillet, *Atlanta Journal*, October 4, 1925, "Not Speaker but Chief Justice."

[24] RBR to Emily Gaillard, September 16, 1936, RBR Sr. Collection, IV, 1936 Senate Campaign, Congratulations, RLPRS.

[25] House *Journal*, 1883, 230.

[26] Correspondence between E. Merton Coulter and RBR Jr., Ina Dillard Russell Stacy's copies, sent her by Richard B. Russell Jr., in author's possession. See also Woodward, *Tom Watson*, 108.

[27] The story of Richard Russell's courtship of and marriage to Minnie Tyler is well recorded in oral family history. For information on the Tyler family I am indebted to their family historians Jane Hampton, Beth Abney, and Priscilla Grant Doster.

[28] VWR gave this detail of Mary's making up the bridal bed.

[29] Author interview with PRP, November 21, 1998.

[30] RBR Sr. Collection, III, Speeches, 1884, RLPRS.

[31] Physical blows were common in the courtrooms of this day and family history reports Richard Russell involved in fights as late as 1920. See J. A. Perry to RBR, April 30, 1907, RBR Sr. Collection, IV, 1907. Ham, *Representative Georgians, Biographical Sketches of Men Now In Public Life with Portraits,* 144-47. Ham was a colleague of

Richard's in the General Assembly and knew of his love and regard for Miinnie and his enthusiasm for their domestic life.

[32] Information concerning the establishment of Georgia Tech, unless otherwise stated, is taken from the following sources: M. L. Brittain, *The Story of Georgia Tech* (Chapel Hill: UNC Press) 18-19; McMath, Bayor, Brittain, Foster, Giebelhaus, and Reed, *Engineering the New South, Georgia Tech, 1885-1985* (Athens GA: UGA Press). The account of the legislative battle is Nat Harris's, *The Autobiography of an Old Man, with Reminiscences of 75 Years* (Macon GA: J. W. Burke, 1925), 202-217

[33] *Atlanta Constitution*, August 14, 1883. B. F. Barksdale to RBR Sr. May 15, 1898; James DuPree to K. C. Bullard [copy sent to RBR] July 23, 1898, RBR Sr. Collection, IV, Campaign 1898, RLPRS.

[34] *Athens Banner-Watchman*, March 1884.

[35] Reap, James, *Athens, A Pictorial History* , chapter two.

[36] RBR Diary, January 3, 1881, RBR Sr. Collection, III. RLPRS.

[37] Bedroom suite extant at the Russell homeplace in Winder. As late as 1998, PRP and CRN still called this suite "Minnie's furniture;" receipts and payment record of other items in RFP at the homeplace.

[38] Even a cursory glance at the Business and Finance papers, I, RBR Sr. Collection, whatever the year, confirms that RBR was constantly in debt but also constantly paying off his debt. See also financial records of all kinds from the Russell Family Papers.

[39] Albert B. Saye, *A Constitutional History of Georgia* (Athens: University of Georgia, 1948) 322-23. Kenneth Coleman, ed., *A History of Georgia*, second edition (Athens: University of Georgia, 1991) 227-29.

[40] RBR diary, November 11, 15, 26, 28,1881, RBR Sr. Collection, III, RLPRS.

[41] Receipts for purchase and sales of these items are found in the RFP.

[42] Augustus Longstreet Hull, *Annals of Athens, 1801-1901*, (Athens, Banner Job Office, 1906. Reprinted 1978, Mary B. Warren, Heritage Papers, Danielsville, Georgia) 388-389; numerous Russell biographies mention his association with this railway.

[43] Ibid., 395-96.

[44] *Peale's Popular Educator Cyclopedia, Historical, Biographical, Scientific and Statistical*, gift of Richard to Minnie, October 3, 1885, with flowers and several clippings therein, extant at the Russell homeplace.

Chapter 5

[1] Every list of accomplishments that RBR made in his later life, and these were numerous, mentions his many activities in Athens business and school life. See *Dictionary of Georgia Biography*.

[2] John Dittmer, *Black Georgia in the Progressive Era 1900-1920* (Urbana, Chicago, London: University of Illinois Press, 1977, 1980) 58-59.

[3] F. McDonald to RBR, April 23, 1888, RBR Sr. Collection, IV, Campaigns, General, 1887-1901, RLPRS.

[4] RFP. All details having to do with Minnie's death are contained in two letters, written by William John Russell, January 10, 1886, and Mary Brevard Russell, January 15,1886, to their brother Robert Lee Russell away on naval duty.

[5] Details of the funeral are taken from Minnie's obituary, extant in the Russell Family Bible. See RFH 1995, 76-78 for the entire obituary and for the poem. See also *Athens Banner Watchman* obituary January 12, 1886.

[6] Patience Russell Peterson discovered the box with this nightgown and her father's note when she was a girl. In 1998 she believed it to be extant at the Russell homeplace.

[7] W. J. Ham, *Representative Georgians, Biographical Sketches of Men Now In Public Life with Portraits* (Savannah Morning News Print, 1887)145.; RBR to J. H. Towns and W. H. Bush, April 6, 1911, RBR to Judge HH Hammond, January 10, 1915, RBR Sr. Collection, III, Misc.,1910-1911 and 1915-1916. W. A. Wilson to RBR, May 6, 1892, RFP, RLPRS.

[8] RBR to Stella Akin, August 15, 1922, RBR Sr. Collection, IV, 1922 Chief Justice Campaign; RBR to M. L. Orr, May 1, 1929, RBR Sr. Collection, III, Education, RLPRS.

[9] See letters to women in the 1922 Campaign file, RBR Sr. Collection, IV, RLPRS, especially to Mrs. J. H. Spratling, August 3, 1922, for details of this initial bill for a women's college; Harris's autobiography gives the account of Little's defense in the battle for Georgia Tech, 215-16.

[10] RBR to C.E. Broyles, June 17, 1898, RBR Sr. Collection IV, Campaign, 1898; Charles R. Russell to RBR, October 6, 1930, RBR Sr. Collection, IV, Campaign, RBR Jr., 1930, Congratulations, RLPRS.

[11] Gilbert, *A Georgia Lawyer*, 66-67.

[12] Richard's notebook, kept during 1890-1892 court sessions, shows the money was variable but that sometimes he collected up to $200. The sheriffs received some of the fines, as did the justices of the peace. Notebook extant in RFP.

[13] Solicitor General Material 1888, RBR Sr. Collection, IV, 1888-1901, RLPRS.

[14] Written notes of MWRG, private collection of Kathryn Hairston Green; Ham, 146-48. RBR to B. B. Bower and Bower to RBR, August 13 and 17, 1898, RBR Sr. Collection, IV, 1898 Campaign, RLPRS.

[15] Curl, Lottie M., "The History of the Georgia State College for Women," Master of Arts Thesis, History Department, George Peabody College for Teachers, 1931. Chapter one. IDR Library, GC/SU. See also *A Centennial History of Georgia College*, chapter one.

[16] See RBR Sr. Collection III, Misc. Pre-1890 folder, RLPRS.

[17] Erwin C. Surrency, *The Creation of a Judicial System: The History of Georgia Courts, 1733 to Present* (Athens: 1999). Ms. in Georgia Room, Hargrett Library, UGA). Gilbert, Chapter VI. Janice and Anne Herman, "Georgia County Courthouses," Pamphlet Series, No. 2, The Georgia Trust for Historic Preservation. Robert H. Jordan and J. Gregg Puster, *Courthouses in Georgia* (Norcross GA: The Harrison Company, 1984).

[18]Clipping regarding William John Russell and Athens Chamber of Commerce, February 14,1964, possibly from *Athens Banner*. RBR Jr. Collection, V, I, Family, RLPRS.

[19]See the *Ledger* in the RFP, RLPRS.

[20] September 9, 1889, WJR [father] to RBR, RFP, RLPRS.

[21] A. C. Hodgson to David C. Barrow, February 5, 1885, David C. Barrow Collection, Hargrett, UGA Libraries.

[22] RFP, photographs.

Chapter 6

[1] The story of Richard's and Ina's courtship that follows comes from family lore, reaffirmed by Patience Russell Peterson, Carolyn Russell Nelson and Virginia Wilson Russell in recent interviews. See also EGR to RBR, July 10, 1892, RFP, RLPRS.

[2] Photograph, RFP. See also *Roots and Ever Green*, first page of gallery.

[3] RBR to IDR, 24 June 1914, IDR Collection. See also *RFH* 1996, 93-94. RLPRS.

[4] Clipping, *Atlanta Journal*, December 11, 1932, "Governor's Mother Honored," by Nelle Womack Hines, IDRS Collection, RLPRS.

[5] Henry Edward "Jeb" Russell Oral History, 7-8, RLPRS.

[6] Information on the Dillards and on Ina's early life comes from family lore, much of it heard by the author at the Dillard Family Reunions at Cherokee Corner since about 1950. Two books self-published by Carlton Dillard, *Back to Old Virginia with Dillard, Daniel and Kin* and *Fielding Dillard (1771-1818) and Descendants*, contain many written accounts from Dillard history and are available at the RLPRS; recent interviews with PRP and CRN; Russell, Ina D., *Roots and Ever Green*, (Athens, UGA Press, 1999) 4-7; Fannie Evans Fussell to IDR, October 6, 1930, IDR Collection, Governor's Race Congratulations; clippings of Oglethorpe Editor Gant on the Fielding Dillards from the IDR Scrapbooks, Box 2/5, IDR Collection, RLPRS.

[7] IDR to [brother] Miles Dillard, April 10, 1888, private collection of Fielding Lewis Dillard, son of Ina's brother Walter Dillard.

[8] RBR to IDR, June 24, 1914, IDR Collection. See also *RFH* 1996, 93-94. RLPRS.

[9] Bessie Cooper Church to IDR, October 3, 1930, Congratulations, 1930, IDR Collection, RLPRS.

[10] The receipts for Ina's piano payments are extant in family papers at the homeplace. Richard did not take up the payments. Ina's sister Annie did, likely because she wanted the piano for her daughter Josie.

[11] Patience Russell [Peterson] dated a young man who told her this story, declaring that his father was her mother's chastised caller.

[12] RFP.

[13] "The American Carlsbad and Its Famous Natural Medicinal Waters, Lithia Springs, Georgia," (promotional pamphlet) Second Edition, Bowden Lithia Springs Co., 1891. Hargrett, UGA Libraries. See also note 4 above, regarding Ina's love of fairy tales.

[14] Carolyn Russell Nelson gave the account of the nightshirt. Virginia Wilson Russell reported under re-examination that Ina told her of her sleepy bridegroom.

[15] J. G. Holland, *Bittersweet, A Poem* (New York: Charles Scribner's Sons, 1867, 1881, 1889) A story involving a husband who was suspected of infidelity but was innocent, the volume is extant at the Russell homeplace.

[16] RBR to IDR, September 23, 1901, IDR Collection, RLPRS. Russell, *Roots and Ever Green*, 22-23, 48-49. In later years, according to CRN, Ina advised her daughters to marry widowers. See also IDR to FMR July 19, 1915, Private Collection of Richard Russell Bowden.

[17] RBR to IDR, March 29, 1901, IDR Collection, RLPRS. Lines from Longfellow's "The Building of the Ship" quoted as an example she followed through life in a letter to her youngest daughter, CLR, April 27, 1937, Private Collection of Carolyn Russell Nelson.

[18] Russell, *Roots and Ever Green,* 21

[19] Ibid., 26.

[20] Ibid., 21-23; RBR to IDR, August 16-17, 1892, IDR Collection, RLPRS

[21] Russell, *Roots and Ever Green*, 28-29; RBR to IDR, January 27, 1892 and March 28, 1894, IDR Collection, RLPRS

[22] Letters of the couple in the early 1890s reveal pleasure in domesticity, joy in their sexual union and affectionate regard. IDR Collection, RLPRS

[23] IDR to RBR, May 4, 1892, IDR Collection, RLPRS.

[24] RBR to IDR, January 27, 1892, IDR Collection, RLPRS; MWRG and ABR reported that their father told them he worried about losing Ina as he had lost Minnie.

[25] Series of letters from Georgia Loan and Trust, January-March 1892; Bank of the University note, February 9, 1892, W.B. Jordan to RBR, February 21, 1892, RBR Collection I, Finances, RLPRS.

[26] LCR to RBR, December 6, 1891, RFP. RLPRS.

[27] Clipping regarding William John Russell in RBR Jr. V, I, Family, dated February 14 ,1964, possibly from *Athens Banner*, RLPRS.

[28] WJR to RBR, February 19 and 23 and March 5, 1892, RFP, RLPRS.

[29] M. L. Ledford to RBR, January 9, 1892 and W. A. Wilson to RBR, May 6, 1892, RFP.

[30] RBR to IDR, September 29, 1892, IDR Collection, RLPRS.

[31] RBR to J. E. Brown, June 27, 1898—see back of letter, RBR Collection IV, 1898 Campaign, RLPRS.

[32] RBR to IDR, August 17 and September 29, 1892, IDR Collection, RLPRS.

[33] WJR to RBR, August 24, 1892, RFP, RLPRS. RBR to IDR, August 17 and 24 1892, IDR Collection, RLPRS.

[34] All details of this campaign, RBR to IDR, October 29, 1892, IDR Collection, RLPRS.

Chapter 7

[1] *Roots and Ever Green*, 23-24; Patience Dillard to Mary Willie Russell, February 27, 1894, RFP. RBR to MWR, March 1, 1894, IDR Collection, RLPRS.

[2] RBR to Dixie (Mary Willie) Russell, 7 March 1893, RFP.

[3] Ibid.; Russell, *Roots and Ever Green*, 24-25.

[4] Ibid., 24-25; RBR to IDR March 31, 1893(I), IDR Collection, RLPRS.

[5] RBR to IDR, March 31, 1893 (II), IDR Collection. RLPRS.

[6] RBR to IDR, September 26, 1893, IDR Collection, RLPRS. Russell, *Roots and Ever Green*, 26.

[7] RBR to IDR, January 27, 1894, IDR Collection, RLPRS.

[8] W.H. Quarterman to RBR, April 11 and 21, 1892, RFP. W. H. Quarterman, to RBR, February 7, 1893, RBR Sr. Collection, I. Business Finance, Misc. 1887-1894; RBR to

IDR, March 31, 1893 (I), IDR Collection, RLPRS. Ingram, *Beadland to Barrow*, 34-45; W. J. Northen, *Men of Mark in Georgia*, IV, 61-64.

[9] RBR to IDR, July 26, 1893, IDR Collection; [Postcard] RBR to RLR, 1881, RBR Sr. Collection, III, Family Correspondence 1872-1899, RLPRS. Ingram, *Beadland to Barrow*, 116.

[10] Russell, *Roots and Ever Green*, 27-28. Family lore records Ina's timidity about the young doctor.

[11] Russell, *Roots and Ever Green*, 29-31; RBR to IDR March 28,1894, IDR Collection, RBR to IDR Jr. [no date], IDRS Collection, RLPRS.

[12] RBR to IDR, January 23, 1894, IDR Collection, RLPRS; Russell, *Roots and Ever Green*, 33-34.

[13] Ibid., 34-37.

[14] HBR to LCR, December 5, 1895, LCR Collection, RLPRS.

[15] WJR (Jr.) to LCR, April 14, 1896, MBR to LCR, October 26, 1896 and January 24, 1897, LCR Collection, Personal, Family, 1896-1907. Family lore is replete with stories on Richard's naming and re-naming of babies. In the RFP a letter from Ina's sister Pipey, perhaps to another Dillard, declares that Richard would like for all the children to be named for him.

[16] RBR to IDR, February 26, 1896, IDR Collection; WJR to LCR, October 7 and 14, 1896, LCR Collection, Personal, Family 1896-1907, RLPRS.

[17] Marion Allen, "Memorial of Chief Justice Richard Brevard Russell, Report of the Proceedings of the Fifty-Sixth Annual Session of the Georgia Bar Association," May 25-27, 1939, 171-77. See also *Georgia Reports* 188, 870-95. Several speakers at Richard Russell's Memorial Proceedings testified to these characteristics. PRP remembered that her father was celebrated in legal circles for the moving speeches he made to juries.

[18] RBR to IDR January 27, 1896, IDR Collection; RBR to J. B. Brown, September 27, 1898, RBR Sr. Collection, IV, 1898 Campaign Correspondence, RLPRS.

[19] RBR to IDR, February 26, 1896, IDR Collection, RLPRS.

[20] RBR to J.E. Brown, June 27, 1898—see back of letter, RBR Sr. Collection IV, 1898 Campaign, RLPRS.

[21] Telegram from J. F. Dillard to IDR, October 26, 1896, IDR Collection, Personal, RLPRS.

[22] HBR to LCR, October 27, and Oct. 1896 and RBR to LCR December 5, 1896, LCR Collection, Family, RLPRS.

[23] Ibid.

[24] Ibid.

[25] WJR Jr. to LCR, April 18, 1897, LCR Collection, Family.

[26] See LCR Collection, Family files, for letters dealing with this failed venture.

[27] Russell, *Roots and Ever Green*, 38-39.

[28] From typed copy of WJR's obituary in IDRS papers, in author's possession. See also RFH 1995, 75.

[29] RFP, RLPRS.

[30] RFH 1995, 75.

[31]RBR to RBR Jr., November 2, 1915, RBR Jr. Collection, V, Correspondence from Parents; RBR to H. H. Hammond, January 10, 1915; RBR Sr. Collection, III, Misc., 1915-16; HBR to Sissie Glover, January 21, 1898, RBR Sr. Collection, III, Family. RLPRS.

[32] A fabled family story; see Fite's account in RBR Jr. biography, another in *Beadland to Barrow*, and G. J. N. Wilson, *The Early History of Jackson County Georgia*, edited and published by W.E. White (Atlanta: Foote and Davies, 1914). Betty Russell Vandiver reports that Franklin County, home of her husband Ernest Vandiver, claims RBR was in their court on the day of his first son's birth, not in Jackson County.

[33] HBR to RBR Jr., November 2, 1897, RBR Jr. Collection, V, Winder Years, Family Corresp., RLPRS.

[34] Russell, *Roots and Ever Green*, 39-40; Jane Bowden Moore gave me the history of her mother's name.

[35] Russell, *Roots and Ever Green*, 40. Ina told this story to all her daughters and daughters-in-law. Versions vary on who took the birth control device out to the back yard.

Chapter 8

[1] HBR to LCR, December 31, 1897, HBR to RBR, January 4, 1898, HBR to LCR undated, HBR to LCR, 9 January 1898, LCR Collection; HBR to 'Sissie," 21 January 1898, RBR Sr. Collection, III, Family 1872-1935; RLPRS. These letters verify the information in the following two paragraphs.

[2] RBR to LCR, July 14, 1896, IDR to LCR, [?] December 1896, LCR Collection, Richard Russell Family,1896-1908, RLPRS.

[3] See 1898 letters of RLR and EGR to LCR in LCR Collection, RLPRS.

[4] Ibid.

[5] RBR to IDR, February 3, 1898, IDR Collection, RLPRS.

[6] RBR to J.B. Brown, September 27, 1898, RBR Sr. Collection, IV, 1898 Campaign, RLPRS.

[7] RBR to LCR, December 5, 1896, LCR Collection, Richard Russell Family, 1896-1908, RLPRS.

[8]Numerous 1898 letters from EGR and RLR to LCR, LCR Collection; spoiled or unsent copies of 'form' campaign letters show the similarity of the two hands. RBR Sr. Collection, Campaigns, General, 1887-1901. See also the Day Book for the Russell Manufacturing Company, LCR Collection; RLPRS.

[9] RBR to IDR, January 23, 1894, September 16, 1899, February 22, 1901, March 7, 1901, IDR Collection, RLPRS.

[10] Ibid., RBR to IDR, March 7, 1901.

[11] RBR to IDR, September 16, 1898, IDR Collection, RLPRS. All subsequent details of this trip are from this letter.

[12] RBR to IDR. October 13, 1898, IDR Collection, RLPRS.

[13] RBR to IDR, October 23, 1898, IDR Collection, RLPRS.

[14] Ibid.

[15] WJR to LCR, October 17, 1898, LCR Collection, William John Russell 1896-1923, RLPRS.

[16] Russell, *Roots and Ever Green,* 44; *Georgia House Journal*, 1898; RBR to IDR, Oct. 17, 1898 telegram, IDR Collection, RLPRS.

[17] HBR to LCR, November 16,1898, LCR Collection, RLPRS.

[18] RBR to IDR, March 7, 1901, IDR Collection, RLPRS.

[19] Reports of PRP, CRN and Jane Bowden Moore.

[20] RBR to IDR, November 22, 1898, IDR Collection, RLPRS.

[21] RBR to IDR, February 24, 1899, IDR Collection, RLPRS.

[22] Rogers, Berto, quoting Judge Arthur G. Powell in *Opinions and Stories of and from the Georgia Courts and Bar* (Oxford NH: Equity Publishing, 1973) 69; RBR to IDR, September 16, 1899, March 29, 1901, IDR Collection; T. Glenn Dorough to RBR, September 17, 1932; R. Terry to RBR, September 18, 1930; Charles R. Russell to RBR October 6, 1930; RBR Sr. IV, General, 1930 and 1932 Campaigns; RLPRS. *Georgia Reports* 188, 879-80.

[23] EGR to LCR, May 18, 1899, LCR Collection, Edward Russell, RLPRS.

[24] See HBR to LCR, all letters 1898 and 1899, LCR Collection, RLPRS.

[25] RBR to IDR Jr., June 21, 1899, IDR Collection, RLPRS.

[26] RBR to IDR, September 16, 1899, IDR Collection, RLPRS.

[27] Patience Dillard (Pipey) to IDR, [October 1902], IDR Collection, RLPRS.

[28] RBR to IDR, August 8, 1900, IDR Collection, RLPRS.

[29] Ina's illness and the beginning of the system of giving babies to the older girls is family history. The positive effects of this policy have been far-reaching. See Russell, *Roots and Ever Green*, 43,46.

[30] Family history. See also RBR to IDR, March 7, 1901, IDR Collection, RLPRS.

[31] RBR to IDR, November 22, 1900 and February 22, 1901, IDR Collection, RLPRS.

[32] Charlotte Machine Company, Engineers, Contractors & Dealers in Cotton Machinery and Cotton Mill Equipment to LCR, February 25, 1898; Day Book of Russell Manufacturing Company, 1901-1903, LCR Collection, RLPRS.

[33] Letters from RLR and EGR to LCR in the years 1896-1900, LCR Collection; Winder became known for a variety of mills in the early days of the twentieth century.

[34] Petition for Charter, LCR Collection; Stock Certificate to EGR, RFP; Stationary indicates the name change around 1901, in both RFP and LCR Collection, RLPRS.

[35] For all information on this trip, including direct quotes, see this series of letters, RBR to IDR, April 7-18ʹ 1901, IDR Collection, RLPRS.

[36] RBR to IDR, September 17, 1901; LCR to EGR, February 24, 1902; RBR to IDR, September 10, 1901; LCR to Wilder Glover, March 2, 1903; IDR and LCR Collections, Personal, Relatives, RLPRS.

[37] Oft-repeated family history; see also RLR to LCR, July 27, 1902, LCR Collection, RLPRS.

[38] See note 37 above; words to hymn in RBR III, Family, RLPRS

[39] PRP reported Mary's aborted courtship. See letters of LCR and MBR from this period to each other in LCR Collection, RLPRS. Lewis and Mary adopted Richard's family as their own after Harriette's death and his family adopted them.

[40]See letters from LCR to EGR and RLR in this period, LCR Collection, RLPRS.

[41] Commendatory Alumni Day Skit, May 1967, 1; newspaper article, source unspecified, July 19, 1943: "William Russell 75; Was First Bicycle Campaigner," RBR Jr. Collection, V, Family. RLPRS.

[42] Campaign letters in LCR Collection; Bar Endorsement in L.G. Hardman Collection, II. Business A. Commerce Office, Box 5, Folder 4, September 11, 1902. RLPRS.

[43] RBR diary, January 1, 1878, RBR Sr. Collection, RLPRS.

[44] E.K. Lumpkin to Marion Smith, October 28, 1905, Manuscript 2345, Box 27, Folder 23, Georgia Room, Hargrett Library, UGA. Reasons for Richard Russell's quarrel with Winder were rarely discussed in the family, probably because Ina minimized it as much as possible. Frank Bondurant remembered that Judge Russell was unpopular in Winder, but that Ina and the children were not. *Roots and Ever Green* shows that they had a congenial playing relationship with Winder.

[45]Ingram, *Beadland to Barrow*, 112-115.

[46]LCR to EGR, September 25, 1902, LCR Collection; reports of PRP and CRN.

[47] RBR to IDR, September 3, 1901, IDR Collection, RLPRS.

[48] See 1902-1903 letters from EGR to LCR, LCR Collection, RLPRS.

[49] Family photo of Ethel, RFP. See letters between Edward, Rob and Lewis at this period, and LCR to RLR, April 23, 1905, LCR Collection. Clipping, IDR Scrapbook, Box 2/5, IDR Collection, RLPRS. PRP and CRN agree that "Aunt Ethel" was concerned about social standing.

[50]Biographical information, Robert Lee Russell, May 24, 1904, LCR Collection, Personal, RLPRS.

[51] MWRG told me this story numerous times, as did PRP.

[52] Written notes of MWRG on her father's life. Undated, private collection of Katherine Hairston Green.

[53] Family history, often repeated by PRP. EGR to LCR, January 1904, LCR Collection, RLPRS; Ingram, *Beadland to Barrow*, 112-116.

[54] Papers View the Candidacy of Judge Russell, RBR Sr. Collection, IV, 1904 Chief Justice Campaign, RLPRS.

[55] It almost certainly was Simmons' age and health that gave Richard the idea that it was time to run against him. If Simmons were re-elected for six years, then died early in office, a sitting Justice would be elevated and become the entrenched incumbent. This is, in fact, what happened. See also editorial from Cobb County paper characterizing Simmons' ability to perform his judicial duties, RBR Sr. Collection, IV, 1904 Campaign; RBR to C. F. Harris, March 5, 1904, private collection of Betty Russell Vandiver.

[56]Russell, *Roots and Ever Green*, 172-73, 234.

[57] Campaign literature, 1904 Race, RBR Sr. Collection, IV, RLPRS.

[58] See all correspondence between IDR and LCR during this year, LCR Collection and Lincoln Co. Voters List marked in IDR's hand, RBR Sr. Collection IV, RLPRS.

[59] RBR to IDR, April 2, 1904; IDR Collection, IDR to LCR, April 13-14 1904, Richard Russell Family, LCR Collection: RLPRS.

[60] RLR(son)to RBR, April 14, 1904, RFH 1997, 127.

[61] A.S. Clay to RBR Sr. March 19, 1904, RBR Sr. Collection, IV. 1904 Chief Justice Campaign, RLPRS.

[62] *Atlanta Constitution*, front page story, April 21, 1904.

Chapter 9

[1] Ina was still amused thirty years later when she told her daughter-in-law Sarah Eaton Russell of this visit from friends in Winder.

[2] See also Ingram, *Beadland to Barrow*, 16-22

[3] Family history. Official Barrow County history is discreetly silent on the Russell opposition to its formation, given that her most distinguished son was a Russell. J. L. Herring to RBR, 24 September 1904; RBR Sr. Collection, IV, General; "A Few Reasons Why a New County Should Be Made with Winder as the County Site," Executive Committee, New County at Winder, LCR Collection, RLPRS.

[4] Family gatherings often heard about the Way patriotism, along with that of the Brevards and Davidsons. See *The Published Records of Midway Church*, a volume belonging to WJR, passed on to son RLR in 1896, LCR Collection. RLPRS.

[5] J. B. Moore, to RBR, March 30, 1905; W.J. Born to RBR, June 8, 1905; Walter R. Brown to RBR, all correspondence; RBR Sr. Collection, IV, 1906 Campaigns.

[6] Clark Howell to RBR, March 4, 1892, RFP, RLPRS.

[7] Clippings, Savannah and Lawrenceville papers, IDR Scrapbooks, IDR Collection, RLPRS.

[8] Dewey Grantham, *Hoke Smith and the Politics of the New South* (Baton Rouge: Louisiana State University Press, 1967) 143; Frank Hughes to RBR, June 6, 1905, RBR Sr. Collection, IV, 1906 Campaign, RLPRS.

[9] E. Merton Coulter to RBR Jr. and RBR Jr., to Coulter, October 25 and November 6, 1958, IDRS Collection, RLPRS.

[10] Little is known about how Walter Brown and Richard Russell became friends, but the record of Brown's support, advice and friendship through many years stands for itself. For his active part in this campaign, see the Walter R. Brown file, RBR Sr. Collection, IV, Campaigns, 1906, RLPRS.

[11] Ibid., Walter R. Brown to RBR, June 30, 1905.

[12] Clipping, "Hon. Richard B. Russell Addresses the Voters of Newton County," All following information regarding his speaking uses this content as representative. IDR Scrapbooks, IDR Collection, RLPRS.

[13] RBR to E.G. Simmons, September 4, 1922, RBR Sr. Collection, IV, 1922 Campaign.

[14] RBR Jr. was famous for going barefoot even in cold weather. See IDRS Oral Interview, RLPRS.

[15] RBR to IDR, June 24, 1914, IDR Collection, RLPRS.

[16] Clipping, IDR Scrapbooks, Box 2/5, IDR Collection, RLPRS.

[17] RBR to IDR, September 27, 1905, IDR Collection, RLPRS.

[18] Family history; see RFH 2000, 35-39.

[19] Author interview with PRP, November 21, 1998; RBR to IDR, March 7, 1901, IDR Collection, RLPRS.

[20] RBR to IDR, February 20, 1921, IDR Collection, RLPRS.

[21] IDR Scrapbooks, IDR Collection, RLPRS.

[22] Doyle Campbell, to RBR, October 25, 1905, RBR Sr. Collection, IV, 1905-1906, RLPRS.

[23] Correspondence of E. K. Lumpkin to Hoke and Marion Smith, October 11–28, 1905. Manuscript 2345, Box 27, Folder 23, Georgia Room, Hargrett Library, UGA. All information regarding Hoke and Richard comes from this series of letters.

[24] The Russell Charter, written when the idea of local option was popular, allowed for a dispensary.

[25] *Monticello News*, November 3, 1905.

[26] RBR to Hoke Smith and Smith to RBR, April 16 and May 7, 1906; "In Crackerland" with Ralph Smith (clipping), RBR Sr. Collection, IV, 1906 Governor's Campaign, RLPRS. RBR Jr. to E. Merton Coulter, note 9 above; Grantham, *Hoke Smith and the Politics of the New South* ,151; see also Clipping "A Joint Discussion," IDR Scrapbooks, IDR Collection, RLPRS. Ralph Smith notes that Russell swept Lumpkin County in the primary.

[27] RBR to IDR, November 14,1905, IDR Collection, RLPRS.

[28] Campaign card, RBR Sr. Collection, IV, 1906 Campaign. See also *RFH*, 1997, 42, RLPRS.

[29] IDR Scrapbooks, various articles, IDR Collection, RLPRS.

[30] W.E. Simmons to RBR Sr., December 15, 1905, RBR Sr. Collection, IV, 1906 Campaign, RLPRS.

[31] RBR to S. A. Hagood, May 5, 1908; RBR to J.A. McDuff, April 5, 1906; RBR to C.E. McGregor, May 11, 1910; RBR Sr. Collection IV, 1906-1911 Campaigns, RLPRS.

[32] See letters between LCR and IDR for 1906, LCR Collection; RBR Sr. Collection, IV, 1906 Campaign. RLPRS.

[33]Transcript of "Georgia Giant," 55; Mary Dillard to IDR, February 18, 1906; Susie Russell to IDR, September 10,1906; many of Richard's letters to Ina mention how her careful management of their funds enabled him to pursue his ambitions; see especially February 18, 1927, IDR Collection, RLPRS.

[34] LCR to RLR, undated, LCR Collection, Family; RBR to Tom Watson April 29, 1910; train schedule, RBR Sr. Collection, IV. 1906 Campaign, RBR to Alice Wrens, July 18, 1922, IV, 1922 Chief Justice Campaign, RLPRS.

[35] Hattie Arnold to IDR, September 7, 1906 and September 10, 1906, IDR Collection, RLPRS.

[36] Clipping, RBR Sr. Collection IV, 1906 Campaign; "Plain Dick Russell as Seen by Editor Jones," IDR Scrapbooks, from the *Toccoa Record*, reprinted in the *Atlanta News*. RLPRS.

[37]Charles R. Thompson to RBR, June 6, 1908; the petition, RBR Sr. Collection, IV, 1906 campaign, RLPRS.

[38] Article from unnamed newspaper, "Judge Richard B. Russell on the Hustings and at Home," July 16, 1906, RBR Jr. Collection, Vertical File; W.O. Perry to LCR, July 10, 1906, LCR Collection, RLPRS.

[39]*Georgian*, July 3, July 16(?),1906. It is possible Selene Armstrong wrote for the *Georgian*. IDR to LCR, RBR Sr. Collection, IV, 1906 Campaign.

[40] A favorite family story. See also "Georgia Giant" transcript, 5, 20, RLPRS.

[41] MBR to LCR, July 26, 1906, LCR Collection, Family. RLPRS.

[42] LCR to MBR, July 13, 1906; WJR to LCR, February 1, 1906 and May 8, 1906; LCR Collection, RLPRS.

[43] RBR to LCR, July 12, 1906, LCR to A.S. Gentry July 19, 1906, LCR Collection, Richard Russell Family, RLPRS.

[44] Grantham, *Hoke Smith and the Politics of the New South* , chapter 9.

[45] This story was told and re-told in numerous articles when RBR Jr. was elected governor in 1930. Clipping, IDR Scrapbooks, Box 4/5 "Russell's Election Answers Prophecy, Prayer of Father" IDR Collection, RLPRS

[46] Opinion of Ina Dillard Russell Stacy, who helped nurse her little brother and was present when he died.

[47]See note 45.

[48] LCR to G. W. Duncan, undated, 1906, LCR Collection, 1903-1906; Jessie D. Harris to IDR, September 11, 1906; EGR and Susie Russell to RBR and IDR, September 9 and 10, 1906; all letters from Hattie Dillard Arnold to IDR, September 7— October 2, 1906; Mary Dillard to IDR, September 9, 1906, IDR Collection, RLPRS.

[49] LCR to EGR, September 21, 1906, LCR Collection; James A. Perry to IDR, May 11, 1950; Clipping regarding Brown telegram at time of Court election, IDR Scrapbooks, IDR Collection, RLPRS.

[50] Walter Brown to IDR, May 17, 1911, IDR Collection, RLPRS.

[51]LCR to EGR, September 21, 1906, LCR; "Dick Russell spent but $4.70," IDR Scrapbook, IDR Collection; RLPRS.

[52] RBR to E.A. Bennett, February 12, 1916, RBR Sr. Collection, IV, 1916 Campaign

[53]Braswell D. Deen. and W. S. Henwood, *Georgia's Appellate Judiciary, Profiles and History* (Norcross GA:, The Harrison Company, 1987) 179.

[54] RBR letters to family from all periods make this statement. It seems likely that the farming did produce some income during most years. It was the one activity outside his law work which he continued over several decades.

[55] Mary Dillard to IDR, February 18, 1906, Hattie Arnold to IDR, August 22, 1907, IDR Collection, RLPRS.

[56] Nita Stroud to IDR, 24 Aug. 1907, IDR Collection, RLPRS. Post card, MWR to "Auntney," August 21, 1907, private collection of Virginia Wilson Russell. The story of the twins' birth was one that Ina enjoyed telling, perhaps because both boys turned out to be robust and lively.

[57]Memory of PRP.

[58] Mary Nancy Green Carmichael, daughter of Mary Willie Russell Green, told this story at the yearly Russell Family Reunion in 1990, at which over one hundred of Richard's and Ina's direct descendants had gathered, including thirty-five living grandchildren, all of whom knew each other as close kin.

Chapter 10

[1] "Judge's Decision Given in Verse," *Atlanta Journal*, January 1909, IDR Scrapbook, IDR Collection, RLPRS.

[2] *Georgia Appeals Reports*, Vols. 1-18. "Court of Appeals of Georgia, 1907-1978" Booklet sponsored under Governor George Busbee, 44-48; see also Arthur Powell, *I Can Go Home Again*, (Spartanburg, S.C.: The Reprint Company, 1984.) 298-300.

[3] *Georgia Reports* 165, Memorial to Chief Justice William Fish, 911.

[4] *Georgia Reports* 188, 875.

[5] Clippings, IDR Scrapbooks, IDR Collection; RBR to Bessie Butler, July 18, 1922, RBR Sr. Collection, IV, 1922 Campaign; RLPRS.

[6] Clippings, "Judge Russell to Run for Governor 08?" and "Brown Issues Address Supporting Watson", IDR Scrapbooks, Box 2/5; RBR to IDR, Feb. 21, 1908, IDR Collection, RLPRS.

[7] Financial sheet, undated, RBR Sr. Collection; II, Legal/Judicial, RLPRS.

[8] EGR to LCR, Jan. 14, 1910; Knitting Mill Daybook, LCR Collection, RLPRS.

[9] Russell, *Roots and Ever Green*, 49-50, 53-54; oral histories of MWRG, IDRS, PERP; RLPRS.

[10] RBR Solicitor General Account Book, converted by Ina into farm and household accounts book, RFP; also Ina's daybook, 1912; RBR to IDR, February 14, 1908, IDR Collection, RLPRS.

[11] RBR to IDR, February 14, 1908, IDR Collection. See also Derieux, James C. "Cheaper by the Baker's Dozen," Colliers Magazine: The National Weekly, vol. 126, no. 10, 2 September 1950, 36-38; 45. RLPRS.

[12] RBR to IDR, February 14 and 21, 1908, IDR Collection, RLPRS.

[13] I have heard Ina Dillard Russell Stacy, Mary Willie Russell Green, and Patience Elizabeth Russell Peterson tell stories of their father's homecomings during this era on many occasions. See also their oral histories, RLPRS. A letter from Patience (Pipey) Dillard to Ina Jr. on her fourth birthday gives her instructions about how to make Papa feel loved and welcome when he comes home. RFP. See also Derieux, James C. "Cheaper by the Baker's Dozen," 36-38, 45.

[14] Many letters in the RBR Sr. Collection, whether political or personal, mention the Judge's Sunday activities. Author interview with Frank Bondurant, Feb. 25, 2002.

[15] See Royal Arcanum files, RBR Sr. Collection III, RLPRS.

[16] RBR to IDR, February 14, 1908, a loving Valentine letter on which Ina wrote THE ONE. IDR Collection, RLPRS.

[17] Russell, *Roots and Ever Green*, 48-49; Louise E. DeWitt to IDR, [1908], IDR Collection, RLPRS.

[18] In addition to the *Dictionary of Georgia Biography* and Cook's *The Governors of Georgia*, see C. Vann Woodward's *Tom Watson, Agrarian Rebel*, 390-93, for the life of Joe Brown and details of this campaign.

[19] RBR to S.A. Hagood, May 5, 1908, RBR Sr. Collection, IV, Campaigns.

[20] MWR to Hattie Arnold (Aunt Hattie), Feb. 25, 1908, RFP; clipping of twins from the *Atlanta Constitution*, IDR Scrapbooks, IDR Collection, RLPRS.

[21]Russell, *Roots and Ever Green*, 49-50; Carlton Dillard, *Fielding Dillard and Descendants* (privately published) 341-342.

[22]ABR told me his father told him this story.

[23] Newspaper clippings and letters of congratulations in the RFP. See also *RFH*, 2000, and RBR Sr. Collection III., Personal, Family 1901-1909, RLPRS.

[24] See all letters from Mary Willie and Ina Jr. to their mother during this school year, in IDRS Collection, RLPRS and in the RFP. See also "No Place for Weakly or Sickly Girls," author's unpublished article on life at G.N.&I.C. 1909-1920. RBR to IDR Jr., Feb. 12, 1912, IDRS Collection, RLPRS.

[25] RBR to Sydney Holderness, March 10, 1901; T.L. Bowden to RBR, May 16, 1910; RBR to B.F. Boykin, April 28, 1910; M.B. Calhoun to RBR, April 28, 1910; RBR Sr. Collection, IV, 1911 Campaign, RLPRS.

[26] RBR to Tom Watson, April 29, 1910.See note 25.

[27] Henry West to IDR, April 22, 1910; IDR Collection; RBR to Mrs. S. J. Tribble, Aug. 9 and 25, 1910, RBR Sr. Collection, IV, 1911 Campaign, RLPRS.

[28] Henry West to IDR, See note 27.

[29] Russell, *Roots and Ever Green*, 50-52

[30] Grantham, *Hoke Smith and the Policies of the New South*, 202-203

[31] RBR to B. Ambrose, July 26, 1910, RBR Sr. Collection, IV, 1911 Campaign, RLPRS.

[32] C.E. MacGregor to RBR, May 20, 1910, RBR Sr. Collection, IV, 1911 Campaign, RLPRS.

[33]RBR to Frank S. Rawson, John R. Dortch, Jack F. Jackson and others, RBR Sr. Collection, IV, 1911 Campaign, RLPRS.

[34] RBR to IDR Jr., Nov. 4,1910, IDRS Collection, RLPRS.

[35] Memories of CRN; written notes of MWRG, Kathryn Hairston Green Private Collection.

[36] Memories of PRP. Hugh Peterson Jr. recalls his mother always pointed out the Peters Mansion as the one Ina liked, now a restaurant called "The Mansion." Notes of MWRG, private collection of Kathryn Hairston Green. Clipping, 1910, Royal Arcanum article, IDR Scrapbooks, IDR Collection, RLPRS.

[37] RBR to FMR, Dec. 3, 1910, private collection of Richard Russell Bow-den.

[38] RBR to FMR and IDR Jr., Oct. 20, 1910, RFP.

[39] Russell, *Roots and Ever Green*, 58-59.

[40] The first two sections of *Roots and Ever Green* give examples of servants moving on.

[41] Russell, *Roots and Ever Green*, 66.

Chapter 11

[1] Copies of reply to papers, RBR Sr. Collection, IV, 1911 Campaign, RLPRS.

[2] Walter Brown to IDR, May 17, 1911; Clipping, IDR Scrapbook; IDR Collection; Invitation, RBR Sr. Collection, IV, Correspondence; RLPRS. Tabloid copy, RFP.

[3] Clipping, "Joe Brown May Not Make Race," *Macon News*, July 27, 1911, RFP; Russell, *Roots and Ever Green*, 69-70.

[4] Clipping from the *Georgian*, c. August 1, 1911, "First-Hand News of the Candidates and Near-Candidates for Governor", RBR Sr. Collection, IV, 1911 Campaign, RLPRS.

[5] RBR to IDR, November 5, 1913, RFP. RBR to Charles Smith and O.E. Smith, August 31, 1926, RBR Sr. Collection IV, 1926 Campaign, RLPRS.

[6] RBR Sr. Collection, III, Personal, Family Correspondence, 1910-1920 shows a heavy burden of school fees in almost every letter. See also RBR Jr. Collection, School Years, IDR Collection and RFP for letters from all the children away at school during this period.

[7] Russell, *Roots and Ever Green*, sections 2 and 3; "Georgia Giant" interview, 55, RLPRS.

[8] Russell, *Roots and Ever Green*, 45.

[9] Ibid., 71

[10] Ibid., 72-74

[11] Ibid., 72-74; RBR to IDR Jr., November 4, 1911, IDRS Collection, RLPRS.

[12] Walter Dillard to RBR, May 14, 1910; L.A. Williams to RBR May 15, 1910; RBR Sr. Collection, IV, 1911 Campaign, RLPRS.

[13] November 4, 1911 Atlanta Speech, copy; "Judge Russell's Issue," *News Herald*, Lawrenceville, Ga., Clipping, "Church Politics" from *Cordele Rambler*; RBR to A. J. Ledford [1916 Campaign]; various clippings, RBR Sr. Collection IV, Campaigns, 1911 and 1916; "Vote for Russell and Save Georgia," article and cartoon, LCR Collection, Political, 1909-1911; RLPRS.

[14] Russell, *Roots and Ever Green*, 71-74.

[15] VWR to author, October 19, 1994; Russell, *Roots and Ever Green*, 64; IDR to FMR, Dec. 5, 1911, Private Collection of Richard Russell Bowden.

[16] November 4, 1911 Speech, RBR Sr. Collection IV, 1911 Campaign, RLPRS.

[17] Russell, *Roots and Ever Green*, 76-78.

[18] Ibid., 80-81.

[19] A famous family tale. See clipping, *Cosmopolitan* magazine, November 1911, RFP.

[20] IDRS oral history, RLPRS.

[21] RBR to RBR Jr., November 5, 1911; RBR Jr Collection, Winder Papers, School Years, RLPRS. Russell, *Roots and Ever Green*, 81-82.

[22] RBR to IDR Jr., October 28, 1911, IDRS Collection; LCR to MBR, November 22, 1911, LCR Collection; RLPRS.

[23] Emory Speer to RBR, Dec. 5, 1911, RBR Sr. Collection IV, 1911 Campaign, RLPRS.

[24] Russell, *Roots and Ever Green*, 82.

[25] Carolyn Russell Nelson, the child born of this union, confirmed she knew this story regarding her conception from her youth.

[26] RBR to FMR and MWR, Dec. 8, 1911. Private Collection of Richard Russell Bowden.

[27] RBR to RBR Jr. Dec. 8, 1911, RBR Jr. Collection, V, D, Winder Years. RLPRS.

[28] HBR to FMR, Dec. 10, 1911. Private Collection of Richard Russell Bowden.

[29] RBR Jr. to RBR, Dec. 8, 1911, RBR Jr. Collection, Winder Years. RLPRS. FMR and MWR to RBR, December 9, 1911, Private Collection of Richard Russell Bowden.

[30] IDR to FMR, Dec. 17, 1911; Private Collection of Richard Russell Bowden.

Chapter 12

[1] Many letters to the children during this period reiterate these themes. See especially RBR to IDR Jr., April 29, 1912, IDRS Collection, and the letters to R. B. Jr. from 1912-1915, RBR Jr. Collection, Winder Papers, School Years, RLPRS.

[2] Entire File on Church/Religion. See especially RBR to G. G. Smith, R.C. Shadburn, and Mrs. J. W. Dougherty; RBR Sr. Collection, III, RLPRS.

[3] Family history skit, "Salute to the Russell Family at UGA," May 6, 1967, RBR Jr. Collection, V, Family, RLPRS.

[4] The exact date of this name change is unknown, but family history maintains that it was changed because of the 1911 election. See Oral History of Mary Willie Russell Green, RLPRS.

[5] Russell, *Roots and Ever Green*, 63-166. The entire section entitled "I Can't Have One of You a Failure, Not One" shows Ina's encouragement of her children. Her themes of working through problems with perseverance are echoed in their father's letters during this period. See IDRS Collection and RFP, RLPRS, and RBR to FMR, Richard Russell Bowden Private Collection.

[6] RBR to IDR Jr., April 29, 1912, IDRS Collection; see all letters in 1912 from RBR Sr. to RBR Jr., RBR Jr. Collection, Winder Papers, School Years, RLPRS.

[7] IDR Jr's diary, January –March 1912, IDRS Collection, RLPRS.

[8] Plans extant in RFP. Patience Russell Peterson told the story of the hotel plans becoming house plans.

[9] Russell, *Roots and Ever Green*, 91-93.

[10] MWR to IDR, May 19, 1912, RFP. Written memories of MWRG, private collection of Kathryn Hairston Green.

[11] Russell, *Roots and Ever Green*, 277.

[12] Memory of PRP; "Georgia Giant," 53-54; William Stueck interview with IDRS, RLPRS.

[13] Russell, *Roots and Ever Green*, 97.

[14] RBR Sr. to IDR, Jr., Nov. 4, 1910, IDRS Collection; RBR Sr. to RBR Jr., March 4, 1912, June 16, 1912, February 5, 1915, 24 Feb. 1915, Nov. 2, 1915, RBR Jr. Collection, Winder Papers, School Years, RLPRS.

[15] Almost all correspondence with his children in school reflects this financial struggle. See especially RBR Sr. to RBR Jr. Dec. 12, 1912; RBR Jr. Collection, Winder Papers, School Years; FMR to RBR, March 1, 1915; HBR to RBR Feb. 14, 1916, RBR Sr. Collection, III, Family, RLPRS.

[16] Russell, *Roots and Ever Green*, 103-104.

[17] R.BR Sr. to RBR Jr. Dec. 12, 1912, see note 15 above.

[18] Ibid.

[19] Ibid.; for more details of farming problems, see also, RBR to IDR Jr., Nov. 29, 1912, IDRS Collection; RBR to RLR, March 1, 1914, RBR Sr. Collection, III, Family;

RBR to RBR Jr., March 8, 1915, RBR Jr. Collection, Winder Papers, School Years, RLPRS.

[20] WJR (brother) to MWR, Dec. 29, 1912, WJR to RBR, April 13, 1913, WJR to IDR, August 31, 1914, RFP.

[21] See RBR Sr. Collection, I, 1900-1906, 1911-1912; RBR Sr. to RBR Jr. Dec. 12, 1912; RBR Jr. Collection, Winder Papers, School Years, RLPRS.

[22] Russell, *Roots and Ever Green*, 106, 108; N.E. McBreyer to IDR and RBR Jr., Oct. 2 and 3, 1930, IDR Collection, 1930 Congratulations; IDR to RBR, on back of letter from E. A. Starr to RBR, March 6, 1914, RBR Sr. Collection, III, Royal Arcanum. RLPRS.

[23] Russell, *Roots and Ever Green*, 111.

[24]ibid., 112-13. see also other letters from the children to RBR in 1913-1914 Nell Brinkley, "A Well-Known Plot—The Father and His Little Ship-of-State," The *Atlanta Georgian*, March 14, 1915, clipping on good fathers, RFP.

[25] Russell, *Roots and Ever Green*, 111.

[26] RBR to RBR Jr. Sept. 28, 1912, RBR Jr. Collection, Winder Papers, School Years. RLPRS.

[27] Ina Dillard Russell Stacy gratefully told this story on her eighty-fifth birthday.

[28] Russell, *Roots and Ever Green*, 119-123.

[29] FMR to IDR, undated, RFP; Interview of IDRS with W. Steuck, 13, RLPRS.

[30] Russell, *Roots and Ever Green*, 119-120; 122-123.

[31] RBR Sr. to RBR Jr., Oct. 6, 1913, RBR Jr. Collection, Winder Papers, School Years, "Georgia Giant," 61, RLPRS.

[32] Exact date is unknown. The school records burned in a fire in 1923.

[33]Clipping, IDR Scrapbooks, RLPRS.

[34] When I heard this family story as a child, it sounded as if the Committee suggested this name, but I suspect it is something Lewis hoped for.

[35]Author interview with Frank Bondurant, Feb. 25, 2002; RBR to son RLR, March 26, 1914, RFP. Correspondence with Pottle, RBR Sr. Collection, III. 1914, RLPRS.

[36] Several copies of this paper are in the RFP, with items concerning the Russells marked.

[37] Unsigned thank you note to IDR, June 27, 1912 and thank you from "Samille" July 25, 1913, RFP; see Russell, *Roots and Ever Green*, and other IDR letters in the Richard Russell Bowden collection for many accounts of visitors at the Russell home. Richard's letters to his wife through the years on her birthday or their anniversary highlight her talents in making their home a haven. See "At the Judge Russell Home", Clipping, IDR Scrapbooks and letters between the couple, IDR Collection, RLPRS.

[38] Russell, *Roots and Ever Green*, 142. RBR Jr. interviewed in "Georgia Giant," 17; OH of FDR Sr., 28-29, RLPRS. Sally Russell, "Homeplace," *Georgia Journal*, Summer 1995, 31-33.

[39] ABR told me this story the first time I heard it, and it is well known to almost everyone in my generation. See also MWRG's written notes, private collection of Kathryn Hairston Green; RFH, 1995, 86-87.

[40]RBR Sr. Collection, IV, Campaigns, 1914. See all letters in this file.

[41] RBR Sr. to RBR Jr., April 20, 1914, RBR Jr. Collection, Winder Papers, School Years; RLPRS. RBR Sr. to IDR, May 20, 1915, RFP.

[42] Bill set a precedent. In the years that followed, other children who became self-supporting helped out younger siblings in school.

[43] Russell, *Roots and Ever Green*, 137-138; Ina Jr.'s early dislike of Winder was a topic of conversation in later years at many family gatherings. See also OH of IDRS, RLPRS.

[44] Russell, *Roots and Ever Green*, 140-143

[45] FMR to IDR, Feb. 15, 1913, RFP.

[46] RBR Sr. to RBR Jr., Dec. 6, 1913, Feb. 5 and 24, 1915, Nov. 2, 1915; RBR Jr. Collection, Winder Papers, School Years. RBR to IDR Jr., 15 May 1915, IDRS Collection, RLPRS.

[47] IDR to FMR, April 17, 1915,Private Collection of Richard Russell Bowden. Several letters from MWR to IDR in the spring of 1915 mention the possible move; see also postcard to PER from IDR, April 29, 1915, RFP.

[48] See entire file on this investigation, RBR Sr. Collection, IV, General; RLPRS. Also RBR to IDR, July 7, 1915, RFP.

[49] Russell, *Roots and Ever Green*, 150-154; see also Miss Dovie's medical records, RBR Jr. Collection, Winder Papers, School Years. RBR to Sylvanus Morris, December 31, 1915, RBR Sr. Collection, III, Family, 1915-1919, RLPRS.

[50] RBR to S.P. Gilbert, March 2, 1916, RBR Sr. Collection, IV, 1916 Campaign, RLPRS.

[51] Russell, *Roots and Ever Green*, 153; Deen and Henwood, 179-180; Clipping, "Georgia Politics News and Views," April 1916, IDR Scrapbooks, IDR Collection, RLPRS; RBR to IDR, Oct. 6, 1915, and March 3, 1916, RFP.

[52] RBR to S. P. Gilbert, see note 50.

[53] Clipping, "Georgia Politics, News and Views," April 1916, IDR Scrapbooks, IDR Collection. RLPRS.

[54] IDR to RLR (son), undated, RFP; Russell, *Roots and ever Green*, 153.

[55]Russell, *Roots and Ever Green*, 156.

[56]Ibid., 156.

[57] Ibid., 157-58.

[58] See RBR Sr. Collection, IV., 1916 Campaign Correspondence, especially letters to J.T. Kendall and C.M. Hudgins.

[59] Ibid., RBR to W.C. Edwards, 16 March 1916.

[60] Ibid., Cartoon clipping from unnamed newspaper.

Chapter 13

[1] "Georgia Giant" interview with RBR Jr. See also correspondence between MBR and LCR during this time, LCR Collection, RLPRS.

[2] Russell, *Roots and Ever Green*, 163-74.

[3] IDR Jr. to RBR, Oct. 3, 1916, IDRS Collection, Family Letters, 1911-1916. Russell, *Roots and Ever Green*, 161-165.

[4]Ibid., 176.

[5] Memory of PRP; see also RBR to RBR Jr. Feb. 2, 1912, RBR Jr. Collection, Winder Years, Parents Correspondence, RLPRS.

[6] Russell, *Roots and Ever Green*, 175,178.

[7] MWRG told me about correcting her beau's English; SGG to IDR, February 11, 1918, IDR Collection, RLPRS.

[8] MWR to RBR, Feb. 11, 1918, IDRS Collection, Family Letters, RLPRS. Details of Richard's letter are inferred from her letter.

[9] Memories of MWRG; MWRG to IDR Sr., March 12, 1918, IDRS Papers, Family Correspondence, RLPRS.

[10] Russell, *Roots and Ever Green*, 179-81. MWRG often told the story of her father on her wedding day.

[11] I heard IDRS tell this story many times. See also her interview with William W. Stueck, RLPRS.

[12] *Georgia Giant*, RLPRS, 61;Russell, *Roots and Ever Green*, 182-83.

[13] HBR to FMR, [?] May 1918, Private Collection of Richard Russell Bowden; several letters of HBR to PER in 1918-1919 mention Harriette's part in cooking at the homeplace. Private Collection of PRP.

[14] Russell, *Roots and Ever Green*, 170, 174-75; postcard MWR to IDR, June 25, [1917?], RFP. IDR to PER, Aug. 18, 1917, Private Collection of PRP.

[15] Fite, *Richard B. Russell, Jr.*, 36; Russell, *Roots and Ever Green*, 182-83.

[16] Ibid., 183; Gordon Green held several patents for his inventions.

[17] MWRG to IDR, Dec. 26, 1918, RFP.

[18] IDR to WBR, Sept. 28, 1920, RFP. Many other letters to her children tell of their busy life at this time. Russell, *Roots and Ever Green*, 187-189.

[19] HBR to PER, April 17, 1920, Private Collection of PRP.

[20] Russell, *Roots and Ever Green*, 185.

[21] HBR to PER, March 29 and April 17, 1920, Private Collection of PRP.

[22] HBR to PER, March 2, 1920, Private Collection of PRP.

[23] RBR to FMR, [undated but can be placed about 1915] Private Collection of Richard Russell Bowden. HBR to PER, April 24, 1920, Private Collection of PRP.

[24] RBR to SGG, Feb. 4, 1920. Author's copy, sent by Mary Nancy Green Carmichael, Aug. 30, 1993.

[25] IDR to FMR, Feb. 16, 1920. Private Collection of Richard Russell Bowden.

[26] Russell, *Roots and Ever Green*, 189.

[27] Fite, *Richard B. Russell Jr., Senator from Georgia*, 39-40.

[28] MWRG told me this story. See also oral history of IDRS, RLPRS.

[29] Russell, *Roots and Ever Green*, 188-89.

[30] Ibid., 189-90.

[31] MWRG to IDR Sr., Feb. 3, 1919, IDRS Papers, Family Correspondence; Gordon Green to RBR, Aug. 28, 1925, RBR Sr. Collection, III, Family. RLPRS.

[32] Russell, *Roots and Ever Green*, 191-194.

[33] IDR Jr. to RLR, Dec. 29, 1921, RFP.

Chapter 14

[1] ABR told me about his father's ailments at this period. RBR to IDR, Feb. 14, 1922; subsequent details are from the series of letters RBR to IDR, Feb. 14– March 3, 1922, IDR Collection, RLPRS.

[2] RBR Jr. and RLR to RBR, February 1922, RBR Sr. Collection, III, Family, RLPRS.

[3] See RBR Sr. Collection, IV, 1922 Campaign, Outgoing Correspondence. Many of these letters detail how his decision was made. RLPRS.

[4] IDR to MWRG, Sept. 19, 1922, Private Collection of Nancy Green Carmichael. For the edited version of this letter, see Russell, *Roots and Ever Green*, 199-202. LCR to Mrs. R. A. Stafford, Aug. 27, 1922, RBR Sr. Collection, IV, 1922 Campaign; RLPRS.

[5] Political Cartoon, RBR Sr. Collection, IV, 1911 Campaign, RLPRS.

[6] "Judge Richard B. Russell To the People of Georgia", Campaign flyer, RBR Sr. Collection, IV, 1922 Campaign. RLPRS.

[7] Numerous letters in the 1922 Chief Justice Campaign file; see especially RBR to Mrs. Geo. C. Owens, July 21, 1922, RBR to Stella Akin, Aug. 15, 1922 and RBR to Mrs. J.H. Spratling, Aug. 3, 1922, RBR Sr. Collection, IV, RLPRS.

[8] Article by Rebecca Felton, RBR Sr. Collection, IV, 1922 Campaign, speeches and material, RLPRS.

[9] See RBR Sr. Collection, IV, 1922 Campaign, for evidence of how the campaign was conducted. Some letters in this file deal with neglected law cases, as well as the campaign.

[10] Ibid. WBR to RBR, Aug. 1, 1922. Author interview with Frank Bondurant, Feb. 25, 2002.

[11] Russell, *Roots and Ever Green*, 197.

[12] RBR to Lella A. Dillard, Aug. 15, 1922; RBR to Walter Dillard, July 17, 1922, RBR Sr. Collection, IV. 1922 Chief Justice Campaign. RLPRS.

[13] RBR Sr. Collection, IV, 1922 Chief Justice Campaign, general, speeches, lists, media material, congratulations. See especially RBR to R.P. Bentley, Aug. 2, 1922, RBR to E. Norman, Aug. 2, 1922, RBR to Mrs. J. Randolph Anderson, July 22, 1922, RLPRS.

[14] Russell, *Roots and Ever Green*, 198-99.

[15] Russell, *Roots and Ever Green*, 199-202; see also IDR to PER, her account to Pat of the ovation, date unknown, Private Collection of PRP. CRN remembers how her father greeted her mother when he came in the house and how her mother would scold, as he hugged her, "Now, Mist'Russell!"

[16] Details of this historic moment are from Russell, *Roots and Ever Green*, 199-202, the unedited letter to MRWR, private collection of Mary Nancy Green Carmichael, and a letter similar in length to PER, Private Collection of PRP.

[17] Clipping, IDR Scrapbooks, Box 2 of 5, RLPRS.

[18] Russell, *Roots and Ever Green*, 202-204. PRP loved to tell this story.

[19] LCR to J. W. McWhorter, Nov. 21, 1922, LCR to Senator Rebecca Felton, Nov. 29, 1922, LCR Collection, Business/Finance and Political, 1918-1923; LCR to WJR 27 November 1922, LCR Collection, Personal, Family. RLPRS.

[20] Russell, *Roots and Ever Green*, 206. Virginia Wilson Russell remembers in written notes to the author [undated] that Richard was always anxious when his daughters or daughters-in-law were pregnant.

Chapter 15

[1] *Georgia Reports*, 188, 891-94; *Georgia Reports,* 178, 890-92.

[2] Author interview with Richard B. Russell III, January 21, 2003.

[3] Ibid. Betty Russell Vandiver to author, June 6, 1999. RBR to J.L. Beeson, May 4, 1931, Office of the President Papers, Box 3, IDR Library, GCS/U.

[4] IDR Scrapbooks,Box 2/5, IDR Collection, RLPRS.

[5] IDR to WBR, July 11, 1923, RFP. See also Russell, *Roots and Ever Green*, 214-15.

[6] Political Cartoon, RBR Sr. Collection, IV, Miscellaneous, RLPRS.

[7] Russell, *Roots and Ever Green*, 211-14. "Georgia Giant," 64, RLPRS.

[8] Fite, 37-59.

[9] RBRSr. to WBR, September 8, 1923, RFP; Russell, *Roots and Ever Green*, 216-17; author interview with Frank Bondurant, Feb. 25, 2002. RBR to IDR Jr. May 15, 1915, IDRS Collection, RLPRS.

[10] Russell, *Roots and Ever Green*, 217.

[11] RBR to WJR (son), Oct. 27, 1931, March 20, 1935, RFP; see also interview with William C. Harris, RLPRS, and RFH 2000, 69-73, RLPRS.

[12] Author interview with PRP, Nov. 21, 1998.

[13] RBR to FMR, April 10, 1918, Private Collection of Richard Russell Bowden. See also RFH 1997, 119-20, RLPRS.

[14] RBR Sr. Collection, III, Misc., RLPRS.

[15] Memories of PRP and CRN. IDR to IDR Jr., Jan. 11, 1926, IDRS Collection, RLPRS.

[16] Russell, *Roots and Ever Green,* 108-10.

[17] Ibid., 196.

[18] Ibid., 218.

[19] *Georgia Reports*, 188, 884-85. Richard B. Russell Sr., "Help Them to Become Good Citizens," article from an unnamed magazine, c. 1933, RBR Sr. Collection, IV, General, RLPRS. CRN gave me this opinion of her father's religious and spiritual journey c. 2002.

[20] Hair, et al., *A Centennial History of Georgia College*, 151-52.

[21] Office of the President, Papers, Box 3, IDR Library, GC/SU Library.

[22] The school history says that Russell first appears on the Board about 1917, and it is believed that Nat Harris (governor, 1915-1917) appointed him. It seems likely he was appointed early in Harris's tenure, rather than later, given his election as Chairman in 1918.

[23] Hair et al., *A Centennial History*, 147.

[24] Ibid., 135-48.

[25] RBR to Marvin M. Parks, Oct. 17, 1925 and Jan. 16, 1926, Office of the President Papers, Box 3, Judge R. B. Russell folder, IDR Library, GC/SU.

[26] Clippings, *Macon Telegraph* and *Atlanta Constitution*, Office of the President Papers, Box 2, Fire of 1924 folder, IDR Library, GC/SU.

[27] Ibid., Marvin M. Parks folder.

[28] Ibid., letters between Beeson and Russell, Beeson folder.

[29] Virginia Russell Black, daughter of FDR Sr., said her father never forgot his shock at these great expectations on his first day at college. FDR to RBR July 26, 1925, RFP.

[30] On February 26, 2000, after reading *Roots and Ever Green*, William Harrison of Barrow County, Georgia, told me the story of how his father, Will Harrison of Bert Day Road, saw a drunk driver damage the judge's wheelbarrow. Harrison asked the judge if he was going to repair it, and he said no. Harrison then asked for it, took it home, repaired it, and used it for many years. William Harrison still has the wheelbarrow but reports it is not usable. See also RFH 1996, 121.

[31] The propensity to predict early death was an old one, which got worse as the end drew near. For dirt digging details, see "Georgia Giant," 55-56; OH of FDR Sr., RFH 1996, 121, RLPRS.

[32] *Crawford W. Long Proceedings in Statuary Hall of the United States Capitol upon the Unveiling and Presentation of the Statue of Crawford W. Long by the State of Georgia*, Sixty-ninth Congress, March 30, 1926. 5-7. Volume extant at the Russell homeplace.

[33] Ibid., see entire speech.

[34] RBR to J. O. Adams, July 2,1926; RBR to Mrs. A. H. Brumby, July 11, 1926; RBR to W. A. Covington, July 5, 1926; RBR Sr. Collection, IV, 1926 Campaign, RLPRS.

[35] see clippings, RBR Sr. Collection, IV, 1926 Campaign. RLPRS.

[36] Fite, *Richard B. Russell Jr.*, 49. Russell, *Roots and Ever Green*, 227-28. Letters from MWRG in the RFP indicate Ina was hoping for a photo.

[37] RBR to LCR, Feb. 2, 1929, LCR Collection, RLPRS.

[38] RBR to J. H. Peebles, July 5, 1926. RBR Sr. Collection, 1926 Campaign. See the personal folder for family involvement. RLPRS.

[39] Robert Lee Russell papers, political, folder 1925-1928, RLPRS; IDR to HER, March 5, 1927, RFP.

[40] HER to RLR, August 27, 1926. RBR Sr. Collection, IV, 1926 Campaign, Personal Correspondence, RLPRS.

[41] Form letters and press releases, RBR Sr. Collection, IV, 1926 Campaign, RLPRS.

[42] Russell, *Roots and Ever Green*, 227; Fite, 48-50.

[43] Clippings, RBR Sr. Collection, IV, 1926 Campaign; see also Russell file, Office of the President, IDR Library, GC/SU.

[44] RBR to Bell Brumby, July 12, 1926, RBR Sr. Collection, IV, 1926 Campaign. RLPRS.

[45] RBR Sr. Collection, IV, 1926 Campaign, Walter George file. RLPRS.

[46] See RBR Sr. Collection, IV, 1926 Campaign for several letters relating to the Ku Klux Klan and the Russell attitude towards it, for example, RBR to John J. Bothan, Aug. 17, 1926. See also IDRS interview with William Stueck, 48-49, RLPRS. See also Reg Murphy article in the *Atlanta Constitution* Jan. 23, 1971, editorial pages.

[47] Clipping, RBR Sr. Collection, IV, 1926 Campaign, RLPRS.

[48] "Democrats, The Negative Power," 29-32. *Time Magazine*, May 19, 1952, discusses the 1952 Presidential race, in which Dick Russell Jr. was a candidate for the Democratic nomination. Its principles clearly apply to the career of Dick Russell Sr. See also Walter Lipmann's "The Indispensable Opposition," in W. H. Stone and Robert Hoopes, *Form and Thought in Prose* (New York: The Ronald Press, 1954) 300.

[49] See "Richard B. Russell to the People of Georgia," speech and RBR to M. E. Crow, July 19, 1926, RBR to W. A. Covington, July 5, 1926, and Edward Russell (nephew) to RBR, July 25, 1931, RBR Sr. Collection IV, 1926 and 1930 [RBR Jr.] Campaigns, RLPRS.

[50] See Fite's excellent discussion of this development, 47-50.

Chapter 16

[1] Russell, *Roots and Ever Green*, 231; RBR to WJR (son) Jan. 5, 1927, RFP.

[2] Fite, *Richard B. Russell Jr.,* 50.

[3] All details in this chapter about Dick Russell Jr.'s early political career are taken from Fite's *Richard B. Russell Jr.,* chapter 3, "Political Apprentice-ship."

[4] Fite, *Richard B. Russell Jr.,* 53-54; Russell, *Roots and ever Green*, 236-37; Interview of IDRS with William W. Stueck, 18-22, RLPRS.

[5] See numerous letters from RBR to HER, 1926-1929, Private papers of Ala Joanna Brewton Russell; Russell, *Roots and Ever Green*, 1923-1930.

[6] Russell, *Roots and Ever Green*, 233.

[7] Family history; see also ABR to HER, [undated] in private papers of Ala Joanna Brewton Russell.

[8] Russell, *Roots and Ever Green*, 223-24; as recently as 2001 CRN told the author that she thought her father would have bought her a Stutz Bearcat if she had asked for it, but she never dared ask for anything without first getting her mother's approval, which she knew she would not get for a car.

[9] RBR to WJR (son) Jan. 5, 1927, RFP; RBR to IDR Jr., January 12, 1926, IDRS Collection, RLPRS.

[10] RBR to HER March 6, 1928, Private Collection of Ala Joanna Brewton Russell.

[11] Russell, *Roots and Ever Green*, 233; HER to RBR, 1927, RBR Sr. Collection, III, Family Correspondence, RLPRS.

[12] VWR, written notes to author on life of Richard Russell Sr., undated.

[13] A favorite remark of IDR Jr. before she met Jean Stacy, whom she married in 1938.

[14] According to Jane Bowden Moore, Margo's daughter, all the Russell daughters, with the possible exception of Carolyn, believed this to be true.

[15] Russell, *Roots and Ever Green*, 234-35; RBR to HER, Oct. 7, 1927, private collection of Ala Jo Brewton Russell. See also Patience (Pipey) Dillard to HER, Oct. 6, 1927, RFP.

[16] RBR to HER, Nov. 4, 1927, private collection of Ala Jo Brewton Russell.

[17] Russell, *Roots and Ever Green*, 242-43.

[18] *Georgia Appeals Court Reports*, October 1919, 664-67, October 1920, 241-49.

[19] Russell, *Roots and Ever Green*, 244, 246.

[20] Ibid., 246-47.

[21] Ibid., 6, 248.

[22] Memorial volume of the *University of Georgia Bulletin*, 1930, prepared by T. W. Reed, in memory of David Crenshaw Barrow and Sylvanus Morris. Copy extant at the Russell homeplace.

[23] *Georgia Reports*, 178, 890-91; 188, 872-874, 892-93. Gilbert, *A Georgia Lawyer*, 138-39.

[24] *Georgia Reports*, 188, 869-895. PRP remembered that her father would not eat properly while living in Atlanta.

[25] Russell, *Roots and Ever Green*, 248.

[26] Ibid., 287.

[27] RBR to HER, Jan. 29, 1930. Private Collection of Ala Joanna Brewton Russell.

[28] Russell, *Roots and Ever Green*, 252-53.

[29] PRP loved to tell the story of how she met Hugh Peterson.

[30] Russell, *Roots and Ever Green*, 254-261.

[31] Oral History of HER, RLPRS.

[32] All details of the campaign are taken from Fite, chapter 4.

[33] RBR to J.L. Beeson, April 26, 1930; Office of the President, Box 3, IDR Library, GC/SU.

[34] Memory of ABR.

[35] Russell, *Roots and Ever Green*, 68.

[36] Memory of PRP and VWR.

[37] Fite, *Richard B. Russell Jr.,* 71.

[38] Ibid., 72; *Cochran Journal*, June 17, 1930.

[39] Family history claims Richard Sr. gave Richard Jr. this advice. See also "Democrats, The Negative Power," 29-32. *Time Magazine*, May 19, 1952. Fite, *Richard B. Russell Jr,* 54-55; Oral History, Robert B. Troutman Sr. RLPRS. See letters from Lewis Russell's women friends in the LCR Collection, Personal, RLPRS.

[40] Russell, *Roots and Ever Green*, 268-69.

[41] See RBR Sr. Collection, IV, Congratulations to Parents, RBR Jr. 1930 Campaign. For character of RBR at this time see Edward Russell (cousin) to RBR July 25, 1931. RLPRS.

[42] *Atlanta Journal*, Oct. 4, 1930.

[43] Ibid.; author interview with Frank Bondurant, February 25, 2002.

[44] Clipping, IDR Scrapbooks, IDR Collection, RLPRS.

[45] RBR to IDR, Dec. 7, 1929, RFP. Russell, *Roots and Ever Green*, 274.

Chapter 17

[1] Russell, *Roots and Ever Green*, 276, 282–84.

[2] Fite, 79-80.

[3] Russell, *Roots and Ever Green*, 286.

[4] Ibid., 286-292.

[5] Ibid., 289.

[6] "Sanger vs. Famous Father of 18," Margaret Sanger Papers Project, Number 29, Winter 2001, 1-4.

[7] Russell, *Roots and Ever Green*, 289; "Sanger vs. Famous Father of 18," 1-4.

[8] Ibid., 2; Opinion of CRN, who reports that she was sensitive to her father's tobacco chewing, but does not recall his chewing on stage ever.

[9] Sanger vs. Famous Father, 3-4; Russell, *Roots and Ever Green*, 290-91; written notes of MWRG, private collection of Kathryn Hairston Green. Sanger's prediction that Russell would be easy prey came true in that she easily won the debate.

[10] Sanger vs. Famous Father, 3.

[11] Memory of PRP.

[12] Clipping, 'My Greatest Thrill," RBR Jr.'s response to the inauguration. IDRS Scrapbook, IDRS Collection, RLPRS.

[13] Written memories of VWR, to author, undated; VWR to RBR April 26, 1932, RFP.

[14] *American Magazine* article, "Father and Son Together Serve Their State" IDR Scrapbooks, 1932, IDR Collection, RLPRS.

[15] Ibid.

[16] IDR to MRB, Jan. 6, 1932, unedited version, Private Collection of Richard Russell Bowden; Russell, *Roots and Ever Green*, 299-300.

[17] Glen Giles to RBR Jr., April 20, 1932; RBR Collection, IV, RBR Jr. Campaign for US Senate. RLPRS.

[18] Memory of CRN.

[19] All details concerning this campaign are from Fite, *Richard B. Russell Jr.,* 101-21, unless otherwise noted.

[20] *Atlanta Constitution*, June 3-4, 1932; *Macon Telegraph*, June 4, 1932; see also "Georgia Giant," 29, RLPRS.

[21] Clipping, IDR Scrapbooks, IDR Collection, RLPRS.

[22] Russell, *Roots and Ever Green*, 307; RFH, 1997, 148.

[23] Russell, *Roots and Ever Green,* 308-09.

[24] Family history. See also Derieux, James C. "Cheaper by the Baker's Dozen," Colliers Magazine: The National Weekly, vol. 126, no. 10, Sept. 2, 1950, 36-38; 45.

[25] A favorite story of ABR. He vowed he was good to his word never to return to a place of that sort, not even as a soldier in Paris after World War II when he was invited to see to a high-class bordello.

[26] Russell, *Roots and Ever Green*, 315-18.

[27] Ibid.

[28] Ibid., 318; Fite,, *Richard B. Russell Jr.,* 122-23.

[29] Russell, *Roots and Ever Green*, 325.

[30] ABR to WJR (son), Oct. 14, 1932, RFP. IDR to RBR Jr. May 2, 1934, RBR Jr. Collection, V. Winder Papers, United States Senatorial Years. RLPRS.

[31] RBR to WJR, (son) March 20, 1935, RFP, RLPRS.

[32] IDR to FMRB, May 9, 1934, Private Collection of Richard Russell Bowden.

[33] IDR to RBR Jr., May 26, 1934, RBR Jr. Collection; IDR to WJR, May 31, 1934, RFP; RLPRS. Memory of CRN.

[34] Russell, *Roots and Ever Green*, 331-32.

³⁵ Favorite story of ABR, who, like his father, shed tears over it.

³⁶ RBR Sr. to WJR, March 20, 1935, RFP, RLPRS.

³⁷ RFH 1996, 123.

³⁸ RBR Sr. to WJR (son), see note 30.

³⁹ IDR 1936 Diary, June 24-25, 1936, IDR Collection, RLPRS.

⁴⁰ IDR Diary, 1936, IDR Collection, RLPRS.

[41] "History of Senator Russell's Family Showing the Years They Have Held Public Office"—Flyer, Robert Lee Russell Collection, Speeches, Talmadge, 1936; IDR's diary entries for summer of 1936, IDR Collection, RLPRS. Photo in Marguerite Russell Bowden's album, private collection of Richard Russell Bowden. Family history reported that the reward was $100 for finding sidewalks, but the photo proves the reward was $10.

[42] Fite gives details about contributions. For cotton bales, see IDR 1936 diary, summer entries, IDR Collection, RLPRS.

[43] Fite, *Richard B. Russell Jr.,* quoting Anderson, 144 [163].

[44] Clipping, IDR Scrapbooks, IDR Collection, RLPRS.

[45] RBR to IDR, Nov. 9, 1936, IDR Collection, RLPRS.

[46] ABR, who was agnostic but had tremendous admiration for his almost-twin brother, told this story many times. See also clippings, IDR Scrapbooks, IDR Collection, RLPRS.

Chapter 18

[1] IDR Diary, 1937, IDR Collection, RLPRS.

[2] Family history. As late as 1999, Jimmie Ruth Hunter of Winder would call me every time I was in town to tell me how the judge made the bus driver wait for her, a young woman with a job in Atlanta.

[3] ABR told me the story of the Braselton brothers refusing the final interest payment. IDR to CLR, April 27, 1937, private collection of CRN.

[4] IDR to CLR, May 7, 1937, private collection of CRN; RBR Jr. to IDR, Jan. 18, 1932, IDR Collection, RLPRS.

[5] IDR to CLR, May 8, 1937, Private Collection of CRN.

[6] Ina likely suffered a stroke, from which she eventually recovered, but without her old energy and verve. IDR to RBR Jr. June 9, 1937, RBR Jr. Collection, Winder Papers, Family, RLPRS. IDR to CLR, Sept. 16, 1937, private collection of CRN.

[7] IDR to RBR Jr., Jan. 18, 1938; RBR Jr. to IDR, Feb. 4, 1938, RBR Jr. Collection, Winder Papers, Family, RLPRS.

[8] AJBR to author, April 16, 1996.

[9] Memory of ABR.

[10] Memory of Sarah Eaton Russell.

[11] W. H. Faust to RBR, August 11, 1938, RFP.

[12] That this romance was a deep and mutually caring love is borne out by the fact that they remained friends and occasionally went out together. Dick sent Pat special gifts on her birthday. When she became engaged to Sal Andretta ten years later, she wrote to tell Dick first. He replied that he was shocked but wished her all happiness. See Fite, *Richard B. Russell Jr., Senator from Georgia*, 170-73; Memories of IDRS and CRN.

[13] *Atlanta Constitution*, December 4, 1938; clippings IDR scrapbooks

[14] *Georgia Reports 188*, 890-91.

[15] ABR told me many times of his father's fear. As a physician he found it remarkable that in spite of this fear, at the last Richard Russell had such an honest sense of his approaching death.

[16] See one such list in RBR Sr. Collection, III, Family 1920-1924.

[17] Written memories of Betty Russell Vandiver and Richard B. Russell III to the author, June 8, 1999 and April 4, 2003; stories heard from Sarah Eaton Russell. This account differs slightly from those published in numerous newspapers at the time of death.

[18] Details of the funeral and other activities as well as of his career, are taken from various newspaper reports of the day found in the Russell Family Papers. The *Winder News*, the *Atlanta Journal* and *Constitution*, and the *Athens Banner-Herald* are the principal sources.

[19] Memories of ABR and Betty Russell Vandiver.

[20] *Georgia Reports* 188, 883.

[21] Funeral remarks by Thomas Walter Reed and Reason Chestnut Bell, RFP.

[22] See son RLR's accounting of the estate, 1939-1948, RFP.

[23] Russell, *Roots and Ever Green*, 340. See also Derieux, James C. "Cheaper by the Baker's Dozen," Colliers Magazine: The National Weekly, vol. 126, n. 10, Sept. 2, 1950, 36-38, 45.

[24] *Georgia Reports 188*, 869-870.

[25] Ibid., 894.

[26] RBRJr. to RBRSr., telegram, April 26, 1936. RBR Jr. Collection, V, Winder, Senatorial Years, RLPRS.

INDEX